T0235355

# Lecture Notes in Artificial Intelligence    9372

Subseries of Lecture Notes in Computer Science

## LNAI Series Editors

Randy Goebel
  *University of Alberta, Edmonton, Canada*
Yuzuru Tanaka
  *Hokkaido University, Sapporo, Japan*
Wolfgang Wahlster
  *DFKI and Saarland University, Saarbrücken, Germany*

## LNAI Founding Series Editor

Joerg Siekmann
  *DFKI and Saarland University, Saarbrücken, Germany*

More information about this series at http://www.springer.com/series/1244

Aditya Ghose · Nir Oren
Pankaj Telang · John Thangarajah (Eds.)

# Coordination, Organizations, Institutions, and Norms in Agent Systems X

COIN 2014 International Workshops
COIN@AAMAS, Paris, France, May 6, 2014
COIN@PRICAI, Gold Coast, QLD, Australia, December 4, 2014
Revised Selected Papers

 Springer

*Editors*
Aditya Ghose
School of Computer Science
University of Wollongong
Wollongong, NSW
Australia

Nir Oren
Department of Computing Science
University of Aberdeen
Aberdeen
UK

Pankaj Telang
Cisco Systems Inc.
Durham, NC
USA

John Thangarajah
Computer Science and Information
 Technology
RMIT University
Melbourne, VIC
Australia

ISSN 0302-9743          ISSN 1611-3349 (electronic)
Lecture Notes in Artificial Intelligence
ISBN 978-3-319-25419-7          ISBN 978-3-319-25420-3 (eBook)
DOI 10.1007/978-3-319-25420-3

Library of Congress Control Number: 2015951952

LNCS Sublibrary: SL7 – Artificial Intelligence

Springer Cham Heidelberg New York Dordrecht London
© Springer International Publishing Switzerland 2015
This work is subject to copyright. All rights are reserved by the Publisher, whether the whole or part of the material is concerned, specifically the rights of translation, reprinting, reuse of illustrations, recitation, broadcasting, reproduction on microfilms or in any other physical way, and transmission or information storage and retrieval, electronic adaptation, computer software, or by similar or dissimilar methodology now known or hereafter developed.
The use of general descriptive names, registered names, trademarks, service marks, etc. in this publication does not imply, even in the absence of a specific statement, that such names are exempt from the relevant protective laws and regulations and therefore free for general use.
The publisher, the authors and the editors are safe to assume that the advice and information in this book are believed to be true and accurate at the date of publication. Neither the publisher nor the authors or the editors give a warranty, express or implied, with respect to the material contained herein or for any errors or omissions that may have been made.

Printed on acid-free paper

Springer International Publishing AG Switzerland is part of Springer Science+Business Media
(www.springer.com)

# Preface

This volume is the 10th in the COIN (Coordination, Organizations, Institutions and Norms in Agent Systems) workshop proceedings series, which began in 2006. The volume contains revised versions of 16 selected papers presented at the two COIN workshops in 2014. The first workshop took place on May 6, 2014, in Paris, France, as an AAMAS workshop, while the second workshop was co-located with PRICAI on December 4, 2014, in Gold Coast, Australia.

The papers in this collection have undergone a substantial process of refinement. Each of the submissions to the workshops was reviewed by at least three Program Committee members. Following the Program Committee's recommendations, accepted papers were revised and presented in the workshop sessions. The authors were subsequently invited to resubmit their papers taking into account the workshop feedback, and these papers underwent another round of reviews. The 16 papers selected for this volume were then revised to address the review feedback, resulting in this volume.

COIN aims to act as a focal point for stimulating discussion, facilitating the emergence of novel ideas, and creating a lively and robust community. Authors and reviewers were therefore encouraged to submit and accept unconventional approaches, particularly if they were driven by ideas from other disciplines. The range of papers in this volume reflect this breadth of scope, ranging from work on formal aspects of normative and team-based systems, to software engineering with organizational concepts, to applications of COIN-based systems, and to philosophical issues surrounding socio-technical systems. We believe that the papers contained in this volume not only highlight the richness of existing work in the field, but also point out the challenges and exciting research that remains to be done in the area, which will no doubt lead to future volumes in this series of workshop proceedings.

Finally, we would like to thank the authors and presenters of papers in the two COIN workshops for their high-quality contributions, and we would also like to acknowledge the efforts of the reviewers, who took time to participate in discussions and provide in-depth feedback to the authors. We believe that the effort put into the reviewing process, and the changes made by the authors in response to the review feedback, is evident in the quality of the papers in this volume.

July 2015

Aditya Ghose
Nir Oren
Pankaj Telang
John Thangarajah

# Organization

## Program Committee

| | |
|---|---|
| Carole Adam | LIG CNRS UMR 5217 - UJF, France |
| Huib Aldewereld | Delft University of Technology, The Netherlands |
| Sergio Alvarez-Napagao | Universitat Politècnica de Catalunya, Spain |
| Tina Balke | University of Surrey, UK |
| Olivier Boissier | ENS Mines Saint-Etienne, France |
| Patrice Caire | University of Luxembourg, Luxembourg |
| Luciano Coutinho | Universidade Federal do Maranhão (UFMA), Brazil |
| Hoa Khanh Dam | University of Wollongong, Australia |
| Marina De Vos | University of Bath, UK |
| Frank Dignum | Utrecht University, The Netherlands |
| Virginia Dignum | Delft University of Technology, The Netherlands |
| Nicoletta Fornara | Università della Svizzera Italiana, Lugano, Switzerland |
| Aditya Ghose | University of Wollongong, Australia |
| Guido Governatori | NICTA, Australia |
| Akin Gunay | Nanyang Technological University, Singapore |
| James Harland | RMIT University, Australia |
| Chris Haynes | King's College London, UK |
| Jomi Fred Hubner | Federal University of Santa Catarina, Brazil |
| Joris Hulstijn | Delft University of Technology, The Netherlands |
| Jie Jiang | Delft University of Technology, The Netherlands |
| Martin Kollingbaum | University of Aberdeen, UK |
| Eric Matson | Purdue University, USA |
| Felipe Meneguzzi | Pontifical Catholic University of Rio Grande do Sul, Brazil |
| Simon Miles | King's College London, UK |
| Tim Miller | University of Melbourne, Australia |
| Pablo Noriega | IIIA-CSIC, Spain |
| Andrea Omicini | Alma Mater Studiorum–Università di Bologna, Italy |
| Nir Oren | University of Aberdeen, UK |
| Julian Padget | University of Bath, UK |
| Jeremy Pitt | Imperial College London, UK |
| Alessandro Ricci | University of Bologna, Italy |
| Juan Antonio Rodriguez Aguilar | IIIA-CSIC, Spain |
| Bastin Tony Roy Savarimuthu | University of Otago, New Zealand |
| Christophe Sibertin-Blanc | University of Toulouse/IRIT, France |

Pankaj Telang            Cisco Systems Inc., USA
John Thangarajah         RMIT University, Australia
Wamberto Vasconcelos     University of Aberdeen, UK
Harko Verhagen           Stockholm University/KTH, Sweden
George Vouros            University of Piraeus, Greece

# Contents

# Utilizing Permission Norms in BDI Practical Normative Reasoning

Wagdi Alrawagfeh[1]([✉]) and Felipe Meneguzzi[2]

[1] Computer Science Department, Memorial University of Newfoundland,
St. John's, NL, Canada
wagdi.alrawagfeh@mun.ca

[2] School of Computer Science, Pontifical Catholic University of Rio Grande do Sul,
Porto Alegre, RS, Brazil
felipe.meneguzzi@pucrs.br

**Abstract.** Norms have been used in multi-agent systems as a standard description of agents' behaviors. A lot of effort has been put into formalizing norms and utilizing them in agent decision making. Such work focuses mostly on two types of norms: prohibitions and obligations; with the unstated assumption that agents are completely aware of all norms. However, agents may have incomplete knowledge about norms in a system for several reasons such as deficient norm identification or because norms are not fixed. In this work we argue that, by assuming that agents do not have complete knowledge of the norms within a system, permission norms are fundamental for modeling unknown normative states. Using Event Calculus (EC), we propose a formal representation of permission norms and we show how to use it in agent normative practical reasoning. We implement a simple mineral mining scenario to demonstrate our work.

**Keywords:** Permission norm · Norm-representation · Normative reasoning

## 1 Introduction

Open Multi-agent Systems contain agents that are heterogeneous, autonomous, self-interested and which can join and leave the system at any time [15,16]. These features make interaction, coordination and collaboration in the system challenging problems. To address such challenges, systems of social norms have been proposed to provide a standard description of desirable behaviors within a society. There are two major approaches regarding the integration of norms into multi-agent systems. The *regimentation* approach where agents must obey norms and do not have choice to violate norms [13]. In this view the agents' behaviors are more predictable; however agents drastically lose their flexibility and autonomy. In the *enforcement* approach, the agents have the choice to comply or violate norms. In order to keep the system stable and encourage agents to

© Springer International Publishing Switzerland 2015
A. Ghose et al. (Eds.): COIN 2014, LNAI 9372, pp. 1–18, 2015.
DOI: 10.1007/978-3-319-25420-3_1

respect norms, agents who violate norms are subject to punishment and those who comply with norms are often rewarded [1, 9, 23].

A substantial amount of recent work focuses on practical normative reasoning using a variety of mechanisms. Panagiotidi and Vasquez-Salceda [22] focus on planning based normative reasoning, in which agents form goals from norms; Criado et al. [10] develop an agent architecture that reasons about agent's objectives based on norms; while Meneguzzi et al. [20] develop a mechanism to steer existing agent behavior towards norm achievement while executing plans to achieve agents' goals. In these efforts, only two types of norms are considered in normative agent decision-making: obligations and prohibitions [2, 17, 19, 21]. In these systems, agents check whether performing a particular behavior complies with obligations or violate prohibitions, making compromises in order to perform norm compliant behavior, but, critically, often ignoring permissions in practical reasoning.

Such design choice seems to stem from the adoption of the sealing principle: "whatever is not prohibited is permitted" [25]. This principle is sound if agents have complete knowledge about the normative states of a particular system, so they can always determine whether some action violates a norm or not. Such clear-cut division of the state-space is illustrated in Fig. 1(a), which depicts an agent's complete knowledge of a system's normative states in accordance with the sealing principle. In this illustration, all states are identified by agents as prohibited (F) or obliged (O) and all states that are not prohibited or obliged are identified as permitted (P). In this case, explicit reasoning about permission norms is not required since permission norms simply represent the absence of prohibition. Royakkers [25] refers to this kind of permission (i.e., one that is not enacted by an authority) as weak permission. However, a different division of state-space is possible. In an alternative system, agents may have incomplete knowledge about normative states. Actions not known to be either prohibited, obliged, or permitted are unknown. Thus, in normative terms, world states can be either obliged, prohibited, permitted, or unknown. The resulting division of the state space is illustrated in Fig. 1(b), which depicts an agent's incomplete knowledge about a system's normative states. In the illustration, agents know some states as prohibited (F), obliged (O), or permitted (P); the rest of the state space is unknown (U). We assume that agents have a mechanism to discover norms as they explore the state-space (see for example [4, 26]). However, when taking permissions into consideration within the reasoning mechanism, an agent should prefer behaviors that are known as permitted over behaviors that are unknown. For example, consider the situation in which an agent needs to navigate from A to B and there are two paths X and Y. If the agent identifies that taking path Y is permitted and taking X is unknown, then a (cautious) rational agent should take path Y rather than X (assuming X and Y have the same cost).

Thus, our contributions in this paper are the following: we develop a practical reasoning mechanism that allows agents to use permission norms to deal with uncertainty about the norms in a society; we present a formal representation

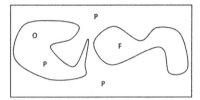 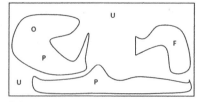

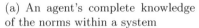

(a) An agent's complete knowledge of the norms within a system

(b) An agent's incomplete knowledge of the norms within a system

**Fig. 1.** F represents prohibition states, O obliged states, P permission states, and U unknown states. P in the shape containing O refers to the implicit permission norm

of permissions suitable to this kind of reasoning in Sect. 3; and we integrate this representation into a normative reasoning strategy that reasons about the usual prohibition and obligation norm in Sect. 4. We show the practicality of our approach empirically in a mineral mining scenario in Sect. 5.

## 2 Background

### 2.1 Jason

Beliefs, Desires and Intentions (BDI) [8] is one of the most widely studied architectures to implement practical reasoning in multi-agent systems. The BDI architecture is also widely used in the definition of agent programming languages, such as the AgentSpeak(L) programming language [24], arguably, the most widely studied such language. Jason [6,11] is a Java-based interpreter for an extended version of AgentSpeak(L) [12]. Agents in Jason use a belief-base that represents knowledge using logic programming constructs that, unlike traditional AgentSpeak(L) allows Prolog-like logical rules in agents definition.

Since we use the AgentSpeak(L) notation throughout this paper, we briefly review the Jason version of its syntax. Agentspeak(L) agent programs have two types of goal: *achievement goals*, represented by a literal prefixed with "!"; and *test goals* represented by a literal prefixed by "?". Goals and belief updates, serve as triggers to the execution of hierarchical plans contained in a plan library. The most basic syntax element in Jason are the predicates, which are represented by alphanumeric strings starting with a lower case character. A predicate represents a fact about the world and may evaluate to either true or false. Predicates may represent propositions (when they have arity 0), or first order relations (with arity greater than zero), in which case they have a number of terms. Terms represent objects in the domain and can be either functions (terms with arity greater than zero); constants (representing specific objects in the domain); or variables, which follow Prolog standard and start with an upper case letter or underscore sign representing an unnamed variable.

The "+" and "−" symbols are used to represent changes in the agent's internal data structure (i.e. the agents beliefs or intentions), and thus represent belief (or alternatively, intention) addition and deletion respectively. A plan is structured as follows: `Triggering-event: Context <- body`. In a plan, the triggering-event part is separated from the context part by the ":" symbol. In rules, the ":-" symbol separates a rule left and right hand sides. A conjunction and a disjunction operators are indicated by the symbols "&" and "|" respectively. For more details on the semantics of Jason, we refer the reader to [7].

## 2.2   Event Calculus

Event Calculus (EC) is a logical framework consisting of predicates and axioms to represent and reason about actions and their effects. EC was originally proposed in logic programming [18] to logically represent that, as a result of executing a particular sequence of actions, some fluents are initiated to be true in a specific time-point and no action occurred that terminates these fluents. Event Calculus is well known by its simplicity in describing concepts and straightforward implementation, since it is based on logic programming. Therefore, several works [5,14] use EC for representing concepts in multi-agent systems. A fluent is a property whose value is subject to change at different points in time. The basic components of EC are actions A, fluents F and time T (See Table 1).

In this paper, we want to represent that sometimes the effect of an action does not hold immediately. Hence, If the occurrence of action A at time T1 initiates the fluent F after T2 where T1 is before T2 then, the basic EC predicate `initiates(A,F,T1)` is not sufficient to represent the delayed effect. Therefore, we extend the basic EC with the following two predicates; `initiatesAt(A,F,T1,T2)` and `terminatesAt(A,F,T1,T2)`:
The `initiatesAt(A,F,T1,T2)` states that the occurrence of action A at time T1 makes fluent F true at T2.
The `terminatesAt(A,F,T1,T2)` states that the occurrence of action A at time T1 makes fluent F false at time T2. We define the predicate `between(A,T1,T2)`, which states that action A occurred after time T1 and before T2.

Below, we summarize the slightly modified basic EC axioms that are important to our work:
$EC1'$: `clipped(T1,F,T3)` ←
`happens(A,T2)` & `terminatesAt(A,F,T2,T3)` & `T1<T2` & `T2≤T3`

**Table 1.** The predicates of event calculus

| Predicate | Meaning |
|---|---|
| `happens(A,T)` | Action A occurs at time T |
| `holdsAt(F,T)` | Fluent F is true at time T |
| `terminate(A,F,T)` | Occurrence of action A at time T will make fluent F false after time T |
| `initiates(A,F,T)` | Occurrence of action A at time T will make fluent F true after time T |
| `initiallyp(F)` | Fluent F holds from time 0 |
| `clipped(T,F,Tn)` | Fluent F is terminated between time T and Tn |
| $<, >, ≤, ≥$ | Standard order relation for time |

This states that fluent F is terminated by the occurrence of action A between times T1 and T3.

EC3′:holdsAt(F,T2)← happens(A,T1) & initiatesAt(A,F,T1,T2) & T1 ≤ T2 & ¬clipped(T1,F,T2)

This states that fluent F holds at time T2 if action A occurred at time T1, fluent F became true at time T2, and F has not been terminated between T1 and T2.


# 3   Norm Representation

In this section, we take the norm representation presented in [3] and expand it with permission norms. Alrawagfeh [3] defines three fluents, one for prohibition norms (fPun(Nid,S)) and two for obligation norms (oPun(Nid,S) and oRew(Nid,R)) to represent that a punishment has been applied (i.e. a violation has occurred) or that a reward has been applied (i.e. fulfillment has occurred). That is, when fluent fPun(Nid,S) becomes true, a prohibition norm has been violated; when oPun(Nid,S) becomes true, an obligation norm has been violated; and when oRew(Nid,R) becomes true, an obligation norm has been fulfilled. In other words, these fluents work like flags raised if a prohibition is violated or an obligation is either fulfilled or violated. Such an approach is unsuitable for defining fluents for permission norms. Regardless of whether the agents act according to a permission norm or not, there is no sanction or reward involved, so defining fluents that refer to a sanction or reward is not suitable for representing a permission norm. Instead of relying only on prohibitions and obligations to choose between plans, we want agents to be able to select a plan based on the number of permitted actions involved.

Thus, we define the fluent pRew(Nid,1) so that it becomes true when a permitted sequence of action(s) has been performed. Plan X is then preferred over plan Y if X has more permitted actions than Y.


## 3.1   Norms

A norm is defined [3] as a tuple N = <D, C, Seq, S, R> where:

- D ∈ {F,O,P} is the deontic type of the norm, F for prohibition, O for obligation and P for permission.
- C is the optional norm's context. The specified sequence of actions is obliged, prohibited or permitted if C is a logical consequence of the agent's belief base. When C is absent, it means that the norm is applicable under any circumstance. C comprises two possible components: $\beta$ and $\alpha$, $\beta$ consists of holdsAt predicates that describe a particular world state, while $\alpha$ is an EC formula to represent a sequence of actions.
- Seq is a sequence of one or more actions that agents are not supposed to perform, have to perform or may perform in case of prohibition, obligation or permission respectively. Note that Seq is different from $\alpha$, since $\alpha$ is part of

the context condition (actions that trigger norm activation) whereas Seq is the object of the norm's deontic type (actions that are forbidden, obliged or permitted).

- S is the sanction to be applied if the norm has been violated or failed to be fulfilled.
- R is the reward that agents may get if they fulfill an obligation.

The punishment and reward in the prohibition and obligation norms represent an incentive for agents to change their behaviors. As we see in the next section, a permission norm gives the agents the possibility of preferring the known permitted actions to unknown actions (actions that are not known to be either prohibited, obliged or permitted). For the purpose of representing the three deontic modalities of norms we adopt the definition of prohibition and obligation from [3] and introduce the definition of permission. Below we define the fluents on which our norm representation is based, followed by the norm representation.

**Definition 1.** *fPun(Nid,S) is a fluent that becomes true if the prohibition norm Nid is violated. The sanction of the violation is S. Nid is a unique number of prohibition norm, where S is an integer representing the sanction value.*

A prohibition norm is represented as follows:
initiatesAt(An,fPun(Nid,S),Tn,Tn+1):- C, happens(A1,T1) & $\cdots$ & happens(An,Tn) & T1<T2< & $\cdots$ & <Tn.

This representation of prohibition norm contains the following parts. D, the deontic type is prohibition; in the left hand side of the definition we use the fPun fluent which refers to a prohibition norm violation state. C is the norm's context. Seq is a sequence of actions, A1,A2, $\cdots$ , An, that is prohibited. S is the sanction value which will be applied on the violator agent. R is empty for prohibition norm.

Our prohibition representation states that: if the actions A1 , $\cdots$ ,An occurred at time T1 , $\cdots$ ,Tn respectively, and the context C was a logical consequence of the agent's belief base, then the sanction that will be applied on the agent after Tn is S. If the order of actions is not important in a norm, then we omit the dependencies among T1,T2,$\cdots$,Tn − 1. However T1,T2,$\cdots$,Tn − 1 should be less than Tn. E.g., if performing actions X, Y and Z in any order is prohibited then we do not need to specify which action X occurs before or after which action.

**Definition 2.** *oPun(Nid,S) is a fluent that becomes true if the obligation norm Nid has not been fulfilled. The punishment issued for this violation is S. Nid is a norm identification number and S is the punishment value.*

**Definition 3.** *oRew(Nid,R) is a fluent which becomes true if the obligation norm Nid has been fulfilled. The variable R refers to the reward value.*

Let $\alpha$ be a, possibly empty, sequence of actions and Seq be a sequence of prescribed actions that is supposed to be performed by an agent. An obligation norm violation occurs if in a particular context (which $\alpha$ is a part of) Seq does not occur. Fluent oPun(Nid,S) becomes true if the obligation norm Nid is violated. The obligation norm fulfillment occurs when Seq occurs in context C. Fluent oRew(Nid,S) becomes true if the obligation norm Nid is fulfilled. We represent obligation norms by two rules; the first rule is shown below:

initiatesAt(Ai,oPun(Nid,S),Ti,Tn+1):- $\beta$ & happens(A1,T1) & $\cdots$ & happens(Ai,Ti) & $\cdots$ & ¬happens(Aj,Tj) | $\cdots$ | ¬happens(An,Tn) & T1< & $\cdots$ & <Ti< & $\cdots$ & < Tj < & $\cdots$ & < Tn.

This representation contains the following parts. D, the deontic type, is an obligation norm; this is so defined because we use the oPun fluent in the left-hand side of the definition, which refers to an obligation norm violation state. C is the norm's context, composed of $\beta$ and $\alpha$, where $\beta$ represents the world's states of the context and $\alpha$ = A1,A2,$\cdots$,Ai. Seq is a sequence of actions (Aj,Aj+1,$\cdots$,An) that is obliged to be performed. S is the sanction value which will be applied on the violator agent.

The first rule states that, if a part of the context C ($\beta$) is a logical consequence from the agent belief base, and a (possibly empty) sequence of actions, $\alpha$, A1,A2,$\cdots$,Ai occurs at time T1,T2,$\cdots$,Ti respectively, and a sequence of actions (Seq) Aj,Aj+1,$\cdots$,An does not occur at Tj,Tj+1,$\cdots$,Tn, then the sanction that may after Tn be applied is S.

The second rule below used to represent obligation norm if the fulfillment of an obligation norm is subject to a reward.

initiatesAt(An,oRew(Nid,R),Ti,Tn+1):- $\beta$ & happens(A1,T1)& $\cdots$& happens(Ai,Ti) & $\cdots$& happens(Aj,Tj) & $\cdots$ & happens(An,Tn) &  T1< & $\cdots$ & <Ti< & $\cdots$ & <Tj< & $\cdots$ & <Tn.

This rule states that, if a part of the context C ($\beta$) is entailed from the agent's belief base, and a (possibly empty) sequence of actions ($\alpha$) A1,A2,$\cdots$,Ai occurs at time T1,T2,$\cdots$,Ti, and a sequence of actions (Seq) Aj,Aj+1,$\cdots$,An occurs at Tj,Tj+1,$\cdots$,Tn, then the reward that might be granted after Tn is R.

**Definition 4.** *pRew(Nid,1) is a fluent that becomes true if a permitted sequence of actions has been performed. Where Nid is the norm identification number (unique number for each permission norm). The second argument of the fluent is used to count the number of permission norms if a plan is performed.*

The permission norm is represented as follows:
initiatesAt(An,pRew(Nid,1),Tn,Tn+1):- C, happens(A1,T1) & $\cdots$ & happens(An,Tn) & T1 <T2< & $\cdots$ <Tn.

This representation contains the following parts. D, the deontic type, is permission; in the left hand-side of the definition we use the pRew fluent which refers to performing a sequence of actions that is permitted. The second argument of the fluent pRew equals one in order to count the number of times a plan complies with permission norms. C is the norm's context. Seq is a sequence of actions: A1,A2,$\cdots$,An, that an agent is permitted to perform.

This representation states that, if the context C is entailed from agent belief base and the sequence of actions A1,A2,$\cdots$,An occur at time T1,T2,$\cdots$,Tn respectively, then after time Tn the fluent pRew(Nid,1) becomes true. We illustrate this representation using the blocks world scenario in the example below.

Suppose we have three colored blocks, red, blue and green, and the following situation: `on(red,blue)`, `on(blue,table)` and `on(green,table)`. If we have a permission norm states that "it is permitted to put green on red if red is not on the table", then this permission norm is represented as follows:

`initiatesAt(on(green,red),pRew(Nid,1),T1,T2):-`
`¬holdsAt(on(red,table),T1) & happens(on(green,red),T1) & T1<T2.`

## 4    BDI Agent Normative Reasoning

In order to develop our normative reasoning mechanism, we leverage the mechanism proposed in [3], and extend it to reason beyond prohibitions and obligations. The mechanism proposed in [3] relies on a definition of "best" plan as a plan of maximum utility (regarding only the value of prohibitions and obligations), among the applicable plans. If we have several "best" plans we call one of them (the one that complies with more permission norms) "safest" plan. We now extend this notion to use permissions in order to find the "safest" plan among the set of best plans. If the agent finds more than one plan with the same maximum utilities, those plans are stored in `BestSet` set. We define the set of safest plans `SafestPl` as the subset of the `BestSet` set which contains those plans that comply with the highest number of permission norms.

We argue that using permission norms in practical reasoning within a normative system is important for at least two reasons. First, if it is the agents' duty to infer norms, the norm identification mechanism can miss some norms. Second, in most systems norms are not fixed; they may change, emerge or vanish. Hence, presuming that "whatever is not prohibited is permitted" is not adequate since it does not account for such missing norms.

We illustrate this argument with the following scenario. Suppose that an agent wants to achieve a goal G and there are several plans for achieving G. Out of those plans the agent finds that the `BestSet` has two plans, P1 and P2, of maximum utilities subject to prohibition and obligation norms. Suppose that P1 has some prohibited action(s) but because of the agent's incomplete knowledge, the agent does not know that. As a result, the agent may mistakenly presume the action(s) as permitted. However, if the agent maintains the permission norms as it does the prohibition and obligation norms, then it can compare P1 and P2 to see which plan complies with the most permitted actions. It will determine which plan is safer.

Figure 2 illustrates the BDI interpreter we describe in this section; white boxes represent the basic BDI interpreter, whereas our additions are drawn using gray boxes. To deal with dynamic norms, the norm identification process needs to be integrated with the normative reasoning strategy in order to update agent's belief base about repealed and emerged norms online. Thus, an agent following our reasoning cycle is able to deal with new norms and norms that have disappeared by norm identification algorithms.

The execution of `Plan` makes fluent `help(Plan)` true if it results in more rewards than punishments (based on the `helpful-rule` presented in [3], and

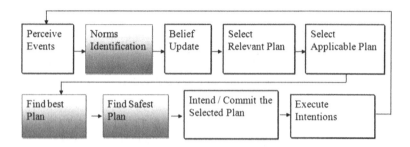

**Fig. 2.** An extended BDI Reasoning processes flow

repeated below). The punishment value comes as a result of violating prohibitions or not fulfilling obligations. The reward value comes as a result of achieving the goal associated with `Plan` and fulfilling obligation norms. We define predicate `goalpreference(G,Points)` to describe the importance of achieving goal `G`, where `Points` is an integer quantifying the achievement of `G`.

**helpful-rule:**
```
initiatesAt(-,help(Plan),T1,T2):-
.findall(V1,holdsAt(oRew(,V1),T2+1),Wins) &
.findall(V2,holdsAt(fPun(-,V2), T2), Losses1) &
.findall(V3,holdsAt(oPun(-,V3), T2), Losses2) &
goalpreference(G,Points) &
(Points + sum(Wins)- sum(Losses1) - sum(Losses2)) > 0
```

Using `helpful-rule`, the agent determines whether a plan is helpful. The righ-hand side of this rule becomes true when the left-hand side finds that all the rewards that can result from executing the current plan (the plan under test) are more than the punishment that can result from executing the same plan. The agent asserts the actions of a plan into a temporary belief base, which is a copy of the agent's belief base, using the `happens` predicate in order to simulate that these actions have occurred, (see Algorithm 1, line 4 and Algorithm 2). Generally, predicate `.findall(V,holdsAt(p(-,V),-),Set)` obtains all the values of `V` where predicate `P` is true. `V` represent the value of a punishment if `p` is `fPun` or `oPun`, or a reward if `p` is `oRew`. Variable `Set` unifies with the set of `V` values. Finally, `sum(Wins)` obtains the rewards that may be granted if `Plan` is executed and `sum(Losses1)` and `sum(Losses2)` unify with the sanctions that can result from executing the plan which an agent is checking.

To use permission norms in the normative reasoning mechanism, we define the `safe(Plan)` fluent which is true if the execution of `Plan` complies with one or more permitted norms (based on the `safe-rule` below). If we have two plans with equal utility, then the plan that complies with more permissions is the safest, since the actions that are unknown might be prohibited. The number of permission norms which a plan complies with is stored in the `Count` variable.

**safe-rule:**
```
initiatesAt(-,safe(Plan),T1,T2):-
.findall(V1,holdsAt(pRew(-,1),T2),Count).
```
We define the following domain-independent axioms using the EC framework. Our Agents implemented these axioms in their normative reasoning mechanism:

- EC1' & EC3' (see Sect. 2.2)
- Ax1: `between(A,T1,T2) :- happens(A, T) & T1 <T & T <T2`
- Ax2: `terminatesAt(*,help(P),T1,T2):- happens(*,T1) & T1<T2`
- Ax3: `terminatesAt(*,safe(P),T1,T2):- happens(*,T1) & T1<T2`
- Ax4: `terminatesAt(*,fPun(I,S),T1,T2):- happens(*,T1) & T1<T2`
- Ax5: `terminatesAt(*,oPun(I,S),T1,T2):- happens(*,T1) & T1<T2`
- Ax6: `terminatesAt(*,oRew(I,S),T1,T2):- happens(*,T1) & T1<T2`
- Ax7: `terminatesAt(*,pRew(I,S),T1,T2):- happens(*,T1) & T1<T2`

In order to terminate fluents, a domain-independent special event * is used as a wild card variable to denote any action. It refers to the fact that the associated fluents become false. These axioms help agents find a potential norm violation/fulfillment that can result from executing the current plan. If we also want the agent to be able to find the potential norm's violation/fulfillment resulting from the combination of actions of the current and the previous plan, we need to add another `happens(*,T2)` predicate to the right-hand side of Ax2 through Ax7. Here, the * action monitors the end point of those fluents that are mentioned in the axioms above. For example, Ax2 will be
`terminatesAt(*,help(P),T1,T3):- happens(*,T1)  &  happens(*,T2)  & T1<T2 & T2<T3`.
The same addition should be added to Ax3 through Ax7.

Using the above domain-independent axioms, `helpful-rule` and `safe-rule`, the agent is able to find the set of best plans (`BestSet`) among the applicable plans; and from the set of best plans, the agent is able to extract the safest plan. We define `Bel` as the belief base that represents the agent's knowledge about the society along with the society's norms represented in EC. `TempBel` is a copy of `Bel`. We also define $\Omega$ to refer to EC1', EC3', Ax1, Ax2, Ax3, Ax4, Ax5, Ax6, Ax7, helpful-rule, `TempBel` and `Bel`.

After `helpful-rule`, the agent uses `safe-rule` to obtain the number of permission norms that a plan complies with. Using the built-in predicate `.findall(V,P,Count)`, the agent obtains all the values of `V` where predicate `P` is true, and adds them to the set `Count`. Note that variable `V` is always unified with the second argument of the fluent `pRew(-,1)` which is always equal to one. Hence, the elements of the set `Count` are all ones and the cardinality of the set `Count` is equal to the number of permission norms that are complied with if `Plan` is executed.

In Algorithm 1, Line 2 we define three empty sets: `UtilSet` to store a set of plans with their utilities, `BestSet` which is used to store the best plans with their utilities and `SafeSet` which stores the best plans with their number of times they comply with permission norms.

**Algorithm 1.** Find Safest Plan

```
 1: function FINDSAFESTPL(Π)
 2:     UtilSet, BestSet, SafeSet ← {}
 3:     for all π ∈ Π do
 4:         TempBel ← InsertAc(π,Bel)
 5:         T ← current time
 6:         if Ω ⊨ holdsAt(help(π),T) then
 7:             utility(π)← Points + sum(Wins) − sum(Losses1) − sum(Losses2)
 8:             UtilSet ← UtilSet ∪ utility(π)
 9:         end if
10:     end for
11:     BestSet ← BestSet ∪ findMaxSetUti{UtilSet}
12:     for all π ∈ BestSet do
13:         TempBel ← InsertAc(π,Bel)
14:         T ← current time
15:         if Ω ⊨ holdsAt(safe(π),T) then
16:             preference(π) ← sum(Count)
17:             SafeSet ← SafeSet ∪ preference(π)
18:         end if
19:     end for
20:     SafestPlan ← findMaxUti{SafeSet} /*findMaxUti{SafeSet} returns the plan of
            maximum preference value (in this case, the one that complies with more
            permission norms)*/
21:     return SafestPlan
22: end function
```

In Algorithm 2, Line 2, the agent finds the sequence of actions of a plan using act(π) function, which is a function that returns the sequence of actions of a given plan π. The agent asserts the actions of plan π using the predicate **happens**, starting from time T, which represents the current time. Note that the added actions have not occurred yet. By adding these actions to the agent's **TempBel** belief base, the agent simulates that it has executed the actions in order to reason about whether the current plan π is helpful or not. In Algorithm 1, Line 6, plan π is helpful if the predicate **holdsAt(help(π),T)** is deduced from **TempBel** belief base. If that is the case, the rewards outweigh losses and the plan of maximum utility is then added to the best plan set **BestSet**. The set **BestSet** will thus have the plans of maximum utilities. As a result of firing the **helpful-rule**, the variables **Points, Wins, Losses1** and **Losses2** are unified with a set of values based on .**findall()** predicate which finds all norms violations and fulfillment. In Line 11, the function **findMaxSetUti()** finds the set of plans of highest utility out of the **UtilSet** and store them in the **BestSet**.

As we see in Algorithm 1, Lines 12–21, the safest plan is found in **BestSet**. At Line 15, if the predicate **holdsAt(safe(π),T)** is deduced from the **TempBel** belief base, this implies that there is at least one permission norm being complied with as a result of executing plan π. In case of executing a plan, the number of times permission norms are complied with is equal to the summation of **Count**

---

**Algorithm 2.** Add plan's actions to agent's belief base

---

1: **function** INSERTAC($\pi$,B)
2:      X $\leftarrow$ act($\pi$)
3:      X = (A1, A2, $\cdots$, An) | Ai is an action of plan $\pi$
4:      T $\leftarrow$ current time
5:      **for** $i \leftarrow 1, n$ **do**
6:          B $\leftarrow$ B $\cup$ happens($A_i$,T)
7:          T $\leftarrow$ T + 1
8:      **end for**
9:      **return** B
10: **end function**

---

set. Plans associated with its summation of `Count` are added to the `SafeSet` set (see Algorithm 1, Line 17). In Line 20, out of the `SafeSet` set, the plan of maximum preference value is selected as the safest plan using the function `findMaxUti()`, which returns the plan of maximum preferences. The safest plan will be ready for execution by adding it to the intentions.

After choosing and performing a plan $\pi$, the `happens` predicate for each action of an executed plan $\pi$ will be added to the `Bel` belief base. Predicate `happens(*,Tn+1)` is added to the belief base after executing the last action of the chosen plan. The purpose of adding the special event * is to terminate the fluents `help`, `safe`, `fPun`, `oPun`, `oRew` and `pRew` after `Tn+1`. This termination is important in order to prevent our agent from re-detecting a past violation. In other words, agents should not be sanctioned more than one time for the same violation. However, we do want to detect violations/fulfillments that may result from combining the current plan and the previous executed plan, which our mechanism is able to do.

## 5   Experiments

For experimental purposes, a mineral mining society adapted from the Gold Miners scenario [7] has been used. In this scenario gold and silver pieces are scattered in a grid-like territory along with agents who want to collect the scattered pieces into their respective depot (one for silver and one for gold). There is a monitor agent in the territory who plays the role of a police officer. The monitor agent is able to observe other agents' actions and is also able to issue sanctions or rewards.

We assume an agent society with three agents ruled by a set of norms, of which the agents are not completely knowledgeable, that is, the agents do not know all norms. One agent uses prohibition and obligation norms in its practical reasoning. The second agent uses prohibition, obligation and permission norms in its practical reasoning. These two agents are both aware of the same prohibition and obligation norms and are in competition with each other. The third agent is the monitor agent. Let us call the first agent the *best-agent*, the second the *best-safest-agent*, and the third the *monitor-agent*. The *best-agent* uses the main

Algorithm presented in presented in [3] in its practical reasoning. The *best-safest-agent* uses Algorithm 1. The norms are represented using EC. The *monitor-agent* uses the `Ax1` to `Ax7` to check if a violation/fulfillment occurred.

## 5.1   Gold and Silver Mining Society

In this society the possible actions which agents can perform are `pick(-)`, `drop(-,-)` and `moveto(-,-)`. The two competitive agents have one continuous goal, `!collect(gold)`. The importance of achieving this goal is specified by the predicate `goalpreference(collect(gold), 10)`. Hence, the value of the importance of achieving the goal `!collect(gold)` is 10.

The grid has two depots, one for gold and one for silver. The grid has 10 gold ores and 10 silver ores. The two agents compete to collect these ores and the game ends when all the ores are collected. In this experiment the potential violation/fulfillment that can result from the current plan and the previously executed plan are taken into consideration. The two agents have the following plans for achieving the goal `!collect(gold)` :

@plan1-1, the agent collects gold to the silver depot.
```
+!collect(gold): free ← !find(gold,X,Y); moveto(X,Y);
pick(gold); moveto(silverDepotX, silverDepotY);
drop(gold,silverDepot).
```

@plan1-2, the agent collects gold to the gold depot.
```
+!collect(gold): free ← !find(gold,X,Y); moveto(X,Y);
pick(gold); moveto(goldDepotX,goldDepotY); drop(gold,goldDepot).
```

@plan1-3, the agent collects gold and silver to their depots.
```
+!collect(gold): free ← !find(gold,X,Y); moveto(X,Y);
pick(gold); moveto(goldDepotX,goldDepotY); drop(gold,goldDepot);
!find(silver,X1,Y1); pick(silver);
moveto(silverDepotX,silverDepotY); drop(silver,silverDepot).
```

@plan1-4, the agent collects two gold ores to the gold depot.
```
+!collect(gold): free ← !find(gold,X,Y); moveto(X,Y);
pick(gold); moveto(goldDepotX,goldDepotY); drop(gold,goldDepot);
!find(gold,X1,Y1); moveto(X1,Y1); pick(gold);
moveto(goldDepotX,goldDepotY); drop(gold,goldDepot).
```

@plan1-5 the agent collects gold and silver and deposits them in the gold depot.
```
+!collect(gold): free ← !find(gold,X,Y); moveto(X,Y);
pick(gold); moveto(goldDepotX,goldDepotY); drop(gold,goldDepot);
!find(silver,X1,Y1); pick(silver); moveto(goldDepotX,goldDepotY);
drop(silver,goldDepot).
```

There are set of prohibition, obligation and permission norms that govern this society. The prohibition and obligation norms given below are known for the three agents:

It is prohibited to drop gold in the silver depot if the gold depot is not full. The sanction value is 5.

```
initiatesAt(drop(gold,silverDepot),fPun(1,5),T1,T2):-
¬holdsAt(full(goldDepot),T1) &
happens(drop(gold,silverDepot),T1) & T1≤T2.
```

It is prohibited to carry more than one gold piece at a time. The sanction value is 10

```
initiatesAt(pick(gold),fPun(3,10),T1,T3):-
happens(pick(gold),T1) & happens(pick(gold),T2) &
¬between(drop(gold,-),T1,T2) & T1<T2 & T2≤T3.
```

It is obligatory to collect silver immediately after collecting gold. The sanction value is 10. The reward of adhering is 10.

```
initiatesAt(pick(gold),oPun(1,10),T1,T4):-
happens(pick(gold),T1) & happens(drop(gold,-),T2) &
happens(pick(gold),T3) & ¬between(pick(silver),T2,T3) &
T1<T2 & T2<T3 & T3≤T4.
```

```
initiatesAt(pick(gold),oRew(1,10),T1,T4):-
happens(pick(gold),T1) & happens(drop(gold,-),T2) &
happens(pick(gold),T3) & between(pick(silver),T2,T3) &
T1<T2 & T2<T3 & T3≤T4.
```

In addition to the previous norms *best-safest-agent* is aware of the following permission norms:

It is permitted to drop gold in gold depot.
```
initiatesAt(drop(gold,goldDepot),pRew(1,1),T1,T2):-
happens(drop(gold,goldDepot),T1) & T1≤T2.
```
It is permitted to drop silver in silver depot.
```
initiatesAt(drop(silver,silverDepot),pRew(2,1),T1,T2):-
happens(drop(silver,silverDepot),T1) & T1≤T2.
```

The *monitor-agent* aware of one further prohibition norm that is unknown to other agents:

It is prohibited to drop silver in the gold depot if the silver depot is not full. The sanction value is 10.
```
initiatesAt(drop(silver,goldDepot),fPun(1,10),T1,T2):-
¬holdsAt(full(silverDepot),T1) &
happens(drop(silver,goldDepot),T1) & T1≤T2.
```

The experiment was executed 10 times and the average was taken. Two values for each agent was recorded: the `calculated-utility` which results from the agent's prediction in case a particular plan is chosen and the `real-utility` which results from the execution of a particular plan. These two values could be different; if an agent did not know that a particular act was prohibited, then the sanction value of performing this act could not be calculated in the `calculated-utility` but it would be included in the `real-utility` (the sanction value would be issued by the monitor agent).

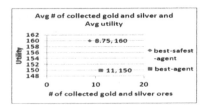
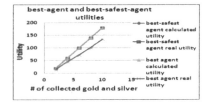

**Fig. 3.** Experiment results

Based on the norms and the five plans above, the *best-agent* and the *best-safest-agent* find the two best plans, both with utility equal to 20 (plan1-3 and plan1-5). Neither agent is aware that plan1-5 violates a prohibition that is unknown to them. Because the *best-agent* has no other information to act upon, it randomly chooses between plan1-3 and plan1-5, chancing a sanction from the *monitor-agent* if plan1-5 is selected. The *best-safest-agent*, however, selects the plan with more permission norms out of the best plans, which is plan1-3 in this case. Thus the *best-safest-agent* successfully avoids receiving a sanction that would have occurred from unknowingly violating a prohibition norm following plan1-5.

The results illustrated in Fig. 3(a) show that the average utility for goals achieved by the *best-safest-agent* is greater than the utility of the *best-agent*. This is because the *best-safest-agent* is able to integrate the permission norm into its normative practical reasoning. However, the *best-agent* collects more gold and silver ores than the *best-safest-agent* because, while the *best-safest-agent* is spending more time in the reasoning process of plan selection, the *best-agent* is able to spend that time mining. The *best-agent*, compared to the *best-safest-agent*, presents the possibility of a higher reward (e.g., because it spends more time collecting gold and silver), but it also presents a higher risk, since it can unknowingly incur sanctions, losing an unknown amount of its reward.

The results in Fig. 3(b) show that the real utility (after plan execution) of the *best-agent* is less than the predicted/calculated utility (before plan execution). This is because the *best-agent* does not utilize permission norms in its practical reasoning. In contrast, the real and calculated utilities were identical for *best-safest-agent*, hence, in Fig. 3(b) the line for the *best-safest* agent calculated utility can't be seen (i.e., it is underneath the *best-safest-agent*'s real utility).

## 6   Summary

In this paper we presented a formal representation of norms and a normative reasoning mechanism based on event calculus. In addition to prohibition and obligation norms, we designed a mechanism that takes permissions into consideration to reason about the "safest" plans to execute. Such safety refers to minimizing uncertainty when an agent operates in environments with no guarantee of full knowledge of norms.

Using simulation experiments we show that when agents have incomplete knowledge about the norms of a system, then permissions have a significant role in practical normative reasoning. Using permission norms gives agents the ability to have preference over plans, i.e., plans containing actions that are known to be permitted over plans that contain actions whose normative status is unknown.

Experimental results show that, using permissions in agent practical reasoning provides agents with an extra tool to avoid norm violations, especially when agents operate in environments with no guarantee of full knowledge of norms. In spite of the fact that, the throughput (i.e. the number of collected ores) of *best-safest-agent* is smaller than the throughput of *best-agent*, who does not use permissions in its reasoning, the ultimate utility of *best-safest-agent* is much higher than *best-agent* (see Fig. 3(a)). This result implies that agents who do not utilize permission norms in their practical reasoning can misbehave and violate unknown norms.

As future work, we plan to do further experiments to study the runtime efficiency of our normative reasoning mechanism. We also aim to compare our *best-safest-agent* with other BDI norm aware agents in the literature.

# References

1. Aldewereld, H., Dignum, F.P.M., García-Camino, A., Noriega, P., Rodríguez-Aguilar, J.-A., Sierra, C.: Operationalisation of norms for electronic institutions. In: Noriega, P., Vázquez-Salceda, J., Boella, G., Boissier, O., Dignum, V., Fornara, N., Matson, E. (eds.) COIN 2006. LNCS (LNAI), vol. 4386, pp. 163–176. Springer, Heidelberg (2007). http://dx.doi.org/10.1007/978-3-540-74459-7_11
2. Alechina, N., Dastani, M., Logan, B.: Programming norm-aware agents. In: Proceedings of the 11th International Conference on Autonomous Agents and Multi-agent Systems, vol. 2, pp. 1057–1064. International Foundation for Autonomous Agents and Multiagent Systems, Richland (2012). http://dl.acm.org/citation.cfm?id=2343776.2343848
3. Alrawagfeh, W.: Norm representation and reasoning: a formalization in event calculus. In: Boella, G., Elkind, E., Savarimuthu, B.T.R., Dignum, F., Purvis, M.K. (eds.) PRIMA 2013. LNCS, vol. 8291, pp. 5–20. Springer, Heidelberg (2013). http://dx.doi.org/10.1007/978-3-642-44927-7_2
4. Alrawagfeh, W., Brown, E., Mata-Montero, M.: Norms of behaviour and their identification and verification in open multi-agent societies. Int. J. Agent Technol. Syst. (IJATS) **3**(3), 1–16 (2011)
5. Artikis, A., Kamara, L., Pitt, J., Sergot, M.J.: A protocol for resource sharing in norm-governed ad hoc networks. In: Leite, J., Omicini, A., Torroni, P., Yolum, I. (eds.) DALT 2004. LNCS (LNAI), vol. 3476, pp. 221–238. Springer, Heidelberg (2005). http://dx.doi.org/10.1007/11493402_13
6. Bordini, R.H., Hübner, J.F.: BDI agent programming in AgentSpeak using *Jason* (Tutorial Paper). In: Toni, F., Torroni, P. (eds.) CLIMA 2005. LNCS (LNAI), vol. 3900, pp. 143–164. Springer, Heidelberg (2006). http://dx.doi.org/10.1007/11750734_9
7. Bordini, R.H., Hübner, J.F., Wooldridge, M.: Programming Multi-agent Systems in AgentSpeak Using Jason. Wiley, Chichester (2007)

8. Bratman, M.: Intention, Plans, and Practical Reason. Harvard University Press, Cambridge (1987)
9. Castelfranchi, C.: Formalising the informal? dynamic social order, bottom-up social control, and spontaneous normative relations. J. Appl. Log. **1**(1), 47–92 (2003)
10. Criado, N., Argente, E., Noriega, P., Botti, V.J.: Towards a normative BDI architecture for norm compliance. In: Fornara, N., Vouros, G. (eds.) 11th International Workshop on Coordination, Organization, Institutions and Norms in Multi-Agent Systems, 30 August 2010, pp. 65–81. Springer, Berlin (2010)
11. Dignum, F., Morley, D., Sonenberg, E.A., Cavedon, L.: Towards socially sophisticated BDI agents. In: Proceedings of the Fourth International Conference on Multi-agent Systems (ICMAS-2000), pp. 111–118. IEEE Press, Los Alamitos (2000)
12. d'Inverno, M., Kinny, D., Luck, M., Wooldridge, M.: A formal specification of dMARS. In: Singh, M.P., Rao, A.S., Wooldridge, M. (eds.) Agent Theories, Architectures, and Languages. LNCS, vol. 1365, pp. 155–176. Springer, Berlin (1998)
13. Esteva, M., Rodríguez-Aguilar, J.-A., Sierra, C., Garcia, P., Arcos, J.-L.: On the formal specification of electronic institutions. In: Sierra, C., Dignum, F.P.M. (eds.) AgentLink 2000. LNCS (LNAI), vol. 1991, pp. 126–147. Springer, Heidelberg (2001). http://dx.doi.org/10.1007/3-540-44682-6_8
14. Fornara, N., Colombetti, M.: Specifying artificial institutions in the event calculus. In: Dignum, V. (ed.) Handbook of Research on Multi-Agent Systems: Semantics and Dynamics of Organizational Models, pp. 335–366. IGI Global, Pennsylvania (2009)
15. Hermoso, R., Billhardt, H., Ossowski, S.: Role evolution in open multi-agent systems as an information source for trust. In: Proceedings of the 9th International Conference on Autonomous Agents and Multiagent Systems, vol. 1, pp. 217–224 (2010), http://dl.acm.org/citation.cfm?id=1838206.1838237
16. Hübner, J.F., Boissier, O., Kitio, R., Ricci, A.: Instrumenting multi-agent organisations with organisational artifacts and agents. Auton. Agents Multi-agent Syst. **20**(3), 369–400 (2010). http://dx.doi.org/10.1007/s10458-009-9084-y
17. Kollingbaum, M.: Norm-governed practical reasoning agents. Ph.D. thesis, University of Aberdeen (2005)
18. Kowalski, R., Sergot, M.: A logic-based calculus of events. In: Schmidt, J., Thanos, C. (eds.) Foundations of Knowledge Base Management. Topics in Information Systems, pp. 23–55. Springer, Berlin (1989). http://dx.doi.org/10.1007/978-3-642-83397-7_2
19. Meneguzzi, F., Luck, M.: Norm-based behaviour modification in BDI agents. In: Proceedings of the 8th International Conference on Autonomous Agents and Multiagent Systems, vol. 1, pp. 177–184. International Foundation for Autonomous Agents and Multiagent Systems, Richland (2009). http://dl.acm.org/citation.cfm?id=1558013.1558037
20. Meneguzzi, F., Vasconcelos, W., Oren, N., Luck, M.: Nu-BDI: norm-aware BDI agents. In: The 10th European Workshop on Multi-agent Systems (EUMAS), London, UK (2012)
21. Oren, N., Vasconcelos, W., Meneguzzi, F., Luck, M.: Acting on norm constrained plans. In: Leite, J., Torroni, P., Ågotnes, T., Boella, G., van der Torre, L. (eds.) CLIMA XII 2011. LNCS, vol. 6814, pp. 347–363. Springer, Heidelberg (2011). http://dx.doi.org/10.1007/978-3-642-22359-4_24

22. Panagiotidi, S., Vázquez-Salceda, J.: Towards practical normative agents: a framework and an implementation for norm-aware planning. In: Cranefield, S., van Riemsdijk, M.B., Vázquez-Salceda, J., Noriega, P. (eds.) COIN 2011. LNCS, vol. 7254, pp. 93–109. Springer, Heidelberg (2012). http://dx.doi.org/10.1007/978-3-642-35545-5_6
23. Pitt, J., Busquets, D., Riveret, R.: The pursuit of computational justice in open systems. AI SOC. 1–20 (2013). http://dx.doi.org/10.1007/s00146-013-0531-6
24. Rao, A.: AgentSpeak(L): BDI agents speak out in a logical computable language. In: Perram, J., Van de Velde, W. (eds.) MAAMAW 1996. LNCS, vol. 1038, pp. 42–55. Springer, Heidelberg (1996). http://dx.doi.org/10.1007/BFb0031845
25. Royakkers, L.M.M.: Giving permission implies giving choice. In: 8th International Workshop on Database and Expert Systems Applications, pp. 198–203. IEEE Press, Los Alamitos, September 1997
26. Savarimuthu, B.T.R.: Mechanisms for norm emergence and norm identification in multi-agent societies. Ph.D. thesis, University of Otago (2011)

# Holonic Institutions for Multi-scale Polycentric Self-governance

Ada Diaconescu[1] and Jeremy Pitt[2]([⊠])

[1] Telecom ParisTech, 46 Rue Barrault,75634 Paris Cedex 13, France
[2] Imperial College London, Exhibition Road, London SW7 2BT, UK
j.pitt@imperial.ac.uk

**Abstract.** Effective institutions are key to the success of self-governing systems, yet specifying and maintaining them can be challenging, especially in large-scale, highly dynamic and competitive contexts. Political economist Elinor Ostrom has studied the conventional arrangements for sustainable natural resource management and derived from these eight design principles for self-governing institutions. One principle, *nested enterprises*, is straightforwardly expressed, but is arguably structural rather than functional, and so is more resistant to declarative specification; yet it also appears to be critical to the effectiveness of complex compositional systems. In this paper, we converge the ideas of holonic systems with electronic institutions, to propose a formalisation of this principle based on *holonic institutions*. We show how holonic institutions provide a structural framework for nested enterprises, which can be designed as composite systems of systems. This, we believe, is compatible with Ostrom's ideas for polycentric governance of complex systems. We use a case study in energy distribution to illustrate these ideas.

**Keywords:** Electronic institutions · Holonic architectures · Multi-agent systems · Self-organising systems · Polycentric governance · Smartgrids

## 1 Introduction

Based on extensive fieldwork examining successful, and unsuccessful, instances of common-pool resource management, Ostrom [17] identified eight common features of the successful instances, some of which were missing from the unsuccessful ones. She then posited these features as design principles for the supply (endowment) of self-governing institutions for sustainable resource management.

These principles are extensively documented [17] and only briefly reminded here (Sect. 4), with the exception of the eighth principle, concerning *nested enterprises*. This principle states that institutions, which consist of conventional rules, are nested within each other, with provision and appropriation systems operating locally at a small-scale (base level) and being organised into multiple layers at larger-scales over wider geographical regions (higher levels).

The principle itself is straightforwardly expressed and is arguably structural rather than functional – i.e., it is more concerned with the structural relationships between institutions than the purposeful functions those institutions are

© Springer International Publishing Switzerland 2015
A. Ghose et al. (Eds.): COIN 2014, LNAI 9372, pp. 19–35, 2015.
DOI: 10.1007/978-3-319-25420-3_2

intended to deliver. As such this principle has proven more resistant to declarative specification than the other principles [20]. Yet, it also appears to be critical to the effective functioning of complex compositional systems operating across multiple scales, with multiple objectives and intricate interdependencies.

For example, reducing global Carbon emissions could be considered as a collective action problem consisting of country-level actors, but regulation by the Kyoto protocol has failed to meet its targets. Indeed, Ostrom herself posed the question: are large-scale collective action problems, with correspondingly large-scale outcomes, better addressed by large-scale government policies [15]? For Ostrom, the answer was equivocal; but generally in the case of climate change, somehow, the system of nested enterprises is failing to provide the appropriate distribution of policy formation, decision-making and self-governance. Therefore, Ostrom argued, policies made at national and international level also required local and regional action and enforcement. Governance had to be *polycentric* – i.e. composed of multiple centres of decision-making [14] – enabling complex, multi-scale systems to cope with complex, multi-criteria problems.

There is, however, a fairly well-established understanding in utilising *holonic architectures* to address complex systems issues, such as scalability, heterogeneity and dynamic adaptability, via the recursive coordination of processes that operate at different granularity levels. Holonic architectures and their key role in creating viable complex systems were introduced by Simon [26], refined by Koestler [9], and progressively adopted in software systems engineering. For instance, Simon argues that holarchy "is one of the central structural schemes that the architect of complexity uses" [26]. Hence, the central question addressed in this paper is: *can holonic architectures be used to implement Ostrom's nested enterprises institutional design principle for polycentric governance?*

Accordingly, we converge the ideas of holonic systems with electronic institutions implementing executable forms of Ostrom's principles [20], and propose a formalisation of the nested enterprises design principle based on *holonic institutions*. The paper is structured as follows. Section 2 reviews the background and motivation for this work, while Sect. 3 introduces the convergence of holonic architectures and electronic institutions. This is the basis for a preliminary study of holonic institutions in Sect. 4, with an illustrative case study of community energy systems in Sect. 5. We conclude that this indicates how holonic institutions could provide a composite system of systems architecture for nested enterprises and inter-linked organisations which, we believe, is compatible with Ostrom's ideas for polycentric governance of complex systems.

## 2    Background and Motivation

### 2.1    Formalising Ostrom's Principles

The primary aim of using Ostrom's principles as the basis for electronic institutions was to address the problem of resource allocation in open computing systems and networks. In open systems, the components effectively form a common pool of resources (CPR) and specify conventional rules concerning provision to, and appropriation of, resources from the common pool. In the absence of a centralised component strictly enforcing the rules, and the possibility of sub-ideal behaviour (from accidental operation, to free-riding and intentional malice), Ostrom's design principles were proposed to supply self-governing institutions which supported sustainable resource management.

In the experiments of [20], six of Ostrom's eight design principles were specified in computational logic. It was shown that, as more principles were added, the electronic institutions moved along the spectrum from failure (usually depleted the resource) through fragility (sometimes depleted, sometimes sustained the resource) to sustainability (usually sustained the resource). This replicated the findings reported by Ostrom in [17, p. 180, Table 5.2].

Of the other two principles, the seventh concerned *no external authorities*, which was effectively implemented since there were no external authorities (although it was *not* shown, in [20], that some form of external authority disrupted an institution's capability to sustain a resource). The eighth principle, *nested enterprises*, was *NR* (not relevant, to borrow the classifier from Table 5.2 cited above): this principle only concerned "CPRs that are parts of larger systems" [17, p. 90]. In [20], there was only a single, base-level CPR.

## 2.2   The Eighth Principle: Nested Enterprises

The eighth principle is highly significant for multiple institutions, more complex systems, or electronic institutions for socio-technical systems. Here, Ostrom's fieldwork indicates a dependence between multiple CPRs. For example, in irrigation systems, there is a CPR for appropriation of water. Given water's tendency to flow downhill, the expectation would be that those at the 'top end' would appropriate all the water, leaving nothing for those at the 'bottom end'. However, this does not (always) happen: it turns out there is a second CPR, for maintenance of the irrigation system, which the top-enders cannot manage on their own. If they appropriate all the water, the bottom-enders don't provision to the maintenance CPR. Therefore it is successful collective action in one CPR which provides the *social capital* [16] for successful collective action in the other; so in fact there are two, asynchronous but co-dependent, CPRs whose inter-operation serves to sustain the resource.

Similarly, in SmartGrids for power management, there has been a shift from the traditional model of *predict and provide* to demand-side management – i.e., given the power available, schedule the demand to fit. This shift has partly been motivated by the increase in stochastic generators and the perceived impossibility of centralised scheduling of millions of dispatchable generators under such constraints. One solution is to form a hierarchy of autonomous virtual power plants (AVPP) [10], and to delegate scheduling to each AVPP in the hierarchy. However, these works mostly focus on the control functions necessary to achieve predefined goals – e.g., avoiding load peaks and maximising provider revenues; based on rules that are known in advance – e.g. switching on and off equipment such as heaters and fridges. They do *not* consider *how* the institutional rules that guide these controls are negotiated, specified or evolved, by members of the socio-technical system, for achieving justice, fairness or conformance objectives.

Finally, while these electronic institutions have been inspired by formalising observations about social systems, it is an open question what happens if such institutions are injected back into the social system, to form a socio-technical system. One example would be a socio-technical system for demand-side power management, or better, demand-side self-organisation. However, such a system would inevitably be part of a much grander socio-technical system, a system of nested enterprises, with base-level concerns (over price, stability and availability, say) to the user, and country-level concerns over Carbon emissions at the top. In other words, this is a system of multi-scale, multi-objective nested enterprises subject to possibly competing policy constraints.

### 2.3 An Example

Consider a single entity producing and consuming resources (a *prosumer*). On its own, it may strike a balance between production and consumption; alternatively at times it may generate more or less resources than are required, which may be wasteful or risk causing a blackout. To avoid these problems, the prosumer can coordinate with others and pool their resources, subject to the self-organisation and mutual agreement of the *rules of engagement*. These rules constitute an institution, in the sense of Ostrom [17].

Suppose that, as in [19], the institution operates in time slices, during which each agent generates resources, computes its resource requirements, provisions resources to the common pool, receives an allocation, and makes an appropriation. There are several *operational-choice* rules involved, for example concerning provision. There are (at least) two alternatives: firstly, that a prosumer in the institution should provision all the resources that it generates to the common pool; secondly, that it only needs to provision any excess beyond its own requirements.

In the framework in [19,20], these rules could be formalised in the Event Calculus (EC) [11] as shown below.

$$\textbf{obl}(H, provide(A, P_a, I)) = true \quad \text{holdsAt} \quad T \quad \leftarrow$$
$$role(A, I) = prosumer \quad \text{holdsAt} \quad T \quad \wedge$$
$$rule(I, provision) = all \quad \text{holdsAt} \quad T \quad \wedge$$
$$generated(A) = P_a \quad \text{holdsAt} \quad T$$
$$\textbf{obl}(H, provide(A, P_a, I)) = true \quad \text{holdsAt} \quad T \quad \leftarrow$$
$$role(A, I) = prosumer \quad \text{holdsAt} \quad T \quad \wedge$$
$$rule(I, provision) = excess \quad \text{holdsAt} \quad T \quad \wedge$$
$$generated(A, I) = G_a \quad \text{holdsAt} \quad T \quad \wedge$$
$$demanded(A, I) = D_a \quad \text{holdsAt} \quad T \quad \wedge$$
$$G_a > D_a \quad \wedge \quad P_a = G_a - D_a$$

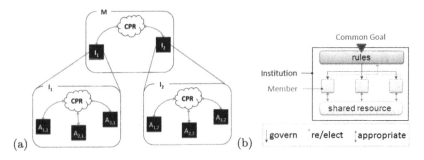

**Fig. 1.** (a) Nested CPR institutions and opaqueness of holons; (b) Conceptual model of a generic institution

The first EC axiom states that, in institution $I$, an agent $A$ occupying the *prosumer* role is obliged to provision everything it generates to the common pool (the provision rule in $I$ is *all*). In the second axiom, the provision rule is *excess*, so the obligation is only to provision the excess difference between what $A$ generated and what it needed.

Note that in an open, decentralised system with autonomous components, as far as the institution is concerned, the prosumers are black boxes, and their 'internals' are unknown; therefore there are other rules to deal with incentives for compliance, monitoring and non-compliance, etc.

However, even within an institution, an *economy of scarcity* may occur when insufficient resources are generated to satisfy all prosumer demands. In this case, it would be beneficial to form 'alliances' with other institutions, and in times of excess it would contribute surpluses to a higher-order common pool, in the expectation of being allocated resources from that common pool in case of a shortfall later on. Note again that participation in the higher-level institution is subject to the mutual agreement of rules of engagement between the institutions; and that just as the prosumers were black boxes to their institutions, the institutions are essentially black boxes to the nested enterprise – the higher-level institution has no knowledge, or any need for any knowledge, of how the components choose to (self)-organise their own affairs (Fig. 1-a).

## 3   Institutions and Holons

It is the nesting of the rules of engagement at different levels of abstraction, and the opacity of components at each level, that suggests a relationship between multiple institutions as nested enterprises and holonic systems architectures. In this section we consider the convergence of institutions and holonics, which will yield the concept of holonic institutions.

### 3.1   Institutions: An Informal Overview

From a systemic perspective, an institution has a *well-defined goal* or objective, which it pursues by enforcing a *set of rules* on its *members*, or participants

(Fig. 1-b). For instance, in the context of electrical power sharing each community member may be entitled to receive a quota of available power for consumption at any one time; or different members may receive different quotas depending on the urgency of their consumption (e.g. medical facilities versus entertainment). Hence, institutions provide the necessary regulations and infrastructure for coordinating the actions of their members, which may otherwise diverge because of their *inherent dissimilarities* (e.g. in individual purposes and/or behaviours). In the absence of effective coordination, groups of non-identical members would most likely fail to achieve a common goal or compromise that would benefit all. An institution's purpose, rules, members and operational context may change over time requiring adequate *adaptations*.

An important question here is related to the manner in which the different functions and membership *roles* of an institution will be implemented. For instance, roles requiring more extensive insights or judgements may be assigned to human operators and performed over longer periods (e.g. redefine common goals and rules, based on knowledge and feedback), while more routine roles may be assigned to automated agents with reactive capacities (e.g. membership control, monitoring, policing and basic conflict resolutions).

## 3.2   Self-organising Electronic Institutions

The framework of dynamic norm-governed systems [1] defined three components: a specification of a norm-governed system; a number of changeable parameters, each with a range of values; and a stack of protocols detailing how to change the specification from one instance to another (i.e. change one parameter value for another). This effectively defined a kind of metric space with 'distances' between one specification instance and another. One way to define the protocol stack was to use an Action Language, such as the Event Calculus (as above). This also enabled constraints to be placed on the transition from one specification instance to another, for example on 'distance', but also some specification instances could be identified as non-normative and moving to them declared invalid.

This framework is very general: therefore in the class of dynamic norm-governed systems, we are interested in the sub-class in which the protocols formalise, in the Event Calculus, six of Ostrom's eight institutional design principles. This sub-class is referred to as self-organising electronic institutions. However, that work stopped short of formalising the eighth principle, and suggested further investigation of nested enterprises in several directions, including "the embedding of institutions within larger institutions, rather than the single layer model implemented here, to form the nested enterprises identified by Ostrom. ... [and the involvement of] third parties and other dependencies which can lead to other, more complex, supply chains" [20, p. 34]. We argue that this further investigation can be facilitated by using the principles of holonic systems.

## 3.3   Holonic Systems

In short, a *holonic system* (or *holarchy*) is composed of interrelated sub-systems, each of which are in turn composed of sub-subsystems and so on, recursively, until reaching a lowest level of 'elementary' subsystems. As emphasised by Koestler [9], each such intermediary sub-system must play a dual role and be both: an autonomous whole controlling its parts; and a dependent part of a supra-system. This helps construct large systems with macro-goals from intermediary components able to achieve partial goals. There are several advantages that holonic structures provide for building viable complex systems [26]. These can be leveraged in applying holonic system principles to electronic institutions (and/or socio-technical systems), offering complexity management support by helping:

- institutions **scale** with the *number* and the *heterogeneity* of their members, since lower memberships in each holon put less strain on the institutional apparatus and decrease the level of internal diversity;
- to integrate institutions with **diverse goals**, since each of them only needs to be aware of the others' observable goals, state and negotiations, rather than of their internal details (e.g. rules and infrastructure);
- to improve an institution's local adaptation **reactivity**, while not directly impacting overall system **stability**, by the way in which the holonic structure modulates overall system dynamics and change propagation;
- system designers to **understand, analyse, simulate, adapt and predict** complex institutions, by allowing them to focus on a single holonic level at a time, with a reduced number of interrelated institutions.

## 4   Holonic Institutions

To benefit fully from these advantages, several important questions concerning holonic institutions have to be addressed:

- Q1: how to compose complementary or conflicting institutions?
- Q2: how to compose institutions at different scales, where each one can play the dual role of an autonomous institution and a semi-autonomous member?
- Q3: how to make holonic institutions adaptable, so that their goals can be achieved when changes occur in their environments, members, feedback on rule inefficiency, constraints from supra-institutions, or goal evolution?
- Q4: how to merge all the concerns above for constructing complex holonic institutions that can achieve their goals?

Figure 2-a depicts a generic conceptual model (abstract architecture) of holonic institutions to help address the questions above. In short, each holonic institution features two complimentary regulatory components implementing their dual roles. *Inward regulation* includes the internal rules, governance and adaptation functions for achieving a goal – as in Fig. 1-b; the difference being that this goal may diverge somewhat from the members' common goal since they agreed to join a supra-institution. *Outward regulation* merges, via conflict resolution and negotiation, the institution's own common goal with the (supra-)institutions' common goals. This results in the compromise goal that the

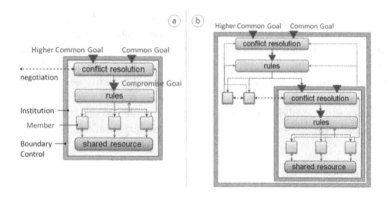

**Fig. 2.** (a) institution *holon* with dual role: inward/selfish &outward/transcendental; (b) supra-institution with several institutions/members

institution agrees to pursue. Each holonic institution is encapsulated within a *membrane* providing *membership-control* functions. At a high level of abstraction, this approach helps address institution composition questions (Q1 and Q2) (Figure 2-b). Institution adaptation relies on feedback from members and from the institution's evaluation of its goal achievement; it is propagated progressively from lower to upper holonic levels (Q3). This component-oriented design helps formalise, understand and analyse composite institutions, providing a key base for addressing the challenge of institutional complexity (Q4).

The above considerations provide a generic architectural overview on the manner in which *holonic institutions* can be constructed and maintained to address the aforementioned questions and achieve the advantages enabled by holonic principles. However, an important consideration is how Ostrom's seven other institutional design principles are impacted, in order to enable the eighth one – i.e. nested enterprises realised by holonic institutions. We will consider each design principle (**Px**) in turn.

(**P1**) **Boundaries**: *"who is and is not a member of the institutions should be clearly defined, as are the resources that are the subject of allocation"*. We propose to encapsulate each institution holon within a special-purpose container, or membrane, which helps isolate a holon's interior from the rest and separate between its internal resources and external environment. This reduces the holon's internal complexity as it only involves a 'manageable' sub-set of the entire system components; and, a predefined set of exchanges with its environment, controlled by its membrane (e.g. message filtering and aggregation). The membrane also exposes the holon's interfaces, allowing holonic institutions and members to appear identically to external observers. They include: the holon's goal; the feedback on purpose achievement; and the inter-holon negotiations, see Fig. 2.

(**P2**) **Congruence**: *"the rules should be congruent with the prevailing local environments (including the profile of the members themselves)"*. This rule will have a decisive impact on the overall shape of the holarchy – i.e. how members group into institutions, and institutions into supra-institutions, recursively. This will impact the size of each holon, as an institution's 'manageable' size will depend on the highest degree of divergence that can be supported over its group members. As stated previously, institutions are about coordinating divergent populations in order to achieve globally advantageous compromises. Hence, each member has to diverge somewhat from its selfish purposes and behaviours in order to benefit from the institution (cf. P6 minimal rights). An institution's internal divergence would have to be limited so as to allow for compromises that are both: sufficiently specific to be effective for achieving the group's purpose; and, sufficiently general to be acceptable to group members. Therefore, successful institution holons are more likely to be obtained by grouping members and institutions with most similarities (e.g. rather than via geometric borders).

(**P3**) **Participation**: *"those individuals who are affected by the collective choice arrangements should participate in their selection"*. To apply this rule, each institution holon must be able to define a common goal as an aggregate of the goals of its members, and use this aggregate goal when participating in the selection of higher-level rules for its supra-holons. Electing representative members to carry-out such negotiations may also be considered. Priorities must be set when participating in several supra-institutions with conflicting goals.

(**P4**) **Monitoring**: *"compliance with the rules should be monitored by the members themselves, or by agencies appointed by them"*. To apply this rule, each institution holon must be able to provide an aggregate estimate of the degree to which it has achieved its goal, or complied to its supra-institutions rules, based on estimates from its internal institution holons, or members.

(**P5**) **Sanctions**: *"graduated sanctions should ensure that punishment for non-compliance is proportional to the seriousness of the transgression"*. To apply this rule, each institution holon must be able to translate, proportionally, external sanctions for the institution to specific sanctions for its members.

(**P6**) **Conflicts**: *"the institution should provide fast, efficient and effective recourse to conflict resolution and conflict prevention mechanisms"*. Each institution holon must be able to detect and resolve conflicts between the common goal of its supra-institution (external) and the own common goal of its individual members (internal). Figure 2 depicts this via a specific *conflict resolution* component, which computes compromises between external and internal goals. These compromises are first *negotiated* with the other members of the supra-institution and then forwarded to the holon's internal members.

(**P7**) **Minimal recognition of rights to self-organise**: *"the rights of appropriators to form their own institutions are not challenged by external authorities"*. Holonic institutions will generally have fewer degrees of freedom in order to be integrated within a higher-level supra-institution, i.e. its autonomy may be limited because more specification instances become non-normative or invalid. This was actually already the case for prosumer members of base level institutions (cf. congruence). The acceptability of constraints and restrictions on rule formation would depend on the benefits expected from joining the institution. The more a member's own goal diverges from an institution's common goal, the bigger the required compromise and so the amount of autonomy that a member will have to surrender for staying in that institution. Similarly, an institutional holon needs to give up an amount of autonomy that is proportional to the difference between its supra-institution's goal (global compromise) and its internal goal. The exact proportionality can also be modulated by various configurations of the sanctions (P5) and boundary control (P1) rules.

In fact, the move towards holonic institutions provides for a much finer-grained separation of rights and powers. It is *not* that specific instances of rules themselves cannot be challenged: it is the *right* to form the institution, and to self-organise its rules, that is at issue. This is the fundamental issue in design principle P7, and is strikingly exposed by holonic systems thinking.

## 5 Case Study for Community Energy Systems

In this section we apply the concept of holonic institutions to the Smart Grids case study in subsect. 2.3. First we discuss Smart Houses as the basic holonic unit. We then introduce the idea of decentralised community energy systems (dCES) as the basic holonic institution unit. This leads to an analysis of multiple dCES as nested enterprises forming holonic institutions, and of the various Smart Grids agencies leading to polycentric self-governance and adaptivity.

### 5.1 Smart Houses

Smart Houses include technical systems that aim to automate *residential services* – e.g. safety and security, home entertainment, control of heating, ventilation and air conditioning – in order to improve owner comfort and experience. Since these systems operate in a social context, Smart Houses become socio-technical systems where several objectives, both technical and social, must be met.

Smart Houses do not operate in isolation and must integrate 'smoothly' within larger socio-technical systems – e.g. smart cities and electric grids. Several authorities with diverse interests and objectives operate at these levels, including city representatives and power grid operators. While each Smart House must remain largely autonomous and pursue its owners' objectives, it must also yield some of its autonomy in order to comply with the more global socio-technical systems that it joins for achieving a broader common purpose.

### 5.2 Decentralised Community Energy Systems

A Community Energy System (CES) is an energy generation, distribution and storage system involving local community ownership and participation. Generally, the differentiation between a nationally and community operated system is the boundary of autonomy – where responsibility for network specification and operation switches from the grid operator to the CES operator [25].

A *decentralised* CES (dCES), illustrated in Fig. 3, is a network of geographically co-located Smart Houses installed with small-scale renewable sources like

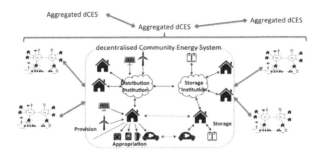

**Fig. 3.** Decentralised Community Energy System (dCES)

photovoltaic (PV) cells or micro wind turbines. At this base level, we assume there is no enterprise-owned Combined Heat and Power (CHP) plant or other large-scale generation: everything is generated in-house (literally), controlled and operated by the residents of Smart Houses. Storage can be provided by in-house batteries or, looking farther ahead, electric vehicles. A group of dCES can be aggregated into a larger institution, as previously discussed.

### 5.3 Holonic Institutions

If we think of an individual Smart House as a single holon, then we can create institutions at the base level by forming a dCES comprising multiple Smart Houses with a set of institutional rules meeting Ostrom's design principles. This allows for a wide range of institutional types. For example, we could have one type of institution whose energy distribution is based on the formalisation of social relationships, such as legitimate claims [19,22], and another type which is primarily market-oriented. Assuming that the minimal membership requirement is met – i.e. to have installed some renewable energy generation and/or micro-storage facility – then two (of many) types of dCES are summarised in Table 1.

In [25], four types of CES were identified: multi-home energy schemes, as suggested here; local energy schemes; district schemes with enterprise collaboration; and, district scheme with large generation. The different types were distinguished according to their ownership model, generation and storage facilities, and grid relationship. This latter could be *grid forming*, if the system operates pre-dominantly independently of the (national) grid (for example in terms of frequency and voltage control); *grid following*, which maintain voltage and frequency using the grid as reference; and, *grid supporting*, if they operate in parallel with the grid for the purposes of importing and exporting power.

It might be that the objective of a type-1 dCES would be grid-forming, while the objective of of a type-2 dCES would be grid-supporting, with the intention to export power through (in the UK) a FIT (feed-in tariff) scheme. Therefore, we can see how a dCES could form different institutional relationships with larger generation schemes, such as CHP plants, to form institutions at a larger scale. The larger scale institutions have different objectives, some technical (e.g.

**Table 1.** Institutional rules for two types of dCES

| dCES Type 1: Social relationship-oriented | |
| --- | --- |
| Ostrom principle | Implementation |
| P1. Membership | By invitation |
| P2. CPR rules | Provision and appropriation according to legitimate claims [19] |
| P3. Participation in rule selection | One member one vote |
| P4. Monitoring | SmartMeter[a] |
| P5. Sanctions | Diminished claims |
| P6. Conflicts | Alternative dispute resolution |
| dCES Type 2: Market-oriented | |
| Ostrom principle | Implementation |
| P1. Membership | By subscription |
| P2. CPR rules | Market-based (e.g. auction) |
| P3. Participation in rule selection | Enterprise appointed management board |
| P4. Monitoring | SmartMeter |
| P5. Sanctions | Cash fines |
| P6. Conflicts | Court hearing |

[a] With caveats, as discussed in Sect. 6

voltage and frequency control), some economic (e.g. import and export of power), and some political (e.g. meeting low-carbon targets). Critically, we can see these larger-scale institutions being realised in the framework of Fig. 2-b.

### 5.4 Polycentric Self-Governance

From a wider perspective, a Smart Grid is, like the water basins of California studied by Ostrom, composed of numerous actors and agencies with different ownership models – e.g. private individual, mutual cooperative, private enterprise, national infrastructure and regulator. Table 2 identifies a number of institutions involved in dCES, together with their associated *common goals* as indicated in Fig. 2.

It is well-known that managing critical infrastructure, like a national energy generation, transmission and distribution network, will necessarily involve multiple agencies with differing (possibly competing or even conflicting) interests, effectively creating a kind of overlay network of relational dynamics which also needs to be resolved. Furthermore, there is some, not always well-understood, inter-connection of public and private ownership that makes the overall system both stable and sustainable.

Therefore, in analysing any such complex system, it is critical to identify the agencies and determine their institutional *common goals* – what each agency (through its institution) is trying to achieve or maintain, by coordination with

**Table 2.** Actors/Agencies in dCES

| Agency (Institution) | Common purpose/typical functions |
| --- | --- |
| Administration | CPR management<br>– operate the servers running CPR Apps<br>– compute the resource allocation<br>– apply membership rules |
| Appropriators | Meet production/storage power goals<br>– provision and appropriate energy (generation and storage)<br>– investment strategy |
| Service providers | Infrastructure and equipment<br>– grid connectivity, voltage and frequency control<br>– installation and maintenance of micro scale generation and storage facilities<br>– market access (e.g. FIT) |
| Ombudsman/courts | Dispute resolution<br>– legal representation<br>– negotiation, mediation and arbitration |
| Regulators | Consumer protection<br>– protect present and future consumer's interests<br>– meeting national and international policy goals |
| Citizens' advocacy | Accountability, pressure, special interests<br>– represent environmental/green energy interests |
| Policy officials | Regulations (at multiple scales)<br>– policy drafting<br>– advice and calibration of CPR/CES rules |
| App entrepreneurs | Software service development<br>– SmartMeter Apps |

other institutions and by the decision-making of its members. Such analysis makes it possible to understand the 'ecosystem' of institutions and how they fit together as collaborators or competitors, based on the nature of their goals and the scope of their influence.

In this way, we believe that all of the institutions (nested enterprises) identified in Table 2 can be organised in a holonic manner. The outcome is twofold. Firstly, that it supports polycentric self-governance at all scales of the system, and in particular supports *subsidiarity* (the idea that problems are solved as close to the local source as possible). Secondly, it encourages the institutions to recognise their role in the overall 'scheme of things' in relation to institutions at the same, higher and lower levels. This is a key requirement for *adaptive* institutions [21] and this establishment of *systems thinking* as a commonplace practice within any one institution is what we may refer to as *institutionalised holonics*.

## 6   Related and Future Work

There are many theories and tools for organisation in multi-agent systems, including MOISE (an organisational model for multi-agent systems) [8], OMACS (organisational model for adaptive computational systems) [3], LAO (logic and organisations) [4], LGI (law governed interaction) [12], electronic institutions [7], and others, but none of these works takes holonic design into account. The issue of multiple interacting institutions has been addressed in [2,18], but only peripherally (at best) consider the concepts addressed here: norm-governed institutions, Ostrom's institutional design principles, holonic system architectures, and polycentric self-governance. Holonic multi-agent systems (HMAS) have been proposed in [23] yet *not* applied to social systems or electronic institutions.

Equally, several works use holonic design patterns to develop technological artefacts and complex systems [29], including traffic control [5], manufacturing plants [28] and (of course) Smart Grids [6]. However, we are not aware of any work that explicitly represents institutional or organisation concepts inside the holon, and reasons with these, with respect to its common goal.

There is much valuable work on a system of systems approach to complexity and self-organisation [27]. To the best of our knowledge, though, the present paper is the first work that has attempted to converge the hitherto disjoint works on self-organising institutions (based on conventional rules formalising Ostrom's design principles) and holonic architectures: i.e. to address both the functional and structural properties of complex CPRs in the context of a single unified framework and its application to a complex system like a Smart Grid.

Evidently, the proposal of holonic institutions and the case study presented in this paper are conceptual rather than actual. In further work, we plan to formalise and implement the concepts both in multi-agent simulation and a Smart Grid testbed, in particular to understand the relationship between structure and macro-level properties such as robustness, stability, resilience and sustainability.

However, in modelling and simulating socio-technical systems of this kind, there are other dimensions to consider. One is the relationship between people and institutions and the incorporation of processes from dynamical social psychology (e.g. [13]) into this framework. Another is the effect that some political/regulatory decisions may yet have on the evolution of the Smart Grid. If the so-called SmartMeter is unbundled (separating the platform from the the grid itself), as advocated by [24], this will have a telling impact on the Smart Grid 'institutional ecosystem'. Modelling this process is essential for understanding and responding to a new wave of innovation (driven by the App Entrepreneur agencies in Table 2) in a constructive and meaningful way.

## 7    Summary and Conclusions

This paper is situated within a broader research programme concerned with the formalisation and operationalisation of Ostrom's institutional design principles to engineer self-* properties for management and control of complex open systems. Specifically, it has focused on the formalisation of the eighth principle: *"For CPRs that are part of larger systems, nested enterprises"*. Since this principle relates more to structure rather than function, it has proved difficult to formalise in a declarative specification, like Principles 1–6, for electronic institutions [20]. Accordingly, the approach that has been proposed in this paper has been based on *structures* and *architectures* rather than rules.

The contribution of this paper is therefore threefold. By converging previously disjoint approaches to the design of complex open systems, one based on electronic institutions [19,20] and the other based on holonic architectures [6], the paper has contributed:

- a critical analysis of Ostrom's eighth institutional design principle for electronic institutions and socio-technical systems;
- an innovative proposal for *holonic institutions*, whereby institutions can be composed and de-composed as nested enterprises, enabling multi-scale polycentric decision-making to be established in the ecosystem of organisations;
- a case study in using holonic institutions for polycentric self-governance in community energy systems (smart grids).

This is, of course, only a first step in developing, demonstrating and applying such concepts. However, if successful, the ultimate contribution of this research could be to enhance polycentric theory, as a branch of political science, with the technology and tools to both analyse and design complex, multi-scale socio-economic, socio-political and socio-technical systems. These in turn would help address complex, multi-scale ecological challenges, such as climate change, just as Ostrom proposed [15].

**Acknowledgements.** Jeremy Pitt was partially supported by the UK EPSRC Grand Challenge project *The Autonomic Power System* (EP/I031650/1).

# References

1. Artikis, A.: Dynamic specification of open agent systems. J. Logic Comput. **22**(6), 1301–1334 (2012)
2. Cliffe, O., De Vos, M., Padget, J.: Specifying and reasoning about multiple institutions. In: Noriega, P., Vázquez-Salceda, J., Boella, G., Boissier, O., Dignum, V., Fornara, N., Matson, E. (eds.) COIN 2006. LNCS (LNAI), vol. 4386, pp. 67–85. Springer, Heidelberg (2007)
3. DeLoach, S.: OMACS: a framework for adaptive, complex systems. In: Dignum, V. (ed.) Multi-Agent Systems Semantics and Dynamics of Organisational Models. IGI Global, Hershey (2009)
4. Dignum, V., Dignum, F.: A logic of agent organizations. Logic J. IGPL **20**(1), 216–283 (2012)
5. Fischer, K.: Holonic multiagent systems – theory and applications. In: Barahona, P., Alferes, J.J. (eds.) EPIA 1999. LNCS (LNAI), vol. 1695, pp. 34–48. Springer, Heidelberg (1999)
6. Frey, S., Diaconescu, A., Menga, D., Demeure, I.: A holonic control architecture for a heterogeneous multi-objective smart micro-grid. In: IEEE 7th International Confrence on Self-Adaptive and Self-Organizing Systems (SASO), pp. 21–30 (2013)

7. García-Camino, A., Noriega, P., Rodríguez-Aguilar, J.: Implementing norms in electronic institutions. In: Proceedings of the Conference on Autonomous Agents and Multi-Agent Systems (AAMAS), pp. 667–673. ACM Press, NewYork (2005)
8. Hübner, J., Sichman, J., Boissier, O.: Developing organised multiagent systems using the MOISE$^+$ model. IJAOSE **1**(3/4), 370–395 (2007)
9. Koestler, A.: The Ghost in the Machine. Hutchinson Publisher, London (1967)
10. Kohler, T., Steghöfer, J.P., Busquets, D., Pitt, J.: The value of fairness: trade-offs in repeated dynamic resource allocation. In: Proceedings 8th IEEE Conference on Self-Adapting and Self-Organising Systems (SASO) (2014)
11. Kowalski, R., Sergot, M.: A logic-based calculus of events. New Gener. Comput. **4**, 67–95 (1986)
12. Minsky, N.: Law-Governed Interaction (LGI): A Distributed Coordination and Control Mechanism. Rutgers University (2005)
13. Nowak, A., Vallacher, R., Kus, M., Urbaniak, J.: The dynamics of societal transition: modeling non-linear change in the polish economic system. Int. J. Sociol. **35**, 65–68 (2005)
14. Ostrom, E.: Beyond markets and states: polycentric governance of complex economic systems. In: Grandin, K. (ed.) Les Prix Nobel, The Nobel Prizes 2009, pp. 408–444. Nobel Foundation, Stockholm (2010)
15. Ostrom, E.: Thinking about climate change as a commons. In: 15th Annual Philip Gamble Memorial Lecture, pp. 1–34. UMass Amherst (2011)
16. Ostrom, E., Ahn, T.: Foundations of Social Capital. Edward Elgar Pub, Cheltenham (2003)
17. Ostrom, E.: Governing the commons. Cambridge University Pressm, Cambridge (1990)
18. Patel, J., Teacy, W., Jennings, N., Luck, M., Chalmers, S., Oren, N., Norman, T., Preece, A., Gray, P., Shercliff, G., Stockreisser, P., Shao, J., Gray, W., Fiddian, N., Thompson, S.: Agent-based virtual organisations for the grid. Multiagent Grid Syst. **1**(4), 237–249 (2005)
19. Pitt, J., Busquets, D., Macbeth, S.: Distributive justice for self-organised common-pool resource management. ACM Trans. Auton. Adapt. Syst. **9**(3), 14 (2014)
20. Pitt, J., Schaumeier, J., Artikis, A.: Axiomatisation of socio-economic principles for self-organising institutions: concepts, experiments and challenges. ACM Trans. Auton. Adapt. Syst. **7**(4), 39:1–39:39 (2012)
21. RCEP: 28th report: Adapting institutions to climate change. Royal Commission on Environmental Protection, The Stationery Office Limited (2010)
22. Rescher, N.: Distributive Justice. Bobbs-Merrill, New York (1966)
23. Rodriguez, S., Gaud, N., Hilaire, V., Galland, S., Koukam, A.: An analysis and design concept for self-organization in holonic multi-agent systems. In: Brueckner, S.A., Hassas, S., Jelasity, M., Yamins, D. (eds.) ESOA 2006. LNCS (LNAI), vol. 4335, pp. 15–27. Springer, Heidelberg (2007)
24. Sanduleac, M., Eremia, M., Toma, L., Borza, P.: Integrating the electrical vehicles in the smart grid through unbundled smart metering and multi-objective virtual power plants. In: 2nd IEEE PES International Conference Innovative Smart Grid Technologies, ISGT Europe 2011, pp. 1–8 (2011)
25. SESIG: Smart Energy Special Interest Group: The role of community energy systems in the UK resilient energy supply. Technical report, Innovate UK (Technology Strategy Board) (2013)
26. Simon, H.: The architecture of complexity. Proc. Am. Philos. Soc. **106**(6), 467–482 (1962)

27. Steghöfer, J.P., Anders, G., Siefert, F., Reif, W.: A system of systems approach to the evolutionary transformation of power management systems. In: GI Jahrestagung, pp. 1500–1515 (2013)
28. Ulieru, M., Brennan, R., Walker, S.: The holonic enterprise: a model for internet-enabled global manufacturing supply chain and workflow management, integrated Manufacturing Systems. Integr. Manuf. Syst. **13**(8), 538–550 (2002)
29. Valckenaers, P., Brussel, H.V., Holvoet, T.: Fundamentals of holonic systems and their implications for self-adaptive and self-organizing systems. In: IEEE SASO Workshops (SASOW) (2008)

# Contextualized Planning Using Social Practices

Virginia Dignum[1] and Frank Dignum[2(✉)]

[1] Delft University of Technology, Delft, The Netherlands
M.V.Dignum@tudelft.nl
[2] Utrecht University, Utrecht, The Netherlands
F.P.M.Dignum@uu.nl

**Abstract.** Intelligent agents increasingly need to be aware of the social aspects of their context in order to take the appropriate action. However, existing techniques and platforms only provide partial solutions for this problem which do not take into account the full consequences of the social context. In this paper we propose to use ideas from social practice theory to support reasoning about action and planning in a social context.

We argue that putting social practices at the heart of the deliberation rather than use them as yet another aspect to be taken care of in the practical planning allows for more efficient planning. We provide a sketch of how this architecture provides some structure in the complexity of the deliberation process and balances between pro-active and reactive behaviour. The approach is demonstrated in a scenario taken from emergency management.

## 1 Introduction

Understanding the social contexts in which actions and interactions take place is of utmost importance for planning one's goals and activities. A system is context-aware if it can extract, interpret and use information about its context to adapt its plans to its current situation. Whereas people are pre-eminently able to understand context, computer systems are notorious for their inability to do so in general.

Social context is defined as the immediate physical and social setting in which something happens or develops. It includes the culture of an individual, and the people and institutions with whom they interact [1]. Within the agent community and in particular the COIN community the social context is often seen as consisting of the norms, organizations and institutions in which an agent is embedded. Subsequently it is investigated how these structures determine the behaviour of agents in application domains. E.g. in [21] we have shown the complexity of adding norms to BDI agents. Similarly in [2] it is shown how organization aware agents can be designed on the basis of BDI agents. From these and similar approaches it becomes clear that adding social context to BDI agents can complicate the deliberation process and often makes the standard deliberation inefficient (especially when used in real-time social environments).

© Springer International Publishing Switzerland 2015
A. Ghose et al. (Eds.): COIN 2014, LNAI 9372, pp. 36–52, 2015.
DOI: 10.1007/978-3-319-25420-3_3

In this paper, we argue that if we see social contexts not as an extra element to be added to an existing deliberation process, but rather as the *foundation* from which the deliberation process starts, it is possible to create more efficient deliberation processes. In a limited way, this has been shown for the case of norms in [15]. There the benefits were shown of using norms in the planning process rather than using them as a filter afterwards. In the current paper we take a broader perspective and include not only norms but all aspects of social context. We furthermore argue that *social practices* can be used to describe this social context in an efficient way.

Social practices give a means to choose between reactive behaviour in standard circumstances and pro-active behaviour that is necessary for social intelligent behaviour.

Existing agent platforms do not give much support to find this balance between pro-active and reactive behaviour. On the one hand, BDI agents, are primarily pro-active, goal driven. BDI implementations such as 2APL [6] or Jason [3], are particularly suitable to identify possible plans given a goal. Thus, for example when more than one plan is possible, 2APL agents are not able to identify which is the most suitable in a given context (the first plan that applies is followed), which may lead to plan revisions down the road, and as such, less efficient performance.

On the other extreme, we have completely reactive agents and Case-based Reasoning systems. These systems identify one possible action (or plan) given a situation by comparing that situation to the rules or known cases. Although this seems similar to the use of context it is limited in the sense that rules or cases are complete descriptions of situations. Only if all parameters are known or estimated can the action be determined. It depends also on the rule or case base whether "similar" cases can be found in order to derive a solution for the situation at hand. Usually this works well in a limited domain, but fails when the domains become dynamic or complex and cases are too scattered to provide answers for most situations.

Finally, Work Practice Modelling has been proposed to support the analysis of complex human-system interactions [19]. The rationale here is that understanding interactions requires going beyond formal procedures and information flows to analyse how people interact with each other. This approach is similar to the one we propose in this paper, but, as is the case in Case-Based Reasoning, current implementations are based on frames, and require the complete filling up of frame slots with situation information, and can thus not be used with incomplete information.

In this paper, we claim that agent plan generation can be enhanced by applying ideas from social practice theory. Social practices can be seen as a middle ground that combines the advantages of goal-directed and Case-Based Reasoning processes, by using social practices as heuristics to guide context-oriented plan identification. Social practice theory seeks to determine the link between practice and context within social situations [20]. Social practices refer to everyday practices and the way these are typically and habitually performed in (much of) a society. Such practices as "going to work", "meeting", or "greeting" are routinely performed and integrate different types of elements, such as bodily and mental activities, material artefacts, knowledge, emotions, skills, and so on [16]. Social practices are similar for groups of individuals at different points of time and location. As such, they can be seen as ways to act in context, i.e. once a suitable practice is identified, people will use it as a 'short cut' to determine an action which does not require elaborate reasoning about the plan to follow. However, social practices are not just mere scripts in the sense of [14]. They support, rather than restrict deliberation about behaviour. E.g. the social practice of "going to work" incorporates usual means of transport that can be used, timing constraints, weather and traffic conditions, etc. So, normally you take a car to work, but if the weather is exceptionally bad the social practice does not force the default action, but rather gives input for deliberation about a new plan in this situation and take a bus or train (or even stay home).

In order to illustrate the major ideas of this paper we consider the development of a serious game to train first responders in a crisis management situation. The use case is a collision of a truck loaded with fluids with a car which has consequently caught fire. The use case is based on our experience designing a serious game for crisis management including such scenarios.

In Sect. 2 we describe how the prototypical approaches described above (goal directed, case based and work practice) would need to model the scenario and what are the main issues. In Sect. 3 we describe social practices and how they can be used in the deliberation cycle of agents. In Sect. 4 we describe how the scenario can be modelled, making use of social practices. Some conclusions and future work are given in Sect. 5.

## 2   Background

In this section, we discuss how activity in context is handled in different frameworks for social deliberation. In particular, we describe 2APL as a typical example of goal-directed approaches, Case-Based Reasoning as an exponent of situation based approaches and Work Practices as an approach in between. Of course, many other approaches exist that take (social) context into account when deciding about actions, but the approaches discussed here highlight the main issues.

### 2.1   2APL

The multi-agent programming language 2APL supports the implementation of individual agents that can perform high-level reasoning and deliberation about their information (i.e., beliefs) and objectives (i.e., goals to achieve) in order to decide what actions to perform [6]. In order to reach its goals, a 2APL agent adopts plans. 2APL provides programming constructs to implement beliefs, goals, actions, plans, events, and three different types of rules that can be applied to generate plans. In particular, 2APL provides *planning goal rules* that implement practical reasoning rules that can be used to generate plans for achieving goals and *practical reasoning rules*, which can be used to expand abstract plans to concrete sequences of actions and to rewrite plans to cope with unforeseen circumstances [5].

A possible way to represent the top level planning goal rules for a fireman agent in the fire fighting scenario as indicated in the introduction is:

```
Goal: handlecrisis
GP/PR rules:
handlecrisis <- victim | inform(medics);save(victim);extinguishfire
handlecrisis <-  | extinguishfire
extinguishfire <- chemical | spray(foam);clean
extinguishfire <- | spray(water);clean
```

The first rule states that whenever the precondition "victim" holds, the goal "*handlecrisis*" can be dealt with by the "*plan*": *inform(medics);save(victim);extinguishfire.* The second rule states that *handlecrisis* can alternatively be handled by the plan *extinguishfire*. This specification makes use of the fact that in 2APL, rules are tried in order, and the first one that is applicable is executed. Thus the agent first checks whether a victim is present and in case there is, it will inform the medics, save the victim and extinguish the fire afterwards. If there is no victim, the condition of the first rule does not apply and the agent follows the second rule: extinguishing the fire. A similar process appears for the "*extinguishfire*" rules. It first checks for chemicals. If they are present it will use foam. If they are not present, it will try the second rule and use water.

A problem with this approach is that if the first rule fails during the execution of the plan, e.g. because the medics cannot be reached, the agent will try the next rule and start extinguishing the fire, even though there is a victim present. This can be avoided by explicitly indicating a precondition to be true or false in order to distinguish the different cases, as in the following two rules:

```
handlecrisis <- victim |
inform(medics);save(victim);extinguishfire
handlecrisis <- not(victim) | extinguishfire
```

However, if in this situation the plan associated with the first rule fails, the second rule is not applicable because there is a victim. In this situation, the agent would just stop, without saving the victim or extinguishing the fire, as it has no applicable plan to follow. Moreover, in the case of conditions involving several criteria, the number of rules would quickly increase such that the different combinations of conditions could be represented.

We are not claiming that the above cases could not in some way be represented in 2APL. However, the example highlights two aspects that are interrelated and mingled in the 2APL representation. The conditions of the rules function as a precondition of the plan in the rule. However, the same conditions are also used for rule selection. The latter necessitates the constructions shown above but can also lead to (unexpected) difficulties as indicated.

By using the idea of social practice we distinguish conditions that are needed for rule selection and preconditions of plans. Thus we do not incorporate the conditions in all the rules, but are checking the context conditions of the social practice first and given those conditions select a subset of the rules that are relevant for the situation. Thus the deliberation is no longer purely goal driven, but is goal plus context driven. This will lead to a more natural specification and (through the modularization of rules based on context) to a more efficient deliberation.

## 2.2 Case-Based Reasoning

Whereas 2APL follows a goal-based approach for selecting actions, Case-Based Reasoning (CBR) is an example of reactive deliberation. CBR uses previous cases (or situations) as the basis for the selection of the next action [17]. The general cycle of CBR follows the following steps:

1. problem formulation
2. retrieve
3. reuse
4. revise
5. retain.

The first step is to formulate the problem. This is important because the way a problem is formulated will determine the query on the case-base, through which the most relevant case is eventually selected. In our scenario this might lead to the following (simplified) problem formulation:

```
fire(house)= no
fire(tanker)= small
contents(tanker)= unknown
fire(car)= no
oil-spillage= no
victims(car)= 2
victims(tanker)= no
...
```

For simplicity, we use here a very simple attribute-value structure, but more complex structures can also be used. With this formulation the case-base is searched for a similar situation. The likelihood of finding a case exactly like the current situation is minimal. Thus one needs some metrics in order to find the most 'similar' case. Without getting into details, we just point to some difficult aspects here. Suppose there is an almost identical case except that it considers also a victim in the tanker. Could we use that case as a basis for the current course of action? As we indicated in the scenario it might be crucial to get information from the truck driver about the load of the tanker. If the driver is unconscious this is not possible, while if the truck driver is not injured he might give that information right away. So, even if the case in the case-base differs in only one parameter it might lead to a quite different course of action.

Given a case from the case-base that is close to the present situation, it has to be checked whether the plan for that situation can be used as it is or should be adjusted. E.g. if in the case from the case-base the first step would be to contact the owner of the tanker to ascertain the contents of it, this could now be just asked from the driver as he is not injured. Although for humans it is reasonably obvious how to make such a revision of the plan it is more difficult to find an algorithm that could calculate the necessary adjustment automatically. Finally, the system should decide whether the present case and its course of action are sufficiently different from the cases in the case base to warrant adding it (in the right place).

Intuitively the example makes clear that in scenarios like the one from Sect. 2 there are many parameters that potentially influence the course of action and even small differences can have big consequences for the course of action to be followed. Thus one needs to have a very large case base to cover all relevant cases such that an appropriate course of action is followed in each situation. In many domains (like crisis management) such a large case base cannot easily be assembled nor is it possible to construct one on the fly, because the consequences of errors are too big to allow for a gradually improving system.

## 2.3 Work Practice Simulation

A last approach relevant to social deliberation is that advocated by the Brahms platform [19]. Brahms is a multi-agent, rule-based, activity programming language. The Brahms language allows for the representation of situated activities of agents in a geographical model of the world. Situated activities are actions that happen in the context of a specific situation, thus their execution is constrained not only by the reasoning capabilities of an agent, but also by the agent's beliefs of the external world, such as where the agent is located, the state of the world at that location and elsewhere, located artefacts, activities of other agents, or communication with other agents and artefacts.

The philosophy of Brahms comes from the realization that work practices in organizations differ from the work flows as described and prescribed by the organization. If it is recognized that ultimately employee behaviours, rather than management practices, are the key to success in organizations [4], then these practices should be described as agent behaviours rather than the official (goal directed) plans. Within Brahms a work practice is defined as the (collaborative) performance of collective situated activities of a group of people who collaborate and communicate, while performing these activities synchronously or asynchronously, by making use of knowledge previously gained through experience in performing similar activities. Differences between formal plans and the work practice can lead to unforeseen results and render organizational plans useless.

The Brahms modelling language is geared towards modelling people's activity behaviour [19]. The Brahms framework consists of several interrelated models. Of particular relevance for this paper is the Activity Model that defines the behaviour of agents and objects by means of activities and workframes. Brahms has an activity-based subsumption architecture by which an agent's activities can be decomposed into sub-activities. Activities can be interrupted and resumed, just as humans can multi-task by switching between different activities. Workframes control when activities are executed based on the beliefs of the agent, and on facts in the world. However, as in CBR, workframes require the full instantiation of all its preconditions in order to be applied.

Our scenario could be modelled through the use of several workframes. One for saving victims, one for checking the tanker load and one for extinguishing the fire. By giving the saving victims framework a high priority it will try to execute first. Thus if the preconditions of the workframe are fulfilled (which will include the presence of victims) it will start saving victims. If the workframe cannot be executed the one with the next highest priority will be executed, etc. If during the extinguishing of the fire suddenly a victim is discovered the framework for saving the victim is automatically fired and the extinguishing workframe is interrupted. This makes the Brahms framework quite flexible. However, it has the same problem as the 2APL framework in that the context and preconditions of the workframes are mixed. Moreover, the agents also do not have a learning capability that might lead to a priority adjustment of workframes after the (failed) execution of activities.

# 3    Social Practices

## 3.1    Social Intelligence and Social Practices

From the previous section, in which we showed some possible problems of using existing techniques and platforms for modelling social deliberation, as exemplified by a crisis management scenario, we can derive the following two requirements for socially realistic behaviour of systems active in real-time environments.

**Context and preconditions for action.** Socially intelligent agents should be able to understand and consider internal (pro-active) drives and external (reactive) drives. In most systems created for social interactions with humans, speed and appropriateness of reaction are leading for the system's behaviour. However, in open, dynamic situations, the socially intelligent agent also has to reason and plan for pro-active drives. So, the framework should maintain both internal and external drives and be able to reason about their relative importance in each situation. Whereas 2APL is strong on the goal based deliberation, it is difficult to incorporate the situation based reactions. This shows in the mix-up of context conditions that are situation based into the pre-conditions of plans for goals. CBR is strong in reasoning from situations, but lacks the goal based deliberation. Brahms seems to better suited to model work practices, but it lacks flexibility in denoting situations and especially does not support learning.

**Learning.** The fact that intelligent agents should be able to learn is obvious. That most agent systems cannot really learn is also a fact. Considering socially intelligent agents, learning is of utmost importance given the need for operation in highly dynamic and open environments and diverse interaction partners. The agent should use its experience to tune its parameters and learn the most effective actions in each situation taking into account both its physical and social effects. However, where physical effects of actions can usually be measured with sensors, the social effects are often not visible and have to be derived from consequent actions of the partners. Thus more subtle sensing and interpretation is needed to learn the most efficient social interaction patterns.

In order to cope with the complexity of combining situation based reactions and goal based planning while taking care of both social and physical aspects of reality and planning in such an environment, we propose to use *social practices* [16]. As described in the introduction, social practice theory seeks to determine the link between practice and context within social situations. That is, social practices aim to integrate the individual with his or her surrounding environment, assessing how that context relates to past, common, experiences, culture and capabilities of the individual. It should be emphasized that social practice theory is a sociological theory that takes social practices as focal point to explain social phenomena. Individuals only play a role in as far as they are 'recruited' by social practices in order for the social practice to be executed. In this paper we look at social practices from the individual's perspective. It should be seen as an addition to the sociological theory not as an explanation or change of that theory. So, social practices certainly seem a good starting point for systems that need to take context into account.

Social practices can be seen as patterns which can be filled in by a multitude of single and often unique actions [16], that endure between and across specific moments of enactment. Through (joint) performance, the patterns provided by the practice are filled out and reproduced. Each time it is used, elements of the practice, including know-how, meanings and purposes, are reconfigured and adapted [18]. Therefore the use of social practices includes a constant learning of the individuals using the social practice in ever changing contexts. In this way social practices guide the learning process of agents in a natural way.

In [18] the social aspect of social practices is emphasized by giving the social practice center stage in interactions and letting individuals be supporters of the social practice. It shows that social practices are shared (social) concepts. The mere fact that they are shared and jointly created and maintained means that individuals playing a role in a social practice will expect certain behaviour and reactions of the other participants in the social practice. Thus it is this aspect that makes the social practices so suitable for use in individual planning in social situations. Because, in this paper, we concentrate on the individual planning we will not see much of the particular social aspects of the social practices, but we like to emphasize that it forms the basis of the success of the individual planning with social practices.

## 3.2   Characteristics of Social Practices

Researchers in social science have proposed a representation of social practices based on three broad categories [12]: materials, meanings and competences.

Based on these ideas, we developed a model to represent social practices that can be used in social deliberation by intelligent systems. Obviously, as is the case with e.g. the representation and use of norms, other representations of social practices are possible given the many dimensions of the use of social practices. Our proposal, depicted in Fig. 1, is especially suitable for use in agent reasoning.

The components of this representation model are as follows:

- *Physical Context* describes elements from the physical environment that can be sensed:
    - *Resources* are objects that play a role in the practice such as fire hose, fire, truck and car in the scenario.
    - *Places* indicates where all objects and actors are located relatively to each other, in space or time.
    - *Actors* are all people and autonomous systems involved, that have capability to reason and (inter)act.
- *Social Context* contains:
    - *Social Interpretation* determines the social context in which the practice is used.
    - *Roles* describe the competencies and expectations about a certain type of actors.
    - *Norms* describe the rules of (expected) behaviour within the practice.
- *Activities* indicate the normal activities that are expected within the practice. Not all activities need to be performed! They are meant as potential courses of action.
- *Plan Patterns* describe usual patterns of actions defined by the landmarks that are expected to occur.
- *Meaning* refers to the social meaning of the activities that are (or can be) performed in the practice. Thus they indicate social effects of actions
- *Competences* indicate the type of capabilities the agent should have to perform the activities within this practice.

Looking at the characteristics of social practices as given in Fig. 1 one can notice some resemblance to the aspects that also play a role in agent organization models (see e.g. [11]). This list can be seen as an analogue of the connection between imposed and emerging norms. Both organizations and social practices give a kind of structure to the interactions between agents. However, organizations provide an imposed (top-down) structure, while the social practices form a structure that arises from the bottom up. Thus where organizational interaction patterns indicate minimal patterns that agents should comply with, the patterns in a social practice indicate minimal patterns that can and are usually used by the agents.

In the next sections, we sketch how we envision the use of social practices in agent deliberations and how they indeed seem to be a useful part of a new architecture for socially intelligent agents.

| Abstract Social Practice | Combat Fire | Going to work |
|---|---|---|
| Physical Context | | |
| Resources | inflammable objects, water, barriers... | Vehicles, money, ... |
| Places | locations of fire, actors and resources,... | Stations, roads,... |
| Actors | Victims, bystanders, colleagues,... | Drivers, co-passengers, ... |
| Social Context | | |
| Social interpretation | Dangerous places, safe places, rescue equipment | Bus driver, train driver... |
| Roles | police, medics, ... | |
| Norms | own safety; public safety | |
| Activities | Identify type of fire; Extinguish fire; Removal victims; Clear area; ensure own/team safety; ... | Choose transport type; buy ticket; drive car; ... |
| Plan patterns | 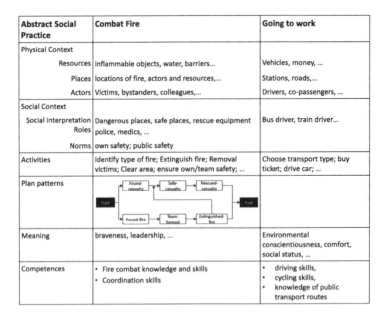 | |
| Meaning | braveness, leadership, ... | Environmental conscientiousness, comfort, social status, ... |
| Competences | • Fire combat knowledge and skills<br>• Coordination skills | • driving skills,<br>• cycling skills,<br>• knowledge of public transport routes |

**Fig. 1.** Social practices

## 3.3 Social Practices in Deliberation

Just by using social practices does not necessarily make agents become socially aware. We also have to have an agent deliberation in which social practices are taken into account at the right moments. In [8,10] we sketched such an agent architecture. We will not describe it fully here again, but just highlight the aspects that are most important for the planning. We assume that sensing is not a passive but also an active process. Active social practices direct the agent's sensing to find objects, actors and events that are expected within that social practice. This leads to reactive but focused sensing based on the current situation.

When the interpretation of the sensed environment in terms of the existing social practices, results in only one possible action, the agent will perform that action directly. However, in cases that there are several possible courses of action, the agent will take into account its motives in order to determine possible goals that are applicable to the sensed environment and generate a plan accordingly. This deliberation can be a complex BDI deliberation or extensions thereof, such as the FAtiMA [7] or BRIDGE [9] deliberations containing emotions, goals, intentions, beliefs, roles, identity, etc. However, due to the context of the social practice the agent can limit the portion of the applicable rules and beliefs and also can use specialized rules for planning (patterns) that are (only) applicable within the social practice.

Alternatively, the drive to search for patterns (and thus the sensing process) can be steered from the agent's motives. E.g., a fireman with a high achievement motive and low avoidance motive will start approaching a fire right away looking for a victim to establish whether a victim can still be saved. Thus we see that the parallel tracks of pro-active and reactive behaviour already start with the sensing behaviour.

Using social practices in deliberation, one can also distinguish the fast and slow reasoning tracks as described by Kahnemann [13]. If a social practice matches the features of a situation to an extend that it dictates a cause of action right away, this leads to a reactive action. E.g. seeing a small fire leads a fireman to use a fire-extinguisher and extinguish the fire (instead of starting to connect the water hoses).

A second fast track is taken when a social practice in combination with a motive also leads to a motivation for a certain type of behaviour. E.g. if a fireman has a strong achievement motive to have all victims saved and it gets the order to proceed from the fire commander he will get to the victim and start to evacuate her (even though he might not have planned the whole activity yet).

If the course of action is not completely determined by the social practice some more *deliberation* takes place.

Figure 2 gives a more detailed overview of the deliberation process.

As in traditional BDI reasoning, by perceiving the current context, an agent will revise its beliefs and goals. The context will also trigger some social practices. That is, some elements of a social practice are filled out by the sensed observations, resulting in more concrete social practices. For example, in the context of the crisis management scenario, the social practice '*rescuing-victim*'

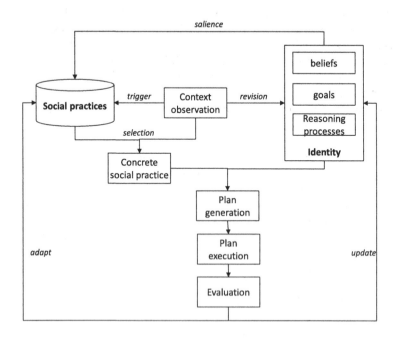

**Fig. 2.** Social reasoning process

is triggered. Further observation of the context will determine whether danger of explosion exists, whether other rescue workers are available, whether the victim is conscious, resulting in the more concrete social practice of '*rescuing-unconscious-victim-in-explosion-danger-together-with-colleague*'. If the agent can establish that the colleague has the same information or because they use a signal when getting in to synchronize the agent can assume that the colleague follows that same social practice and the rescue can be done efficiently without negotiating the coordination (because that is included in the social practice plan patterns). The agent will then generate a plan for this social practice based on its identity (beliefs, goals and reasoning process). Thus it should be emphasized that the social practices do not replace the traditional deliberation of BDI agents. They give a background and patterns that can be used for the plan deliberation. This will increase efficiency and also allows for dividing context checks and pre-conditions of actions and plans.

Notable in the above scenario is that the social practices take a leading role in organizing possible courses of action. Thus we do not have either a fixed set of plans per goal nor do we have a large set of plans that have to be searched. Because the social practices combine material and social aspects one can start from either side and check the appropriateness of the other aspect for the current situation. This avoids having to reason separately about both aspects and combining them afterwards. Having the social practices also can instantiate elements in the deliberation if they are already clear from the context, such as the roles and expected goals. Other times social practices overrule elements like emotions thus bypassing deliberation about this element.

In order to facilitate their use, social practices should be stored in an efficient and easy to use way. Case Bases such as used in CBR provide seem to be suitable structure for the management and maintenance of social practices. The practices can be linked based on some (prominent) features and generalizations. Thus, for example, the relation between practices related to crisis management is based on the type of incident and parties involved. Generalizations also play a major structuring role. E.g. all fire fighting practices can be related to a general fire fighting practice. This allows for inheritance and all the usual reasoning over hierarchies.

Given the fact that agents will have many social practices, the question also arises how they choose a practice when several practices seem applicable in a situation. Several strategies can be designed for these situations. One is that the agent checks which social practice will most likely further its own (social) goals and motivations. The agent can also check its experience and choose the social practice that led most often to a successful interaction. So, it plays on safe. Many more strategies can be designed to make the choice. It is important to note that there is not a single possible best strategy to make this choice. The social practices function more as background and guideline than as obligations. Thus it is not necessary that in each situation a unique social practice fits. If more practices fit one will be chosen and its effects evaluated. If it worked well and the choice was based on an aspect not yet considered before, this aspect might be added (conditionally). In this way the social practices form a flexible and evolving structure to support the adequate deliberation of the agents.

## 4   Scenario

In this section we illustrate how social practices can be used to model and implement the scenario of Sect. 2. When the fire brigade gets to the accident it might have heard about the situation already and assume it is in the *tanker fire* practice. If the firemen did not hear this yet, the first thing they will do is check which objects are on fire (this might be part of the social practice of "*arriving at an incident*"). The concrete social practice of "*tanker fire*" is exemplified in Fig. 3.

In this case, the firemen can start right away using this social practice of tanker fire to deliberate about their next actions. Notice that they might do this as well even if they have not seen the car that has been hit. As the situation unfolds they will continuously check whether the physical resources present match those expected give the social practice. The information about physical

| Concrete Social Practice | Tanker Fire |
|---|---|
| **Physical Context** | |
| Resources | Tanker, car, fire truck, water resource, |
| Places | Geometric position of all objects |
| Actors | Truck driver, car driver, passenger, firemen, policemen, bystanders |
| **Social Context** | |
| Social interpretation | Victim in danger, explosion risk, chemical health hazard, safe distance |
| Roles | Victim, firemen, tanker driver, police, bystander |
| Norms | police takes care of road safety<br>Fireman determines risk of explosion<br>Fireman has power to order evacuation<br>Fireman has power over police , victim and medics |
| Activities | Identify type of fire; Extinguish fire; Removal victims; clear area; ensure own/team safety; close roads; first aid to victim,... |
| Plan patterns | Determine truck load **before** evacuate victims<br>Evacuate victims **before** extinguish fire |
| Meaning | Safety first |
| Competences | • Domain knowledge and skills: know type fire<br>• Coordination skills : know who to call about fire/victims<br>**Choice/deliberation skills:**<br>• When explosion high choose to evacuate all<br>• When victim quick to help choose free victim first<br>• When fire extinguished choose clear debris<br>• When situation safe choose open roads<br>• ... |

**Fig. 3.** Concrete social practice tanker fire

resources, places and actors can also give rise to (additional) sensing in order to fill in parameter values and objects that are present.

Given the physical context asserted, the social context is filled as far as possible. Some of the social context is given by the social practice. E.g. a person sitting in a car that has collided with the tanker that is now on fire will be a "victim". However, the social practice also prescribes that an interpretation should be made that indicates whether the situation should be classified as "*chemical health hazard*". Again this might be simple if the truck load is known, but otherwise might give rise to an explicit process to ascertain the truck load and whether this load can give rise to a chemical health hazard.

The social context also indicates a number of aspects that will be important for the execution and coordination of actions from the social practice. The roles indicate the type of actors that potentially interact within this practice. The norms indicate constraints and expectations of (inter)actions within this social practice. E.g. the firemen expect the police to ensure the safety of the road. This means that they will not check this safety whenever the police is around.

The next consideration in the social practice is the competencies that are needed to execute the actions within this social practice. E.g. in order to ascertain whether there is a chemical health hazard the fireman needs to have knowledge about chemicals and particularly about the dangers of these in high temperatures. If the social practice indicates that the first thing to do is to ascertain chemical health hazards and the fireman has too little knowledge about chemicals or no knowledge about the truck load he needs to take action to remedy this lack of knowledge. Also, if the fireman has no experience with extinguishing certain types of chemicals and has no complete knowledge he might decide to just evacuate the scene instead of trying to extinguish the fire. Thus in this way

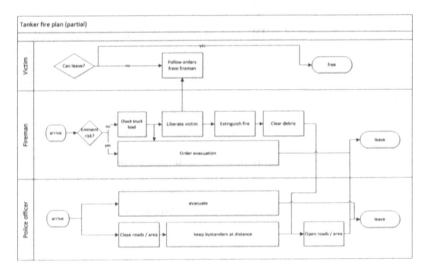

**Fig. 4.** Concrete plan

the competencies influence the particular actions that are executed or avoided within the social practice.

Finally, the plan patterns indicate that the fireman first determines the chemical hazard before evacuating victims. The victims have to be evacuated before he starts extinguishing the fire. These patterns determine a kind of default patterns that are assumed to hold for all ways in which the social practice is used. Note that the patterns in this case only give very sparse constraints on the behaviour. Thus the fireman has a lot of freedom to fill in the actual plan resulting from the social practice. Given his personality, experience, goals and emotions he can deliberate to come to a concrete plan as shown in Fig. 4.

## 5   Discussion and Conclusion

Intelligent agents increasingly need to be more socially aware of their context in order to take the appropriate action. We have shown how current techniques and platforms only provide partial solutions for this problem through the use of these approaches in a simple scenario. Of course, this does not mean that current platforms are not usable, but rather that they have problems modelling a scenario in which aspects are present that play a prominent role for socially intelligent behaviour.

In this paper, we have argued for the use of social practices as part of a new agent architecture that should facilitate socially intelligent behaviour. It puts social context and social motives at the heart of the deliberation rather than use them as additional modules. We have sketched how this architecture provides some structure in the complexity of the deliberation process, facilitates the combination of social and physical aspects of a situation, integrates fast and slow thinking patterns as described in the psychology literature, and balances between pro-active and reactive behaviour. As such it can be seen as combining the features of goal directed (BDI) architectures as exemplified by 2APL, situation based reasoning as performed in CBR and workframe based deliberation as done in Brahms.

The use of social practices for social intelligent agents also led to the realization that the concept is not very well defined and thus needs to be made more precise and formal in order to serve as a basis for implementations. In this paper we have shown a first step towards this goal. Two aspects are important in this respect. First, social practices can be seen as a kind of emerging organizations. Taking this seriously led to the realization that many concepts of organization models can be very well used to describe aspects of social practices as well. However, one should bear in mind that social practices do not have the kind of imposed normative flavour but rather have the flavour of emerging norms.

The second aspect that should be further explored is the way social practices should be structured with respect to each other. Do we need abstraction hierarchies? As a first step it seems that using similar structures as used in case based reasoning is promising. However, more research with large quantities of practices should be done to make this more precise.

Because in this paper we have focussed on the use of social practices by the agents we have not touched upon the fact that social practices emerge and evolve in social interactions. Therefore an important characteristic of them is that they are partially shared. This means that when a fireman starts the tanker fire practice it can expect a certain type of behaviour from the policeman involved as they share the same practice. A shared social practice thus can serve as a background for facilitating coordination and also for solving problems in coordination protocols (due to a changed environment or social context).

# References

1. Barnett, E., Casper, M.: A definition of "social environment". Am. J. Public Health **91**(3), 465–465 (2001)
2. Boissier, O., van Riemsdijk, M.B.: Organisational reasoning agents. In: Ossowski, S. (ed.) Agreement Technologies. Law, Governance and Technology Series, vol. 8, pp. 309–320. Springer, Dordrecht (2013)
3. Bordini, R.H., Hubner, J.F., Wooldridge, M.: Programming Multi-agent Systems in AgentSpeak using Jason. Wiley, Chichester (2007)
4. Colvin, A., Boswell, W.: The problem of action and interest alignment: beyond job requirements and incentive compensation. Hum. Resour. Manag. Rev. **17**, 38–51 (2007)
5. Dastani, M.: Modular rule-based programming in 2APL. In: Giurca, A., Gasevic, D., Taveter, K. (eds.) Handbook of Research on Emerging Rule-Based Languages and Technologies: Open Solutions and Approaches, pp. 25–49. IGI Global, Hershey (2009)
6. Dastani, M.: 2APL: a practical agent programming language. Auton. Agents Multi-agent Syst. **16**(3), 214–248 (2008)
7. Dias, J., Mascarenhas, S., Paiva, A.: FAtiMA modular: towards an agent architecture with a generic appraisal framework. In: Bosse, T., Broekens, J., Dias, J., van der Zwaan, J. (eds.) Emotion Modeling. LNCS, vol. 8750, pp. 43–55. Springer, Heidelberg (2014)
8. Dignum, F., Dignum, V., Jonker, C., Prada, R.: Situational deliberation; getting to social intelligence. In: Computational Social Science and Social Computer Science: Two Sides of the Same Coin, June 2014
9. Dignum, F., Dignum, V., Jonker, C.M.: Towards agents for policy making. In: David, N., Sichman, J.S. (eds.) MAPS 2008. LNCS, vol. 5269, pp. 141–153. Springer, Heidelberg (2009)
10. Dignum, F., Prada, R., Hofstede, G.J.: From autistic to social agents. In: AAMAS 2014, pp. 1161–1164, May 2014
11. Dignum, V.: A model for organizational interaction: based on agents, founded in logic. Ph.D. thesis, SIKS Dissertation Series 2004-1, Utrecht University (2004)
12. Holtz, G.: Generating social practices. JASSS **17**(1), 17 (2014)
13. Kahneman, D.: Thinking, fast and slow. Farrar, Straus & Giroux (2011)
14. Minsky, M.: A framework for representing knowledge. In: Collins, A., Smith, E. (eds.) Readings in Cognitive Science, pp. 156–189. Morgan Kaufmann, San Mateo (1988)
15. Panagiotidi, S., Vázquez-Salceda, J., Dignum, F.: Reasoning over norm compliance via planning. In: Aldewereld, H., Sichman, J.S. (eds.) COIN 2012. LNCS, vol. 7756, pp. 35–52. Springer, Heidelberg (2013)

16. Reckwitz, A.: Toward a theory of social practices. Eur. J. Soc. Theor. **5**(2), 243–263 (2002)
17. Richter, M.M., Weber, R.O.: Case-Based Reasoning: A Textbook. Springer, Berlin (2013)
18. Shove, E., Pantzar, M., Watson, M.: The Dynamics of Social Practice. Sage, London (2012)
19. Sierhuis, M., Clancey, W.J., van Hoof, R.J.J.: Brahms an agent-oriented language for work practice simulation and multi-agent systems development. In: Seghrouchni, A.E.F., Dix, J., Dastani, M., Bordini, R.H. (eds.) Multi-Agent Programming, pp. 73–117. Springer, New York (2009)
20. Smolka, A.L.B.: Social practice and social change: activity theory in perspective. Hum. Dev. **44**(6), 362–367 (2001)
21. VanHee, L., Aldewereld, H., Dignum, F.: Implementing norms? In: Hubner, J.F., Petit, J.-M., Suzuki, E. (eds.) Proceedings International Joint Conference on Web Intelligence and Intelligent Agent Technology, pp. 13–16 (2011)

# Modelling the Impact of Role Specialisation on Cooperative Behaviour in Historic Trader Scenarios

Christopher K. Frantz[1]([✉]), Martin K. Purvis[1], Bastin Tony Roy Savarimuthu[1], and Mariusz Nowostawski[2]

[1] Department of Information Science, University of Otago, Dunedin, New Zealand
{christopher.frantz,martin.purvis,tony.savarimuthu}@otago.ac.nz
[2] Faculty of Computer Science and Media Technology,
Gjøvik University College, Gjøvik, Norway
mariusz.nowostawski@hig.no

**Abstract.** We analyse two well-established historic trader scenarios from the area of comparative economics known as the Maghribi Traders Coalition and the contemporary Genoese traders, which contrast the otherwise comparable individualistic Genoese and collectivistic North-African trader societies by the institutions they used to sustain cooperative behaviour. We employ agent-based modelling to test a previously unexplored aspect, namely whether a unified role structure (unifying the contrasting investor and merchant perspectives – something that could have characterised one of the two communities in question, the Maghribis) could have been a contributing factor to sustain cooperation for the collective group of Maghribi Traders. To model the emerging institutions, we utilise a continuous notion of deontics that supports the adoption of norms from an experiential perspective. Our simulation results support the idea that experiencing economic transactions from different perspectives increases the convergence performance towards stable behaviour, and supports the enforcement of cooperation by informal means, such as norms, based on their stronger normative alignment.

**Keywords:** Institutions · Role specialisation · Maghribi Traders Coalition · Genoese traders · Norms · Rules · Dynamic Deontics · Social simulation · Multi-agent systems

## 1 Introduction

In recent decades the importance of institutions as a fundamental element to determine economic success has gained strong reflection in economic literature. Notable works include North's seminal work [13], but also more recent efforts such as Robinson and Acemoglu's [1] and Greif's [9].

Recent achievements modelling norm emergence using multi-agent systems ([2,11,18]) demonstrate the suitability to represent those subtle social

ⓒ Springer International Publishing Switzerland 2015
A. Ghose et al. (Eds.): COIN 2014, LNAI 9372, pp. 53–71, 2015.
DOI: 10.1007/978-3-319-25420-3_4

coordination mechanisms in silico. We build on that effort and show how perspective-taking can drive differing norm understandings without prescribing specific norms ex ante.

To realise this, we capitalise on the previously introduced Dynamic Deontics [6] that relax the otherwise rigid categorisation of prescriptions into *may*'s, *must*'s and *must not*'s.

In the next section (Sect. 2), we introduce Dynamic Deontics in detail, before presenting the trader scenarios and their historical context (Sect. 3) in order to derive a simulation model that allows us to generate behavioural norms based on reinforcement learning (Sect. 4). The final Sect. 5 discusses the simulation results.

## 2    Dynamic Deontics

A conceptual foundation of this work is the notion of Dynamic Deontics introduced by previous work [6]. Conventionally, the notion of discrete, interdefinable deontics (often represented using the deontic primitives *must, must not,* and *may*) based on deontic logic [19] is appealing and offers a clear interpretation of associated prescriptions. However, to model the emergence of norms and institutions (especially when we cannot make presumptions about pre-existing norms) as well as the dynamics associated with this, we use a continuous notion of deontics. This enables agents to operate along a *deontic range* spanning from the extreme of proscriptions (or prohibitions) via permissions to prescriptions (or obligations), as illustrated in Fig. 1.

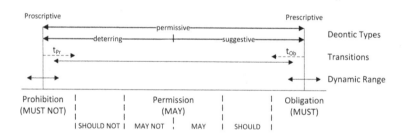

**Fig. 1.** Dynamic deontic range

Note that this approach is not related to dynamic deontic logic [12], which attempts to resolve the ambiguities of 'ought-to-do' and 'ought-to-be' in standard deontic logic. Our approach does not entail a refinement of deontic logic, but uses the term 'dynamic' to describe the expanding and contracting boundaries of the deontic range.

In the remainder of this section we will briefly explore the central characteristics of Dynamic Deontics and discuss possible operationalisation approaches.

## 2.1  Characteristics

**Continuous Notion of Deontics** – Concrete deontics associated with a given action or outcome can be allocated along the deontic range and shift continuously, including moderate movements along the range, varying across short time frames. However, norms (and institutions in general), can potentially likewise shift from one deontic extreme to the other. An example of this is the societal attitude towards homosexuality, which in the past decades experienced a considerable shift from (former) legal prohibition towards increasing acceptance. A similar example is the societal attitude towards spanking of children as a punitive measure. To make the continuous notion more compatible with customary linguistic usage, we can allocate terms along this range to express the varying extent of normative prescriptiveness. For this work here, we operationalise common norm understandings and employ the terms *must not, should not, may not, may, should* and *must*, which we allocate in *deontic compartments* of equal size along the deontic range. However, the choice of deontic terms and their number is flexible. Likewise the range and compartment may not be necessarily conceived symmetric respectively equally sized. However, in this context, we concentrate on the core idea of compartmentalising different institutions in order to simplify their interpretation.

**Stability** – Adopting a continuous understanding implicitly suggests the situational shift of norms. However, a core characteristic of institutions (and thus norms) is their stability [15]. Once successfully established, they exhibit 'stickiness' and change resistance which opens up an arena for potential norm violations. If a model exhibits stability properties itself, we can observe the emerging stabilisation towards the outer extremes without explicit operationalisation (*Modelling Variant 1*). However, depending on the model objectives and underlying assumptions about institutional change (see [10]) this characteristic can be represented using the metaphor of hysteresis. Stability can be modelled using discrete tolerance zones around the deontic extremes (denoted as $t_{Pr}$ and $t_{Ob}$ in Fig. 1), in which institutions, if penetrating those extremal deontic compartments for sufficiently long time, become engrained and stable (*Modelling Variant 2*). If in such state, institutions likely require strong reinforcement to give up this stability and shift back into an adaptive state, which allows their resumed movement along the deontic scale. Translating this into simulation models, it can be operationalised by counting simulation rounds for which a particular statement remains in the extremal ends of the deontic range, with thresholds for their establishment and dissolution. An alternative, continuous operationalisation could establish increasing levels of friction along the range towards the deontic extremes (*Modelling Variant 3*), avoiding the discrete tolerance zones at the outer ends.

**Dynamic Deontic Range** – A final important aspect is the dynamic nature of the deontic range. Individuals experience the world subjectively and absorb feedback in a varying fashion. As an example imagine individuals moving in culturally diverse environments in which different, potentially conflicting, influences coexist. An individual might be inclined to incorporate those different aspects and develop a wide deontic range with greater degrees of tolerance ('openness'), i.e. a wider range between his deontic extremes, his no-go's. This can be seen in contrast to individuals that adopted existing rigid political or cultural rule-sets, and act within rather narrow boundaries of permissiveness, but in case of uncertainty quickly resort to stable internalised rules. We thus suggest that the deontic range changes throughout an agent's lifetime, widening with experience, but also narrowing if experiential stimuli cease.

## 2.2   Operationalisation

The Dynamic Deontics concept itself does not prescribe a specific operationalisation, but for our purpose, here of modelling the establishment of institutions (and norms in particular), we adopt an experiential perspective and do not rely on predefined norms.

For this paper we operationalise those using reinforcement learning (RL, specifically Q-Learning [20]), and use the mean of a sliding window across the highest and lowest Q-values as the deontic range boundaries. The middle point of the scale (normative centre) is the mean of the upper and lower boundary values, which depend on the situational Q-values. The discounting characteristics associated with Q-Learning reflect the dynamic adaptation, i.e. expansion or retraction, of the deontic range over time. The operationalisation of stability follows the *Modelling Variant 2* introduced in Subsect. 2.1; stability characteristics are represented by the time range of Q-values within the tolerance zones around the deontic extremes (e.g. number of rounds), the values of which are specified as part of the simulation parameter set.

Doing so, at any time during simulation runtime, an agent's Q-values can be resolved to deontic terms associated with the respective compartment along the deontic scale, such as *may not*, *should not* or *must not*.

Even if the norm assignment to compartments across the deontic range is not accurate, the intuition of the individualised norm understanding and its varying strength is retraceable. This categorisation simplifies the interpretation of the differentiated norm understandings, especially given that the core interest is not centred around a precise accurate representation of what an agent 'thinks', but instead to provide a situational understanding of the overall normative landscape.

Important to note at this stage is that the chosen operationalisation adopts a consequentialist perspective in opposition to the traditional deontic perspective, in which individuals evaluate their norm compliance behaviour based on given norms or rules. In this case, individuals need to learn which behaviour provides them with the best outcome, shaping behavioural norms from experience. In this context the role of the Dynamic Deontics is not to prescribe rules. Instead this operationalisation extracts deontic values from the existing RL instances maintained by each agent in order to derive the agents' understanding of normative behaviour.

# 3   Historic Trader Scenarios

We use Dynamic Deontics for the exploration of scenarios from the area of comparative economics. A core topic in this area is to analyse the impact of institutions on the development of economies, thus asking the question why some, often more closed, societies could rely on informal mechanisms to assure cooperation, while societies made up of weaker social ties had to rely on legal instruments, i.e. formal institutions, to bind agents to their commitments.

An interesting example is Avner Greif's comparison of long-distance trading in 12th century Genoa, which is considered an important early historical example for the systematic use of formal institutional mechanisms. He contrasts this with what he called the *Maghribi Traders Coalition*, a contemporary homogeneous group of traders that were unified by their cultural background and beliefs, and operated along the North African coast.

Greif's work [9] combines rational choice theory with game-theoretical analysis to show that Maghribi traders could sustain cooperation, among other aspects, based on the high cost that was associated with non-cooperation. As a central characteristic of their group, Greif elaborates on the information transmission mechanisms employed by Maghribi traders. They maintained communicative ties by frequent exchange of letters among associates by means of which they shared market information and coordinated agency services for each other. However, they used such medium not only to manage their business operations (which usually extended to remote ports across the Southern part of the Mediterranean basin), but likewise to share information about fellow traders, suggesting a fast spread of information,[1] should a trader attempt to misreport profits when acting as an agent for a remote associate.

Maghribis, named by their geographical descent ('West') within the Arabic world, were in fact traders from Jewish communities in nowadays Tunisia that were united by their operation in a culturally contrasting Islamic environment, making it hard for outsiders to enter their group. Accordingly, likewise high exit costs were associated with defecting from cooperation.

Genoa, on the other hand, was different in its structure. It operated in opposition to other influential city states, such as Venice, and relied on a constant influx of foreigners to sustain its development. Consequently, binding features were limited, which facilitated easy defection from business commitment, given the limited effect of informal enforcement.[2] Consequently, Genoa had to rely on formal institutions, such as commercial courts and associated legal instruments, to sustain cooperation. Trade operations in Genoa's open society thus neatly contrast with the kinds of interactions in the closed Maghribian trader community.

For our simulation model, we adopt the comparative nature of the scenario, but concentrate our focus on an aspect that has been mentioned in historical

---

[1] Goldberg [7] allocates the fraction of communication dedicated to such gossip at around 20 percent.

[2] At that time Genoa had more than 30,000 citizens [9].

commentaries but not explored in previous analyses: individuals involved in Genoese long-distance trade were stratified into different roles, a characteristic that is reflected in the dominantly used institutional mechanism, the 'commenda', namely

- investors ('commendatores') that supplied funds and goods for travels to remote trade locations, and
- actual merchants ('tractatores') that ran the actual operation, thus bearing the laborious share of the agreement.[3]

Given Genoa's central role as trading port, long-distance trade was seen as an investment opportunity that attracted rich citizens as well as foreigners, who often did not have any trade experience themselves or ceded that part of their enterprise to a third party (see van Doosselaere [17] for an overview of the structure in commenda relationships). The actual merchants, however, were often opportunists themselves, or workless artisans that saw the adventure of long-distance trade as a promising temporary job opportunity.

The Maghribi traders, in contrast, had cultivated a rigorous apprenticeship system, in which young aspiring traders operated under the supervision of an often unrelated experienced trader. In this process apprentices would be increasingly embedded in the trade operations (and information transmission aspects) and so could eventually establish themselves as full traders – a process which could last more than a decade [8]. A second characteristic was the unification of the investor and merchant roles. While senior traders tended to concentrate on the investment aspect, as part of the trader coalition, the reciprocity-based informal rule system still required them to process agent services for other traders (or at least store their goods at no expense). So the clear role differentiation as found with the Genoese did not exist in the Maghribi case.

Based on the available information we hypothesise that, notwithstanding the core differences between open vs. closed societies, the role stratification in the Genoese trader community and their unified character in the Maghribian case could have been an important difference that might have driven cooperation based on informal mechanisms. We postulate that Maghribi cooperation was largely facilitated by the mutual interest to sanction violators, and more so, by the desire of the potential violators not to be detected, knowing that they themselves, when acting as an 'investor', could be cheated if delegating their goods-handling to fellow traders. So even in the attempt of cheating, they still had an incentive to sustain cooperation to suppress cheating by others. In the Genoese trader community, opportunistic merchants could not expect to undertake multiple journeys with the same investor, and were, unless affiliated with a family firm, hardly ever in the position to take up the investor role. Given this role separation, merchants did not have any incentive to avoid non-cooperative behaviour unless he could exercise control by formal means or private-order enforcement (e.g. retaliation against family members).

---

[3] In this text we use 'trader' to capture both roles and use 'investor' and 'merchant' to address the respective specialised roles.

## 4   Model

To test the hypothesis that the Maghribis' integrated role understanding could have been fundamental to drive cooperative behaviour, we have developed an agent-based simulation model that captures the essence of the aforementioned scenarios. We start with a basic scenario that employs the commission-based trading metaphor. During each round traders can randomly choose fellow traders to whom they wish to send goods and expect profit in return. Instead of modelling the entire trade interaction in detail, we concentrate on the essential decisions, namely whether goods-receiving agents cooperate or withhold profits. As part of this scenario, each round an agent (Investor 'Inv') chooses a random trade partner (Merchant 'Mer') before sending him goods. The receiver can then decide whether to trade fair and return realized profits, or to cheat, and withhold profits. The investing party (Inv) then reacts to the merchant's behaviour using the reaction he considers suitable based on his experience. For this purpose Inv has selected reactions at its disposal. For given actions with corresponding reactions, we specify the effects in terms of payoffs for individual action-reaction combinations as shown in Table 1. To memorise the respective feedback, agents use reinforcement learning from which we can derive their respective norm understanding using the Dynamic Deontics operationalisation introduced in Sect. 2.

Central to this is the integrated nature of the memory structure (used to internalise feedback from actions and reactions) and the operationalisation of Dynamic Deontics as part of the simulation infrastructure (see also [6]). To represent the experiential aspect, reinforcement is associated with action-reaction pairs (e.g. [TRADE FAIR, PAY COMMISSION]), since feedback information entails the combination of action and reaction, independent of whether they act as investors or merchants. Further, choosing action-reaction combinations allows the use of this memory structure independent of the role stratification, i.e. the RL instance can be used to store experience from a merchant's perspective ('What reaction followed my action?') as well as investor's perspective ('What reaction did I choose to address a given action?'). We use the integrated RL memory instance as a mechanism to unify all memory entries by the action the statement describes. As a consequence, for each action, the deontic associated with

**Table 1.** Action reaction feedback combinations

| Action-Reaction combinations | | Utility from Actions | |
|---|---|---|---|
| Action (Mer) | Reaction (Inv) | for Mer | for Inv |
| TRADE FAIR | FIRE | $-2$ | $-1$ |
| TRADE FAIR | RETALIATE FAMILY | $-3$ | $-1$ |
| TRADE FAIR | PAY COMMISSION | $1$ | $1$ |
| WITHHOLD PROFIT | FIRE | $-1$ | $0$ |
| WITHHOLD PROFIT | RETALIATE FAMILY | $-3$ | $1$ |
| WITHHOLD PROFIT | PAY COMMISSION | $2$ | $-2$ |

that action needs to be derived from all potential consequences (i.e. reactions) an individual has faced, e.g. the action 'TRADE FAIR' may have been usually reciprocated with 'PAY COMMISSION', but potentially also with 'FIRE' and 'RETALIATE FAMILY' at different times.

The intuitive approach to derive the deontic to be associated with the given action is to calculate the sum of all individual Q-values. This offers an integrated picture of the individual's experience. However, as actions hardly co-occur, this representation may not be faithful to the individual's perception and neither reflect an individual's fear of uncertainty, a central driver for the establishment of institutions. Instead of adding the Q-values, we thus choose the most extreme Q-value, representing an individual's expected greatest gain or pain.

To operationalise this, we derive the deontic from the Q-value with the greatest deviation (extremal) from the centre of the deontic range ($c_{deonticRange}$) towards the direction indicated by the sum of all Q-values (*deontic bias*). With $stmt$ representing individual statements and $d(stmt_{l,i})$ as the deontic value for the $i$th statement on nesting level $l$, we can say[4]

$$extremeDeontic(stmt_l):=[(\sum_{i=0}^{count_{(l+1)}} d(stmt_{(l+1),i})) > c_{deonticRange}] \begin{cases} \texttt{true}, & max(d(stmt_{(l+1)})) \\ \texttt{false}, & min(d(stmt_{(l+1)})) \end{cases}$$

The extreme deontic is applied unless the sum of the Q-values is located at the deontic range centre $c_{deonticRange}$, in which case the Q-values associated with action-reaction pairs cancel each other out. In that case, the deontic range centre itself describes the action's deontic (which, under the assumption of a symmetric deontic range, resolves to *may*), i.e.

$$d(stmt_l):=[(\sum_{i=0}^{count_{(l+1)}} d(stmt_{(l+1),i})) = c_{deonticRange}] \begin{cases} \texttt{true}, & c_{deonticRange} \\ \texttt{false}, & extremeDeontic(stmt_l) \end{cases}$$

To illustrate our mapping from RL to the deontic range value associated with an action, we show in Fig. 2 how deontic terms are derived from a situational deontic range for a given agent ranging from around -30 to 20.1. Based on the deontic range and the reinforcement values, the figure displays the different Q-values associated with various reactions (e.g. retaliate against family, pay commission, fire) grouped by the action 'WITHHOLD PROFIT' (represented in the nADICO syntax [5]) and derives the action's deontic term using the aforementioned principle.

Before discussing the entire agent execution cycle, we briefly discuss the intuitions associated with the value choices (shown in Table 1): Being fired after trading fair has a negative impact on the merchant who operated truthfully. For the sanctioning investor, however, this is likewise of negative impact, given that he sanctions a compliant merchant. Similarly, retaliation against a compliant merchant's family is counterintuitive. Private-order enforcement of contractual

---

[4] The following formalisations use Iverson brackets to model the conditional substitution of the assigned expression.

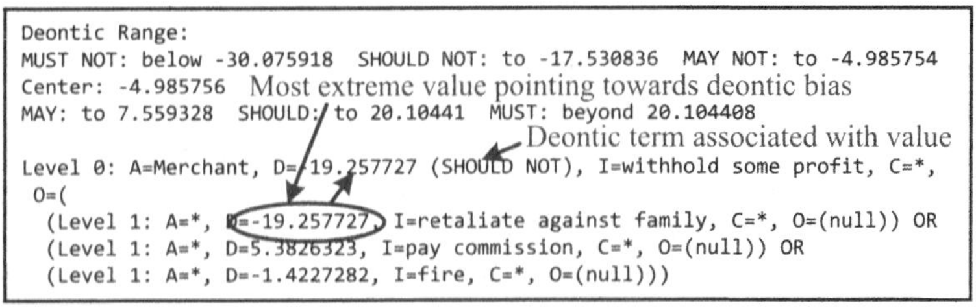

```
Deontic Range:
MUST NOT: below -30.075918   SHOULD NOT: to -17.530836   MAY NOT: to -4.985754
Center: -4.985756   Most extreme value pointing towards deontic bias
MAY: to 7.559328   SHOULD: to 20.10441   MUST: beyond 20.104408
                                          Deontic term associated with value
Level 0: A=Merchant, D=19.257727 (SHOULD NOT), I=withhold some profit, C=*,
  O=(
    (Level 1: A=*, D=-19.257727, I=retaliate against family, C=*, O=(null)) OR
    (Level 1: A=*, D=5.3826323, I=pay commission, C=*, O=(null)) OR
    (Level 1: A=*, D=-1.4227282, I=fire, C=*, O=(null)))
```

**Fig. 2.** Example for deriving deontic term from situational deontic range

obligations was very well present in medieval Genoa [17], given that pursuing the legal track was cumbersome and time-consuming [4], making private-order enforcement against cheating merchants a realistic option. Paying the commission to a compliant merchant is considered the regular outcome if cooperation should be sustained. The lower payoffs associated with this imply that both parties had the general expectation that the commitments associated with their trade interaction (i.e. being paid for fair trading) would be honoured. For the negative case of a non-compliant merchant, payoffs are amended. Withholding profit and being fired as a consequence has mild negative feedback for the merchant (who indeed cheated) and neutral feedback for the investor (who identified and fired a cheater). Retaliation against family has a strongly negative feedback, as it possibly is the greatest threat associated with non-compliance. However, given the elicited satisfaction for the sanctioner, we associate a mild positive feedback for this reaction.[5] As a final aspect, paying commission to an unloyal merchant has a negative effect for the investor, and is highly rewarding for the cheater. Note that this work is based on historical scenarios, which constrains an authentic representation. Nevertheless, instead of putting the emphasis on precision, we rather seek to improve the understanding of an otherwise unexplored aspect of the scenarios based on available information.

Given this overview on the infrastructural aspects, we can return to the discussion of the scenario. Our model of the trader scenario allows the representation of a characteristic that sets apart different society types, using Simmel's social circles [16] as a metaphor. Following this understanding, in more homogeneous societies (in line with North, Wallis and Weingast's primitive societies [14]) we can find a lower extent of role specialisations. Thus roles in such societies are of more general nature, allowing members to develop a more unified understanding of roles and overlapping social circles, rather than a differentiated and stratified role experience (which we postulate for the more individualistic Genoese society). This drives our hypothesis that a more integrated role understanding of traders in the Maghribi society (i.e. taking the perspective of both investor and merchant at different times) could have been a contributor to the more compliant behaviour without need for formal institutions.

---

[5] Neuro-scientific findings [3] support the idea that performing punishments can elicit feelings of reward, especially if they are considered 'deserved'.

The basic execution cycle is shown in Algorithm 1. It does not differentiate between different roles for investors and merchants. We thus interpret it as a representation of the Maghribi trading behaviour (denoted as 'Maghribi version'). Note that we include the choice to activate norm enforcement. If choosing to exploit, an agent chooses an action based on the Q-values associated with it. In this context norm enforcement refers to the sanctioning of other merchants' actions, using the memorised action-reaction combination associated with the highest Q-value, or if not existent, a randomly chosen reaction. The Genoese variant of the algorithm (see Algorithm 2) introduces the role specialisation discussed in Sect. 3. Agents are thus instantiated as either investors or merchants and take actions only related to their respective role. If acting as merchants, they engage in exploration and exploitation of actions (with a bias towards exploitation, see Table 2). If norm enforcement is activated, investors can sanction unrelated merchants' behaviours in addition to applying sanctions according to their action-reaction Q-values.

---

**Algorithm 1.** Agent Execution Cycle – Maghribi version

---

1 Decide whether to *explore* or *exploit* in this round;
2 **if** *exploring* **then**
3    | Pick random action from action pool;
4 **else**
5    | Pick action with highest Q-value from action pool;
6    | **if** *norm enforcement activated* **then**
7    | | Sanction action taken by randomly chosen agent using sanction with
8    | |   highest Q-value;
9    | | Memorize feedback from sanction choice;
10 **end**
11 Execute picked action and apply to randomly chosen agent;
12 Memorize reaction and make action-reaction combination (with valence representation of feedback) visible to other agents;
13 Update deontic range;
14 Check Q-values for stability (shifts from/to obligation or prohibition norms);
15 Apply discount factor to all memory entries;

---

We test both scenarios using the same parameter set shown in Table 2. The different scenarios sketched here allow us to specify four possible configurations:

– Scenario 1 – Role Unification w/o Norm Enforcement
– Scenario 2 – Role Unification with Norm Enforcement
– Scenario 3 – Role Specialisation w/o Norm Enforcement
– Scenario 4 – Role Specialisation with Norm Enforcement

We ran each scenario for 20,000 rounds. The high number of rounds was chosen to allow the stabilisation of changing norm understandings in the given simulation. The simulation outcomes are discussed in the following section.

---

**Algorithm 2.** Agent Execution Cycle – Genoese version

---

1  During setup: Assign either investor or merchant role;
2  Decide whether to *explore* or *exploit* in this round;
3  **if** *exploring* **then**
4     **if** *is merchant* **then**
5        Pick random action from action pool;
6  **else**
7     **if** *is merchant* **then**
8        Pick action with highest Q-value from action pool;
9     **if** *is investor &norm enforcement activated* **then**
10       Sanction action taken by randomly chosen agent using sanction with
11         highest Q-value;
12       Memorize feedback from sanction choice;
13 **end**
14 **if** *is merchant* **then**
15    Execute picked action and apply to randomly chosen agent;
16    Memorize reaction and make action-reaction combination (with valence
      representation of feedback) visible to other agents;
17 Update deontic range;
18 Check Q-values for stability (shifts from/to obligation or prohibition norms);
19 Apply discount factor to all memory entries;

---

## 5   Simulation Results

As explained previously, throughout the simulation runtime agents develop a normative understanding of the different actions aligned with the deontic compartment in their respective deontic range (e.g. *must not, should not, may not, may, should, must,* etc.). We can thus show the progression in the developing norm understanding using time-series diagrams in which the different understandings for a particular action accumulate to 100 percent (i.e. each agent has a normative attitude towards an action). Combining both actions in one diagram thus provides us with a macro-view of the normative landscape. Given our interest in the developing normative understanding, we concentrate on this aspect in our analysis. Given the vast number of possible combinations of actions and deontics, we highlight the essential findings for each scenario. To do this, we show a representative simulation run for each scenario and interpret the displayed dynamics.

### 5.1   Role Unification Without Norm Enforcement

For the first scenario (Maghribi-like), individuals adopt both roles, investor and merchant, throughout the simulation runtime, but do not engage in norm enforcement (i.e. sanctioning of merchants in observed trade interaction with another investor). Instead, agents operate purely based on experiential learning from feedback they receive for chosen actions (and the reaction chosen by their counterpart).

**Table 2.** Simulation parameters

| Parameter | Value |
|---|---|
| Number of agents | 100 |
| Tolerance zone around extreme deontics $(t_{Pr}, t_{Ob})$ | 0.05 of deontic range amplitude |
| Norm establishment threshold | 100 rounds |
| Norm destruction threshold | 200 rounds |
| Deontic range history length | 100 rounds |
| Memory discount factor | 0.99 |
| Exploration probability | 0.1 |

Looking at the simulation results for this configuration (Fig. 3), we can observe that most agents quickly converge to the understanding that they can act selfishly and cheat repeatedly. They mostly act in a compliant manner, which is driven by the integrated roles in which they act. If situationally acting as merchant, cheating is a beneficial option. When acting as an investor, in contrast, cheating is not desirable. However, as investors they can likewise exploit their agent, e.g. by firing him despite compliant behaviour. But by integrating the different perspectives, over time up to 70 percent of all agents converge to the understanding that they *must* trade fair, mirrored by around 20 to 30 percent that think they *must not* trade fair. The remainder (less than 10 percent) believe they *should* trade fair.

It is important to understand that both actions cannot simply be assumed complementary and mirror each other. Firstly, the evaluation relies on the reinforcement (i.e. continuous experience) of the different actions in combination with reactions chosen by the counterpart, which may vary for different actions. Secondly, the norm understanding provided here is derived from the Q-values of individual agents, but that does not necessarily reflect their situational choice as the choice of actions is based on the individual Q-values, not aggregated ones from which we derived the overall perspective. This way agents can maintain in principle conflicting norms (e.g. based on negative reinforcement for individual actions), but solely base their choice on the highest Q-value, which allows them to overrule the extracted normative understanding.

## 5.2   Role Unification with Norm Enforcement

Another outcome can be observed when including norm enforcement (Fig. 4) in the Maghribian scenario. This configuration is the closest match to the institutional setup in the real Maghribian society. Individuals acted in role unity and are aware of constant norm enforcement (see Sect. 3). In this simulation model norm enforcement introduces a bias towards the investor role. Agents judge other agent's behaviour from the investor perspective, i.e. interpret it as if they had been subject of that action, and reinforce their reaction choice. As a consequence of this, agents acting as situational merchants need to expect multiple reactions

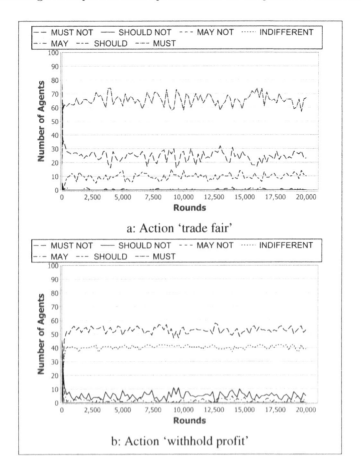

Fig. 3. Role unification, no norm enforcement

to their action, an aspect that considers the uncertainty about both occurrence of consequences ('Will I be sanctioned?') and chosen measure ('What will the sanction be?') associated with norms, as opposed to precisely prescribed consequences in the context of laws or rules. The result of this shift (Fig. 4) is a societal perspective on compliant behaviour. After initial low measures for compliant behaviour (*must* trade fair), the norm enforcement (once sufficiently explored and settled in individual agents) leads to a fully cooperative trader society. In parallel, agents adjust their understanding of withholding profit and arrive at a majority of agents that think they *should not* cheat (around 60 percent). Complementing this, a stable fraction of 20 percent persist that they *must not* cheat. The reason for the lower convergence towards extreme values is the lesser reinforcement of the action 'withhold profit', because agents more strongly reinforce fair trading as opposed to cheating. This aspect is an artefact caused by the operationalisation using the discounting mechanism of reinforcement learning.

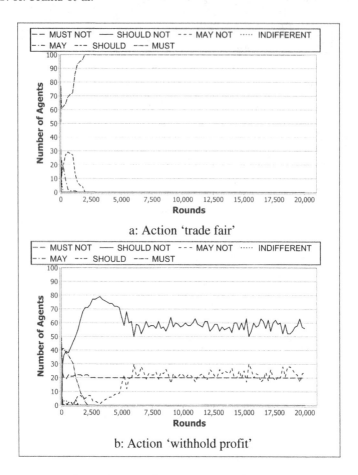

**Fig. 4.** Role unification, norm enforcement

## 5.3   Role Specialisation Without Norm Enforcement

Introducing role specialisation requires further considerations in order to maintain comparability of simulation results. In the Maghribi case each agent could act as investor and merchant, enabling each individual to act as a merchant (and thus either trade compliantly or cheat). Simply separating the roles would render us with 50 active merchants and 50 purely reactive investors as opposed to the Maghribian case where each individual could act as a merchant. To reflect the effect of role stratification and establish comparable outcomes, for the role-specialised Genoese scenario we double the number of agents to maintain the same number of acting merchants. All other parameters remain unchanged, and so we increase the number of agents to 200 for all remaining simulations.

Analysing the simulation outcomes for this configuration (Fig. 5), we observe that traders nearly fully converge to the understanding that they *must not* trade fair, framed with around 5 percent that retain a weaker normative understanding

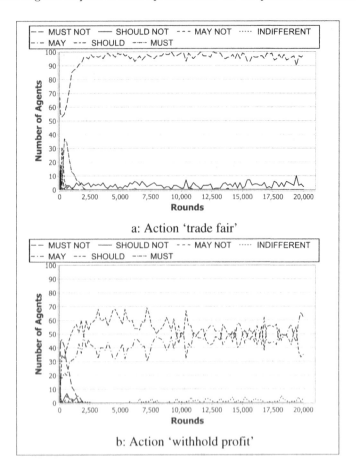

Fig. 5. Role specialisation, no norm enforcement

and believe that they *should not* trade fair. Regarding the action 'withhold profit', agents provide a more divided view; agents are largely equally divided (but shifting over time) between *may* and *should* withhold profit. The general trend points towards a stronger dominance of the weaker *may* withhold profit.

The scenario described here is closer related to the actual, historical Genoese society. We can clearly see that role specialisation could not have sustained cooperative behaviour without the introduction of formal mechanisms that afforded legal commitments of participating individuals. Given their individualised roles, individuals would never be able to perform the perspective taking as done implicitly in the context of role unification (i.e. both roles fulfilled by same trader at different times). But given the exploratory possibilities of our simulation setup, we complement our simulation runs by exploring how norm enforcement would impact our modelled Genoese case.

## 5.4    Role Specialisation with Norm Enforcement

The activation of norm enforcement in addition to role specialisation adds an artificial aspect in the sense that it ignores the fact that Genoa was an open society, in which constant influx of new merchants and investors limited the effect of society-internal normative enforcement (although private-order enforcement is indeed documented as sanctioning mechanism [9]). However, in the scenarios presented here, the number of agents is constant. Neither do we model trader generations nor an open society. However, introducing norm enforcement allows us to explore the hypothetical case of norm enforcement in a closed society with role specialisation.

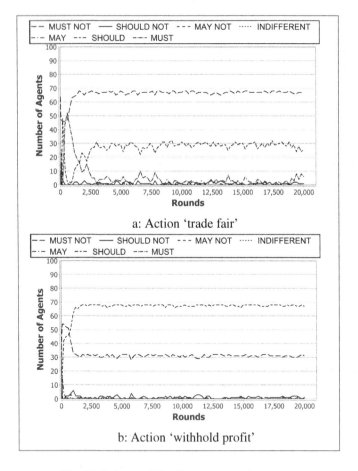

a: Action 'trade fair'

b: Action 'withhold profit'

**Fig. 6.** Role specialisation, norm enforcement

The results for this configuration (Fig. 6) show that norm enforcement by investors could indeed have an impact on the normative attitude of merchants towards compliant trading. Around 30 percent of merchants share the view that merchants *should* trade fair. The dominant attitude, however, remains that merchants *must not* trade fair (nearly 70 percent). In this case, this distribution is contrasted with 70 percent of traders who think they *should* withhold profit and 30 percent maintaining that they *must not* withhold profit as a reaction to norm enforcement they experienced.

It is important to stress again, that this scenario ignores further characteristics of that society, but the isolated perspective on role stratification supports the presumption that it could have played an important role in preventing the society from maintaining cooperative behaviour based on informal means.

# 6    Discussion, Conclusions and Outlook

This work addresses important scenarios from the area of comparative economics, the Maghribi Traders Coalition and its Genoese counterpart, both of which are some of the earliest well-documented historical examples for long-distance trade by in/formal means. Particular focus lies on a specific previously documented but unexplored aspect, namely the question whether the role specialisation in the Genoese society could have made the difference in driving the society towards stronger reliance on formal institutional mechanisms to assure compliance. Their historical counterpart, a North African trader collective – called 'Maghribis' – could maintain cooperation based on informal means but shared a unified role understanding. We model and explore differing outcomes for the characteristics of role specialisation and norm enforcement in otherwise unchanged scenarios. Our findings support the hypothesis that the normative understanding of the individualistic Genoese society, at least in part, drifted apart over time based on the specialisation of individuals.

The experiments described here bear further interesting findings: Looking at the model, even in the informally regulated society norm enforcement remains the important driver for fully compliant behaviour. However, even without norm enforcement, around 70 to 80 percent (*must* and *should* trade fair) of traders act compliantly. Norm enforcement in the Maghribi society initially produces diverse compliance levels (nearly 100 percent for *may*, *should* and *must*), which fully converge to the prescription (*must*) to trade fair. For role specialisation we cannot observe such behaviour. The individualistic specialised perspective drives selfish behaviour. The hypothetical case of introducing norm enforcement drives a more diverse understanding with a significant minority of around 30 percent internalising the understanding that compliant behaviour is desirable (*should*). This leaves to suggest that even in specialised societies, normative influence still proves to be supportive for achieving a socially desirable outcome. However, the sketched simulation models an idealised social representation. The simulation scenario focuses on the essential representation of the social features of interest, but omits specific societal characteristics (open vs. closed society) and the consideration of possible psychological components. This includes a limitation to the fixed representation of utilities as well the lacking consideration of situational, rather than randomised, choice of compliance behaviour. This is hardened by the challenge to find more grounded data on the historic societies. But even though this analysis specifically focuses on the Maghribi Trader Coalition and their Genoese counterpart, the results bear general value in that they support the hypothesis that role specialisation in combination with the assumption of the selfish individual potentially supports antisocial behaviour, insofar as individuals do not have mutual awareness about their individual preferences. This challenges the ability to regulate behaviour in a normative fashion driving increasing formalisation of institutions in open specialised societies.

Beyond the simulation outcomes it is worthwhile to discuss the concept of Dynamic Deontics used to operationalise the simulation model. It is important to reemphasise that the operationalisation showcased here adopts a purely consequentialist perspective and does not explicitly preimpose normative statements or rules, but agents experience feedback from both their actions and their social environment in a greenfield approach. Dynamic Deontics allow us to represent the society's normative understanding on an individual level (see memory sequences shown in Fig. 2) as well as collective level (see time-series charts shown in Sect. 5). By mapping normative understandings onto deontic terms the salience of established norms becomes accessible, which allows us to follow the dynamics in which norms emerge and stabilise.

The operationalisation presented here does not exploit the full capabilities of the Dynamic Deontics concept. Agents can in principle develop independent normative understandings for individual actions (see the operationalisation in Subsection 2.2). However, the current action representation is too simplistic to capture different situational contexts. To allow a more comprehensive application, we intend to introduce a more complex action representation that incorporates context, with the use of statements in the nADICO syntax [5] as a starting point (which is briefly highlighted in Fig. 2). Further aspects that require future exploration (and highlighted previously [6]) include the allocation of deontic terms along the deontic scale, but likewise the assumption of symmetry of deontic compartments. Those refinements will naturally rely on empirical input based on user studies to establish the necessary grounding. We are further investigating mechanisms that allow the meaningful aggregation of individual normative understandings beyond the simplified conflation of individual deontic compartments in time-series.

Concluding, we believe that Dynamic Deontics is an intuitively accessible concept that offers the potential to incorporate the representation of different mindsets, such as cultural or social backgrounds (e.g. by different experiences and deontic scale widths), as well as preimposed norms, which may potentially change over time. Moreover, the inclusion of different contexts and experiences may pave the path towards a representation of morality (here: the agent's ability to infer what is 'good' or 'bad' based on the developed deontic scale derived from contextual experience) within individual agents.

# References

1. Acemoglu, D., Robinson, J.: Why Nations Fail: The Origins of Power, Prosperity, and Poverty. Crown Business, New York (2012)
2. Andrighetto, G., Villatoro, D., Conte, R.: Norm internalization in artificial societies. AI Commun. **23**(4), 325–339 (2010)
3. de Quervain, D.J.-F., Fischbacher, U., Treyer, V., Schellhammer, M., Schnyder, U., Buck, A., Fehr, E.: The neural basis of altruistic punishment. Science **305**(5688), 1254–1258 (2005)
4. Epstein, S.A.: Secrecy and Genoese commercial practices. J. Medieval Hist. **20**(4), 313–325 (1994)
5. Frantz, C., Purvis, M.K., Nowostawski, M., Savarimuthu, B.T.R.: nADICO: a nested grammar of institutions. In: Boella, G., Elkind, E., Savarimuthu, B.T.R., Dignum, F., Purvis, M.K. (eds.) PRIMA 2013. LNCS, vol. 8291, pp. 429–436. Springer, Heidelberg (2013)
6. Frantz, C., Purvis, M.K., Nowostawski, M., Savarimuthu, B.T.R.: Modelling institutions using dynamic deontics. In: Balke, T., Dignum, F., van Riemsdijk, M.B., Chopra, A.K. (eds.) COIN 2013. LNCS, vol. 8386, pp. 211–233. Springer, Heidelberg (2014)
7. Goldberg, J.L.: Choosing and enforcing business relationships in the eleventh century mediterranean: reassessing the 'Maghribī traders'. Past & Present **216**(1), 3–40 (2012)
8. Goldberg, J.L.: Trade and Institutions in the Medieval Mediterranean: The Geniza Merchants and their Business World. Cambridge University Press, New York (2012)
9. Greif, A.: Institutions and the Path to the Modern Economy: Lessons from Medieval Trade. Cambridge University Press, New York (2006)
10. Kingston, C., Caballero, G.: Comparing theories of institutional change. J. Inst. Econ. **5**(2), 151–180 (2009)
11. Mahmoud, S., Griffiths, N., Keppens, J., Luck, M.: Efficient norm emergence through experiential dynamic punishment. In: ECAI 2012, pp. 576–581 (2012)
12. Meyer, J.-J.C.: A different approach to deontic logic: deontic logic viewed as a variant of dynamic logic. Notre Dame J. Formal Logic **29**(1), 109–136 (1988)
13. North, D.C.: Institutions, Institutional Change, and Economic Performance. Cambridge University Press, New York (1990)
14. North, D.C., Wallis, J.J., Weingast, B.R.: Violence and Social Orders: A Conceptual Framework for Interpreting Recorded Human History. Cambridge University Press, New York (2009)
15. Scott, W.R.: Approaching adulthood: the maturing of institutional theory. Theor. Soc. **37**(5), 427–442 (2008)
16. Simmel, G.: The Sociology of Georg Simmel. Free Press, New York (NY) (1964). Originally published (1908)
17. van Doosselaere, Q.: Commercial Agreements and Social Dynamics in Medieval Genoa. Cambridge University Press, Cambridge (2009)
18. Villatoro, D., Andrighetto, G., Sabater-Mir, J., Conte, R.: Dynamic sanctioning for robust and cost-efficient norm compliance. In: Walsh, T. (ed.) Proceedings of the 22nd International Joint Conference on Artificial Intelligence, IJCAI 2011, vol. 1, pp. 414–419. AAAI Press (2011)
19. von Wright, G.H.: Norm and Action: A Logical Enquiry. Routledge & Kegan Paul, London (1963)
20. Watkins, C.: Learning from delayed rewards. Ph.D. thesis, Cambridge University, Cambridge (UK) (1989)

# Severity-Sensitive Robustness Analysis in Normative Systems

Luca Gasparini[(✉)], Timothy J. Norman,
Martin J. Kollingbaum, and Liang Chen

Department of Computing Science, University of Aberdeen, Aberdeen, UK
{l.gasparini,t.j.norman,m.j.kollingbaum,l.chen}@abdn.ac.uk

**Abstract.** Norms specify ideal behaviour. Agents, however, are autonomous, and may fail to comply with the ideal. Contrary to Duty obligations can be used to specify reparational behaviour that mitigates the
effects of a violation. In addition to specifying reparational behaviours,
it is important to understand how robust a system is against possible
violations. Depending on what kind of system property we want to preserve, non-compliance with different norms may be of varying severity.
We propose a method for analysing robustness of normative systems,
with support for Contrary to Duty obligations. We introduce violation
severity as a concept orthogonal to reparational behaviour and specify it
by means of a partial order over norms. We use this severity partial order,
together with normative specifications, to rank the possible worlds from
the most to the least compliant. In this way, we are able to use model
checking to analyse robustness to a certain severity, or whether it is possible to achieve a certain goal, without violating any norm of a given
severity.

## 1 Introduction

In multi-agent systems (MAS), a normative system specification consists of a set
of constraints (norms) that specify the ideal behaviour of agents. Norms declare
how agents should behave within a social context, what they should refrain from
doing or what undesirable outcomes to avoid. Sub-ideal behaviour may, however,
vary in severity. For example, the consequences of revealing restricted information is undesirable, but less severe than revealing secret information ("restricted"
and "secret" being common information security classifications). Implicit in this
example is the idea that severity is viewed as a series of levels, or, more accu-
rately, represents a partial ordering over norm violations. This is, we believe,
the best way to think of the notion of severity from the perspective of system
robustness. We are interested in reasoning about how robust a system may be
to some *level* of severity, given some situation, often in which some kind of norm
violation is inevitable. The common alternative is to view violation severity in
terms of penalties (i.e. anticipated loss of utility). This, however, leaves the way
open to significant fallacies in reasoning. Consider, for example, prison terms

© Springer International Publishing Switzerland 2015
A. Ghose et al. (Eds.): COIN 2014, LNAI 9372, pp. 72–88, 2015.
DOI: 10.1007/978-3-319-25420-3_5

imposed on individuals in a jurisdiction for certain crimes. Suppose that a typical term for a robbery is 6 months, and a murder 25 years. Should we infer that committing a murder (gently or not!) is equivalent to a series of 50 robberies? Penalties for norm violation are imposed *post hoc*, typically by authorities. Violations may even be excused if the alternative would have been less desirable; e.g. an under-cover policeman choosing between engaging in robberies or committing a murder to gain trust.

Where norms capture the ideal, agents operate autonomously and, hence, their actual behaviour may violate norms. Norm violations may be accidental, due to unanticipated consequences of activities, or deliberate, for example, in order to achieve a goal that would not be possible otherwise. It is, therefore, important to account for and consider the consequences of violations. One way of addressing this issue is to define Contrary To Duty (CTD) obligations. These are structures that describe what an agent should do when a violation occurs. CTD obligations can be used to define a behaviour that mitigates the effects of a violation. In traditional deontic logic frameworks, CTD obligations often lead to inconsistencies [2]. For this reason, a number of logics have been proposed to capture and correctly reason about CTD obligations [12,13].

In addition to specifying behaviours that may mitigate the effects of a violation through CTD obligations, it is important to understand how robust a normative system is to potential future violations. For example, we may want to determine if certain desired properties are preserved even if a subset of agents in the system fail to comply with the ideal. [1] introduced the idea of verifying robustness of normative systems. They developed a logic, Norm Compliance CTL (NCCTL), for the definition of robustness-related properties. In their model the transitions between possible worlds of a Kripke structure are divided into those allowed (green) and forbidden (red), according to a normative specification. Using NCCTL it is possible to specify properties such as "if a subset of agents comply with the normative system (i.e. do not activate any forbidden transition), it is guaranteed that a certain (un)desired property will (not) hold". In a related work, [10] developed a model checking tool (NorMC) that enables the verification of a NCCTL property for a specified model. Model checking [3] is a formal verification technique that, given a model specification, and some properties, determines whether these properties hold. Properties can be specified using various temporal logic formalisms, such as Linear Temporal Logic (LTL) and Computation Tree Logic (CTL) (or its extension CTL*).

One open question in robustness analysis of normative systems, however, is how to reason about (non) compliance of CTD obligations. Moreover, we believe that, when analysing the robustness of normative systems, it is important to take into account the severity of violations. Our idea is based on the observation that, if our objective is to preserve certain safety properties of a system, some norms are more important than others. In fact, while a system could accept a number of violations of a certain kind, some properties might cease to hold even with only one (more severe) violation of another kind.

Our aim is to develop methods to reason about the robustness of normative systems, taking into consideration both violation severity and CTD obligations. We apply model checking to analyse robustness, under different compliance standards. We build upon a preference-based approach to define obligations proposed by [13] and use the preference relation to derive a ranking of the worlds according to their "ideality level"; i.e. according to how compliant these worlds are with the enforced normative system. Moreover we introduce a preference relation between obligations that specifies, for each obligation, how severe its violation would be. The preference relation between worlds is computed in such a way that worlds that violate less severe obligations or fewer obligations of the same severity are preferred. Different ranges of ranking levels are then computed according to the severity of the obligations that are violated in such worlds. This results in a partition of the world-space that is encoded in a model suitable for an off-the-shelf model checker. Further, we discuss how severity ranges are used to query the model checker about robustness-related properties and the feasibility of a given plan if we constrain ourselves to a certain severity range. Before presenting our model, however, we present an intelligence, surveillance and reconnaissance (ISR) scenario that helps illustrate the motivations behind our research.

## 2   ISR Scenario

We consider as an example a coalition of three agents that includes a patrol boat, an unmanned aerial vehicle (UAV) and a helicopter of the sea-guard conducting surveillance of a restricted area. In order for the coalition to achieve its mission, either the helicopter or the UAV needs to monitor the restricted area. If an unauthorized boat is discovered in the restricted area, one of the three agents must intercept the vehicle. The behaviour of the three agents is guided by the normative system specified in Example 1.

*Example 1.* Sea-Guard.

1. The UAV must monitor the area.
2. If the UAV does not monitor the area, the helicopter must monitor the area.
3. If an unauthorized vehicle is in the area, one of the three agents must intercept the vehicle.
4. If no agent intercepts the vehicle, one of the three agents must send a report to the head-quarters.
5. The UAV must not reveal its location.

There are, in addition to normative constraints, practical constraints that restrict possible solutions to achieve the mission goals. Neither the helicopter nor the UAV can monitor and intercept at the same time, and, by deploying the UAV to intercept the unauthorized vehicle, its position is revealed. It is easy to see that norms 2 and 4 are CTD obligations, describing behaviours that should be performed in order to mitigate the effect of violations of norms 1 and 3 respectively. As discussed before, another way of addressing the issue of non-compliance could be to develop a normative system that is robust to violations. Considering our example, we assume that the objective is to preserve the security property: "no unauthorized vehicle is to enter the restricted area, without being reported". However it is preferred that unauthorized vehicles be intercepted. We want to be able to specify that, if our main concern is to preserve these two properties, obligation 3 or at least 4 must be always complied with, while we could accept some violations of norm 1 or 5. Moreover, in order for the coalition to be operative, we want to specify that it is more important to guarantee that there is at least one agent monitoring (either the UAV or the helicopter) rather than to avoid revealing the location of the UAV. We address this problem by defining a partial order between norms that specifies for each norm, how severe its violation is. We then want to use the normative and severity specifications to compute a ranking of the possible worlds, according to their level of compliance with the set of norms, giving more importance to violations of more severe obligations. In other words, keeping at the first level the worlds that are fully compliant, we want to give higher ranking values to the possible worlds that violate more severe obligations, or more obligations of the same (or incomparable) severity. Our aim is to apply model checking to ask questions such as: is it possible to always intercept or report a boat without going through states that are above a certain severity level; i.e. without violating any norm that is as severe as a given level?

## 3 Formalization

Given a normative specification, our aim is to compute a preference relation between the possible worlds that reflects the level of compliance of the worlds with a set of norms. We then use this preference relation to build a ranking of possible worlds. Such a ranking can be used to partition the world-space in different severity ranges, and encode them into a model suitable for a model-checker. By doing so, we can verify different properties of a system, taking different assumptions about its level of compliance; i.e. verify how robust our system is against failures to comply with norms.

Our semantics is based on Prohairetic Deontic Logic (PDL)[13], where dyadic (conditional) obligations are represented through a preference relation between worlds. As claimed by [13], this formalization allows us to correctly represent most of the scenarios involving CTD norms. Note that, like PDL, this is not a conflict-tolerant deontic logic and it requires a conflict-free normative specification. We do not address the problem of checking whether a normative specification might result in some conflicts between two or more norms, but see [14] for an example of an approach to addressing this problem. Together with a set of norms, we declare a strict partial order relation between norms that specifies the relative severity of their violation. A preference relation over possible worlds is computed using both normative and severity specifications.

We define a model $M = \langle W, B, V, OS, R, P_o \rangle$ where:

- $W = \{w_1, \ldots, w_i, \ldots, w_n\}$ is a set of $n$ possible worlds.
- $B$ is a set of boolean atoms. The set of well formed boolean formulae $f$ is defined as $f ::= b \mid (\neg f) \mid (f \wedge f) \mid (f \vee f) \mid (f \rightarrow f)$, where $b \in B$.
- $V : W \rightarrow 2^B$ is a valuation function that assigns to each world $w$ the set of boolean atoms that hold in $w$.
- $OS = \{O_1 = \mathbf{O}(\alpha_1 \mid \beta_1)), \ldots, O_m = \mathbf{O}(\alpha_m \mid \beta_m)\}$ is a normative specification, where $\alpha_i$ and $\beta_i$ are two boolean formulae. $\mathbf{O}(\alpha_i \mid \beta_i)$ represents an obligation to achieve (or maintain) $\alpha_i$ that applies to the worlds where $\beta_i$ holds.
- $R \subseteq W \times W$ is an accessibility relation, where $(w_i, w_j) \in R$, or alternatively $w_j \in R(w_i)$, if it is possible, from world $w_i$, to access $w_j$ through a transition. A transition is an event that could lead to a change on the environment; e.g. actions performed by one or more agent, or non-deterministic events. While transitions are not used to compute the ranking of the possible worlds, we need to encode them in the model.
- $P_o \subseteq OS \times OS$ is a partial order over obligations that reflects the relative severity of their violation. Given two obligations $O_i$ and $O_j$, $(O_i, O_j) \in P_o$ means that a violation of $O_i$ is considered more severe than one of $O_j$. $P_o$ is a transitive relation, thus, if we consider a graph $G$, where each node represents an obligation, and each edge a member of $P_o$, we say that violating $O_a$ is more severe than violating $O_b$ (alternatively $O_a \succ_o O_b$) if and only if the node representing $O_b$ is reachable from $O_a$ through the edges of $G$.

As typical in such models, prohibitions are defined in terms of obligations. Saying that a world that satisfies $a$ is prohibited whenever $b$ holds ($\mathbf{F}(a \mid b)$) is equivalent to saying that there is an obligation to achieve or maintain $\neg a$ whenever $b$ holds ($\mathbf{O}(\neg a \mid b)$). Moreover, we assume that all the worlds that are not explicitly prohibited are permitted. Let $\alpha$ and $\beta$ be two boolean atoms in $B$, boolean formulae satisfaction is defined as:

- $w_i \models \alpha$ iff $\alpha \in V(w_i)$.
- $w_i \models \neg\alpha$ iff $\neg(\alpha \in V(w_i))$.
- $w_i \models \alpha \wedge \beta$ iff $(w_i \models \alpha)$ and $(w_i \models \beta)$.

The other boolean operators are defined as usual.

The choice of using a partial order to specify the severity of obligations, rather than defining a fully ordered sequence of obligations, is motivated by the fact that we might have sets of obligations that are not comparable in terms of severity. We believe that our approach represents many real world scenarios, where the violation of a certain norm is less desirable than several other violations, and provides the necessary flexibility to define complex structures.

In the following we define *compliance* of a world with an obligation, and *coherence* of an ordered pair of worlds with an obligation. These two concepts will be used to compute a preference relation between possible worlds, where a world $w_i$ is preferred to $w_j$ ($w_i \succ_w w_j$) if and only if it is more compliant with the normative specification.

**Definition 1.** A world $w_i$ is *compliant* with an obligation $O_j = \mathbf{O}(\alpha_j \mid \beta_j)$ if $w_i \models \neg\beta_j \vee \alpha_j$: i.e. if the obligation does not apply to $w_i$ or it is already satisfied. We denote this by $compliant(w_i, O_j)$.

**Definition 2.** Given an ordered pair of worlds $(w_i, w_j)$ where $w_i, w_j \in W$ and an obligation $O_k \in OS$, we define the following:

$$coherent((w_i, w_j), O_k) \equiv compliant(w_i, O_k) \wedge \neg compliant(w_j, O_k)$$
$$incoherent((w_i, w_j), O_k) \equiv compliant(w_j, O_k) \wedge \neg compliant(w_i, O_k)$$

We define $P_w \subseteq W \times W$ as a strict partial order that defines a preference relation between worlds. We write $(w_i, w_j) \in P_w$ or alternatively $w_i \succ_w w_j$ if $w_i$ is preferred to $w_j$ according to the normative system specification. $P_w$ is computed from $M$ according to the following rule:

$$w_i \succ_w w_j \leftrightarrow \exists\, O_k \in OS \text{ s.t. } (coherent((w_i, w_j), O_k) \wedge \atop (\nexists\, O_l \in OS \text{ s.t. } \neg(O_k \succ_o O_l) \wedge incoherent((w_i, w_j), O_l))) \tag{1}$$

Informally, we say that $w_i$ is preferable to $w_j$ if $w_i$ complies with an obligation $O_k$ that is violated by $w_j$, and all the obligations $O_l$ (if any) that are violated by $w_i$ and for which $w_j$ is compliant, are less severe than $O_k$. If we assume that all obligations are incomparable in terms of severity, the statement $\neg(O_k \succ_o O_l)$ holds for any pair of obligations and $P_w$ becomes equivalent to the preference relation between worlds defined by [13]. Note, however, that while the preference relation of PDL semantics is reflexive, $P_w$ is a strict one; thus, whenever $\alpha \succ_w \beta$ holds, we can say that $\alpha$ is preferred to $\beta$. Formally, if we denote by $\succeq_{PDL}$ the preference relation used to define the semantics for PDL, we have $w_1 \succ_w w_2 \equiv (w_1 \succeq_{PDL} w_2) \wedge \neg(w_2 \succeq_{PDL} w_1)$.

The second condition of (1) is needed to avoid the so called "strong preference problem" [13]: considering the two worlds $w_1 \models a \wedge \neg b$ and $w_2 \models \neg a \wedge b$, without such conditions, a normative system with two obligations $O_1 = \mathbf{O}(a \mid true)$ and $O_2 = \mathbf{O}(b \mid true)$ would result in two conflicting preference relations $w_1 \succ_w w_2$ (according to $O_1$) and $w_2 \succ_w w_1$ (according to $O_2$). Introducing our second condition, and assuming that the two obligations are incomparable according to $P_w$, we have no preference between these worlds. When we specify $O_a \succ_o O_b$ we want to say that a violation of $O_a$ is more severe than a violation of $O_b$, thus we want to obtain a ranking where $w_1$ is preferred to $w_2$. We obtain this by restricting the second part of the equation, introducing the condition $\neg(O_k \succ_o O_l)$. Doing so, we have a preference relation $(w_i, w_j)$ only if it is incoherent with obligations $O_l$ that are less severe than the obligation $O_k$ such that $coherent((w_i, w_j), O_k)$. Considering the previous example, since $O_a \succ_o O_b$, we have only $w_1 \succ_w w_2$.

**Definition 3.** Given a set of possible worlds $W$ and a strict partial order relation $P_w$ on $W$, we define the ranking of the set as a function $ranking_{(P_w)} : W \rightarrow \mathbb{N}$ where:

- $ranking_{(P_w)}(w_i) = 1$ if there is no $(w_j, w_i) \in P_w$.
- $ranking_{(P_w)}(w_i) = max[ranking_{(P_w)}(w_j) : (w_j, w_i) \in P_w] + 1$, otherwise.

Dividing the worlds by their ranking, we obtain a partition of the set $W$, in which states in the same subset can be considered equally compliant. We call the ranking of a possible world $w_i$ according to $P_w$ the *ideality level* of $w_i$. When verifying robustness properties, we want to reason about what properties hold when we consider only violations of a certain severity. Let $ranking_{(P_w)}(O_i)$ be the world with minimum (more compliant) ranking such that we have a violation of $O_i$. We can state that all the worlds with ranking lower than $ranking_{(P_w)}(O_i)$ can be considered more compliant than a world that violates $O_i$, while all the worlds with higher ranking violate obligations that are at least as severe as $O_i$. We define for each obligation $O_i$ the *severity range of* $O_i$, alternatively *severity_$O_i$*, as the set of worlds that have ranking lower than $ranking_{(P_w)}(O_i)$. Severity ranges can be used to verify how robust a system is to violations of a certain severity, or to verify the feasibility of a certain workflow/plan, restricting ourselves to worlds that violate only obligations that are less severe than a given one.

In the following section, we detail how we compute the strict partial order relation $P_w$ for a model $M$ and, given that, the $ranking_{(P_w)}$ of the possible worlds in $W$.

## 4    Normative Ranking of Possible Worlds

In this section, we introduce two algorithms. The first uses the set of possible worlds, the set of obligations enforced and the severity relation to compute the partial order relation between worlds $P_w$. The second computes a ranking of the possible worlds into *ideality levels*, from the best (most compliant) world to the worst (least compliant).

### 4.1    Computing $P_w$

Algorithm 1 computes a preference relation $P_w$ that satisfies (1). In lines 1–6, for each enforced obligation $O_1$, we loop through all the possible worlds $w_1$ that are compliant with $O_1$, and for each of them we create preference relations to all non-compliant worlds $w_2$. From line 8 to 22 we loop again through all the obligations and remove all the preference relations $(w_1, w_2)$ that are incoherent with the current obligation $O_1$. Note that, we delete a relation $(w_1, w_2)$ only if we can find no other obligation $O_2$ that is more severe than the current one $(O_2 \succ_o O_1)$ and such that $coherent((w_i, w_j), O_2)$ (variable to_delete in lines 11–16). In other words the relation is not removed if it is imposed by a more severe obligation. Recall from the definition of $P_o$ that, checking whether $O_2 \succ_o O_1$ reduces to checking graph reachability in $G$, with complexity linear in the number of obligations. Since, in the worst case, we have to perform the reachability test $n^2m^2$ times, where $n$ is the number of obligations and $m$ the number of

---

**Algorithm 1.** Algorithm for computation of preference relation

---

1: **for all** $O_1 = \mathbf{O}(a \mid b) \in OS$ **do**
2:     **for all** worlds $w_1$ such that $compliant(w_1, O_1)$ **do**
3:         **for all** worlds $w_2$ such that $\neg compliant(w_2, O_1)$ **do**
4:             add the relation $(w1, w2)$ to $P_w$.
5:         **end for**
6:     **end for**
7: **end for**
8: **for all** $O_1 = \mathbf{O}(a \mid b) \in OS$ **do**
9:     **for all** worlds $w_1$ such that $\neg compliant(w_1, O_1)$ **do**
10:         **for all** worlds $w_2$ such that $compliant(w_2, O_1)$ **do**
11:             **boolean** $to\_delete = $ **true**
12:             **for all** $O_2 = \mathbf{O}(c \mid d) \in OS$ **do**
13:                 **if** $(O_2 \succ_o O_1) \wedge compliant(w_1, O_2) \wedge \neg compliant(w_2, O_2)$ **then**
14:                     $to\_delete = $ **false**
15:                 **end if**
16:             **end for**
17:             **if** $to\_delete$ **then**
18:                 delete $(w_1, w_2)$ from $P_w$
19:             **end if**
20:         **end for**
21:     **end for**
22: **end for**

---

worlds, it is convenient to pre-compute the transitive closure of $G$ (e.g. using the Floyd-Warshall algorithm [6] with complexity $O(n^3)$) so that we can test reachability in $O(1)$ time. Applying Algorithm 1 to a set of worlds $W$, a set of obligations $OS$ and a severity relation $P_o$, we obtain as output a partial order relation $P_w$ that respects (1). For all the $(w_i, w_j) \in P_w$ we can say that $w_i$ is preferable to $w_j$ according to the normative specification enforced: if we consider the obligations violated in the two worlds, there is at least one obligation violated in $w_j$ that is more severe than all the obligations violated in $w_i$, or $w_j$ violates more obligations at the highest severity level for which the number of violations is not equal between the two worlds.

## 4.2  Computing the Ranking

Once we have computed $P_w$, we can rank the worlds according to Definition 3, obtaining a ranking where the more compliant worlds are in a higher position; i.e. are associated with a lower ranking number. To do so, we extend the topological sorting algorithm developed by [9], computing the ranking while sorting the worlds in a linear extension of the partial order. The original topological sorting algorithm performs, at each iteration, the following steps: firstly, it takes all the nodes with indegree equal to 0 (i.e. no incoming edges) and inserts these nodes at the end of an ordered list (no_incoming; then it takes the first element of the no_incoming list, inserts it at the end of the list ordered_list), and deletes all its outgoing edges from the `relations` list. We observe that a node $w_i$ is inserted into the `no_incoming` list when the last node $w_l$ such that $(w_l, w_i) \in P_w$ has been deleted. Since topological sorting deletes nodes in an order that respects the partial order (and thus the ranking), all the previously deleted nodes have ranking lower than or equal to that of $w_l$. It follows that $ranking_{(P_w)}(w_i)$ must be equal to $ranking_{(P_w)}(w_l) + 1$. Every time we add a node to the `no_incoming` list, we assign to the node a ranking equal to the ranking of the last node we removed from the graph incremented by 1.

We now apply the algorithms proposed in Sects. 4.1 and 4.2 to our ISR example, firstly assuming all the obligations to be equivalent in terms of severity, and after that, specifying the severity relations between obligations.

## 5   Detailed Example

The norms summarized in Example 1 can be formalized as in Table 1, where the proposition $m_u$ stands for "The UAV is monitoring the restricted area", $m_h$ for "the helicopter is monitoring the restricted area", $rep$ stands for "the unauthorized vehicle has been reported" and $r_u$ for "the location of the UAV has been revealed". We use a single variable $rep$ instead one variable for each agent who might send a report in order to limit the space of possible worlds and make our presentation more compact. Variables $i_u$, $i_b$ and $i_h$ represent the UAV, the boat and the helicopter respectively intercepting the unauthorised boat. In formalizing the normative system, we assume that an unauthorized vehicle has entered the restricted area. This is the reason why norm $O_3$ is unconditionally active. We do this in order to simplify the example. It is possible, however, to add a variable *boat* to the model and modify the normative specification accordingly. Norm 3, for example, would become $\mathbf{O}(i_u \lor i_b \lor i_h \mid boat)$.

Considering all the possible values for the boolean variables $m_u$, $m_h$, $rep$, $r_u$, $i_u$, $i_b$ and $i_h$, we compute the list of possible worlds (Table 3). In listing these, we do not consider all those that do not satisfy the constraints in Table 2. While constraints 3, 4 and 5 are causal constraints that allow us to capture only the subset of worlds that are meaningful, constraints 1, 2 and 6 should be encoded as norms; these are standard operating procedures in the scenario that guide an optimal allocation of resources. We declared them as causal constraints,

Table 1. Norms formalization.

| Id | Norm |
|----|------|
| $O_1$ | $\mathbf{O}(m_u \mid \top)$ |
| $O_2$ | $\mathbf{O}(m_h \mid \neg m_u)$ |
| $O_3$ | $\mathbf{O}(i_u \lor i_b \lor i_h \mid \top)$ |
| $O_4$ | $\mathbf{O}(rep \mid \neg(i_u \lor i_b \lor i_h))$ |
| $O_5$ | $\mathbf{O}(\neg r_u \mid \top)$ |

**Table 2.** Sea guard scenario: possible worlds constraints

| Id | Constraint |
|----|-----------|
| 1 | $\neg m_u \vee \neg m_h$ |
| 2 | $(\neg i_b \wedge (\neg i_u \vee \neg i_h)) \vee (\neg i_u \wedge \neg i_h)$ |
| 3 | $i_u \rightarrow r_u$ |
| 4 | $\neg m_u \vee \neg i_u$ |
| 5 | $\neg m_h \vee \neg i_h$ |
| 6 | $\neg rep \vee \neg(i_u \vee i_b \vee i_h)$ |

again to simplify our scenario. Constraint 1 says that either the UAV or the helicopter, but not both, can monitor the area at a certain instant of time. In the same way, constraint 2 says that no more than one agent will be deployed to intercept at each instant of time. Constraint 3 states that if the UAV is deployed for interception, then its position will be revealed. Constraints 4 and 5 state that both UAV and helicopter are not able to monitor the area while intercepting targets. Constraint 6 allows us not to consider the worlds in which an unauthorized boat is both reported and intercepted.

Using Algorithm 1, we compute the preference relation $P_w$. For example, we have $w_3 \succ_w w_{22}$ because $coherent((w_3, w_{22}), O_4)$ (same for $O_5$) and there is no obligation $O_i$ such that $incoherent((w_3, w_{22}), O_i)$. We apply Algorithm 1 (Sect. 4.2) to the preference relation in order to compute a ranking that satisfies Definition 3. As a result, we obtain an ordered sequence of worlds, with a numeric value that represents their ranking. Part of this ranking is shown in Table 4. Worlds $w_9$ and $w_{13}$, with $ranking_{(P_w)}(w_9) = ranking_{(P_w)}(w_{13}) = 1$, are the only two possible worlds that are compliant with all the obligations, while world $w_{22}$, with $ranking_{(P_w)}(w_{22}) = 6$ is the only world that violates all 5 obligations.

Since all the violations are considered equally severe, the ranking depends only on the number of possible violations. For example, $w_3$ has ranking equal to

**Table 3.** Possible worlds for the sea guard example.

| Id | World | | | | | | |
|----|-------|---|---|---|---|---|---|
| | $\ldots$ | | | | | | |
| $w_3$ | $\neg i_h$ | $rep$ | $\neg i_b$ | $\neg m_h$ | $\neg r_u$ | $m_u$ | $\neg i_u$ |
| $w_9$ | $\neg i_h$ | $\neg rep$ | $i_b$ | $\neg m_h$ | $\neg r_u$ | $m_u$ | $\neg i_u$ |
| $w_{13}$ | $i_h$ | $\neg rep$ | $\neg i_b$ | $\neg m_h$ | $\neg r_u$ | $m_u$ | $\neg i_u$ |
| $w_{16}$ | $\neg i_h$ | $\neg rep$ | $\neg i_b$ | $m_h$ | $r_u$ | $\neg m_u$ | $i_u$ |
| $w_{22}$ | $\neg i_h$ | $\neg rep$ | $\neg i_b$ | $\neg m_h$ | $r_u$ | $\neg m_u$ | $\neg i_u$ |
| | $\ldots$ | | | | | | |

**Table 4.** Ranking without considering severity specification

| R | Id | World | | | | | | |
|---|-----|-----------|----------|----------|----------|---------|----------|----------|
| 1 | $w_9$ | $\neg i_h$ | $\neg rep$ | $i_b$ | $\neg m_h$ | $\neg r_u$ | $m_u$ | $\neg i_u$ |
| 1 | $w_{13}$ | $i_h$ | $\neg rep$ | $\neg i_b$ | $\neg m_h$ | $\neg r_u$ | $m_u$ | $\neg i_u$ |
| 2 | $w_3$ | $\neg i_h$ | $rep$ | $\neg i_b$ | $\neg m_h$ | $\neg r_u$ | $m_u$ | $\neg i_u$ |
| | | ... | | | | | | |
| 3 | $w_{16}$ | $\neg i_h$ | $\neg rep$ | $\neg i_b$ | $m_h$ | $r_u$ | $\neg m_u$ | $i_u$ |
| | | ... | | | | | | |
| 6 | $w_{22}$ | $\neg i_h$ | $\neg rep$ | $\neg i_b$ | $\neg m_h$ | $r_u$ | $\neg m_u$ | $\neg i_u$ |

2 because it violates only norm $O_3$, while $w_{16}$ has ranking equal to 3 because the UAV is intercepting, and thus both norms $O_1$ and $O_5$ are violated.

As stated in Sect. 2, since our main objective is to preserve the properties $i_u \lor i_h \lor i_b$ and, whenever $i_u \lor i_h \lor i_b$ does not hold, to preserve $rep$, we want to be able to specify that violations of $O_3$ or $O_4$ are more severe than other violations. Moreover, since we want to specify that having someone monitoring the area is more important than not revealing the UAV location, we want to say that violations of $O_2$ are more severe than violations of $O_1$ and $O_5$. In other words, observing again worlds $w_3$ and $w_{16}$, we want to specify that $w_3$ is to be considered worse than $w_{16}$, even if fewer obligations are violated, because the unauthorized boat is not intercepted. To obtain a ranking that respects these two properties, we need to specify a partial order between violations and compute $P_w$ and $ranking_{(P_w)}$ accordingly. Figure 1 represents the severity relation in our example. The graph G is built according to the definition of $P_o$. Each node represents an obligation, while an arrow from $O_i$ to $O_j$ represents the relation $O_i \succ_o O_j$. Note that, from the transitivity property of the partial order, since $O_3$ and $O_4$ are both preferred to $O_2$, and $O_2$ is preferred to $O_1$ and $O_5$, we also have that $O_3$ and $O_4$ are preferred to $O_1$ and $O_5$.

The resulting partial order $P_w$ is just a refinement of the previous one; i.e. all the relations computed without considering obligation severity are still valid when considering any severity specifications. Compared to the preference relation

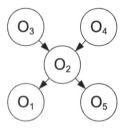

**Fig. 1.** Sea-guard example: severity partial order between norms

**Table 5.** Ranking considering severity of norms

| R | Id | World | | | | | | |
|---|---|---|---|---|---|---|---|---|
| 1 | $w_9$ | $\neg i_h$ | $\neg rep$ | $i_b$ | $\neg m_h$ | $\neg r_u$ | $m_u$ | $\neg i_u$ |
| 1 | $w_{13}$ | $i_h$ | $\neg rep$ | $\neg i_b$ | $\neg m_h$ | $\neg r_u$ | $m_u$ | $\neg i_u$ |
| | . . . | | | | | | | |
| 3 | $w_{16}$ | $\neg i_h$ | $\neg rep$ | $\neg i_b$ | $m_h$ | $r_u$ | $\neg m_u$ | $i_u$ |
| | . . . | | | | | | | |
| 6 | $w_3$ | $\neg i_h$ | $rep$ | $\neg i_b$ | $\neg m_h$ | $\neg r_u$ | $m_u$ | $\neg i_u$ |
| | . . . | | | | | | | |
| 15 | $w_{22}$ | $\neg i_h$ | $\neg rep$ | $\neg i_b$ | $\neg m_h$ | $r_u$ | $\neg m_u$ | $\neg i_u$ |

obtained without considering the severity specification, we have, for example, that $w_{16} \succ_w w_3$. This is because $coherent((w_{16}, w_3), O_3)$ and there is no obligation $O_i$ more severe than $O_3$ such that $incoherent((w_{16}, w_3), O_i)$ (violations of $O_1$ and $O_5$ are both considered less severe than violations of $O_3$).

The resulting ranking, computed according to $P_w$, is shown in Table 5. Even considering the severity of obligations, the most and least compliant worlds remain the same as in Table 4; i.e. the ones that comply with all the norms and the ones that violate all of them. Our purpose is to query the model checker in order to check what properties hold under different severity ranges; i.e. if we restrict the set of reachable worlds to the ones that violate obligations with severity lower than a certain threshold. Recall that $P_w$ is calculated such that worlds that violate more severe obligations have a lower ranking. Looking at our example, with $ranking_{(P_w)} \geq 6$, we have all the worlds for which $O_3$ is violated, and with $ranking_{(P_w)} \geq 10$ all those that violate $O_4$. At first sight it would seem that $O_3$ is preferred to $O_4$, but this happens because $O_4$ is a CTD obligation, active only in the case of violation of $O_3$. With $ranking_{(P_w)} \geq 4$ we have worlds that violate $O_2$ or more severe obligations. With $ranking_{(P_w)} \geq 2$ we have worlds that violate $O_1$, $O_5$, or more severe obligations. Our approach for severity-sensitive robustness verification is to use these values to label different severity ranges, each of them associated with an obligation, and use these labels to write queries for the model checker.

In the following section, we show how we can do so by using the PRISM [11] model checker. We encode the ranking in a PRISM model and show what kind of properties we can check using Computation Tree Logic (CTL) [3].

## 6  Checking Robustness

By ranking the worlds according to their ideality level we obtain a partition of the set of possible worlds. In order to verify properties about the system under different ideality levels, we can encode this partition into a model suitable for a model checker. This enables us to use model checking to ask questions such as

```
1     ...
2     formula L1 = (!i_h & !rep &  i_b & !m_h & !r_u &  m_u & !i_u) |
3        (i_h & !rep & !i_b & !m_h & !r_u &  m_u & !i_u );
4     ...
5     formula ideality_level = (L1)?(1):((L2)?(2):((L3)?(3):((L4)?(4)
6        :((L5)?(5):((L6)?(6):((L7)?(7): ... )))))))))))))))));
7     ...
8     formula severity_03 = ideality_level < 6;
9     ...
10    module M1
11       i_h: bool init false; i_b: bool init true; i_u: bool init false;
12    ...
13       true -> (1.0):(r_u'= !r_u)&(i_u'=(r_u)?(false):(i_u));
14
15       true -> (1.0):(i_h'=!i_h)&(i_u'=(!i_h)?(false):(i_u))
16          &(i_b'=(!i_h)?(false):(i_b))&(m_h'=(!i_h)?(false):
17          (m_h))&(rep'=(!i_h)?(false):(rep));
18    ...
```

**Fig. 2.** PRISM model for boat example

what properties hold in each ideality level or what behaviours are feasible if we constrain ourselves to a subset of the ideality levels. In Fig. 2, we encoded the ranking of Table 5 into a model suitable for PRISM.

In Lines 14–16, we define all the variables of our model. From line 3, we write a formula for each level $L_1$ to $L_{15}$. These are boolean formulae that return true if and only if the model is in the given ideality level. In lines 7–8, we use the if-else construct of the PRISM modelling language to write a formula that returns an integer value corresponding, at each instant of time, to the current *ideality_level*. In lines 10–11, we define, for each obligation $O_i$, a boolean formula that is true if the system is currently in the severity range of $O_i$. Lines 13–24 describe the PRISM module, with its variables and transitions. When defining the possible transition, we can specify a probability $p$ of occurrence and a guard. Each transition is fired with probability $p$ when the guard holds. In this model we assume that all transitions have the same probability and we define the transitions so that only the possible worlds in Table 3 are reachable.

By encoding the ideality levels and severity ranges as PRISM formulae, we can use them to specify CTL properties as we do with standard variables. For example, we can ask whether it is possible to reach a world where an unauthorized boat is neither intercepted nor reported, if we restrict the world-space to the severity range defined by $O_5$ (2). The operator $\mathbf{E}\,\phi$ asks whether there exists a path (execution) such that the property $\phi$ holds. $\alpha\,\mathbf{U}\,\beta$ ($\alpha$ until $\beta$) is a path formula that is true for a path where we can find a world $t$ such that $\beta$ holds in $t$ and $\alpha$ holds in all the preceding worlds.

$$\mathbf{E}\ [severity\_O5\ \mathbf{U}\ (\neg(i\_u \lor i\_h \lor i\_b \lor rep) \land severity\_O5)] \qquad (2)$$

Considering a slightly extended model for our scenario where we can have more than one unauthorized vehicle to intercept at the same time, we could ask whether it is possible to intercept four vehicles avoiding a state where no vehicles are monitoring the area. In a similar way, if we are modelling a scenario involving collaborating workflows and some normative constraints, we could ask the model checker if it is possible to complete a specified workflow without reaching a state that is above a certain severity range:

$$\mathbf{E}\ [(severity\_O5)\ \mathbf{U}\ (goal\_state \land (severity\_O5))] \qquad (3)$$

## 7   Discussion

Compared to the approach by [1], where the set of transitions is divided into allowed and forbidden, we use a more fine-grained partitioning, dividing states into different levels of ideality. In the field of fault tolerant systems, deontic logic is used to distinguish between correct and faulty behaviours of a system. CTD-like obligations represent behaviours that are meant to repair a fault in the system. [7] proposed RoCTL*, a logic for the specification and verification of robustness properties. RoCTL* enables quantification over the number of failures and the verification of properties such as "it is guaranteed that, with fewer than $n$ violations, a property $\phi$ will hold". However there is no distinction between different kinds of violation and no means to specify different severity levels for them.

The reader might argue that the introduction of violation severity does not increase the expressiveness of our model. In fact, given a desired ranking of worlds $RA$, it is always possible to define a normative system that uses only CTD norms, and that would result in the desired ranking $RA$. Denoting by $L_i$ the boolean expression that identifies all the worlds at the $i$-th level, in the following we show how it is possible to define such a normative system.

- $\mathbf{O}(L_1 \mid true)$
- $\mathbf{O}(L_2 \mid \neg L_1)$
- $\mathbf{O}(L_3 \mid \neg L_1 \land \neg L_2)$
- $\ldots$
- $\mathbf{O}(L_n \mid \land_{i=1}^{n-1} \neg L_i)$

However, in order to do so, it would be necessary to know in advance the desired ranking of worlds and this is not always trivial. Moreover our approach enables a more straightforward and natural formalization for the same normative system.

The PRISM model checker supports Probabilistic CTL (PCTL), an extension of CTL that enables the expression of properties involving probabilities about events. In our model (Fig. 2) we assumed that all the transitions occur with the same probability (lines 19–27). By introducing probability values for violations of norms, we could ask the PRISM model checker to compute the likelihood that some undesired situations will happen. An interesting application of our model, together with the probabilistic features of PRISM, would be to compute the conditional probability that a certain (un)-desired property will hold, given that we restrict our model to be inside a certain severity range. A method to evaluate the risk of violating a certain norm in the context of electronic contracts has been proposed by [5].

Currently, we are only able to analyse static scenarios with a well defined configuration and there is no support for the representation of complex workflows where the goal of the coalition, or some environmental constraints could change at run-time. We can start to address this problem by verifying the robustness of the system in some representative worst case scenarios. Another way to improve our model would be to allow the expression of obligations that must be fulfilled before a certain deadline occurs. Such obligations would be violated only when the deadline has expired. Both these limitations have been addressed in related research [8], where we introduced CÒIR[1], a normative language that supports the definition of CTD obligations, collective and event-driven imperatives with deadlines. We give an operational syntax and semantics for CÒIR, and implement a CÒIR monitoring component using the Maude [4] rewriting logic framework. We then discuss how the Maude LTL model checker allows us to verify robustness and correctness-related properties of a scenario governed by a set of CÒIR norms.

Another limitation of our model is given by the fact that we define the severity preference between elements of the set of norms, $OS$, rather than subsets of $OS$. There may be situations in which the violation of two or more norms taken individually would have moderate severity but, when combined, would have more severe consequences. We plan to generalise our model in this manner and explore the consequences of using a relation $P_o \subseteq 2^{OS} \times 2^{OS}$ computationally and in modelling real-world scenarios.

We are also exploring the possibility of specifying different compliance assumptions for different autonomous agents in a system, in the same way that [1] do in NCCTL [1]. It would be interesting, for example, to be able to ask the model checker about properties of the system in the event of different subsets of agents remaining in different severity ranges.

## 8   Conclusions

In this paper, we have proposed a method for verifying the robustness of a normative system. This is done by partitioning the set of predictable possible worlds according to their level of compliance. We encode the partition in a model suitable for the PRISM model checker so that a world satisfies the property $L_i$ (Lines 3–5 of Fig. 2) if it is in the $i$th level of the ranking. In this way, we are able to use model checking to verify what properties of interest hold at each level. We derive our ranking by computing a preference relation $P_w$ between possible worlds that reflects the given normative specification. We then divide the worlds into different compliance levels so that if $w_i \succ_w w_j$, $w_j$ will be in a

---

[1] CÒIR is the Scottish Gaelic for obligation.

higher level than $w_i$. To do so, we propose an algorithm inspired by the topological sorting algorithm [9]. Computing the preference relation is based on the semantics of Prohairetic Deontic Logic which captures most of the traditional contrary to duty benchmarks. In order to represent different levels of severity for obligation violations, we introduce a partial order over obligations. We say that an obligation $O_k \succ_o O_l$ if a violation of $O_k$ is considered more severe than a violation of $O_l$. The preference relation between possible worlds is computed so that $w_i \succ_w w_j$ holds if and only if $w_j$ violates more severe obligations or more obligations at the same level of severity. This allows us to verify properties of worlds that are compliant only with some norms and to represent CTD obligations.

**Acknowledgments.** This research was sponsored by Selex ES.

# References

1. Ågotnes, T., Van der Hoek, W., Wooldridge, M.: Robust normative systems and a logic of norm compliance. Log. J. IGPL **18**(1), 4–30 (2010)
2. Chisholm, R.M.: Contrary-to-duty imperatives and deontic logic. Analysis **24**(2), 33–36 (1963)
3. Clarke, E.M., Grumberg, O., Peled, D.: Model Checking. The MIT Press, Cambridge (1999)
4. Clavel, M., Durán, F., Eker, S., Lincoln, P., Martí-Oliet, N., Meseguer, J., Talcott, C. (eds.): All About Maude - A High-Performance Logical Framework. LNCS, vol. 4350. Springer, Heidelberg (2007)
5. Fagundes, M.S., Ossowski, S., Luck, M., Miles, S.: Using normative Markov decision processes for evaluating electronic contracts. AI Commun. **25**(1), 1–17 (2012)
6. Floyd, R.W.: Algorithm 97: shortest path. Commun. ACM **5**(6), 345 (1962)
7. French, T., Mc Cabe-Dansted, J.C., Reynolds, M.: A temporal logic of robustness. In: Konev, B., Wolter, F. (eds.) FroCos 2007. LNCS (LNAI), vol. 4720, pp. 193–205. Springer, Heidelberg (2007)
8. Gasparini, L., Norman, T.J., Kollingbaum, M.J., Chen, L., Meyer, J.J.C.: Verifying normative system specifications containing collective imperatives and deadlines. In: Proceedings of the 14th International Conference on Autonomous Agents and Multiagent Systems (2015)
9. Kahn, A.B.: Topological sorting of large networks. Commun. ACM **5**(11), 558–562 (1962)
10. Kazmierczak, P., Pedersen, T., Ågotnes, T.: NORMC: a norm compliance temporal logic model checker. In: Kersting, K., Toussaint, M. (eds.) Frontiers in Artificial Intelligence and Applications, pp. 168–179. IOS Press, Amsterdam (2012)
11. Kwiatkowska, M., Norman, G., Parker, D.: Advances and challenges of probabilistic model checking. In: Proceedings of the 48th Annual Allerton Conference on Communication, Control, and Computing, pp. 1691–1698 (2010)

12. Prakken, H., Sergot, M.: Contrary-to-duty obligations. Stud. Log. **57**(1), 91–115 (1996)
13. van der Torre, L., Tan, Y.H.: Contrary-to-duty reasoning with preference-based dyadic obligations. Ann. Math. Artif. Intell. **27**(1–4), 49–78 (1999)
14. Vasconcelos, W.W., Kollingbaum, M.J., Norman, T.J.: Normative conflict resolution in multi-agent systems. Auton. Agent. Multi-Agent Syst. **19**(2), 124–152 (2009)

# Building an Artificial Primitive Human Society: An Agent-Based Approach

Marzieh Jahanbazi[✉], Christopher Frantz, Maryam Purvis, and Martin Purvis

Department of Information Science, University of Otago, Dunedin, New Zealand
Marzieh.Jahanbazi@Postgrad.otago.ac.nz,
{Christopher.Frantz,Maryam.Purvis,
Martin.Purvis}@otago.ac.nz

**Abstract.** The model presented here is mainly concerned with building an artificial society from the bottom-up by specifying their basic social structural elements and institutional meta-roles based on the CKSW (Commander, Knowledge, Skill, Worker) societal meta-model. In this paper our focus is to introduce different types of interactions and outline the degree to which they affect the sustainability of the modeled artificial society. The main motivation is to develop a model that can show institutional changes with minimum set of externally defined triggers to drive changes at the micro level.

**Keywords:** Social structure · Agent-based modeling · Primitive societies · CKSW · Knowledge sharing

## 1 Introduction

Agent-based Modelling [1] has found increasing application to the study of societies in order to gain a deeper understanding of their complex nature [2–8]. Similar to [8], our broader aim is to examine the transitions between different types of state organizations and the emergence of new institutions. Rather than inserting new institutions into a model, our concern is to examine how institutional behavior may emerge from the presence of, ideally, more primitive behavioural aspects. Our model is an extended version of the model described by [9] which builds on previous work by Younger [10], who performed observational studies of Pacific Island societies to ground his study.

Our aim is to take advantage of ABM's ability to define complex agent interactions among themselves as well as their environment. While this is a common goal of most agent-based simulations, we intend to reconstruct the development of modern societies from the onset, determining their socio-economic and institutional development based on the nature of the societal configuration (for which we borrow the CKSW meta-role model), but also the interactions facilitated by different types of leadership, sharing of knowledge and skills. Starting from the institutional onset of primitive societies, our model contains a wide set of societal characteristics, such as kinship, leadership, in-group and between group interactions, mate-selection, gene mutation, institutional changes (by means of introducing rules to change the current rules), social stratification (by defining different class membership), reputation networks, reciprocity, conflict

© Springer International Publishing Switzerland 2015
A. Ghose et al. (Eds.): COIN 2014, LNAI 9372, pp. 89–96, 2015.
DOI: 10.1007/978-3-319-25420-3_6

resolution and finally fulfillment of survival, societal and civil needs. Most researchers look at societies from specific perspectives such as social structure [8, 9, 11], demographic change [12], biological evolution [13], economic development [14, 15] or mortality consequences market collapse [16], while our model aims to make all of these aspects work simultaneously with each other.

## 2    Background

In summary, the model uses the CKSW societal and institutional framework introduced in [17, 18]. The CKSW meta-role can be used both to model agent's internal module and their preference toward different opportunities and, at society level, to define different social classes. In the CKSW meta-role model, the commander class (C) represents leaders and those who are in charge of decision making and have the power to influence and control others. The knowledge class (K) has the responsibility to maintain, create, control and transmit institutional knowledge. The skilled class (S) is those who have "Know how" knowledge and their role is crucial in sustaining every society's economics. And finally, the worker class (W) represents a general working population of the society which mostly uses the tools provided by the skilled class to produce goods or services. CKSW is also consistent with the structures [16] used in simulation of market development.

In the present work we extend the model with particular focus on a more detailed representation of social interactions. This includes a more refined *representation of knowledge and information sharing*, as well as introducing *reciprocity-based food sharing* and *proactive knowledge querying*. One of the reasons behind selection of these features lies in the need to address the issues we face when scaling up the base model. We further apply an incremental approach to introduce all CKSW classes step by step as defining all of them at once might cause unpredicted and surprisingly complicated phenomena. Furthermore, specialization and development of division of labor and skill happened after transition from hunter-gatherers to settled agricultural societies [14]. Therefore, at this step we only introduce a few developed aspects of the agents' K element.

### 2.1    Simulation Environment and Settings

Agents in our model encapsulate different attributes which corresponds to their different roles and requirements such as demographic attributes, personality (aggression, altruism, physical ability and loyalty level), kinship, and internal CKSW role variables which are new to the model. Just as a summary of basic actions defined in [9], Algorithm 1 describes a sample high level overview of a follower agent's daily activities, with italicized items indicating novel model additions. Each simulation run includes 40000 ticks (time units) which allows agents to sustain their society over ten generations (an agent dies of old age if he reaches 4000 ticks). The results explored in this paper consider two village settings, each with its own leader who orders its people to collect food daily and redistribute this food based on his altruism level. Working class agents are obliged to follow leader's order base on their loyalty and after that they can share, steal, take revenge or socialize.

**Algorithm 1.** Simplified Follower Agent's Daily Activities

```
At every time unit
    Perform unintentional task (Consume energy, grow older, and check for death condition)
    Check the conditions to perform actions that are not restricted by time (mate selection, procreation,
    observations of other nearby agent's activities)
    If Clock <= (Length of Day * Loyalty) and (Leader is issuing orders) : /* Agent is following orders */
        Move toward one of known food sources
        If reached to the target food source
                Collect as much as agent's carrying capacity
                Look further if food level is not enough
                Eat if there is still food at this area.
                Move back to nearest village storage
                Deposit food into village storage
    Else :   /* Agent is free of any obligation */
        Eat from the food carrying if agent is hungry
        Move back to food source if the agent does not carry food and there is no food at home patch
                Collect food
        Store food at home patch
        Share
        Steal (high aggression, high hunger, no food, low altruism)
        Ask for food (Low aggression, high hunger, no food, collocated with a known agent)
        Share normative reputation (High knowledge capability)
        Ask for food source location (High knowledge capability, low number of known food sources)
        Take revenge
```

*Relationships.* Since the focus of new features lies in the relationships among agents, we describe the novel capabilities and features in more detail:

Relationships are defined as Netlogo directed Links. New relationships are created either by direct interaction with an agent or by observing another agent within their visibility range. An agent can improve its relationship status with others by sharing food.

To reflect the notion of bounded rationality [19], i.e. an agent's limited capability to retain knowledge about all other agents and experiences, there is a forgetting mechanism which helps agents to determine which links to forget. First, agents filter and retain all extreme relationships independent of age and frequency. This reflects the common understanding that extreme events are not forgotten, even if they happened a long time ago. Therefore, agents will not forget a murder scene, or someone who shared a lot of resources with them. Second, agents sort their other links based first on age and then on frequency. The candidate link for deletion is the one with the oldest age and lowest frequency, which would imply that agents may have met each other some time ago, but they did not maintain any relationship.

In summary, the relationship values are used by agents for the following activities: (a) choosing a mate, (b) spreading their own interaction experience with another agent, (c) considering revenge if they hold a negative relationship value against another agent, (d) considering previous relationship with agent if asked for food by another agent,

(e) selecting an agent to share with, since agents are more likely to share with others who helped them (i.e. based on reciprocity [20, 21] ) or whom they observed performing acts of sharing.

*Knowledge Capability.* Going beyond [9] we have introduced *Knowledge capability* as one of CKSW meta-role attributes. An agent's *Knowledge capability* is relevant to the spreading of information both about other people's reputations and about *Food source* locations. Only those agents with higher *knowledge capability* than the mean *knowledge capability* in their current community will share information in this manner. Also, an agent will ask others for *Food source* locations if it has a high *knowledge capability*.

## 3  Experimental Settings and Results

In order to test the effect of each new feature, we ran the experiments for each feature combination (enabled, disabled) with 20 different random seeds. Output measures defined in this section are those which are significantly influenced by each feature. Mean population size is the average number of alive agents at each time step and it captures the fact that population does not experience rapid decline or growth. On the other hand, the number of total agents in the simulation shows total births and deaths of agents. A very high number is an indicator of society's inability to sustain itself and death happens before agents reach old age (i.e. reducing the mean life span). Summary of the experimental results is presented in this section.

*1. Observing other agents' behaviour.* While in [9] agents only witness crimes, we added observation of all social activities including sharing as well. Observing fellow agents' sharing behavior initially produces counterintuitive results. Since observation of sharing increases the relationship levels towards observed agents. Instead of actually promoting sharing, it helps observed sharers to quickly find a mate. This effectively reduces the number of actual sharing events, since only single agents[1] engage in proactive sharing with others. Married agents drive population growth, but since resources are limited, this can cause disorder in the society based on increasing hunger levels. This is in agreement with Gooding [5] who argues that population rise (without increasing resources) will lead to rising starvation and a decline in life span. There is a significant correlation of 0.94 between activating this feature and total population in the simulation. It also decreases agents' life spans (correlation−0.96). The first column of Table 1 summarizes the correlation figures between this feature and different output measures.

*2. Considering Knowledge Capability when spreading opinion about other agents.* Introducing knowledge-dependent sharing, only a subset of agents with high *knowledge capacity* involves in spreading their personal opinion about known agents. Thus in the refined model fewer people share their opinion about other agents' activities; uninformed agents have to be directly involved in an interaction or witness it.

---

[1] They do so in order to create more links and thus increasing their chance of finding mate.

**Table 1.** Correlation between different features and output measures(empty cell means no correlation).

| Output measures/feature number | 1 | 2 | 3 | 4 | 5 |
|---|---|---|---|---|---|
| Mean age at death | −0.97 | +0.68 | | | |
| Mean value of relationships | +0.90 | +0.89 | +0.30 | +0.59 | −0.47 |
| Number of thefts | +0.77 | | −0.46 | +0.68 | −0.60 |
| Number of sharing | −0.71 | −0.55 | −0.67 | +0.89 | −0.70 |
| Rate of death by age | −0.96 | +0.58 | | | +0.50 |
| Rate of death by hunger | +0.77 | −0.60 | | −0.91 | |
| Rate of death by revenge | +0.87 | +0.56 | −0.51 | +0.92 | +0.30 |
| Rate of death by violence | +0.69 | −0.43 | +0.42 | +0.88 | −0.77 |

The main difference between this scenario's outcome (see second column of Table 1) and the previous one's is that instead of increasing total number of agents, this variant allows agents to live longer, which increases the mean population size of each simulation round (correlation 0.9) and the average age of agents at death (correlation 0.67). While violence and hunger rates are going down, death due to revenge increases. One possible explanation is the extended mean lifespan of agents. Over time, agents build up more relationships with others and there is a higher probability for having a negative relationship values with other agents, and even more time to act upon their negative relationships. In effect, the *knowledge capability* mechanism reflects the systematic construction of knowledge-based relationship networks, which begs the question of how far it may affect structural aspects of a society's social network – an aspect we will explore further in future work.

*3. Considering current relationship value when sharing.* In the earlier model [9], the only condition for sharing was (a) agent's altruism level, (b) carrying resources and (c) collocating with another agent who does not carry food. In the present refinement agents only share food if the target agent shared with them previously. However, higher numbers of single agents will inhibit population maintenance, so knowing that one of the pre-requisites of finding a mate is to have a high reputation, we allow single agents to share (and thereby enhance their reputations) without considering their existing relationship value with the person whom they share with.

Similar to limiting the number of agents who share knowledge, this feature limits the number of agents that sharing agents share food with. Intuitively it makes sense that agents prioritize fellow agents they have existing relationships with. In effect it thus reinforces current relationships instead of creating new ones. The indirect effect of the feature is to keep the population in a more balanced state and to reduce the amount of stealing and death due to violence. Similar to the second feature (consideration of knowledge level for sharing of information), it may have a larger impact on the emergent societal connectivity and relationship structure.

*4. Collecting for self.* This feature essentially reflects the economically selfish agent. Since these agents have the opportunity to collect more food, their likelihood of dying from hunger de-creases. However, the mean level of food carried by agents rises, which makes them likely targets for agents without food, significantly affecting stealing behaviour. On the upside, giving agents the ability to carry higher levels of food gives them more sharing opportunities. This features thus leads to more sharing, but also makes them targets of violence and revenge (see forth column in Table 1), thereby effectively crowding out death due to hunger. This feature is interesting, because it has significant social effects. Activating selfish agent understanding increases existential well-being, but challenges personal well-being by increasing selfishly motivated threats of violence. In our view this feature effectively reflects individualistic traits and offers a precursor of why systematic state-based enforcement is necessary to sustain socio-economic development in the long run.

5. *Asking for Resources.* In addition to stealing behavior, hungry (but not too aggressive)[2] agents will ask for food instead of stealing it. If agents respond positively to each other's sharing requests, the tendency for stealing declines markedly and more agents live to old age. However, since some agents might refuse to reciprocate, the average relationship value goes down. This is observed in cultures where the norm of gift-giving reciprocity is dominant: those who do not follow the norm will be sanctioned in one way or another. In our model the effective sanction for not returning the favors is the loss of relationship value and accompanying loss of reputation.

# 4 Discussion

Our results show that the introduction of inter-agent knowledge-sharing can have far-reaching effects on overall societal outcomes. For example allowing agents to choose whom they share with, and determining whether they should expect anything in return for sharing, can have a significant impact on average population size and thus the vital statistics of death causation. We believe this demonstrates an advantage of using agent based modeling compared to other more conventional social science methodologies, because it allows one to see the inter-relationships between input variables as well as relationships between input and output variables. On the other hand, it introduces a new set of challenges in defining social models and the relationship among different settings and configurations. It necessitates more extensive testing and sensitivity analysis to make sure changes are isolated and are in response to a single variable change. Our approach is to take into account a wide range of feature and configuration combinations, which requires extensive explorative analysis.

In the pursuit of extending our model to reflect features considered relevant to retrace the progression from primitive societies to more complicated ones, we added several basic agent behaviours relevant in primitive societies to our previous, more conventional model described in [14]. The novel additions include (a) observing other agents' behaviour, (b) considering Knowledge Capability when spreading opinion about other agents, (c) share only with reciprocator agents, (d) collecting for oneself (e) ask for resources in return for sharing.

---

[2] High level of aggression in combinations with low altruism and high hunger level drive stealing behaviour.

Looking at the overall effect, the first three features impact the relationship network of the agents, with the first one supporting the expansion the network, while the latter ones, in principle, constrain its growth. These can have a considerable impact on the emergent societal structure. Collecting for oneself reveals how selfish acts can affect the society and what new institutions may be needed to compensate for this exploitative group behaviour. Requesting aid (asking for sharing reciprocity) highlights the importance of maintaining relationship links (as is demonstrated in primitive "gift economies").

## 5 Conclusion and Future Direction

In this paper we have argued that some intuition-based rules of interaction can lead to wide-ranging social effects, shaping a society's developmental path. Particular features explored here which we deem of significant importance are the ability to engage in *selfish food collection* as well as *knowledge sharing based on preexisting relationships structures*. The former (food collection) points to the increasing relevance of coercive enforcement to control violence, thus indicating a demand for institutional innovations. At the same time the sharing of knowledge based on preexisting links defines a process structural formation with lasting impact on the social configuration and stratification ('classes'), which likewise reinforces and shapes new relationships. We employ the K element of the CKSW meta-role model in order to inform the principal structural configuration of any society. Using the meta-role model in conjunction with an emergentist perspective on institutional evolution, this work represents an incremental step in a process of providing the structural scaffolding (social structures) and the behavioural regularities (institutions) that arise from a set of interconnected simple agent activities. We believe that agent-based modeling as applied here presents a promising way to explore societal development based on the complex effects of relatively simple interactions and social mechanisms, knowing societies cannot be simply reduced to the latter. A natural progression of this work is to introduce the skilled class – the 'Know How' -, enabling us to investigate the role of trade and production on the institutional and socio-economic development in artificial societies.

## References

1. Gilbert, N., Troitzsch, K.: Simulation For The Social Scientist. McGraw-Hill International, New York (2005)
2. Edmonds, B., Lucas, P., Rouchier, J., Taylor, R.: Human Societies: Understanding Observed Social Phenomena. In: Edmonds, B., Meyer, R. (eds.) Simulating Social Complexity, pp. 709–748. Springer, Heidelberg (2013)
3. Tesfatsion, L.: Agent-based computational economics: growing economies from the bottom up. Artif. Life **8**, 55–82 (2002)
4. Epstein, J.M.: Generative Social Science: Studies in Agent-Based Computational Modeling. Princeton University Press, Princeton (2007)
5. Epstein, J.M., Axtell, R.L.: Growing Artificial Societies Social Science from the Bottom Up. The MIT Press, Cambridge (1994)
6. Gooding, T.: Modelling society's evolutionary forces. J. Artif. Soc. Soc. Simul. **14** (2014)

7. Gotts, N.M., Polhill, J.G., Law, A.N.R.: Agent-based simulation in the study of social dilemmas. Artif. Intell. Rev. **19**, 3–92 (2003)
8. Vanhée, L., Ferber, J., Dignum, F.: Agent-based evolving societies. In: Proceedings of the 2013 International Conference on Autonomous Agents and Multi-agent Systems. pp. 1241–1242. International Foundation for Autonomous Agents and Multiagent Systems (2013)
9. Jahanbazi, M., Frantz, C., Purvis, M., Purvis, M., Nowostawski, M.: Agent-Based Modelling of Primitive Human Communities. Intelligent Agent Technology, Warsaw (2014)
10. Younger, S.: Leadership, violence, and warfare in small societies. J. Artif. Soc. Soc. Simul. **14** (2011)
11. Axtell, R.L., Epstein, J.M., Dean, J.S., Gumerman, G.J., Swedlund, A.C., Harburger, J., Chakravarty, S., Hammond, R., Parker, J., Parker, M.: Population growth and collapse in a multiagent model of the Kayenta Anasazi in Long House Valley. Proc. Natl. Acad. Sci. US Am. **99**(3), 7275–7279 (2002)
12. Billari, F.C., Ongaro, F., Prskawetz, A.: Introduction: agent-based computational demography. In: Billari, F.C., Prskawetz, A. (eds.) Agent-Based Computational Demography, pp. 1–17. Springer, Heidelberg (2003)
13. Hammond, R.A., Axelrod, R.: The evolution of ethnocentrism. J. Confl. Resolut. **50**, 926–936 (2006)
14. Macmillan, W., Huang, H.Q.: An agent-based simulation model of a primitive agricultural society. Geoforum **39**, 643–658 (2008)
15. Huang, H.Q., Macmillan, W.: A generative bottom-up approach to the understanding of the development of rural societies. Agrifood Res. Rep. **68**, 296–312 (2005)
16. Ewert, U.C., Roehl, M., Uhrmacher, A.M.: Hunger and market dynamics in pre-modern communities: insights into the effects of market intervention from a multi-agent model. Hist. Soc. Res. Sozialforsch. **32**, 122–150 (2007)
17. Purvis, M.K., Purvis, M.A.: Institutional expertise in the Service-Dominant Logic: Knowing how and knowing what. J. Mark. Manag. **28**, 1626–1641 (2012)
18. Purvis, M., Purvis, M., Frantz, C.: CKSW: a folk-sociological meta-model for agent-based modelling. In: Social.Path Workshop (2014)
19. Simon, H.A.: A behavioral model of rational choice. Q. J. Econ. **69**, 99–118 (1955)
20. Gouldner, A.W.: The norm of reciprocity: a preliminary statement. Am. Sociol. Rev. **25**, 161–178 (1960)
21. Francesco, G.: Reciprocity: Weak or strong? what punishment experiments do (and do not) demonstrate. Behav. Brain Sci. **35**, 1–15 (2012)

# Designing for Planned Emergence in Multi-agent Systems

Kathleen Keogh[1,2(✉)] and Liz Sonenberg[2]

[1] School of Engineering and Information Technology,
Federation University Australia, P.O. Box 663, Ballarat, VIC 3353, Australia
[2] Department of Computing and Information Systems,
The University of Melbourne, Melbourne, VIC, Australia
k.keogh@federation.edu.au

**Abstract.** We present an approach for designing organization-oriented multi-agent systems (MASs) to allow improvisation at run time when agents are not available to exactly match the original organizational design structure. Working with system components from an existing MAS organizational meta-model, OJAzzIC, the approach sets out five stages for the design process. We illustrate the design approach with an incident response scenario implemented in the Blocks World for Teams (BW4T) environment, and show how agents at runtime can improvise - for example they can adopt tasks even if those tasks do not precisely match a predefined role.

**Keywords:** Multi-agent systems · Coordination · Adaptation · Organizations

## 1 Introduction

People coordinating in dynamic environments can do so based on predefined roles, but also can operate with a degree of flexibility that allows individual improvisation to achieve shared tasks. Indeed, meso-level control has been shown to improve coordination and provide structure and collective responsibility to otherwise ad hoc teams of people [24]. Meso-level mediation and control has also been argued to ensure that micro-level, operational decision making does not interfere with or cause undesirable macro outcomes [20]. Similar multi-level approaches have been used in the design of multi-agent systems (MASs) for some time [6].

When designing and implementing a MAS, generally the process includes adopting a conceptual framework, developing a platform independent design, detailed design then implementation [23]. A more generic software engineering approach involves following a process of adapting and reusing existing meta-models to create an organizational model for agents (e.g. [1,22]). Our focus is on organizational meta-models and approaches that provide organizational structures and frameworks that can be instantiated with some flexibility - to

© Springer International Publishing Switzerland 2015
A. Ghose et al. (Eds.): COIN 2014, LNAI 9372, pp. 97–113, 2015.
DOI: 10.1007/978-3-319-25420-3_7

govern agents' behaviour but still allow improvisation – i.e. a form of planned emergence [20].

An organization-oriented MAS is one that is not considered primarily in terms of individual agent mental states, but involves organizational concepts such as roles, groups, tasks and interaction protocols, thus the focus is on what relates the structure of an organization to the externally observable behavior of its agents. The structure needs to be general enough to allow for context based adaptation at run time but specific enough to constrain agent's behaviour where necessary. An organizational meta-model defines a representation of the MAS organization, with the choice of meta-model driven by the domain requirements. Organization-aware agents then can prioritise goal selection based on organizational information as well as individual goals [5,8]. Improvisation can be thought of as allowing agents flexibility to ignore or adapt role descriptions based on which agents are available. The conceptual framework requires us to adopt models for goals, roles, organizations and the domain. Sterling and Taveter refer to this as the conceptual viewpoint [23].

In this paper we address requirements drawn from complex, dynamic domains such as emergency management, where flexibility and improvisation is required. Characteristics of such settings include interdependencies between tasks, distributed coordination between members and adaptive, emergent behaviour. Appropriate knowledge sharing between agents is important, as is behaving with awareness of collective objectives, so that organizational goals can be as important as individual goals. We have previously addressed these requirements in the specification of an organizational MAS meta-model OJAzzIC [16,17]. The meta-model specifies necessary components and relationships. In this paper we outline a process for the design of such organization-oriented MASs. The need for improvisation requires specific features and the contribution of this paper is to highlight the issues to be considered at design time regarding the meta-model and the way it is used to specify an organization that supported run-time improvisation.

The OJAzzIC meta-model provides a conceptual framework that builds on features from OperA+ [14], OMACS [7] and SharedPlans [11], and has been designed for situations when agents cannot rely on pre-scripted plans or pre-defined roles for coordinated behaviour, but must dynamically coordinate knowledge and plans. To describe the systems design approach, we adapt O-MaSE [9], an organisation-based multi-agent software engineering methodology. At design-time, the system requirements are described using goals and tasks, agents are defined in terms of capabilities and potential roles that could be enacted at run-time. Organizations are defined based on domain related roles and responsibilities. Agents are aware of the organizational structures and at run-time engage in organizational reasoning to prioritise goal selection based on organizational policies as well as individual goals.

In the execution model behind OJAzzIC, organizational reasoning at run-time includes an agent committing to social policies to ensure that appropriate knowledge sharing and coordinated behaviour occurs within the organization. The social policies operate as a meso-level, place explicit obligations on the agent within an organization regarding coordination of knowledge and plans, and also allow the creation of adhocracies to facilitate coordination between emerging collectives of cooperating agents [17]. Our implemented scenario, developed in the Blocks World for Teams (BW4T) environment [15], demonstrates features in OJAzzIC that facilitate improvisation at run time. In specifying a series of issues to be addressed during the design phase, we highlight the need to identify complexities of the requirements in a domain and consider these at design time where possible.

In the next section, we provide a brief overview of the OJAzzIC meta-model then introduce our design considerations. In Sect. 4 we elaborate on each of the stages in the design process using an example system we built for an incident response scenario. In Sect. 5, we reflect on our findings, follow this in Sect. 6 with pointers to related work, then offer some concluding observations in Sect. 7.

## 2    OJAzzIC Overview

OJAzzIC [16,17] provides a meta-model based on a layered specification. High level modeling completed at design time provides flexibility and allows for improvisation at run time. The improvised behaviour is similar to that observed in a jazz musician who follows a high level score then improvises to add detail during a performance. This flexibility supports planned emergence, when agents dynamically combine to form a complex system [20]. In OJAzzIC, meso-level policies can be defined at design time and instantiated at run time to facilitate coordination by creating an ad hoc organization of agents (i.e. an *adhocracy*) [17]. An adhocracy is temporarily formed to achieve coordination between agents with a shared objective. Each organization provides a context for coordination. While an organization exists, all members know who else is involved so that appropriate

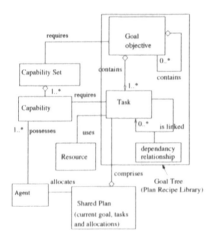

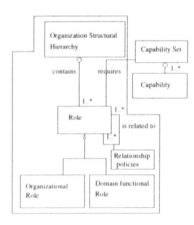

**Fig. 1.** Goal Task Model in OJAzzIC related to capabilities

**Fig. 2.** Role Model in OJAzzIC

knowledge can be shared and so that individuals can mutually adjust their own plans to fit in with others. Social policies in OJAzzIC explicitly define behaviour for role adoption, selection of goal objectives and communication obligations [17]. To provide flexibility, in addition to agents enacting a role, agents may adopt tasks or be allocated based on capabilities [7,16]. Figures 1 and 2 show the design time models in OJAzzIC indicating how capabilities relate to goals and roles. More details can be found in [16,17]. A distinctive feature in OJAzzIC that addresses the requirement of planned emergence is one that allows for responsibilities in a role to be split and shared by multiple individual coordinating agents, without a centralized coordinator. In OJAzzIC, as shown in Figs. 1 and 2, agents may play roles and thus possess the appropriate role based capabilities, but agents may possess capabilities apart from role allocations so, if permitted, agents can improvise at a micro level (operational level) and 'fill in' where there is a need even if they do not match the required role description exactly.

## 3  Design Considerations

### 3.1  Scenario

To highlight design considerations and illustrate our requirements and proposed design approach, we use an incident response scenario used previously [13]. The scenario involves multiple agencies involved in rescuing injured individuals from a disaster area. Two agencies are involved: a medical agency (Medics) and a law enforcement agency (Officers). Medics are responsible for the rescue of injured parties and delivery to an ambulance; the objectives of the Officers include clearing away fights that break out between Bystander agents and clearing Bystanders as delegated by Medic agents. Bystander agents are from two opposing football teams and fights may break out that need to be resolved by separating fans into different areas.

The system is implemented using BW4T [15] and agents using the GOAL programming language [12]. Locations in the disaster scene are represented by rooms in a blocks world environment. Each room may contain injured individuals. Only one agent is permitted in a room at a time, so a Bystander agent in a room must be cleared before a Medic agent can enter the room to rescue an injured party. The domain is complex and dynamic enough to require considerable flexibility and coordination in agent behaviour. The problem involves first searching for injured participants, then coordinating the rescue. If there is no agent available to adopt a role, multiple agents may be able to coordinate in order to achieve the associated objective.

### 3.2  Design Questions

Considering the desire for flexibility to improvise at run time, a number of issues must be considered at design time regarding agent knowledge and awareness:

*What type of adaptation is required in the system?* Organizational adaptation can involve structural adaptation of an existing organization as well as reallocation of roles used within the organization. It may also involve a revision of tasks chosen to achieve an objective. As a dynamic domain situation involves the possibility that agents may leave and enter the organization, the re-allocation of agents to tasks is also important. If new organizations can be instantiated at run-time, then at design time, if this can be anticipated, organizational policies and triggers for creation can be determined. Organizational policies can also be specified to guide dynamic coordination of knowledge and goal prioritisation.

*How complete and adaptable are roles specified during design?* The system requirements may be represented as a set of goals and a decomposition of goals and related tasks to be completed. In many MAS organizational approaches, the next step is to identify a set of organization/s and roles responsible for such tasks. It is common for roles to be directly associated with objectives or goals within an organizational MAS (e.g. [3,14,19]), so agents are associated with a role to determine the activities the agent may adopt. We seek to enable agents to dynamically adopt responsibility for tasks outside role-specific definitions where appropriate to achieve system goals. We also seek to enable agents to form adhocracies at run time in order to facilitate an awareness and context for coordinated behaviour [16]. These requirements lead us to adopt the notion of representing agents as individuals with particular capabilities and relationships separate from role specific definitions. Agents may adopt or be assigned predefined roles, however roles can be split and agents may also be matched to potential tasks using individual capabilities.

*How much autonomy should be given to agents in terms of choosing tasks outside of a role specification?* For example, the task of clearing away bystanders might be fulfilled by any agent type within the vicinity. However, rescuing an injured agent and moving them to the ambulance might only be adopted by an agent enacting the Medic role. If there is no specific 'Medic in charge', the Medic agents may agree amongst themselves who is rescuing each injured agent. Questions around leadership roles or domain specific roles and responsibilities should be considered in the design. The system design can be configured with flexibility where it is anticipated that agents may need to dynamically revise objectives and agent allocations to roles or tasks.

*Which potential adhocracies can be identified at design time?* Adhocracies emerge dynamically during a scenario and can cross existing organizational boundaries. These organizations persist over some time to assist with coordination of particular objectives and to facilitate inter-organizational coordination. The motivation to create an adhocracy is triggered by a need for coordinated behaviour or knowledge sharing commitments. During design, anticipate situations when adhocracies may form and triggers for their creation. Create social policies to define the triggers for creating and finalising adhocracies.

## 3.3    Designing an OJAzzIC Based System

Based on our experience and considering the questions posed in Sect. 3.2, we adopt steps in the design process based on an adaptation on the O-MaSE methodology. (For each step, the equivalent task in O-MaSE is shown in brackets.) Tasks in O-MaSE map well to produce corresponding OJAzzIC components and are consistent with our approach. Our approach is not linear, refinement and review may result in repeating steps. In O-MaSE, goals are used to define the objectives of the organization, whilst roles are used to define abstract positions within the organization that can achieve a given goal or set of goals. In O-MaSE, unlike OJAzzIC, there is no provision for splitting roles. Our approach differs from others in separating the design of a problem solution into two distinct design components: the problem design represented as a set of goals and tasks and the resources available described in terms of agent types and organizations. By keeping these distinct, we aim for more flexibility at run time. We do not presume a direct relationship between roles responsible for a goal and agents available to adopt roles. If there is not a direct match between the goals and the available agents' roles, then adoption of goals can emerge at a lower level based on agent capabilities and the capabilities required to achieve a task.

We have implemented a simple incident response system using this process in order to clarify the design approach.

1. Define the Goal Model (O-MaSE:Model goals, Refine goals, Model domain, Model plans, Model protocols)
   - Create a high level goal decomposition of system objectives.
   - Break objectives into tasks that may be achieved by agents individually.
   - Where possible identify multiple alternatives to achieving an objective.
   - Identify dependencies between tasks and objectives, paying attention to requirements of synchronisation - e.g. before(task1,task2), concurrent(task1,task2).
   - Identify autonomy and control associated with each objective or task. Identify for each task or objective if it must be associated with any particular role.
2. Define the Organizational Model (O-MaSE:Model organizational interfaces, Model roles)
   - Identify long term organizations agents may belong to.
   - Define default agent types and domain roles associated within each organization.
   - Identify any inter-agent relationships.
3. Define the Agent Capabilities Model (O-MaSE:Define roles, Model agent classes, Model capabilities)
   - List capabilities to be given to particular agent types.
   - Identify capabilities required to achieve each task and thus required to fulfill each domain role.
4. Define the Role Model (O-MaSE:Define role goals)
   - Identify roles that agents of a particular type may be able to adopt within each organization (domain roles and structural roles). e.g. Medic, Leader

- Identify responsibilities associated with roles within each organization. Map organizational roles to objectives they are responsible for.
- Identify role relationships (e.g. dependency, authority, right to delegate etc.).
5. Establish Social Policies to be adopted within the run-time organizational contract (O-MaSE:Define protocols, Model policies)
   - role adoption responsibilities. e.g. Medic will prioritise locating injured then rescuing injured
   - knowledge sharing obligations. e.g. Medic will tell other Medics when an injured agent has been located or a rescue has been completed
   - organizational adhocracy creation triggers e.g. in rescue domain, if inter-agency coordination is required, a new adhocracy will be created to ensure appropriate communication and coordination occurs.
   - obligations between agents to establish shared organizational plans for coordinated tasks before goal actions are adopted.

In Sect. 4, we describe each stage in more detail using illustrations from our case study.

## 4 Incident Response Demonstration System

### 4.1 Define the Goal Model

Defining the goal model involves the following steps: Create a high level goal decomposition of system objectives and where possible, break objectives into tasks that may be achieved by agents individually. After decomposing objectives into a Goal Tree, identify if multiple alternatives plans exist to achieving an objective; Identify dependencies between tasks and objectives, paying attention to requirements of synchronisation; and Identify autonomy and control associated with each objective or task. Identify for each task or objective if it must be associated with any particular role. Based on the objectives and tasks, design plans and action specifications for how to achieve these.

Figure 3 shows a goal decomposition tree for the incident response scenario.

A design decision should be made regarding autonomy and initiative: For each task - can it be actioned by any agent with the necessary skills (capabilities) or must it be adopted only by one specific type of agent or an agent fulfilling a particular role? Our system may be configured to treat the task of removing blocking bystanders as a task that is only allocated to Officers, either as part of their role, or as a task delegated by request from a Medic, or as a task that Medic agents may also adopt by initiative if they are available. In our system, the feature allowing a Medic agent to clear bystanders using their initiative if available to do so may be turned on or off.

For each objective (landmark), it should be possible to identify at least one plan for how that objective can be achieved. The plan contains a list of states that must be achieved toward the final objective and a list of tasks or goals that will lead to successfully reaching the objective state.

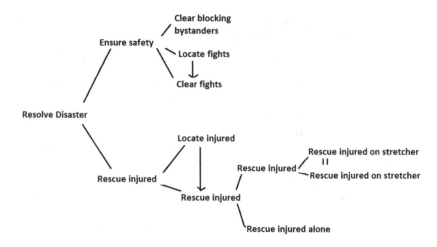

**Fig. 3.** Goal tree - incident response system

For example, within our test system the plan for locating injured involves checking all rooms for injured and at least locating one injured agent. The plan definition is as follows:*plan(injuredLocPlan, injuredLocatedLmk, [checkedRooms, injuredLocated], injuredLocatedGoal).* The corresponding Landmark objective injuredLocatedLmk is defined as:

$$landmark(injuredLocatedLmk, [checkedRooms, injuredLocated],$$
$$[at(Ag, \_), injured(Ag)]).$$

### 4.2   Define the Organizational Model

It is necessary to identify long term organizations agents may belong to and the agent types associated with each organization. Also, it is important to consider adhocracies that may form and anticipate these and incorporate these at design time. Although this hasn't been implemented in our test system at this stage, the OJAzzIC model allows for the dynamic formation of adhocracies at run time.

In our demonstration run-time system, three organizational structures are created at design time: medicOrg, officerOrg and combinedOrg. For each organization, a list of objectives, a list of member agents, a set of roles and plans are identified. The organizational belief set is initialised to include the name of each org. The syntax *org(Org, Objlist, Memberlist, Rolelist, CurrPlanID, BeliefSet)* defines an organization. The specification of each org is as follows:

Based on the initial goal decomposition, high level objectives are allocated to particular organizations. For example, the overall goal objectives allocated to the Medic organization are to rescue injured and transport injured to hospital using ambulances. The Officers organization has responsibility for the ensure safety objective. Within each organization agent types can be identified. These types may have a set of associated related roles they are capable of enacting.

org(medicOrg, [injuredRescuedLmk], [medic1,medic2,medic3], [medic], [injuredRes-
cuePlan], [orgname(medicOrg)])

org(officerOrg,    [injuredLocatedLmk,    blockingBystanderRemovedLmk,    fight-
LocatedLmk,    fightStoppedLmk],    [officer1,officer2,officer3],    [officer],    [injured-
LocPlan,blockingBystanderRemovedPlan,fightLocatedPlan,fightStoppedPlan],
[orgname(OfficerOrg)]).

org(combinedOrg,    [blockingBystanderRemovedLmk],    [medic1,    officer1],
[medic,officer], [blockingBystanderRemovedPlan], [orgname(combinedOrg)])

Do all agents have the same capabilities or are some more specialised? For each
agent type identified, what capabilities does that agent type have? The answer
to this design question may impact upon flexibility in the final system when
adapting to changes in agent availability. In our system, all Medic agents have
the capabilities required to locate injured and enact a basic rescue. Medic agents
also have the capability to remove blocking bystanders. We can also allocate to
particular Medic agents the capability to perform a rescue on stretcher. Based
on the capability set, the agents may be allocated to roles in the run time model
or allocated (or adopt) responsibility for specific tasks.

When basic organizations have been identified, the designer needs to think
about adhocracies that may form during a simulation. Adhocracies are organizations that are created in order to facilitate coordination between agents across
organizational boundaries. For example, an Officer and two Medic agents need
to work together to clear a safe exit for a complex rescue in an area of the rescue zone where access is limited due to a room collapse[1]. This complex rescue
may require multiple coordinated activities and so an agreed plan for action
and communication between these agents is required. In such a case, forming an
adhocracy organizational structure is beneficial to ensure that agents are coordinated. At design time, if such an adhocracy can be anticipated, then triggers
for the creation of an adhoc organization with members from both Medic and
Officer agents based on the anticipated particular domain situation can be specified. The combinedOrg is a relatively simple test adhocracy based on Medic
agent medic1 and Officer agent officer1 both being in an organization responsible for removing blocking bystanders. The presence of this organization means
that when these agents perform the task of removing blocking bystanders, they
will be obligated by social policies within the organization to keep each other
updated about progress on this task.

### 4.3   Define the Agent Capabilities Model

For each agent type, we list the capabilities they possess. The capabilities can
be used to match agents to tasks in the system. The capabilities can also be
associated with roles that are responsible for particular objectives as shown in
Fig. 1.

---

[1] room collapse is not implemented in the current system.

The agent capabilities model provides knowledge to enable organization-aware reasoning in terms of goal selection. In our example, Medic agents have capabilities to locate injured, rescue injured and remove blocking bystanders. Officer agents have capabilities to find fights, clear fights and remove blocking bystanders. In addition to the domain capabilities, organization aware agents have reasoning abilities to consider the organizational objectives when choosing to adopt a goal. An agent will first consider adopting an active landmark objective if it is an organizational objective and the agent is in a role that is responsible for that particular objective. Second, the agent will consider adopting an active landmark from within an active scene in which the agent is involved (no organizations involved). Third, the agent will consider adopting an objective if the agent is capable of fulfilling all tasks in an objective (apart from role allocations). Fourth, the agent will consider adopting a task that is part of a current objective if the agent is capable of achieving that task. When an agent has a list of considered objectives, the agent will select a goal to adopt based on a prioritisation of these objectives. For example, the Officer agent will prioritise locating fights over stopping fights and lastly removing blocking bystanders. These priorities, decided at design time, are specified by the order of rules in the program module or by explicitly defining priorities as policies.

### 4.4   Define the Role Model

The role model describes roles and responsibilities (objectives) associated with each role within the organization. A role has an associated capability set that defines the capabilitie(s) required in an agent to fulfill that role. Figure 2 shows the role model in OJAzzIC and how it relates to the capabilities. An agent may adopt or be allocated a role. In our system, for example, a medic role is defined as follows:

$$role(medic, [injuredLocatedLmk, injuredRescuedLmk,$$
$$blockingBystanderRemovedLmk, rescueOnStretcherLmk]).$$

This specifies that the medic role is responsible for the named objectives.

When specifying the role model, it is necessary to identify roles that agents may be able to adopt within each organization. These may include domain roles such as Medic or Officer and structural roles e.g. Leader. For each role, identify the responsibilities that should be associated with that role in terms of which objectives that role is responsible for achieving. In the above example, the medic role is responsible for four landmark objectives: injuredLocatedLmk, injuredRescuedLmk, blockingBystanderRemovedLmk and rescueOnStretcherLmk. Following the definition of roles, then role relationships can be identified (e.g. dependency, authority, right to delegate etc.). For example, Medic agents can delegate to Officer agents to clear blocking bystanders as there is a hierarchical dependency between the Medic and the Officer, defined as follows:

$$dependency(medic, officer, [blockingBystanderRemovedLmk], hierarchical).$$

## 4.5   Establish Social Policies

At this stage, we establish social policies to be adopted within the organizational contract. We are focused on social policies to facilitate coordination between cooperating agents. We are not concerned with defining sanctions to impose on non-compliant agents although clearly in a broader open application, defining such consequences may be essential to controlling an agent society. In OJAzzIC agents are aware of the policies at an internal agent-level. The types of social policies to consider include [17]:

- Role adoption responsibilities. e.g. Medic will prioritise locating injured then rescuing injured.
- Knowledge sharing obligations. e.g. Medic will tell other Medics when an injured agent has been located or a rescue has been completed
- Organizational adhocracy creation triggers e.g. in rescue domain, if inter-agency coordination is required, a new adhocracy will be created to ensure appropriate communication and coordination occurs.
- Obligations between agents to establish shared organizational plans for coordinated tasks before goal actions are adopted.

Social policies also make explicit the priorities to aid agents in their reasoning, selection and adoption of goals. Priorities for goal adoption eg. Medic agents low priority to remove blocking bystanders; priorities for role adoption e.g. Medic agents can be allocated the Medic Role; and priorities for communication - e.g. within an organization, inform all others of task progress.

The follow social coordination policies are directly implemented in our test incident response system:

- An agent A can delegate a task to agent B in order to achieve an objective if the agent A is playing a role with authority to delegate to role that B is enacting.
- If an agent A completes a task which another agent B is dependent upon, then agent A should tell agent B the task is completed.
- If agent A and agent B share an objective and agent A completes the objective, then agent A should tell agent B it has been completed.
- If agent A and agent B are both involved in the same scene, then when an objective in that scene is completed, then the agent, A should inform other agents in the scene, B that it has been completed.
- If agent A and agent B are both members of an organization O, then when an objective for that organization is completed, then the agent, A should inform other agents in the scene, B that it has been completed.

## 5   Observations

We implemented our scenario with organizationally aware Officer and Medic agents, and also built a comparison implementation using unaware Medic and Officer agents with the capabilities of a Medic and Officer respectively, but no organizational reasoning, awareness or capabilities. The latter agents could be coordinated by using an external coordinator, an organizational middleware agent, to allocate objectives to these agents. Our observations are primarily based on the performance of the organizationally aware agents. Following the design approach and considering which requirements can be given flexibility helped the run time system to behave with that flexibility. Agents could show initiative to adopt tasks outside role allocation. Agents engaged in knowledge sharing within each organization so that coordinated behaviour occurred.

In the following discussion, we focus on the objective: rescuing an injured agent, to highlight the knowledge sharing benefits gained by our organizationally aware agents. The organizational instance defines which other agents to share with. Unsurprisingly, the organizationally aware agents share information that enables them to be more coordinated in their behaviour than a more basic agent. In the unaware system, with no coordinated knowledge sharing, each basic medic agent, when allocated the rescue task has to first individually search the potential locations and identify where the injured agents are, before planning a rescue. However, in the organization-aware agent system, as soon as any medic agent locates an injured agent, this knowledge is shared with all other medic agents by sending a message to each. This allows the organization-aware medic agents to focus on the rescue task sooner. Further analysis is required as our test system is expanded to focus on agents coordinating their actions to collaborate and achieve a shared goal (when a role is split or when the goal requires multiple agents working together). We are currently working to implement the shared rescue task where 2 medic agents perform a complex rescue using a virtual stretcher. In this case, the 2 collaborating agents create commitments to each other to form the agreement on a shared plan to work together with the stretcher rescue. Once they have both adopted this goal, they will remain committed to each other until the objective is reached.

When rescuing, the medic agent creates a specific goal to rescue a particular agent based on current beliefs as to the location of that injured agent. When an injured agent is delivered to the ambulance, the environment changes and all agents are able to perceive that change and update their beliefs. When a medic agent no longer believes that a particular agent is injured, any active goal to rescue that agent is dropped. When allocated the rescue objective, organization-aware Medic agents, due to their social policy for sharing beliefs send a message to all other medic agents when the rescue of a particular injured agent has been completed. In this case, with access to beliefs about rescued agents, the organization-aware agent can choose to adopt goals to rescue injured agents only if they have not already been rescued. This avoids the creation of redundant goals. Table 1 shows a sample of messages sent and received by medic agent, medic3 during a run of the system. Medic3 shares relevant beliefs with medic1 and medic2 because they are in an organization: medicOrg. Medic1 and medic2 in turn update their own beliefs when informed by medic3. Social policies describe these obligations.

**Table 1.** Selection of messages and beliefs from medic3

| Messages | Beliefs |
|---|---|
| sent(medic1,rescued(23)) | clearingRoom('DropZone') |
| sent(medic2,rescued(23)) | occupiedclearRoom('DropZone') |
| received(medic2,rescued(23)) | rescued(23) |
| received(medic1,rescued(23)) | injuredRescued(23) |
| sent(medic1,rescued(22)) | informed(rescued(23)) |
| sent(medic2,rescued(22)) | rescued(22) |
| received(medic2,rescued(22)) | informed(rescued(22)), at('DropZone') |

# 6   Related Work

Within the field of agent oriented software engineering, there have been proposals for structures and concepts in general meta-models that could be used
as components to design and build MAS [22]. Some have attempted to create
generic meta-models for MAS that could be adapted to particular situations,
for example, FAML [3]. These approaches are helpful to provide process and
perhaps automate the design and implementation of systems. However, being
generic, these meta-models do not address specific details or requirements such
as adaptability and flexibility. Agüero and colleagues propose an organizational
meta-model that could be used to create an organizational model, however the
inner specifics of the organizational structure are left to a lower level of specification [1]. In our work, we use OJAzzIC as a meta-model that defines the
organizational structure and behavioural policies used to instantiate MAS organizations. OJAzzIC is not a generic meta-model, but a meta-model with specific
features that allow for flexibility in task allocation and improvisation of roles.

A number of methodologies for agent-oriented MAS design have been proposed. A good overview is provided in [23]. We draw attention particularly to
organization centered approaches: OperA+ [14] and OMACS [7]. Determining
an appropriate organizational MAS design for any given scenario is an open
research problem, with some taking an empirical approach [10] and others defining generic meta-models by combining existing models e.g. JaCaMo [4] and
FAML [3]. FAML does not attempt to address the specific requirements of adaptability and flexibility. Flexibility in terms of role adoption is addressed within
OperA by including capabilities in role specifications and using a gate-keeper
agent to allocate roles dynamically [2]. In this case, the gate-keeper agent selects
an agent to play a role based on the agent matching the required capabilities. If
an agent does not possess all the required capabilities, the role is not assigned.
Similarly, OMACS achieves flexibility enabling goals and agent roles to be linked
by matching capabilities dynamically. In OJAzzIC, an individual agent or set of
agents may possess the capabilities to achieve a task or objective without necessarily being allocated directly to a role. We take the approach that agents do
not need to be formally allocated to all roles, particularly when an unexpected

situation emerges requiring an individual agent to improvise. We are not alone in specifying individual agent types to describe the system requirements [18].

Within an organizational model, social relationships are defined using abstractions such as roles, interactions, norms and policies. In models such as OperA+ and OMACS, the organizational model defines a set of roles that achieve the system goals. OperA+ represents multi-organizational interactions in two dimensions: specification (the organizational structure defined in terms of roles) and enactment (agents enacting roles). In FAML, there is a distinction made between design-time specification of organizations and run-time instantiation models. This is similar to OJAzzIC. The social models in OperA+ and JaCaMo are similar to our social contract. OperA+ does not suit our requirements because it needs agents available at run time with an exact match to be able to enact the organizational roles, so flexibility relies on careful specification of the organization at design time defining alternative atomic or composite roles. JaCaMo is also built on an assumption that roles can be predefined at design time, although it makes explicit the possibility that a number of potential schemes can be defined with high level guidelines for instance stating the number of roles required. This enables some flexibility at run time, although still requires that agents who are able to enact the required roles are available.

Norms, rights and rules can be defined to constrain agent behaviour within roles, (e.g. OperA+) or policies can be defined at design time with associated commitments enacted at run time (e.g. OJAzzIC, O-MaSE). In FAML, the design time organization has associated policies defined for it. OJAzzIC social policies are consistent with the organizational policies in FAML except that in FAML policies are agent-external design time classes, whilst in OJAzzIC agents are aware of the policies at an internal agent-level. In OJAzzIC, organizations are run time entities created based on organizational definitions. Policies can be defined for a particular organization at design time, then are adopted in the organization in a run time contract of commitments between agents in the organization.

## 7   Conclusion

The previously introduced organizational MAS meta-model OJAzzIC specifies components and relationships intended to support the development of adaptive organisation-oriented MASs. In this paper we outlined a process for the design of such MASs. We proposed a number of questions to be considered during the design stage, in particular, we suggested explicitly considering flexibility, coordination, adaptability, autonomy and adhocracies that could be created. The process of making explicit choices about elements of the system that can be specified at design time was helpful in clarifying the requirements of the system overall. In particular, in trying to identify where flexibility and potential emergence can be anticipated and planned at design time, we can create a framework for run time instantiation of organizations. Each organization provides a context for agents regarding knowledge sharing and coordination. Additionally, we have found it possible within the described meta-model to achieve flexibility in terms of agents adopting tasks outside predefined roles. The organizational reasoning model when identifying potential goals to consider includes goals that the agent is capable of as well as goals the agent is responsible for due to role enactment. We did not focus on dynamic coalition formation or optimisation of coordination algorithms for the dynamic formation of MAS (e.g. [21]). However such work is relevant and could inform the automatic creation of adhocracies in response to dynamic and complex situations. Rather, here we focus on the organizational meta-model and processes to be considered in designing MAS with agents that embody appropriate awareness of the organizational structure. We address issues around the knowledge sharing and coordination related knowledge that agents require in order to successfully coordinate behaviour.

Our approach shows promise for building MASs capable of flexible run time behaviour and we plan to conduct further trials to assess how organization-aware agents cope with other challenges: for example if an agent leaves the system, tasks are potentially unallocated creating a setting where remaining agents make a run time decision to adopt unallocated tasks. In future, we also intend to support implementation of policies that enable agents to achieve appropriate coordination by creating adhocracies at run time.

Our design approach addresses the requirements of flexibility and improvisation. At design time to enable run-time adaptation, macro level roles and tasks that achieve system objectives are to be specified. At run time, adhocracy formation and instantiation of policies guide the sharing of knowledge and plans between organization-aware agents in a particular context. This moves us closer to the aim of facilitating planned emergence within agent organizations.

**Acknowledgments.** We thank the anonymous reviewers and those who have given feedback on the presentation – all of which helped improve this paper.

# References

1. Agüero, J., Rebollo, M., Carrascosa, C., Julián, V.: Developing virtual organizations using MDD. In: Proceedings of Workshop on Agreement Technologies (WAT 2009), pp. 130–141 (2009)
2. Aldewereld, H., Dignum, V., Jonker, C.M., van Riemsdijk, M.B.: Agreeing on role adoption in open organisations. KI-Künstliche Intelligenz **26**(1), 37–45 (2012)
3. Beydoun, G., Low, G., Henderson-Sellers, B., Mouratidis, J.J.H., Gomez-Sanz, J., Gonzalez-Perez, C.: FAML: a generic metamodel for MAS development. IEEE Trans. Softw. Eng. **35**(6), 841–863 (2009)
4. Boissier, O., Bordini, R., Hübner, J., Ricci, A.: Unravelling multi-agent-oriented programming. In: Shehory, O., Sturm, A. (eds.) Agent-Oriented Software Engineering, Springer-Verlag Heidelberg (2014)
5. Corkill, D., Durfee, E., Lesser, V., Zafar, H., Zhang, C.: Organizationally Adept Agents. In: 12th International Workshop on Coordination. Organization, Institutions and Norms in Agent Systems (COIN@AAMAS 2011), pp. 15–30. Taipei, Taiwan May 2011

6. Corkill, D.D., Lesser, V.R.: The use of meta-level control for coordination in a distributed problem solving network. In: Bundy, A. (ed.) Proceedings of the 8th International Joint Conference on Artificial Intelligence, pp. 748–756. William Kaufmann (1983)

7. DeLoach, S.A.: OMACS: a framework for adaptive, complex systems. In: Dignum, V. (ed.) Multi-Agent Systems: Semantics and Dynamics of Organizational Models. IGI Global: Hershey, PA (2009) ISBN: 1-60566-256-9

8. DeLoach, S.A.: O-MaSE: an extensible methodology for multi-agent systems. In: Shehory, O., Sturm, A. (eds.) Agent-Oriented Software Engineering, Springer-Verlag, Heidelberg (2014)

9. DeLoach, S.A., Carlos, G.-O.J.: O-MaSE: a customizable approach to designing and building complex, adaptive multiagent systems. Int. J. Agent Oriented Softw. Eng. 4(3), 244–280 (2010)

10. Franco, M.R., Sichman, J.S.: Comparing and evaluating organizational models: a multi-agent programming contest case study. In: Pre-proceedings The 17th International Workshop on Coordination, Organisations, Institutions and Norms, AAMAS (2014)

11. Grosz, B., Kraus, S.: The evolution of SharedPlans. In: Wooldridge, M., Rao, A. (eds.) Foundations of Rational Agency. Applied Logic Series, vol. 14, pp. 227–262. Springer, Netherlands (1999)

12. Hendriks, K., Dix, J.: GOAL: a multi-agent programming language applied to an exploration game. In: Shehory, O., Sturm, A. (eds.) Agent-Oriented Software Engineering, pp. 235–258. Springer-Verlag, Heidelberg (2014)

13. Jensen, A., Alderwereld, H., Dignum, V.: Dimensions of organizational coordination. In: Hindriks, K., de Weerdt, M., van Riemsdijk, B., Warnier, M. (eds.) Proceedings of the 25th Benelux Conference on Artificial Intelligence, pp. 80–87 (2013)

14. Jiang, J., Dignum, V., Tan, Y.-H.: An agent based inter-organizational collaboration framework: OperA+. In: Proceedings of Web Intelligence/IAT Workshops, pp. 21–24 (2011)

15. Johnson, M., Jonker, C., van Riemsdijk, B., Feltovich, P.J., Bradshaw, J.M.: Joint activity testbed: blocks world for teams (BW4T). In: Aldewereld, H., Dignum, V., Picard, G. (eds.) ESAW 2009. LNCS, vol. 5881, pp. 254–256. Springer, Heidelberg (2009)

16. Keogh, K., Sonenberg, L.: Adaptive Coordination in Distributed and Dynamic Agent Organizations. In: Cranefield, S., van Riemsdijk, M.B., Vázquez-Salceda, J., Noriega, P. (eds.) COIN 2011. LNCS, vol. 7254, pp. 38–57. Springer, Heidelberg (2012)

17. Keogh, K., Sonenberg, L.: Coordination using social policies in dynamic agent organizations. In: Balke, T., Dignum, F., van Riemsdijk, M.B., Chopra, A.K. (eds.) COIN 2013. LNCS, vol. 8386, pp. 83–102. Springer, Heidelberg (2014)

18. Miller, T., Lu, B., Sterling, L., Beydoun, G., Taveter, K.: Requirements elicitation and specification using the agent paradigm: the case study of an aircraft turnaround simulator. IEEE Trans. Software Eng. 40(10), 1007–1024 (2014)

19. Odell, J.J., Nodine, M., Levy, R.: A metamodel for agents, roles, and groups. In: Odell, J.J., Giorgini, P., Müller, J.P. (eds.) AOSE 2004. LNCS, vol. 3382, pp. 78–92. Springer, Heidelberg (2005)

20. Pitt, J., Bourazeri, A., Nowak, A., Roszczynska-Kurasinska, M., Rychwalska, A., Rodriguez, I., Santiago, M., Sanchez, M.L., Florea, M., Sanduleac, M.: Transforming big data into collective awareness. Computer 46(6), 40–45 (2013)

21. Ramchurn, S., Farinelli, A., Macarthur, K., Jennings, N.: Decentralized coordination in robocup rescue. Comput. J. **53**(9), 1447–1461 (2010)
22. Seidita, V., Cossentino, M., Hilaire, V., Gaud, N., Galland, S., Koukam, A., Gaglio, S.: The metamodel: a starting point for design processes construction. Int. J. Softw. Eng. Knowl. Eng. **20**(04), 575–608 (2010)
23. Sterling, L., Taveter, K.: The Art of Agent-Oriented Modeling. MIT Press, Cambridge (2009)
24. Valentine, M.A., Edmondson, A.C.: Team scaffolds: how meso-level structures support role-based coordination in temporary groups, Harvard Business School, Working Paper (2014)

# Supporting Request Acceptance
# with Use Policies

Thomas C. King[(✉)], M. Birna van Riemsdijk,
Virginia Dignum, and Catholijn M. Jonker

TU Delft, Delft, The Netherlands
{t.c.king-1,m.b.vanriemsdijk,m.v.dignum,c.m.jonker}@tudelft.nl

**Abstract.** This paper deals with the problem of automating the contribution of resources owned by people to do work for others. This is by providing a means for owners of resources to maintain autonomy over how, when and to whom their resources are used with the specification of use policies governing resources. We give representations of *requests* for resource usage as a set of conditional norms and a *use policy* as specifying what norms should and should not be imposed on a resource (i.e. a set of meta-norms). Our main contribution is a reasoner built on the Event Calculus, that detects conflicts between requests and use policies, determining whether the request can be accepted.

## 1 Introduction

Increasingly, detailed environmental data is needed to support governments and citizens in making decisions affected by environmental conditions. Such decisions include determining where to go to avoid flooded areas or deciding how city water infrastructure can be improved based on its current effectiveness. Getting detailed data requires a large number of sensory resources, such as dense networks of precipitation sensors to monitor the rain.

Crowdsensing [9] is a means to cost-effectively acquire detailed data by requesting the use of the mobile sensors people already own (i.e. crowdsourcing them), such as rain sensors on citizens' bicycles. We view a request for the use of a resource posed to its owner as a request for the owner to agree to the imposition of norms (obligations and prohibitions [1]) on the resource. An example of a request is for an ongoing agreement such as: 'a resource is obliged to collect rain data when at a specific location and it is prohibited to turn the sensor off until the data is collected'. Given a large number of such agreements, detailed data can be gathered through the crowdsourcing of sensors.

However, if there are many requests for the use of a resource, feasibility demands the automation of their acceptance and rejection. Yet, the automation must respect an owner's desire to maintain autonomy over how, when and for whom their resource is used. Owners of resources need a means to specify a *use policy* governing how their resource may be used, and an automated process should reject requests if they conflict with the use policy. Whilst existing work

© Springer International Publishing Switzerland 2015
A. Ghose et al. (Eds.): COIN 2014, LNAI 9372, pp. 114–131, 2015.
DOI: 10.1007/978-3-319-25420-3_8

detects conflicts between norms (see [1]), such as when something is simultaneously obliged and prohibited, there lacks a way to detect conflicts between requests and use policies.

We address these issues by proposing a means to specify a use policy governing how a resource may be used, and an automated reasoner for rejecting requests if they conflict with the use policy. We view a use policy as specifying which norms should and should not be imposed. To exemplify, a use policy for a mobile sensor might state that anyone using it should be obliged to make a payment, and prohibit the prohibition of the sensor from being turned off. Given that a use policy obliges and prohibits the imposition of norms, we view it as a set of norms about norms, called *meta-norms*.

Our proposed reasoner therefore detects conflicts between a request to use a resource and the meta-norms of a use policy that governs it, supporting the acceptance and rejection of requests. To detect conflicts we model norms and meta-norms in the Event Calculus [14], a logic of events and their effects over time. This allows us to determine if norms and meta-norms coincide and therefore detect if there are circumstances under which there are conflicts.

In the rest of the paper we first give an overview of existing work in the area (Sect. 2). Then, we give an overview of our approach (Sect. 3). In Sect. 4 we introduce the specification languages for requests and use policies and their informal meaning. The formal operational semantics are specified using the Event Calculus in Sect. 5. In Sect. 6 we illustrate the proposal with a formalisation of a running example. In Sect. 7 we describe an implementation of our proposal. We draw conclusions in Sect. 8.

## 2   Related Work

Our proposal fits into the broad area of normative multi-agent systems (see [1] for a recent literature survey), the formal study of which is deontic logic (see [8]). Much work has been done on reasoning about normative agreements such as contracts and compliance with norms (e.g. [5,10,18,21,22]) and multi-agent organisational frameworks for the verification of organisations as networks of contractual agreements (e.g. [7,12]). However, we focus on a pre-agreement stage, where the novelty of our proposal is the application of meta-norms to govern resource use.

There is already much work on reasoning about normative conflicts (for a review see [1]). In particular, Vasconcelos, Kollingbaum and Norman [19] provide a normative conflict checking and resolution formalism based on logic and constraint programming. Unlike our work, they do not consider conflicts between norms and meta-norms, nor do they consider conditional norms and meta-norms about events. Instead, they detect normative conflicts between coinciding temporal obligations and prohibitions, where compliance with both is impossible. The advantage of their approach is that it enables expressing norms with constraints such as a prohibition to stay within an area. A conflicting norm would then be an obligation to be in a smaller part of that area.

Like our proposal, the work of Günay and Yolum [11] use the Event Calculus to detect normative conflicts. They consider conflicts between social commitments (norms bound to agents as a part of an agreement). Unlike our proposal, they do not consider meta-norms or conflicts between norms and meta-norms. Instead, they consider conflicts in terms of different simultaneous obligations to perform tasks that cannot coincide. For example, two obligations to rent the same car to different people at the same time.

In reasoning about meta-norms, López, Luck and D'Inverno [15] propose a kind of legislative meta-norm to govern which norms an agent may issue or abolish. Their meta-norms define which norms can be introduced into the system and when. Unfortunately, they do not provide an implementation level mechanism for checking meta-norm/norm conflicts based on their operational semantics as we do.

Boella and Torre [3] also propose a kind of meta-norm acting as a permission issued by a higher authority to block the imposition of norms by lower level authorities. Using input/output logic (a logic of conditional norms [16]), their formalism produces for a given situation what may be obliged by lower-level authorities given everything that is permitted by higher-level authorities. The main difference with our work is that they give permissions the role of derogation and do not consider obligatory meta-norms. Furthermore, unlike in the aforementioned work, we detect conflicts between temporal norms and meta-norms (conditional norms with deadlines and conditional meta-norms). The temporal aspect affects whether specific norms and meta-norms can simultaneously hold such that they cause conflict.

Finally, Wansing [20] treats both obligatory and prohibitory meta-norms in deliberative-stit logic as being norms about the action of imposing norms. This is in a setting where there is a hierarchy of authorities, so for example, one authority obliges a lower authority to forbid an even lower authority. Like Wansing, we define a meta-norm as being about the event of a norm being imposed. We also explicitly represent norms as being from one authority to another, and meta-norms are implicitly so. Unlike Wansing's work, our work contributes a meta-norm/norm conflict detection mechanism.

In summary, there is much work on detecting conflicts between norms. There is also much work on reasoning about certain kinds of meta-norms. However, as far as we know there are no proposals for reasoning about conflicts between conditional norms and meta-norms about events, or the application of meta-norms to resource governance.

## 3   Overview

Throughout the paper we consider a scenario where a municipality wants detailed statistics of rain hitting the ground. Specifically, near a newly built water square – an above-ground area that is both a recreational square, and a place

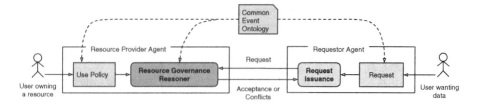

**Fig. 1.** Overview

to store rain water temporarily until there is capacity in the sewage system to handle the water[1].

Assuming there is no dense network of stationary rain sensors in the area, the municipality might opt to make an ongoing agreement with the mobile sensors of people that frequent or pass by the square. Such that, whenever they are near the square they will collect and send rain data. For example, by recruiting users with an app on their mobile phone that communicates with rain sensors on their umbrella or bicycle to collect rain data, such that the sensors transmit the rain data they gather to their mobile phones which then send it to the requestor.

For simplicity we consider a process between two agents, depicted in Fig. 1. These are: the resource provider agent governing a resource owned by a user and a requestor agent used by someone who wants to request use of the resource. The process begins with the data-requesting user specifying the terms of the request, using the lexicon of a common ontology describing events. Their requestor agent then poses the request to the resource provider agent. The owner of the resource has specified the terms of its use policy, using the same common ontology of events.

The resource provider agent detects conflicts between the use policy and request. This supports the automated governance of resources, so the resource provider agent refuses requests that conflict with the use policy.

There are two types of conflict to consider. The first occurs if the request does not impose a norm in circumstances where the use policy obliges it to be imposed (e.g. an obligation to oblige a requestor to provide payment). The second type of conflict occurs if the request would impose norms in circumstances where they are prohibited by the use policy (e.g. a prohibition on prohibiting the free movement of a resource).

In this paper, we focus on the reasoning about requests for resources governed by use policies, including the representations of requests and use policies. An overview of the resource governance reasoner architecture is given in Fig. 2.

The resource governance reasoner we propose takes as inputs an ontology of events (what can happen), a request, and a use policy. The ontology of events is used to generate a sequence of events for the normative evaluator. The normative evaluator determines for the given event-sequence which norms and meta-norms hold simultaneously and when. This is according to the (meta-)norms' conditions

---

[1] http://www.raingain.eu/en/actualite/rotterdam-inaugurates-first-large-scale-square-water-storage-greenery-and-sport.

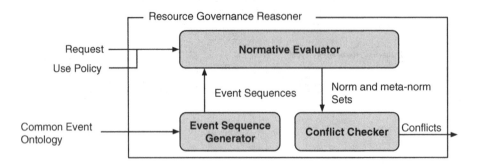

**Fig. 2.** The architecture of the reasoner

which describe what event causes the (meta-)norm to hold, or as is commonly used in the literature 'to be detached' [1] (the intuition is similar to the of the law of detachment/modus ponens in classical logic). Simultaneously detached norms and meta-norms are output as sets for the conflict detector. As a result, the reasoner returns the conflicts between a request and a use policy.

We model norms and meta-norms, detached and terminated according to a sequence of events, by using the Event Calculus [14] as the underlying formalism.

## 4    Requests and Use Policies

In this section we introduce the languages of requests as a set of norms and use policies as a set of meta-norms (Sect. 4.1), then we proceed to discuss how norms and meta-norms relate to each other in terms of conflicts (Sect. 4.2).

### 4.1    Representations

We use requests to represent what a requestor would like a provider to agree to doing and a use policy to govern what a provider agent will agree to. We begin with an example to motivate our representations of requests.

**Example.** (Part One, Requestor) Rachel wants to monitor the level of rainfall around a newly built water square. There is no dense network of static sensors, so she wishes to make use of the existing mobile sensors people carry to gather the data. Thus, she requests people to make an ongoing agreement to provide her with precipitation data. The terms of the request are that whenever someone enters the water square, rain data should be gathered. Once data is gathered it should be sent before the sensor leaves the area around the station. The sensor should not be turned off until data has been gathered.

Norms concern agents, so we assume a set of agent names $Ag$. Norms are about events, which can be generated by or concern specific agents (e.g. an agent entering an area), or the environment (e.g. rain starting to fall). Thus, events are either non-agentive, denoted as propositions, or agentive denoted as propositions with an agent name in the subscript.

**Definition 1.** (Events) Let *EnvProp* with typical element *EP*, and *AgProp* with typical element *AP* be mutually disjoint sets of propositions, respectively denoting non-agentive and agentive events. Also let *Ag* be a set of agent names with typical element *a*. The set *Ev* is the set of all elements *ev* expressible in the language:

$$ev ::= EP \mid AP_a$$

Norms are obligations and prohibitions, respectively denoted with a deontic type of $O$ or $F$. Norms oblige or prohibit an agent to ensure an aim $A$ happens (an event) possibly before a deadline $D$ (also an event).

A norm can be detached (become active) [1], either unconditionally or on the condition of an event happening. If a norm's detachment is conditional on an event, we say it is a conditional norm, otherwise it is an unconditional norm. Conditional norms are represented as a rule with the conditional event $C$ placed in the antecedent and a norm as the consequent.

Finally, we follow the notion that when a norm is detached it is imposed on a debtor denoted with *DE*, towards a creditor denoted with *CR*. For example, a debtor can be an agent obliged to provide data within one minute towards a creditor requesting it, or a debtor can be an agent obliged to pay for data towards an agent providing the data.

**Definition 2.** (Norm) Let $O$ and $F$ respectively denote the deontic types of obligation and prohibition, $DE, CR \in Ag$ be debtor and creditor agents, and $C, A, D \in Ev$ be events respectively denoting the condition, aim and deadline of the norm. An unconditional norm is denoted with $\langle ucn \rangle$ and a conditional norm is denoted with $\langle cn \rangle$. The set of norms $N$ is the set of all elements $\langle n \rangle$ expressible in the language defined as:

$$
\begin{aligned}
\langle n \rangle \quad &::= \quad \langle cn \rangle \mid \langle ucn \rangle \\
\langle cn \rangle \quad &::= \quad C\ THEN\ \langle ucn \rangle \\
\langle ucn \rangle \quad &::= \quad O_{DE:CR}(A\ BEFORE\ D) \mid F_{DE:CR}(A\ BEFORE\ D) \mid \\
&\qquad O_{DE:CR}(A) \mid F_{DE:CR}(A)
\end{aligned}
$$

A request to use a resource, is the set of norms that if the request is accepted will be imposed on the resource.

**Definition 3.** (Request) A request $R$ is a set of norms such that $R \subseteq N$.

Thus we can formalise the request $R$ of Rachel (*rac*), to a resource owned by a person called Peter (*pet*), as:

$$R = \{enter\_water\_square_{pet} \; THEN \; O_{pet:rac}(gather\_rain\_data_{pet}$$
$$BEFORE \; send\_data_{pet}),$$
$$enter\_water\_square_{pet} \; THEN \; O_{pet:rac}(send\_data_{pet}$$
$$BEFORE \; leave\_water\_square_{pet}),$$
$$enter\_water\_square_{pet} \; THEN \; F_{pet:rac}(sensing\_off_{pet}$$
$$BEFORE \; gather\_rain\_data_{pet})\}$$

Use policies are used to govern a resource, such that requests that impose norms that are unacceptable in how, when and for whom the resource is used are detected as conflicting with the use policy. Conflicts then cause a request to be automatically rejected, avoiding a user's resource from being used in ways they do not want. We use the following example to motivate the expressivity of our use policy representation.

**Example.** (Part Two, Provider) Peter has a cellphone app that can measure rainfall in a location by communicating using bluetooth with a sensor on his umbrella. Peter usually carries his cellphone and umbrella with him, including when he walks past the water square. He is willing to donate the use of his sensing resource, but only if he does not have to stay in any particular area. His cellphone uses up a lot of energy when collecting data, so he wants to be allowed to turn the sensing off when the battery's energy becomes low. Finally, if he is obliged to provide data, then he wants to be paid within one day.

We represent a use policy as a specification of what norms should and should not be detached under specific circumstances. That is, it is a set of norms about norms, or meta-norms. This specification can be compared against a request.

Meta-norms can be conditional on an event or a norm being detached. For example, on the condition an obligation for data to be provided is detached, then it is obligatory for the agent that should be sent data to provide payment.

An unconditional meta-norm is detached by default, whilst a conditional meta-norm is detached on the condition an event occurring, or a norm specified in the condition is detached. Both conditional and unconditional meta-norms oblige or prohibit the detachment of a norm. Whilst (non-meta) norms have deadlines affecting whether they are detached simultaneously with conflicting meta-norms, for brevity we do not examine the case where a meta-norm also has a deadline. However, the framework can easily be extended to meta-norms with deadlines.

**Definition 4.** (Meta Norms) Let $n, n' \in N$ denote norms, and $C \in Ev$ be an event. An unconditional meta-norm is denoted with $\langle ucmn \rangle$ and a conditional meta-norm is denoted with $\langle cmn \rangle$. The set $MN$ is the set of all elements $\langle mn \rangle$ expressible in the language defined as:

$$\langle mn \rangle \quad ::= \quad \langle cmn \rangle \mid \langle ucmn \rangle$$
$$\langle cmn \rangle \quad ::= \quad n \; THEN \; \langle ucmn \rangle \mid C \; THEN \; \langle ucmn \rangle$$
$$\langle ucmn \rangle \quad ::= \quad O(n') \mid F(n')$$

A use policy is a set of meta-norms.

**Definition 5.** (Use Policy) A use policy $UP \subseteq MN$ is a set of meta-norms.

To exemplify, we formalise Peter's use policy $UP$ which specifies how Rachel may use his resource, where his resource is denoted with *pet*, as[2]:

$$UP = \{O_{pet:rac}(send\_data_{pet} \; BEFORE \; leave\_water\_square_{pet}) \; THEN$$
$$O(O_{rac:pet}(pay_{rac} \; BEFORE \; tomorrow)),$$
$$F(O_{pet:rac}(send\_data_{pet} \; BEFORE \; leave\_water\_square_{pet})),$$
$$battery\_depleted_{pet} \; THEN \; F(F_{pet:rac}(sensing\_off_{pet} \; BEFORE$$
$$gather\_rain\_data_{pet}))\}$$

## 4.2 Conflict

Taking Rachel's request and Peter's use policy, we can intuitively see there are conflicts, which should be identified by the resource governance reasoner.

**Example.** (Part Three, Conflict) Rachel's request has been posed to Peter's agent in control of providing the resource. Rachel wants data sent before Peter's sensor leaves the water square area, however, Peter has stated that he wants to be free to move. If Rachel's request is accepted then Peter will be prohibited from turning his sensor off, yet, he has stated that when his cellphone's battery is depleted he must be allowed to do so. Finally, once Peter has fulfilled an obligation to provide data, he demands to be paid before tomorrow, but Rachel's request does not include such an obligation.

The normative reasoner identifies sets of norms and meta-norms that hold simultaneously given some circumstances (a sequence of events), a request, and a use policy. Meanwhile the conflict-detector takes as input sets of simultaneously holding norms and meta-norms and identifies conflicts by comparing those sets.

The conflict detector identifies two types of conflict. The first type of conflict is where a meta-norm holds that obliges a norm to be detached, but that norm is not detached. Conversely, the second type of conflict is where a meta-norm holds that prohibits a norm from being detached, but that norm is detached. We define conflict in terms of a set of norms and meta-norms that hold simultaneously. We assume the sets of norms and meta-norms to be self-consistent and focus on conflicts between norms and meta-norms.

**Definition 6.** (Conflict) Let $N' \subset N$ be a set of unconditional norms and $MN' \subset MN$ be a set of unconditional meta-norms, denoting all of the simultaneously detached norms and meta-norms for some circumstances. We say that there is a conflict between $N'$ and $MN'$ if either of the following holds:

$$(n \in N' \; and \; F(n) \in MN') \; or \; (n \notin N' \; and \; O(n) \in MN')$$

---

[2] More general use policies are possible by extending the framework with variables. This would allow non-specific debtors and creditors to be specified, and the expression of meta-norms about norms where we are not concerned with exact terms.

To exemplify, consider a sequence of events generated by the event sequence generator component, that can hypothetically happen after the request is accepted, where Peter enters the water square and then the battery on his phone is depleted. For this situation, assuming nothing else has happened, the sets $DN$ and $DMN$ are the respective sets of simultaneously detached norms from Rachel's request and meta-norms from Peter's use policy:

$$DN = \{F_{pet:rac}(sensing\_off_{pet} \ BEFORE \ gather\_rain\_data_{pet})\}$$
$$DMN = \{O(O_{rac:pet}(pay_{rac} \ BEFORE \ tomorrow),$$
$$F(F_{pet:rac}(sensing\_off_{pet} \ BEFORE \ gather\_rain\_data_{pet})),$$
$$F(O_{pet:rac}(send\_data_{pet} \ BEFORE \ leave\_water\_square_{pet}))\}$$

Both types of conflict are identified in this example when these sets of norms and meta-norms are compared. The first, is that a norm forbids turning the sensing off, yet a meta-norm is simultaneously detached that forbids such a prohibition. Similarly, a norm obliges Peter to send data before he leaves the water square, but such an obligation is prohibited by a detached meta-norm. Finally, a meta-norm obliges the obligation for payment to be provided, but such an obligation is not detached at the same time.

## 5   The Event Calculus Normative Model

In this section we give the operational semantics for the detachment and termination of norms and meta-norms, and when they produce conflicts between a use policy and a request. We first re-introduce the Event Calculus (Sect. 5.1) which we subsequently use to define the operational semantics (Sect. 5.2).

### 5.1   Event Calculus

The Event Calculus is a logical-formalism specified by Kowalski and Sergot [14] for reasoning about events and their effects on which fluents hold and when. The Event Calculus provides an ontology of predicates (Table 1) for specifying in an Event Calculus theory the effects of events on initiating and terminating fluents, and what events happen at which time *points* (a narrative). The same ontology also provides predicates that specify, given the Event Calculus, an Event Calculus Theory and a narrative, which fluents hold at specific time *intervals*.

We choose the Event Calculus due to its modelling of inertial fluents and its efficient implementations [2,4,6]. Inertial fluents are required because we treat norms and meta-norms as fluents, and the informal notions of detached norms and meta-norms mean they continue to be detached until either their aim or deadline occurs. Efficiency is important, due to the time constraints that can be expected when accepting or rejecting a request.

Although many variations of the Event Calculus exist [17] we use the *simple* Event Calculus, where from here-on we usually omit the word simple. In the

**Table 1.** The event calculus ontology of predicates

| Predicate | Meaning |
|---|---|
| broken_during(P, Start, End) | P is terminated between time points Start and End. |
| happens_at(E, T) | The event E happens at time T. |
| holds_at(P, T) | The property P holds at time T. |
| holds_for(P, Start, End) | The property P holds from time points Start until End. |
| initially(P) | The property P holds at the first time point. |
| initiates_at(E, P, T) | The event E initiates the property P at time T. |
| terminates_at(E, P, T) | The event E terminates the property P at time T. |

following, we give an axiomatisation of the Event Calculus adapted from [6] with the addition of a commonly used axiom for an initial state.

Axioms are given as Prolog-style horn-clauses. Following the convention, symbols starting with upper-case denote variables and lower-case denote constants. Since the Event Calculus explicitly deals with time, we assume an infinitely countable set of time instances $\mathbb{T}$ with typical element $t_i$ where $i \in \mathbb{N} \cup \{\infty\}$. The operators $<$ and $\leq$ are assumed to be specified for all members of the set $\mathbb{T}$, with the expected meaning. Finally, $\neg$ is interpreted as negation-as-failure, making the Event Calculus non-monotonic.

The first axiom, EC1, states that any fluent stated to initially hold is initiated at the first time point.

$$initiates\_at(initially(P), P, 0) \leftarrow initially(P) \tag{EC1}$$

The next two axioms specify the intervals fluents hold for. Axiom EC2 states that a fluent holds in an interval beginning immediately after the initiation event and ending at the termination event. Axiom EC3 deals with the case where there is no terminating event for a fluent.

$$\begin{aligned} holds\_for(P,\ Start,\ End) \leftarrow\ &initiates\_at(Ei,\ P,\ Start) \wedge \\ &terminates\_at(Et,\ P,\ End) \wedge \\ &End > Start \wedge \\ &\neg broken\_during(P,\ Start,\ End) \end{aligned} \tag{EC2}$$

$$\begin{aligned} holds\_for(P,\ Start,\ t_\infty) \leftarrow\ &initiates\_at(Ei,\ P,\ Start) \wedge \\ &\neg broken\_dduring(P,\ Start,\ t_\infty) \end{aligned} \tag{EC3}$$

Axiom EC4 states that a fluent is broken during an interval if a terminating event occurs during that interval. We specify the axiom such that it provides a 'weak-interpretation' of the initiates_at predicate [6], where the same initiation event occurring consecutively does not imply there was a terminating event in-between.

$$\begin{aligned} broken\_during(P,\ Start,\ End) \leftarrow\ &terminates\_at(E,\ P,\ T) \wedge \\ &Start < T < End \end{aligned} \tag{EC4}$$

Finally, axiom EC5 states which time points a fluent holds at.

$$holds\_at(P,\ T) \leftarrow holds\_for(P,\ Start,\ End) \wedge Start < T \leq End \qquad \text{(EC5)}$$

Given the Event Calculus specification, the effects of events can be specified using the schemas EC6 for the initialisation of a fluent and EC7, taken from [5].

$$initiates\_at(E,\ P,\ T) \leftarrow happens\_at(E,\ T) \wedge holds\_at(P_1, T)$$
$$\wedge ... \wedge holds\_at(P_n, T) \qquad \text{(EC6)}$$

$$terminates\_at(E,\ P,\ T) \leftarrow happens\_at(E,\ T) \wedge holds\_at(P_1, T)$$
$$\wedge ... \wedge holds\_at(P_n, T) \qquad \text{(EC7)}$$

## 5.2   Normative Evaluation and Conflict Checking

Our normative evaluation and conflict checking semantics uses the Event Calculus for reasoning about which norms and meta-norms hold when, and when they conflict. The two resource governance reasoner components (see Fig. 2), the Normative Evaluator and the Conflict Checker, are defined as sets of Event Calculus rules.

In the following, we use the predicates $o/4$ and $f/4$ to respectively represent obligations and prohibitions, with the first two parameters respectively being the debtor and creditor, the third the aim, and the fourth the deadline event or $\perp$ to indicate no deadline. $o/1$ and $f/1$ are predicates representing meta-norms, where the parameter is a norm. We use the predicate $ifthen/2$ to represent conditional and unconditional norms and meta-norms, the first parameter is the condition or $\top$ if it is unconditional, the second parameter is the norm or meta-norm.

As with work on social commitment modelling [5] we assume that two events cannot occur at the same time. However, we make an exception for the event of a norm being detached, which can often occur at the same time as a non-detachment event and other norms being detached.

*Normative Operational Semantics.* The operational semantics of norms and meta-norms correspond to the Normative Evaluator component (see Fig. 2), specifying when a norm or meta-norm is and is not detached. The semantics are specified with axioms for the $initiates\_at/3$ and $terminates\_at/3$ Event Calculus predicates, which state an event (the first term) respectively detaches or terminates a norm or meta-norm (the second term) when the event happens (the last term). These axioms are defined with respect to the $happens\_at/2$ predicate which describes when an event happens.

The first two axioms state that any unconditional norm holds initially.

$$initially(o(DE,\ CR,\ A,\ D)) \leftarrow ifthen(\top, o(DE,\ CR,\ A,\ D))$$
$$\text{(Obl. Uncond. Norm Detachment)}$$

$$initially(f(DE,\ CR,\ A,\ D)) \leftarrow ifthen(\top, f(DE,\ CR,\ A,\ D))$$
$$\text{(Pro. Uncond. Detachment)}$$

Obligatory meta-norms have different detachment semantics from norms. An unconditional obligatory meta-norm is detached initially only if it is not simultaneously satisfied with the detachment of a norm. We do not check if the norm it obliges is *already* detached. Although this is certainly possible, we take the meaning of an obligatory meta-norm to be that it obliges the detachment of a norm at the time it is itself detached. If the obligatory meta-norm is satisfied as soon as it is detached, then there is no conflict and so it will not be taken into account by the conflict checker.

$$initially(o(Norm)) \leftarrow ifthen(\top, o(Norm)) \wedge \neg initially(Norm)$$
$$\text{(Obl. MN Uncond. Detachment)}$$

Unconditional prohibitory meta-norms, however, are detached regardless of whether the norm they prohibit is detached. Thus, their detachment follows the same form as norms, formulated in the next axiom.

$$initially(f(Norm)) \leftarrow ifthen(\top, f(Norm)) \qquad \text{(Pro. MN Uncond. Detachment)}$$

The next two axioms, give the conditional detachment of norms, stating that when the condition of a conditional norm happens, the norm is detached.

$$initiates\_at(C, o(DE, CR, A, D), T) \leftarrow ifthen(C, o(DE, CR, A, D)) \wedge$$
$$happens\_at(C, T)$$
$$\text{(Obl. Cond. Detachment)}$$

$$initiates\_at(C, f(DE, CR, A, D), T) \leftarrow ifthen(C, f(DE, CR, A, D)) \wedge$$
$$happens\_at(C, T)$$
$$\text{(Pro. Cond. Detachment)}$$

The next axiom states that a conditional obligatory meta-norm is detached when its condition occurs, unless it is satisfied at the same time with the detachment of the norm it obliges (as with its unconditional variant). Again, if the obligatory meta-norm is detached and simultaneously satisfied, the conflict checker will not take it into account, because there is no conflict.

$$initiates\_at(C1, o(Norm), T) \leftarrow ifthen(C1, o(Norm)) \wedge happens\_at(C1, T) \wedge$$
$$\neg initiates\_at(C2, Norm, T)$$
$$\text{(Obl. MN Cond. Detachment)}$$

Conditional prohibitory meta-norms have the same detachment semantics as conditional norms.

$$initiates\_at(C, f(Norm), T) \leftarrow ifthen(C, f(Norm)) \wedge happens\_at(C, T)$$
$$\text{(Pro. MN Cond. Detachment)}$$

We treat the detachment of a norm as an event, the event of the norm being imposed on an agent. This is required for the detachment of meta-norms that are conditional on the event of a norm being detached and the satisfaction of obligatory meta-norms which is the event of a norm being detached.

$$happens\_at(o(DE,\ CR,\ A,\ D),\ T) \leftarrow ifthen(C, o(DE,\ CR,\ A,\ D)) \land$$
$$happens\_at(C, T)$$
$$\text{(Obl. Detachment Event)}$$

$$happens\_at(f(DE,\ CR,\ A,\ D),\ T) \leftarrow ifthen(C, f(DE,\ CR,\ A,\ D)) \land$$
$$happens\_at(C, T)$$
$$\text{(Pro. Detachment Event)}$$

We now turn our attention to the termination of detached norms. A detached obligation is terminated if its aim is achieved, whilst a detached prohibition is terminated if its deadline occurs. Thus, although we do not explicitly model violations, under these semantics a norm persists after it is violated until it is fulfilled. Alternative semantics can be accommodated for in the future.

$$terminates\_at(A, o(DE,\ CR,\ A,\ D), T) \leftarrow happens\_at(A, T)$$
$$\text{(Obl. Aim Termination)}$$
$$terminates\_at(D, f(DE,\ CR,\ A,\ D), T) \leftarrow happens\_at(D, T)$$
$$\text{(Pro. Deadl. Termination)}$$

As with obligatory norms, obligatory meta-norms are terminated when their aim (the detachment of a norm) occurs:

$$terminates\_at(Norm, o(Norm), T) \leftarrow happens\_at(Norm,\ T)$$
$$\text{(Obl. MN Aim Termination)}$$

Prohibitory meta-norms, like their norm counterparts, are not terminated when their aim occurs (a norm they prohibit is detached). Thus, due to not having a deadline, they are not terminated at all.

*Conflict Detection Semantics.* The conflict detection semantics correspond to the Conflict Checker component (see Fig. 2). The semantics are given as axioms for the predicate *conflict/3*, which states a meta-norm is causing conflict (the first term), from when (the second term) and until when (the last term). As conceptually defined in Definition 6, conflict is detected based on which norms and meta-norms hold for the same period of time.

The first type of conflict occurs when a meta-norm obliges the detachment of a norm and that norm is not detached. If this is the case, then the obligatory meta-norm will hold for some time until it is satisfied. If the obligatory meta-norm holds, then the norm it obliges was not detached at the same time or subsequently and so there is a conflict.

$$conflict(o(Norm), Start, End) \leftarrow holds\_for(o(Norm), Start, End)$$
$$\text{(Obl. MN Conflict)}$$

The final axiom states that given two overlapping intervals where a norm holds and a prohibitory meta-norm holds, there is a conflict if the norm is prohibited by the meta-norm. We assume two predicates $minimum(T, T', Min)$ and $maximum(T, T', Max)$ for defining when two periods of time, $T, T' \in \mathbb{T}$, overlap. The predicate $minimum/3$ holds iff $Min$ is the minimum of the two time points, and the predicate $maximum/3$ holds iff $Max$ is the maximum.

$$conflict(f(Norm), Start, End) \leftarrow holds\_for(f(Norm), MNStart, MNEnd) \land$$
$$holds\_for(Norm, NStart, NEnd) \land$$
$$maximum(NStart, MNStart, Start) \land$$
$$minimum(NEnd, MNEnd, End) \land Start < End$$
$$\text{(Pro. MN Conflict)}$$

## 6   Illustration

In this section we illustrate how our formalism works for the running example of Rachel's request and Peter's use policy. First, we assume the following narrative is produced by a sequence generator component (to be sure all conflicts are detected, all possible event sequences would need to be checked):

$E1 = happens\_at(enter\_water\_square_{pet}, 1)$, $E2 = happens\_at(battery\_depleted_{pet}, 2)$,
$E3 = happens\_at(gather\_rain\_data_{pet}, 3)$, $E4 = happens\_at(send\_data_{pet}, 4)$

From this narrative, we can infer the following norm detachment events:

$E5 = happens\_at(O_{pet:rac}(gather\_rain\_data_{pet} \ BEFORE \ send\_data_{pet}), 1)$,
$E6 = happens\_at(O_{pet:rac}(send\_data_{pet} \ BEFORE \ leave\_water\_square_{pet}), 1)$,
$E7 = happens\_at(F_{rac:pet}(sensing\_off_{pet} \ BEFORE \ gather\_rain\_data_{pet}), 1)$

Given these events, Fig. 3 depicts which norms, meta-norms and conflicts hold and when.

As we intuitively expect, there is a conflict because Peter is obliged to send data, but Rachel is not obliged to pay him. Another conflict occurs because Peter is forbidden from turning his device off, but because his phone's battery has become low he wants to maintain this right. Finally Peter is obliged to send data before leaving the water square, but such an obligation is forbidden.

## 7   Implementation

Our proposal is implemented [13] for a prototype crowdsensing system used to gather rain data with user's mobile sensing devices (such as rain sensors on bicycles) in a simulated environment. The prototype, using NetLogo[3], simulates

---

[3] A multi-agent modelling environment http://ccl.northwestern.edu/netlogo/.

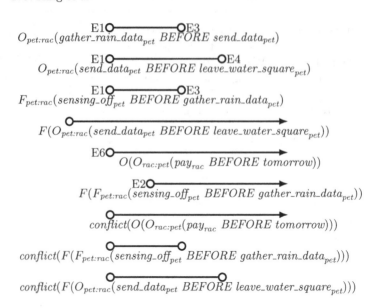

**Fig. 3.** An example with several conflicts. — indicates the interval a fluent holds for, O–O is a terminated interval, whilst O→ is an interval that continues forever.

users in a crowdsensing system. Users can request other users to gather rain data and form an ad-hoc network to help transmit the data. Users can also respond to requests by providing rain data and participate in an ad-hoc network to help transmit the data.

Each user in the system has a use policy governing their resource and a resource governance reasoner, implemented in Prolog, for the automated acceptance and rejection of requests for the use of their resource on the basis of its use policy. Our implementation uses pre-formulated requests (sets of norms) for users to send to others and provides a graphical user interface for the editing of Use policies governing the devices of the individual simulated users.

The proposal in this paper closely corresponds to our implementation. Two Definite Clause Grammars (DCGs) are specified corresponding to the formal definition of the norm and meta-norm specification languages defined earlier, with an appropriate lexicon for the rain gathering scenario. The DCGs are used to check the requests and use policies are well-formed.

The resource governance reasoner consists of Prolog theories that directly correspond to the rules for the operational semantics specified in this paper, and a combinatorial Event Sequence Generator for producing Event Calculus narratives. We combine a request, a use policy, the operational semantics for the normative evaluator and conflict checker, and Event Calculus narratives into a single Prolog theory which we query for conflicts using a Prolog engine.

# 8  Conclusions

In this paper our main contribution was a novel temporal event-based reasoner for determining if there are conflicts between a request to use a resource and a use policy governing a resource's usage. This allows owners of resources to maintain autonomy over how, when and to whom their resources are used. Taking the notion of a request for the use of a resource as a set of norms, we gave a representation of a use policy, specifying what norms a request should and should not impose on a resource under some circumstances, as a set of meta-norms. Our reasoner detects whether a request can be accepted with respect to a use policy or if there are conflicts necessitating rejecting the request. Conflicts are detected based on whether there is a context in which conflicting norms and meta-norms are detached simultaneously.

There are many interesting avenues for future work, we go over some of the most immediate extensions here. Extending the representation of meta-norms to include an 'Or Else' option, such as 'you should not oblige me to do X, but if you do then you should not forbid me to do Y' would syntactically represent a preferential ordering among norms. Coupled with a suitable semantics, this can support better decision making in a resource governing agent. For example, when negotiating requests which are better to accept when there are many offered. Extending our work to support negotiation would also require a mechanism to revise requests to be more preferential. Supporting counter-offers to be made to the agent requesting the use of the resource by modifying the original request and sending it back according to a negotiation protocol.

Finally, our proposal is limited in that we use propositions as the terms of norms and meta-norms. This makes sense since it allows us to express concrete norms in a request. Extending the representation to make use of variables in first-order logic as in the work of [19] would increase expressivity. For example allowing a user to express meta-norms such as 'you are prohibited from obligating me to do anything' and also meta-norms with constraints such as 'you are forbidden from obliging me to pay you anything over €10'.

**Acknowledgements.** Thomas C. King—supported by the SHINE (http://www.shine.tudelft.nl) project of TU Delft. Authors would like to thank anonymous reviewers of COIN-14 for their helpful comments.

# References

1. Andrighetto, G., Governatori, G., Noriega, P., van der Torre, L.: Normative multi-agent systems. Dagstuhl Follow-Ups **4**, 135–170 (2013)
2. Artikis, A., Sergot, M., Paliouras, G.: Run-time composite event recognition. In: Proceedings of the 6th ACM International Conference on Distributed Event-Based Systems, pp. 69–80. ACM Press, New York (2012)
3. Boella, G., van der Torre, L.: Permissions and obligations in hierarchical normative systems. In: Proceedings of the 9th International Conference on Artificial Intelligence and Law, pp. 109–118 (2003)

4. Chesani, F., Mello, P., Montali, M., Torroni, P.: A logic-based, reactive calculus of events. Fundamenta Informaticae **105**(1–2), 135–161 (2010)
5. Chesani, F., Mello, P., Montali, M., Torroni, P.: Representing and monitoring social commitments using the event calculus. Auton. Agent. Multi-Agent Syst. **27**(1), 85–130 (2012)
6. Chittaro, L., Montanari, A.: Efficient temporal reasoning in the cached event calculus. Comput. Intell. **12**(3), 359–382 (1996)
7. Dignum, V.: A model for organizational interaction: based on agents, founded in logic. Ph.D. thesis. University of Utrecht, Utrecht, The Netherlands (2003)
8. Gabbay, D., Horty, J., Parent, X., van der Meyden, R., van der Torre, L. (eds.): Handbook of Deontic Logic and Normative Systems, vol. 1. College Publications, London (2013)
9. Ganti, R., Ye, F., Lei, H.: Mobile crowdsensing: current state and future challenges. IEEE Commun. Mag. **49**(11), 32–39 (2011)
10. Governatori, G.: Representing business contracts in RuleML. Int. J. Coop. Inf. Syst. **14**(2–3), 181–216 (2005)
11. Günay, A., Yolum, P.: Detecting conflicts in commitments. In: Sakama, C., Sardina, S., Vasconcelos, W., Winikoff, M. (eds.) DALT 2011. LNCS, vol. 7169, pp. 51–66. Springer, Heidelberg (2012)
12. Hübner, J., Sichman, J.S., Boissier, O.: A model for the structural, functional, and deontic specification of organizations in multiagent systems. In: Bittencourt, G., Ramalho, G.L. (eds.) Advances in Artificial Intelligence. LNCS **2507**, 118–128 (2002)
13. King, T.C., Liu, Q., Polevoy, G., de Weerdt, M., Dignum, V., van Riemsdijk, M.B., Warnier, M.: Request driven social sensing (demonstration). In: Lomuscio, A., Scerri, P., Bazzan, A., Huhns, M. (eds.) Proceedings of the 13th International Conference on Autonomous Agents and Multiagent Systems (AAMAS 2014), Paris, France (2014)
14. Kowalski, R., Sergot, M.: A logic-based calculus of events. New Gener. Comput. **4**(1), 67–95 (1986)
15. López, FLy, Luck, M., D'Inverno, M.: A normative framework for agent-based systems. Comput. Math. Org. Theor. **12**(2–3), 227–250 (2006)
16. Parent, X., van der Torre, L.: Input/output logic. In: Gabbay, D., Horty, J., Parent, X., van der Meyden, R., van der Torre, L. (eds.) Handbook of Deontic Logic and Normative Systems, vol. 1, pp. 499–544. College Publications, London (2013)
17. Shanahan, M.: The event calculus explained. In: Veloso, M.M., Wooldridge, M.J. (eds.) Artificial Intelligence Today. LNCS (LNAI), vol. 1600, pp. 409–430. Springer, Heidelberg (1999)
18. van Riemsdijk, M.B., Dennis, L.A., Fisher, M., Hindriks, K.V.: Agent reasoning for norm compliance a semantic approach. In: Proceedings of the 12th International Conference on Autonomous Agents and Multiagent Systems (AAMAS 2013), pp. 499–506, Saint Paul, Minnesota, USA (2013)
19. Vasconcelos, W.W., Kollingbaum, M.J., Norman, T.J.: Normative conflict resolution in multi-agent systems. Auton. Agent. Multi-Agent Syst. **19**(2), 124–152 (2008)
20. Wansing, H.: Nested deontic modalities: another view of parking on highways. Erkenntnis **49**(2), 185–199 (1998)

21. Yolum, P., Singh, M.: Reasoning about commitments in the event calculus: an approach for specifying and executing protocols. Ann. Math. Artif. Intell. **42**(1–3), 227–253 (2004)
22. Yolum, P., Singh, M.P.: Flexible protocol specification and execution: applying event calculus planning using commitments. First Int. Joint Conf. Auton. Agents Multiagent Syst. Part **2**, 527–534 (2002)

# Coordination Mechanisms in Multi Objective Setups: Results of an Agent-Based Simulation

Stephan Leitner$^{(\boxtimes)}$ and Friederike Wall

Faculty of Management and Economics, Alpen-Adria Universität Klagenfurt,
Universitätsstraße 65-67, 9020 Klagenfurt, Austria
{stephan.leitner,friederike.wall}@aau.at

**Abstract.** In this paper, we analyze how different modes of coordination and different approaches of of multi objective decision making interfere with organizational performance and speed at which performance improves. The investigation is based on an agent-based simulation of a stylized hierarchical business organization. In particular, we employ a model based on the idea of NK-fitness landscapes, where we map multi objective decision making as adaptive walk on multiple performance landscapes. In our model, each landscape represents one objective. We find that the effect of coordination mode on performance and speed of performance improvement is critically shaped by the choice of multi objective decision making approach. In certain setups, more complex approaches of multi objective decision making turn out to be less sensitive to the choice of coordination mode.

**Keywords:** Coordination mechanism · Hierarchical organizations · Multi objective decision making · Simulation · NK-Model

## 1 Introduction and Research Question

During the last decades, changing environments have brought organizations to revise their management approaches. In fact, today the major challenges are increased complexity and the need to consider multiple potentially conflicting objectives in decision making simultaneously, instead of focusing solely on one performance measure. For these developments, there are several lines of explanation. First, rapid technological change and growing globalization increase the levels of complexity and turbulence and lead to intensified competition [9]. Second, the consideration of different stakeholder interests in decision making has become critical for organizational success [7]. Third, the call for sustainability claims to balance economic, ecologic and social objectives [5,38]. The literature on organizational theory recognizes goal conflicts that stem from divergent interests and preferences between organizational members [6] but widely ignores conflicts due to multiple competing objectives. This is where we place our research: We particularly focus on goal conflicts stemming from organizations pursuing multiple objectives. Developing innovative ideas and products as well as being

© Springer International Publishing Switzerland 2015
A. Ghose et al. (Eds.): COIN 2014, LNAI 9372, pp. 132–147, 2015.
DOI: 10.1007/978-3-319-25420-3_9

very cost efficient at the same time might be an example for conflicting objectives. Hierarchies typically help in assuring cost efficiency via the improvement of (production) activities with respect to speed and quality. Being innovative, in contrast, often requires more space for creative and (sometimes) unconventional employees. However, space for creativity is not necessarily in line with the idea of hierarchies. Another illustrative example might be that maximizing the corporations' shareholder value as well as considering ecologic interests at the same time are potentially conflicting objectives. However, such objectives are not necessarily conflicting in every case. Think, e.g., of BP and the oil platform 'Deep Horizon'. The ecologic consequences of this catastrophe were tremendous. At the same time, the catastrophe had an negative impact on BP's equity price (which, after the catastrophe, dropped drastically).

It is in the tradition of organizational science to develop efficient organizational structures, where particular focus is often put on how to design incentives and individual performance measures so that the corporate performance is maximized (given conflicting objectives on the individual level, like, e.g., diverging time horizons between the decentral managers and the corporation as a whole) [8, 11, 29]. We follow this tradition. In particular, we focus on conflicting objectives not on the individual level but focus on conflicts between multiple organizational objectives and their consequences for the design of efficient organizational structures. This captures situations in which multiple corporate objectives are broken down to the individual level via multiple performance measures. Such multiple (and potentially conflicting) corporate goals evoke a higher need of coordination. The particular focus, here, is to align the involved individuals' varying behavior in a way which aligns their decisions to the overall strategy in the best possible way. What, however, makes coordination much more complex is that increasing complexity leads to more interdependencies among decisions (cf. [22]). In order to illustrate such interdependencies think, e.g., of scarce (financial) resources: Investments by one department decrease the available resources for all other departments. Investment into production capacity could, e.g., reduce the available financial resources for building up sophisticated distribution channels. Even though both aspects (capacity and sophisticated distribution channels) might be essential for a corporate objective, which, e.g., might be to fulfill the market's demand and, thereby, maximizing revenues. If multiple objectives are added on top of this complexity, coordination becomes even much more complex. However, in order to assure the efficiency within organizations, coordination is necessary across both objectives and individual decisions. Organizations can face this challenge with changes in their organizational design. In particular, the choices of coordination mode and method of multi objective decision making are promising regulating variables in order to increase the efficiency of the organizational structure [22].

The performance of multi objective decision making methods is widely investigated for the individual level, but rarely researched for the context of hierarchical organizations and different intensities of interdependencies among decisions. In addition, it is rarely investigated how suitable specific coordination modes are for certain setups of multi objective decision making approach and decision interdependencies across objectives. We take account of this research gap and provide new insights into the suitability of a set of multi objective decision making policies and coordination mechanisms for multi objective setups. In order to do so, we utilize a variant of the NK-model [12,13]. In particular, we map multi objective decision making as adaptive walk on multiple performance landscapes with each landscape representing one objective.[1]

With respect to multi objective decision making policies, we investigate the relatively simple, but widely utilized, methods of assigning (i) equal weights to each objective and (ii) satisficing approaches (i.e., fixing aspiration levels). However, assigning equal weights, at least to some extent, can be interpreted as not taking particular care of the conflicting objectives and equally promoting their achievement without stating any preferences. With respect to the coordination mode, we investigate the extreme cases of (a) centralized decision making (with decentralized units proposing strategies for the future, where the central unit composes an overall strategy out of the proposals), and (b) autonomous decentralized decision making (where corporate departments autonomously decide and operate their favored strategy). Please note that we do not intend to develop very sophisticated methods of multi objective decision making or coordination mechanisms that promise a high performance. We do rather want to test the performance of deploying the set of investigated methods and mechanisms to particular setups. In particular, we aim at answering how the choice of coordination mechanisms and the choice of multi objective decision making policy interfere with each other (with respect to organizational performance). By doing so, we particularly address the following issues:

– **How sensitive is the achieved performance to the choice of coordination mechanism given particular multi objective decision making policies?** In particular, in Sect. 3.1 we investigate the efficiency of the investigated coordination modes in the case of equally weighted objectives. We show that in the case of equally weighted objectives, it does not make a significant difference whether departments can make their decisions autonomously or the central unit is in charge of making the final decision. In Sec. 3.2, we focus on satisficing approaches and show that decentral coordination only brings very slight increases in performance as compared to the central coordination mode. However, we reveal that it is superior to fix aspiration levels not for the objective which is more difficult to achieve but for the less complex objective (with respect to interdependencies among decisions).

---

[1] In order to investigate the research question, we apply a simulation approach. In particular, simulation appears to be a powerful research method that allows mapping hierarchical organizations, different modes of coordination, interacting agents and different methods of multi objective decision making. Due to the potential complexity and unpredictability of repeated simple patterns, formal modeling would lead to intractable dimensions [2]. Controlling the multitude of issues and disentangling effects of variables under research from other effects would find the boundaries of empirical research [33]. Simulation, on the contrary, appears to be a powerful method to face the complexity of the outlined research problem (cf. also [15–19]).

– **Which multi objective decision making policy appears to be appropriate with respect to the degree of interdependence among decisions?** In Sect. 3.3, we evaluate performances across multi objective decision making policies and show that for equally complex objectives, equal weighting (or not caring particularly which objective to follow) leads to organizations being better off. For different complex objectives to be pursued concurrently, aspiration level approaches appear to be superior to weighting approaches. However, the efficiency of satisficing approaches critically hinges on the complexity of the objective the aspiration level is fixed for.

Organizations usually benefit from the actions and decisions taken by their (human) members. Here, both the organizational structure and the informal communication and interaction among agents play an important role with respect to the organization's success. It has already been recognized that enhancing multi agent systems with concepts stemming from organizational theory allows for investigating coordination and communication mechanisms as well as the structure of interactions (among agents and decisions) [13,14,23]. However, one central question is how to translate organizational structures and the structure of interactions into models of multi agent organizations. Typically, the global behavior (or the overall organizational objective) is captured by the organizational structure (e.g., in terms of coordination mechanisms or information flows) whereas the autonomous agents make their decisions in a local and autonomous process [3,35]. By employing variants of the NK-model [13], different coordination mechanisms have been intensely investigated by Siggelkow and Rivkin [30]. In another line of research, they also utilized the idea of the NK-model and focused on investigating interdependencies among different organizational design elements, like, e.g., hierarchies, information flows, incentive systems [27]. In [28], the particular focus is put on patterns of interactions among decisions. Ethiraj and Levinthal [6] were among the first to investigate organizations pursuing multiple objectives but, however, did not take into account organizational structures. We follow this tradition and design a model of a multi agent organization considering multiple objectives and hierarchical structures and investigate the impact of organizational design elements (embodied in the organizational structure) on the corporations performance [35].[2]

## 2  Simulation Model

We employ a simulation model based on the NK-model, which was originally introduced by Kauffman et al. [12,13,40]. We decided for the NK-model because it has explicitly been designed in order to investigate interactions among its components. Based on the basic NK-model [12,13,40] and relevant extensions by Ethiraj and Levinthal [6], we map multi objective decision making as adaptive

---

[2] A more extensive review of models of agent organizations, autonomous agents in organizations, and approaches to build agent organizations can be found at [3,4,14,35,37].

walk on multiple performance landscapes (cf. also [20–22]). In our model, each decision affects performance on multiple performance landscapes, where each landscape represents one objective.

In order to give an extensive description of our model, we elaborate on the following three aspects in detail: (1) the design of hierarchical organizations, (2) the representation of the performance landscapes, and (3) the mapped methods of multi objective decision making.

## 2.1   The Hierarchical Design

We map organizations as systems of interdependent choices [25], i.e., we conceptualize agents to search along a multi-dimensional decision space for optimal configurations rather than making decisions in a single-dimensional setup [26]. For each objective the decision problems are represented by the respective performance landscapes. The number of decisions, $N$, and the architecture of performance landscapes are constant along the observation period.

Our organizations face a ten-dimensional decision problem, where each decision can be solved in two ways, i.e., in each period $t \in \{1, ..., T\}$ agents make decisions $n^{i,t} \in N$ with $n^{i,t} \in \{0,1\}$ and $i \in \{1, ..., |N|\}$. Due to the binarity of single decision-making alternatives, there exist $2^{|N|}$ different configurations for the overall decision problem, which are expressed by the vectors $C = \left(n^{i=1}, ..., n^{i=|N|}\right)$. The configuration of decisions for period $t$ is denoted by $C^t = \left(n^{i=1,t}, ..., n^{i=|N|,t}\right)$. The starting configuration $C^{t=0}$ is chosen randomly.

Decisions $n^{i,t}$ affect the performance of all objectives $g \in G$. In each period $t$ and for each objective $g$, the decisions $n^{i,t}$ make a contribution $p_g^{i,t}$ to overall performance $P_g^t$. Due to interdependencies among decisions, the performance contribution $p_g^{i,t}$ may additionally to decision $n^{i,t}$ be affected by $K_g^i$ other decisions, which are denoted by $n_k^{j,t}$ where $i, j \in \{1, ..., |N|\}$, $k \in \{1, ..., K_g^i\}$ and $i \neq j$.[3] Considering interdependencies, for each period $t$ and each performance contribution $p_g^{i,t}$ the function $f_g^i$ randomly draws a value from uniform distribution $U[0,1]$, i.e.,

$$p_g^{i,t} = f_g^i \left(n^{i,t}; n_{k=1}^{j,t}, ..., n_{k=K_g^i}^{j,t}\right) \tag{1}$$

where $i, j \in \{1, ..., |N|\}$, $i \neq j$ and $0 \leq p_g^{i,t} \leq 1$. Whenever any of the coupled decisions changes, the value for $p_g^{i,t}$ is redrawn. We map all $p_g^{i,t}$ to contribute to the performance per objective equally. Hence, performance $P_g^t$ results in the normalized sum of performance contributions $p_g^{i,t}$, i.e.,

$$P_g^t = \frac{1}{|N|} \sum_{i=1}^{|N|} p_g^{i,t} \tag{2}$$

---

[3] Please note that superscript $i$ indicates the single decision $n^{i,t}$, which is directly related to performance contribution $p_g^{i,t}$. This performance contribution might be affected by decisions other than the one indexed by $i$, for the other decisions, we utilize superscript $j$.

The stylized organizations consist of decentralized units $d \in D$ and one central unit $h$. With respect to prior research (e.g. [6]), the mapping of hierarchical structures appears to be a novelty. We map organizations to consist of three decentral units where two units are in scope of three decisions and one unit is in scope of four decisions (cf. also Fig. 1 and [22], the solid lines represent our corporation's decentral structure). For each $d$, we denote the set of decisions within the area of responsibility as $N^{own_d}$, while the other units' decisions are given by $N^{res_d}$.

We map the decentralized decision makers as agents that seek to enhance their individual utility via incremental changes (for their utility functions cf. Sect. 2.3). Efforts for stepwise improvement go along with the literature on organizational learning [1] and prior modeling efforts (e.g. [28]), while the agents' selfishness is consistent with the economic literature [10]. Due to bounded rationality [31], agents do not envision all possible alternative configurations of departmental decisions $N^{own_d}$. They randomly discover two alternative configurations that differ in one or two decisions from the status quo (cf. also [20–22,36]).

Along with the status quo, the decentral units $d$ evaluate three alternative configurations of decisions. Each department is eligible to propose two alternative configurations of $N^{own_d}$ for the next period. All departments rank two of the alternative configurations under evaluation with respect to which alternative is perceived to provide the highest improvement in individual utility. Depending on the limitation of proposals, one alternative (i.e., that configuration of decisions that promises the least performance) is discarded and, hence, not considered in the order of preference. The ranking for departmental decisions $N^{own_d}$ is denoted by vectors $V_r^{own_d,t}$ with $r = \{1,2\}$ indexing the assigned rank.

We analyze the effects of design options on overall performance. The computational model considers alternative choices in the mode of coordination of decisions and in the incentive scheme as options of organizational design. One further design-determinant considered in our research, is the structuring of the decentral units with respect to (cross-unit) interdependencies among decisions (cf. Sect. 2.2)

The mode of coordination determines how the overall configuration of decisions for the following period $t + 1$ is selected. Hence, the mode of coordination is one of the major design options [41]. In our model, we consider two different coordination modes: (1) fully decentralized coordination, and (2) a central mode of coordination. In the case of *full decentralization*, the decentral units decide and act autonomously in their areas of responsibility $N^{own_d}$ [24]. The overall configuration of decisions $C^{t+1}$ for period $t + 1$ results as concatenation of the top-ranked alternative configurations $V_1^{own_d,t}$. In the case of the *central mode of coordination*, the decentral units send proposals $V_i^{own_d,t}$ to the central unit where all proposals are evaluated with respect to overall performance (cf. Eq. 5). The central unit evaluates concatenations of all proposals $V_i^{own_d,t}$ and residual decisions according to the status quo $D^{res_d,t}$ and selects that proposal that promises the highest performance.

One further crucial design factor is the incentive scheme. The incentive scheme is reflected the subunits' utility functions (cf. Sect. 2.3) and, hence, affects the outcome of the ranking of alternatives directly. We consider a linear incentive scheme where for every period $t$ the decentralized units $d$ are rewarded on the basis of performance $P_g^t$ of each objective $g$. In particular, the departments' incentives depend on the performance of intra-unit decisions $N_g^{own_d,t}$ and residual decisions $N_g^{res_d,t}$ with different weights denoted as $w_g^{own_d}$ and $w_g^{res_d}$, respectively. For the current investigation, we analyze incentive schemes that put more weight on intra-unit than on residual performance, what may causes a divergence of interest between the decentral units $d$ and the central unit $h$. We set $w_g^{own_d} = 1$ and $w_g^{res_d} = 0.5$.

## 2.2    Representation of the Performance Landscapes

The level of complexity within hierarchical organizations critically depends on the nature of interdependencies among decisions [32]. In particular, complexity is a function of the choice of design options and the organizational environment. On the one hand, interdependencies among decisions are dictated by the decision problem itself [30]. On the other hand, organizations can face this given complexity by considering interdependencies among decisions in the structure of their decentralized units. Building units or assigning decision rights with respect to interdependencies among decisions might affect performance crucially.

According to Sect. 2.1, we describe interdependencies among decisions by parameter $K_g^i$. Increasing interdependencies $K_g^i$ lead to performance landscapes to be more rugged [13]. With respect to the mapped search strategies (incremental improvement), a lower level of interdependencies leads to more starting configurations of decision $C^{t=0}$ to be in basin of attraction of the global maximum while increasing interdependencies $K_g^i$ lead to a larger number local maxima [39], i.e., configurations of decisions where performance can not be further improved. Once an organization reaches such a trap, the status quo of the configuration of decisions is likely to be constant for the remaining observation periods [6].

We follow the basic NK-framework [12, 13, 40] and use interdependence matrices in order to represent functional dependencies among decisions. In particular, we use one interdependence matrix for each objective the mapped organizations follow. Due to the $|N|$-dimensionality of the decision problem, all matrices $M$ are of size $|N| * |N|$. The set of decisions $N$ is assigned to the vertical axis while the horizontal axis represents payoff functions $f_g^i$ (cf. Fig. 1). In our mapping, the performance contribution $p_g^i$ is functionally depended on decision $n^i$ in all cases. Additionally, a 'x' in cell $m_{ij}$ with $i, j \in \{1, ..., |N|\}$ and $i \neq j$ shows that decision $n^i$ additionally to performance contribution $p_g^i$ affects performance contribution $p_g^j$. Consequentially, empty cells $m_{ij}$ indicate that there is no functional dependency among decision $n^i$ and performance contribution $p_g^j$.

We limit our research to three exemplary natures of interactions (cf. also [22]). In the case of level of interdependencies *low* the decisions within a subunit are fully interdependent but there is no cross-unit interdependence. Hence,

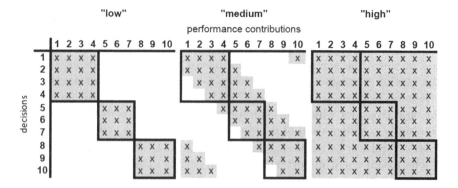

**Fig. 1.** Interdependence matrices (cf. also [22])

decisions $N^{own_d}$ do not affect residual performance. For each decentralized unit $d$, the $K$-values are constant along intra-unit decisions, i.e. $K_g^i = |N^{own_d}| - 1$ (cf. Fig. 1, panel 'low'). This pattern of interactions is comparable to the modular setup of organizations as investigated by Rivkin and Siggelkow [28]. With reference to small world networks, the level of interdependencies *medium* is characterized by a high level of clustering [34]. The interdependencies among decisions are mainly clustered along the main diagonale of the matrix $M$, $K_g^i = 4$ along all decisions. This pattern of interactions results in intra-unit decisions $N^{own_d}$ being partly interdependent but they are also partly interacting with the other departments' decisions. Unit-performance is reciprocally dependent on other units' decisions but intra-unit decisions also affect residual performance (cf. Fig. 1, panel 'medium'). We also map a (3) *high* level of interdependencies where all decisions are fully interdependent, i.e. $K_g^i = 9$ (cf. Fig. 1, panel 'high').

### 2.3  Methods of Multi Objective Decision Making

We map two different methods of multi objective decision making. On the one hand, we analyze the effectivity of (1) a decision making policy where each objective is equally weighted. On the other hand, we map a (2) satisficing approach where aspiration levels are fixed for certain objectives (cf. also [22]).

In the case of (1) *equal weighting*, decision makers do not have to explicitly articulate preferences for single objectives, they rather decide for all objectives to be pursued with the same importance. Consequently, with respect to multiple objectives and the linear incentive scheme (as stated in Sect. 2.1) in the case of equal weighting, the decentralized units' utility function results in

$$U_d^t = \sum_{g=1}^{|G|} \left( w_g^{own_d} \frac{\sum_{i \in N^{own_d}} p_g^{i,t}}{|N^{own_d}|} + w_g^{res_d} \frac{\sum_{i \in N^{res_d}} p_g^{i,t}}{|N^{res_d}|} \right). \tag{3}$$

In order to operationalize the (2) *satisficing approach*, we introduce aspiration levels $s_g \in \{0, 1\}$ that are constant for the entire observation period. The function $f^g(s_g) = g$ defines the single objective $g$ the aspiration level $s_g$ is fixed for. Decision makers seek to, at least, satisfy the aspiration levels before they consider the other objectives in the evaluation of alternatives (cf. Sect. 2.1). The period in which the aspiration level is achieved or exceeded is denoted by $t^{s_g}$. In the case of aspiration level approaches, for periods $t \leq t^{s_g}$ our agents solely pursue one objective, i.e., objective $f^g(s_g) = g$. Once the performance $P^t_{f^g(s_g)}$ of the objective $g$ for which the aspiration level is fixed exceeds the stated level, no alternative configuration of decisions that leads to $P^t_{f^g(s_g)}$ falling below the aspiration level will be realized. Similar to method (1), for periods $t > t^{s_g}$ organizations assign equal importance to all objectives. The corresponding utility functions results in

$$
U^t_d = \begin{cases} w^{own_d}_{f^g(s_g)} \frac{\sum_{i \in N^{own_d}} p^{i,t}_{f^g(s_g)}}{|N^{own_d}|} + w^{res_d}_{f^g(s_g)} \frac{\sum_{i \in N^{res_d}} p^{i,t}_{f^g(s_g)}}{|N^{res_d}|} & \text{for } t \leq t^{s_g} \\ \sum_{g=1}^{|G|} \left( w^{own_d}_g \frac{\sum_{i \in N^{own_d}} p^{i,t}_g}{|N^{own_d}|} + w^{res_d}_g \frac{\sum_{i \in N^{res_d}} p^{i,t}_g}{|N^{res_d}|} \right) & \text{for } t > t^{s_g}. \end{cases}
$$

$$(4)$$

While decentralized units aim at maximizing their own utility functions (cf. Eqs. 3 and 4), the central unit seeks to maximize overall performance. With respect to the mapped methods of multi objective decision making, the central unit's utility functions result in

$$
U^t_h = \begin{cases} \frac{1}{|G|} \sum_{g=1}^{|G|} P^t_g & \text{if equal weighting} \\ P^t_{f^g(s_g)} & \text{if satisficing approach, for } t \leq t^{s_g} \\ \frac{1}{|G|} \sum_{g=1}^{|G|} P^t_g & \text{if satisficing approach, for } t > t^{s_g}. \end{cases}
$$

$$(5)$$

In the case of equal weighting and satisficing approaches (for periods $t > t^{s_g}$), the central unit aims at maximizing overall performance while considering all objectives simultaneously. If aspiration levels are fixed, for periods $t \leq t^{s_g}$ also the central unit solely takes into account the objective the aspiration level is fixed for (cf. Eq. 5).

## 3   Results

Each organization is in charge of taking ten decisions and pursuing two objectives simultaneously. Performance is observed for 100 periods. Thus, we set $|N| = 10$, $|G| = 2$ and $T = 100$. The hierarchical setup of the computational model corresponds to Sect. 2.1. All results are based on 450 landscapes per objective, each with 20 adaptive walks. The results for each combination of different levels of interdependencies are based on 9,000 simulation runs. We report two performance measures. On the one hand, we report achieved performances after 100 periods $P^{t=100}_g$ as a snapshot of final performance (cf. Eq. 2). On the other hand, we report the average performance per objective $g$ over the observation period $T$ and all 9,000 simulation runs as measure for performance over time $P^{avg}_g$, i.e.

$$P_g^{avg} = \frac{1}{9{,}000 \cdot T} \sum_{j=1}^{9{,}000} \sum_{t=1}^{T} P_g^{t,j} \tag{6}$$

with $j$ indexing the simulation runs. $P_g^{avg}$ can also be regarded as a condensed measure of the speed of performance improvement over all 100 periods [30]. Furthermore, the measures for overall performance are given by the averaged performance contributions of all objectives, i.e., $P_{all}^{t=100} = 1/|G| \sum_{g=1}^{|G|} P_g^{t=100}$ and $P_{all}^{avg} = 1/|G| \sum_{g=1}^{|G|} P_g^{avg}$.

We investigate effect of the choice of coordination mode on performance and effectivity of multi objective decision making methods in two steps. First, we analyze effects of design options on performance separately for each multi objective decision making method. This is to answer the question how sensitive performance in certain multi objective decision making approaches is to the choice of coordination mode. In a second step, we analyze performance across multi objective decision making methods. This allows for answering the question which decision making mode appears to be appropriate in given setups of interdependencies among decisions. Furthermore, implications on hierarchical design in the case of a given decision making method can be derived from the presented results.

**Table 1.** Equal weighting.

| Interdependencies obj 1/obj 2 | Final performances | | | Average performances | | |
|---|---|---|---|---|---|---|
| | $P_1^{t=100}$ | $P_2^{t=100}$ | $P_{all}^{t=100}$ | $P_1^{avg}$ | $P_2^{avg}$ | $P_{all}^{avg}$ |
| **Panel A: coordination mode: central** | | | | | | |
| *low/low* | 0.8984 | 0.8994 | 0.8989 | 0.8941 | 0.8949 | 0.8945 |
| *low/medium* | 0.8777 | 0.8737 | 0.8757 | 0.8734 | 0.8694 | 0.8714 |
| *medium/medium* | 0.8515 | 0.8475 | 0.8495 | 0.8479 | 0.8437 | 0.8458 |
| *low/high* | 0.8515 | 0.8508 | 0.8512 | 0.8478 | 0.8474 | 0.8476 |
| *medium/high* | 0.8215 | 0.8334 | 0.8274 | 0.8186 | 0.8303 | 0.8245 |
| *high/high* | 0.8089 | 0.8084 | 0.8087 | 0.8070 | 0.8063 | 0.8066 |
| **Panel B: coordination mode: decentral** | | | | | | |
| *low/low* | 0.8987 | 0.8975 | 0.8981 | 0.8957 | 0.8945 | 0.8951 |
| *low/medium* | 0.9004 | 0.8705 | 0.8855 | 0.8967 | 0.8638 | 0.8803 |
| *medium/medium* | 0.8599 | 0.8596 | 0.8598 | 0.8530 | 0.8525 | 0.8527 |
| *low/high* | 0.8961 | 0.8415 | 0.8688 | 0.8909 | 0.8310 | 0.8609 |
| *medium/high* | 0.8457 | 0.8323 | 0.8390 | 0.8369 | 0.8198 | 0.8284 |
| *high/high* | 0.8121 | 0.8153 | 0.8137 | 0.7989 | 0.8023 | 0.8006 |

Incentivisation: $w_g^{own,d} = 1$ and $w_g^{res,d} = 0.5$. Results are based on 450 landscapes each with 20 adaptive walks. obj = objective, confidence intervals vary from 0.002 to 0.005 on the 99.9 % level.

### 3.1    The Choice of Coordination Mode in the Case of Equal Weighting

We find that in the case of equal weighting in the central as well as in the decentral coordination mode increasing complexity leads to decreasing final and average overall performance. Not surprisingly, pursuing objectives with the same levels of interdependencies lead to the same levels of final and average overall performances (cf. Table 1).

For the choice of coordination mode, final performances indicate that in most cases the decentral coordination mode is superior to the central mode. This is also partly reflected in the average performances. In particular in the case *low/medium*, the decentral coordination mode leads to a significantly higher speed of performance improvement while in the extreme cases (i.e. *low/low* and *high/high*) no sensitivity can be observed. So, in the majority of cases the decentral coordination mode leads to higher levels of final overall performances even though the concrete incentive scheme (cf. Sect. 2.1) causes a divergence of interest between central $h$ and decentral units $d$.

On the single objective level, results suggest that with decentral coordination in mainly all combinations of objectives with different levels of complexity final and average performances increase for the objective with the less complex interactions and decrease for the other one. Due to higher performances on the overall level in the decentral mode of coordination, the increasing effect appears to be higher than the decreasing effect.

### 3.2    The Choice of Coordination Mode in the Case of Satisficinig Approaches

Similar to the case of equal weighting, in the case of satisficing approaches both performances decrease with increasing complexity of interdependencies among decisions. As expected, when our organizations pursue two objectives with the same complexity of interdependencies among decisions, final and average performances achieve the same level in the single objective as well as in the overall performance perspective and for both the central and the decentral coordination mode. In the case of objectives with the same complexity of interdependencies, the choice of which objective the aspiration is to be fixed for does not affect performance measures. (cf. Tables 2 and 3).

In most cases, for final and average overall performances, at best, marginal increases with decentral coordination can be observed. However, in most scenarios performance does not appear to be significantly sensitive to the mode of coordination.

Conventional wisdom suggests to fix aspiration levels for that goal that is perceived to be more difficult to accomplish. Applying aspiration levels to the objective with the more complex interactions appears to be beneficial with respect to performance. Counterintuitively, for setups with different levels of complexity, we find that fixing aspiration levels for the less complex objective leads to significantly superior final overall performance and a higher speed of performance improvement in the central as well as for the decentral coordination mode.

**Table 2.** Satisficing approach, aspiration level for objective one: $s_1 = 0.8$.

| Interdependencies | Final performances | | | Average performances | | |
|---|---|---|---|---|---|---|
| obj 1/obj 2 | $P_1^{t=100}$ | $P_2^{t=100}$ | $P_{all}^{t=100}$ | $P_1^{avg}$ | $P_2^{avg}$ | $P_{all}^{avg}$ |
| **Panel A: coordination mode: central** | | | | | | |
| *low/low* | 0.9090 | 0.8818 | 0.8954 | 0.9030 | 0.8700 | 0.8865 |
| *low/medium* | 0.9065 | 0.8503 | 0.8784 | 0.9005 | 0.8393 | 0.8699 |
| *medium/medium* | 0.8857 | 0.7849 | 0.8353 | 0.8794 | 0.7762 | 0.8278 |
| *low/high* | 0.8996 | 0.8293 | 0.8645 | 0.8938 | 0.8201 | 0.8570 |
| *medium/high* | 0.8784 | 0.7850 | 0.8317 | 0.8729 | 0.7768 | 0.8248 |
| *high/high* | 0.8568 | 0.7117 | 0.7842 | 0.8526 | 0.7073 | 0.7799 |
| **Panel B: coordination mode: decentral** | | | | | | |
| *low/low* | 0.9122 | 0.8783 | 0.8952 | 0.9104 | 0.8715 | 0.8910 |
| *low/medium* | 0.9166 | 0.8505 | 0.8836 | 0.9146 | 0.8422 | 0.8784 |
| *medium/medium* | 0.8907 | 0.7983 | 0.8445 | 0.8851 | 0.7889 | 0.8370 |
| *low/high* | 0.9130 | 0.8259 | 0.8695 | 0.9110 | 0.8166 | 0.8638 |
| *medium/high* | 0.8871 | 0.7888 | 0.8379 | 0.8817 | 0.7795 | 0.8306 |
| *high/high* | 0.8573 | 0.7134 | 0.7853 | 0.8482 | 0.7074 | 0.7778 |

Incentivisation: $w_g^{own_d} = 1$ and $w_g^{res_d} = 0.5$. Results are based on 450 landscapes each with 20 adaptive walks. obj = objective, confidence intervals vary from 0.002 to 0.003 on the 99.9 % level.

### 3.3 Evaluation Across Multi Objective Decision Making Methods

After having outlined the sensitivity of performance measures on organizational design elements separately for each policy of multi objective decision making, the following section analyses differences in performances between decision making approaches.

For scenarios with two objectives that show the same level of interdependencies among decisions, we find that the method of equal weighting appears to be superior with respect to final overall performance and average overall performance, in the central as well as in the decentral coordination mode. The difference between performances in the case of equal weighting and performances in the case of aspiration level approaches increases with the level of interdependencies is. For both final performance and speed of performance improvement the difference reaches a slightly higher level in the case of the decentral mode of coordination as compared to the central coordination mode.

In setups with two objectives of different complexity, in most cases performance does not appear to be sensitive to the choice of multi objective decision making approach as long as the aspiration level is fixed for the objective with the less complex interactions among decisions. As a consequence of the results presented in Sect. 3.2, applying the aspiration level to the objective with the more complex interactions leads to a higher difference between performances. Hence,

**Table 3.** Satisficing approach, aspiration level for objective two: $s_2 = 0.8$.

| Interdependencies | Final performances | | | Average performances | | |
|---|---|---|---|---|---|---|
| obj 1/obj 2 | $P_1^{t=100}$ | $P_2^{t=100}$ | $P_{all}^{t=100}$ | $P_1^{avg}$ | $P_2^{avg}$ | $P_{all}^{avg}$ |
| **Panel A: coordination mode: central** | | | | | | |
| low/low | 0.8814 | 0.9076 | 0.8945 | 0.8967 | 0.9016 | 0.8856 |
| low/medium | 0.8197 | 0.8945 | 0.8571 | 0.8098 | 0.8877 | 0.8488 |
| medium/medium | 0.7918 | 0.8876 | 0.8397 | 0.7826 | 0.8815 | 0.8321 |
| low/high | 0.7338 | 0.8616 | 0.7977 | 0.7296 | 0.8569 | 0.7932 |
| medium/high | 0.7146 | 0.8606 | 0.7876 | 0.7103 | 0.8561 | 0.7832 |
| high/high | 0.7080 | 0.8568 | 0.7824 | 0.7037 | 0.8525 | 0.7781 |
| **Panel B: coordination mode: decentral** | | | | | | |
| low/low | 0.8803 | 0.9089 | 0.8946 | 0.8734 | 0.9073 | 0.8903 |
| low/medium | 0.8324 | 0.8917 | 0.8620 | 0.8226 | 0.8860 | 0.8543 |
| medium/medium | 0.7980 | 0.8901 | 0.8441 | 0.7885 | 0.8848 | 0.8366 |
| low/high | 0.7389 | 0.8609 | 0.7999 | 0.7328 | 0.8517 | 0.7922 |
| medium/high | 0.7144 | 0.8588 | 0.7866 | 0.7084 | 0.8495 | 0.7789 |
| high/high | 0.7132 | 0.8587 | 0.7859 | 0.7070 | 0.8495 | 0.7783 |

Incentivisation: $w_g^{own_d} = 1$ and $w_g^{res_d} = 0.5$. Results are based on 450 landscapes each with 20 adaptive walks. obj = objective, confidence intervals vary from 0.001 to 0.004 on the 99.9 % level.

determining the objective the aspiration level is to be fixed for affects overall performance crucially—besides the choices of coordination mode and multi objective decision making policy.

## 4  Implications and Conclusion

Our results indicate that final and average performances and speed of performance improvement subtly depend on the choice of design elements of hierarchical organizations. We find that building the decentral structure with respect to cross-unit interdependencies among decisions affects performance crucially. Increasing the level of overall complexity in general leads to a decreasing performance and a decreasing speed of performance improvement. Furthermore, advanced knowledge of the effects of the choices of coordination mode and multi objective decision making policy appears to be a critical factor of success for the design of hierarchical organizations.

In case of *equal weighting*, decentral coordination leads to significantly higher performances than central coordination as long as cross-unit decision interdependencies are not too complex. With respect to performance, for the design of hierarchical organizations this implies that the choice decentral coordination is superior to central coordination.

For the case of *satisficing approaches*, performance is de facto non-sensitive to the choice of coordination mode. Counterintuitively, our results suggest that fixing aspiration levels for the objective with the less complex cross-unit inter-dependencies affects performance and speed of performance improvement positively. For the building of a decentral structure and the assignment of decision rights to decentralized units this could mean that interactions of that objective the aspiration level is fixed for should be particularly considered.

The *evaluation across methods of multi objective decision making* indicates that equal weighting is superior in cases where all objectives are of the same level of interdependencies. In cases of objectives with different levels of cross-unit interdependencies, the favorable choice of multi objective decision making policy critically depends on the level of complexity of the objective the aspiration level is fixed for.

At the same time, our research suffers from some limitations. Future research might investigate the generalizability of our results to setups with more than two objectives being followed concurrently. This also applies to the three exemplary levels of decision interdependencies. Future research might also want to investigate a wider range of natures of interdependencies among decisions.

# References

1. Cyert, R.M., March, J.G.: A Behavioral Theory of the Firm, 2nd edn. Blackwell, Oxford (2005)
2. Davis, J.P., Eisenhardt, K.M., Bingham, C.B.: Developing theory through simulation methods. Acad. Manag. Rev. **32**(2), 480–499 (2007)
3. Dignum, V., Dignum, F.: A logic of agent organizations. Logic J. IGPL **20**(1), 283–316 (2012)
4. Dignum, V., Vázquez-Salceda, J., Dignum, F.P.M.: OMNI: introducing social structure, norms and ontologies into agent organizations. In: Bordini, R.H., Dastani, M., Dix, J., El Fallah Seghrouchni, A. (eds.) PROMAS 2004. LNCS (LNAI), vol. 3346, pp. 181–198. Springer, Heidelberg (2005)
5. Elkington, J.: Cannibals with Forks: The Triple Bottom Line of 21st Century Business. Capstone, Oxford (1999)
6. Ethiraj, S.K., Levinthal, D.: Hoping for A to Z while rewarding only A: complex organizations and multiple goals. Organ. Sci. **20**(1), 4–21 (2009)
7. Freeman, R.E.: Strategic Management. A stakeholder approach, Pitman, Boston (1984). (Pitman series in business and public policy)
8. Guest, D.E.: Human resource management and performance: a review and research agenda. Int. J. Hum. Resour. Manag. **8**(3), 263–276 (1997)
9. Hamel, G., Prahalad, C.K.: Competing for the future. Harvard Bus. Rev. **72**(4), 122–129 (1994)
10. Jensen, M.C., Meckling, W.H.: The nature of man. J. Appl. Corp. Finance **7**(2), 4–19 (1994)
11. Jensen, M.C., Murphy, K.J.: Performance pay and top-management incentives. J. Polit. Econ. **98**(2), 225–264 (1990)
12. Kauffman, S.: The Origins of Order: Self-Organization and Selection in Evolution. Oxford University Press, New York (2010)

13. Kauffman, S., Levin, S.: Towards a general theory of adaptive walks on rugged landscapes. J. Theor. Biol. **128**, 11–45 (1987)
14. Keogh, K., Sonenberg, L.: Adaptive coordination in distributed and dynamic agent organizations. In: Cranefield, S., van Riemsdijk, M.B., Vázquez-Salceda, J., Noriega, P. (eds.) COIN 2011. LNCS, vol. 7254, pp. 38–57. Springer, Heidelberg (2012)
15. Leitner, S.: Information Quality and Management Accounting. Lecture Notes in Economics and Mathematical Systems, vol. 664. Springer, Heidelberg (2012)
16. Leitner, S.: A simulation analysis of interactions among intended biases in costing systems and their effects on the accuracy of decision-influencing information. Centr. European J Operat. Res. **22**(1), 113–138 (2014)
17. Leitner, S., Behrens, D.A.: On the robustness of coordination mechanims involving incompetent agents. In: Leitner, S., Wall, F. (eds.) Artificial Economics and Self Organization. Lecture Notes in Economics and Mathematical Systems, vol. 669, pp. 191–203. Springer, Heidelberg (2014)
18. Leitner, S., Behrens, D.A.: On the fault (in)tolerance of coordination mechanisms for distributed investment decisions. Centr. European J Operat. Res. **23**, 253–271 (2015)
19. Leitner, S., Wall, F.: Simulation-based research in management accounting and control: an illustrative overview. J Manage. Contr. **26**(2–3), 105–129 (2014)
20. Leitner, S., Wall, F.: Effectivity of multi criteria decision-making in organisations: Results of an agent-based simulation. In: Osinga, S., Hofstede, G.J., Verwaart, T. (eds.) Emergent Results of Artificial Economics. Lecture Notes in Economics and Mathematical Systems, vol. 652, pp. 79–90. Springer, Berlin, Heidelberg (2011)
21. Leitner, S., Wall, F.: Unexpected positive effects of complexity on performance in multiple criteria setups. In: Hu, B., Morasch, K., Pickl, S., Siegle, M. (eds.) Operations Research Proceedings 2010. Operations Research Proceedings, pp. 577–582. Springer, Berlin, Heidelberg (2011)
22. Leitner, S., Wall, F.: Multiobjective decision making policies and coordination mechanisms in hierarchical organizations: results of an agent-based simulation. Sci. World J. 2014, 12 (2014). http://dx.doi.org/10.1155/2014/875146
23. Levinthal, D.A.: Adaptation on rugged landscapes. Manag. Sci. **43**(7), 934–940 (1997)
24. Mintzberg, H.: The Structuring of Organizations: A Synthesis of the Research. Prentice-Hall Internat, London (1979)
25. Porter, M.E.: What is strategy? Harvard Bus. Rev. **74**(6), 61–78 (1996)
26. Rivkin, J.W.: Imitation of complex strategies. Manag. Sci. **46**(6), 824–844 (2000)
27. Rivkin, J.W., Siggelkow, N.: Balancing search and stability: interdependencies among elements of organizational design. Manag. Sci. **49**(3), 290–311 (2003)
28. Rivkin, J.W., Siggelkow, N.: Patterned interactions in complex systems: implications for exploration. Manag. Sci. **53**(7), 1068–1085 (2007)
29. Sadedin, S., Guttmann, C.: Promotion of Selfish Agents in Hierarchical Organisations. In: Padget, J., Artikis, A., Vasconcelos, W., Stathis, K., da Silva, V.T., Matson, E., Polleres, A. (eds.) COIN@AAMAS 2009. LNCS, vol. 6069, pp. 163–178. Springer, Heidelberg (2010)
30. Siggelkow, N., Rivkin, J.W.: Speed and search: designing organizations for turbulence and complexity. Organ. Sci. **16**(2), 101–122 (2005)
31. Simon, H.A.: A behavioral model of rational choice. Q. J. Econ. **69**(1), 99–118 (1955)
32. Simon, H.A.: The architecture of complexity. Proc. Am. Philos. Soc. **106**(6), 467–482 (1962)

33. Sprinkle, G.B.: Perspectives on experimental research in managerial accounting. Acc. Organ. Soc. **28**(2–3), 287–318 (2003)
34. Uzzi, B., Amaral, L.A., Tschochas-Reed, F.: Small-world networks and management science research: a review. European Manag. Rev. **5**, 77–91 (2007)
35. van der Vecht, B., Dignum, F., Meyer, J.-J.C., Dignum, V.: Organizations and autonomous agents: bottom-up dynamics of coordination mechanisms. In: Hübner, J.F., Matson, E., Boissier, O., Dignum, V. (eds.) COIN@AAMAS 2008. LNCS, vol. 5428, pp. 17–32. Springer, Heidelberg (2009)
36. Wall, F.: The (benefical) role of informational imperfections in enhancing organisational performance. In: LiCalzi, M., Milone, L., Pellizzari, P. (eds.) Progress in Artificial Economics. Computational and Agent-Based Models, Lecture Notes in Economics and Mathematical Systems, vol. 645, pp. 115–126. Springer, Heidelberg, London, New York (2010)
37. Wall, F.: Agent-based modeling in managerial science: an illustrative survey and study. Rev. Manag. Sci. 1–59 (2014). doi:10.1007/s11846-014-0139-3
38. Wall, F., Leitner, S.: Die Relevanz der Nachhaltigkeit für unternehmerische Entscheidungen. Controlling-Zeitschrift für erfolgsorientierte Unternehmensführung **24**(4/5), 255–260 (2012)
39. Weinberger, E.D.: Local properties of Kauffman's N-K model: a tunably rugged energy landscape. Phys. Rev. A **44**(10), 6399–6413 (1991)
40. Weinberger, E.D., Kauffman, S.: The NK model of rugged fitness landscapes and its application to maturation of the immune response. J. Theor. Biol. **141**, 211–245 (1989)
41. Zimmerman, J.L.: Accounting for Decision Making and Control, 7th edn. McGraw-Hill, New York (2011)

# Destabilising Conventions Using Temporary Interventions

James Marchant[(✉)], Nathan Griffiths, Matthew Leeke, and Henry Franks

Department of Computer Science, University of Warwick, Coventry, UK
{james,nathan,matt}@dcs.warwick.ac.uk, hpwfranks@googlemail.com

**Abstract.** Conventions are an important concept in multi-agent systems as they allow increased coordination amongst agents and hence a more efficient system. Encouraging and directing convention emergence has been the focus of much research, particularly through the use of fixed strategy agents. In this paper we apply temporary interventions using fixed strategy agents to destabilise an established convention by (i) replacing it with another convention of our choosing, and (ii) allowing it to destabilise in such a way that no other convention explicitly replaces it. We show that these interventions are effective and investigate the minimum level of intervention needed.

**Keywords:** Convention emergence · Norms · Coordination · Intervention

## 1 Introduction

In multi-agent systems (MAS) coordinated actions help to reduce the costs associated with incompatible choices and increase the efficiency of a system. However, in many domains such behaviour cannot be enforced, as there is no centralised control and a lack of *a priori* knowledge of which actions clash. In practice, many systems rely on the evolution of *conventions* as standards of behaviour adopted by agents with no, or little, involvement from system designers. Understanding how these conventions emerge, how they can be influenced, and how aspects such as topology affect them is an active research area [5,7,10,15,18].

Conventions have been shown to support high levels of coordination without the need to dictate action choices in a top-down manner. Facilitating the emergence of high-quality conventions in a short period of time, without requiring prior computation, is an area of ongoing research. Much work has focussed on the emergence of conventions given only agent rationality and the ability to learn from previous choices. Small numbers of fixed strategy agents (agents who choose the same action regardless of others' choices) have been shown to influence the conventions that emerge and to increase the speed of adoption [7,8,15].

The ability to remove, as well as establish, conventions allows correction or replacement of adopted actions. In domains where the desirability of actions can change over time, being able to cause such a change is beneficial to the system as

© Springer International Publishing Switzerland 2015
A. Ghose et al. (Eds.): COIN 2014, LNAI 9372, pp. 148–163, 2015.
DOI: 10.1007/978-3-319-25420-3_10

a whole. Additionally, understanding how to cause this shift gives insights into what makes a convention robust to outside influence.

In this paper, we examine what is needed to *destabilise* an established convention. We propose temporarily inserting agents, known as *Intervention Agents* (IAs), with strategies that differ from the established convention to influence a population into discarding that convention. The insertion of IAs is equivalent to incentivising individuals to take particular actions, for example through reward or payment. We show that a small proportion of IAs placed at targeted locations in the population for a sufficient duration can destabilise an established convention, replacing it with another of our choosing. We also show that conventions can be destabilised in such a way that we are not required to select a replacement, and instead we can allow a new convention to emerge.

The remainder of this paper is structured as follows. In Sect. 2 we introduce the related work on convention emergence and the role of fixed strategy agents. Sections 3 and 3.1 present our model of convention emergence and metrics for characterising conventions. In Sect. 3.2 we present our model of IAs for convention destabilisation. We describe our experimental settings in Sect. 4, and present our results in Sect. 5. Finally, in Sect. 6 we present our conclusions.

## 2   Related Work

*Conventions* can be viewed as socially-accepted rules, in the form of expected behaviour, amongst agents. There is no explicit punishment for acting against the convention, but doing so increases the likelihood of coordination problems and costs. Thus a convention can be thought of as "an equilibrium everyone expects in interactions that have more than one equilibrium" [20]. Conventions can emerge from local agent interactions [5,10,17,19] and support coordination by placing *social constraints* on the actions that are available to the agents [16]. As such, conventions differ from *norms* (although the terms are often used interchangeably in the literature [12,15]) as the latter typically involve punishments for failure to adhere to the expected behaviour [2,3,9,14]. Norms generally require additional abilities or overheads to facilitate this punishment. We do not assume that agents are able to punish others (or even to observe their defection), and instead focus on conventions as a lightweight method of supporting coordination.

In this work we examine convention emergence where the only assumptions on agent behaviour are rationality and a (limited) *memory* of past interactions. This setting has been widely studied [5,8,15,19] and is able to support effective convention emergence. Walker and Wooldridge [19] were amongst the first to produce a formal model of convention emergence with few assumptions about the underlying agent architecture. They present a model in which a global convention emerges where agents choose their action based solely on observations of others. Sen and Airiau [15] explore social learning as a method for convention emergence, where agents learn the best action choice based on the payoff of their interactions. They show that convention emergence is possible with minimal additions to agents' abilities (for example, no memory of interactions is required) and without assuming public interactions. However, the work is limited by several simplifications: there is no connecting topology restricting agent interactions and the convention space contains only two possible conventions. In general, larger convention spaces and connecting topologies are commonplace.

The underlying topology has been shown to have a significant effect on convention emergence [4,5,10,18]. Much of the work investigating topology has been restricted to a small convention space (typically with just two actions). More recent work has explored the effect of increasing the number of available actions and has shown that doing so typically increases the time taken for convergence [7,8,13].

## 2.1  Fixed Strategy Agents

Sen and Airiau [15] demonstrated that a small number of fixed strategy agents, that always choose the same action regardless of others' actions, were sufficient to cause a population to adopt this action as a convention. This indicates that, at least in some circumstances, small numbers of agents are able to influence much larger populations. Franks et al. [6,7] examined the effectiveness of fixed strategy agents when agent interactions are restricted by a social network topology in a large convention space. They showed that the topology affects the number of fixed strategy agents required to influence convergence speed, and that *where* such agents are placed is crucial to the extent of their influence. Placement by metrics such as degree or eigenvector centrality has substantial benefits over random placement on speeding up convergence.

## 2.2  Destabilisation of Conventions

There has been relatively little work that explores destabilising established conventions. Previous work on fixed strategy agents focuses on promoting convention emergence, by introducing such agents at the beginning of population modelling. Our hypothesis is that fixed strategy agents can also be used to destabilise existing conventions. Villatoro et al. [17,18] explored a similar concept of destabilisation as part of convention emergence. They consider meta-stable subconventions, which are secondary conventions amongst subsets of the population that persist due to their stability. Meta-stable subconventions impede the emergence of more general conventions and can prevent full adoption. Villatoro et al. describe methods for preventing and removing meta-stable subconventions by identifying and targeting particular topological structures. Although related to our work, their approach focuses on subgroups of the population whereas we focus on the whole population. Moreover, Villatoro et al. have the aim of destabilising meta-stable subconventions to enable full emergence of a single convention, while our aim is more broadly to destabilise existing conventions.

## 3  Convention Emergence Model

Conventions emerge as a result of agents in a population selecting the same action and learning the best strategy (action choice) over time. We assume that a population consists of a set of agents, $Ag = \{1, ..., N\}$, who select from a number of actions, $\Sigma = \{\sigma_1, \sigma_2, ..., \sigma_n\}$. Each timestep each agent selects an interaction partner from its neighbours, and both partners choose an action from $\Sigma$. The individual payoff for each agent is determined by the combination of action choices. In this paper we adopt the n-action coordination game, such that interaction partners receive a positive payoff if they select the same action and a negative payoff if their actions differ. The 2-action coordination game is often used in exploring convention emergence, but we expand to the n-action coordination game to avoid restricting the number of possible conventions as discussed above.

Each agent chooses the action that it believes will result in the highest utility based on its previous interactions. We also assume an element of exploration, such that with probability $p_{explore}$ agents will choose a random action from those available. In this regard our model adopts the approach of Villatoro et al. [18] by using a simplified Q-Learning algorithm for both partners in an interaction to update their strategies.

We assume that agents are situated on a topology that restricts their interactions such that agents can only interact with their neighbours. Further, we consider small-world and scale-free networks which exhibit properties that reflect those observed in real-world environments such as power law degree distributions and clustering. We also consider random networks as a baseline.

### 3.1 Convention Metrics

In order to characterise convention establishment we need a measure of when a convention exists and when agents should be considered as members of that convention. Much work in the field uses Kittock's criteria in which a convention is said to have emerged when 90 % of the non-fixed strategy agents, when not exploring, select the same action [10]. However this offers no insights into emerging conventions until after they have become established, or of their decline if they are subsequently destabilised. Additionally, this measure relies on observation of agent internals to know when they are exploring and their preferred action. Thus, we propose a finer grained set of metrics for characterising convention emergence, from which we will define our strategies for destabilisation.

We introduce a number of new metrics (modified from [19]). We begin by formalising what it means to say an agent chose an action:

$$chose_x(\sigma, t) \iff \exists i : i \in par_x(t) \wedge self_x(i, t) = \sigma \tag{1}$$

where $self_x(i, t)$ is the action chosen by agent $x$ in interaction $i$ in timestep $t$, and $par_x(t)$ is the set of interactions that $x$ participated in during timestep $t$.

We can then define the set of agents that have chosen a given action $\sigma \in \Sigma$ during timestep $t$ as:

$$chosen(\sigma, t) = \{x | x \in Ag \wedge chose_x(\sigma, t)\} \tag{2}$$

We also require a way of defining whether we consider an agent to be a member of a convention or not, and of establishing the *existence* of a convention. Due to exploration, full adherence to a single strategy is unlikely to occur. It is useful to quantify an agent's *adherence* to a strategy of choosing $\phi$ as the probability of that agent choosing $\phi$ in any potential interaction at time $t$:

$$adh(x, \phi, t) = P(self_x(i, t) = \phi \mid i \in par_x(t)) \tag{3}$$

Note that since in general action selection is likely to be relatively complex, we may not be able to establish adherence exactly. We can determine an estimate based on the agent's interaction history, by considering the proportion of the last $\lambda$ interactions in which the agent selected $\phi$.

We subsequently define the set of conventions $\Phi_t$ that exist in a population at time $t$ as follows:

$$\phi \in \Phi_t \iff \exists x : x \in chosen(\phi, t) \land adh(x, \phi, t) > \gamma \tag{4}$$

That is, a given action $\sigma$ is considered to be a convention at time $t$ if there is at least one agent choosing that action with a probability greater than some threshold $\gamma$. This characterisation allows us to capture the notion of a personal convention analogous to that of a personal norm. We use $\phi$ to denote an action that is also a convention and $\sigma$ to denote an action that may or may not be a convention. This distinction allows us to separate actions selected by chance, exploration or some other process and those selected with sufficient frequency to be considered conventions.

We define the average adherence to a strategy of choosing $\sigma$ to be the mean adherence across the agents that chose $\sigma$ in a timestep:

$$averageAdh(\sigma, t) = \frac{\displaystyle\sum_{x \in chosen(\sigma, t)} adh(x, \sigma, t)}{|chosen(\sigma, t)|} \tag{5}$$

We assume that the temporal variance of $adh$ is low, such that an agent who satisfies $adh(x, \phi, t) > \gamma$ at time $t$ is likely to satisfy it at $t + 1$ (Walker and Wooldridge [19] discussed that since strategy change typically incurs a cost we can expect the number of strategy changes to be minimised).

We define a convention as *established* if the average adherence is greater than the *convention establishment threshold* $\beta$, a model-wide parameter:

$$estbl(\phi, t) \iff \phi \in \Phi_t \land averageAdh(\phi, t) > \beta \tag{6}$$

Finally, we can define the extent to which agents are part of a convention. We denote agents as *members* of a convention if they currently adhere to it with probability greater than or equal to $\beta$:

$$member(x, \phi, t) \iff estbl(\phi, t) \land adh(x, \phi, t) \geq \beta \tag{7}$$

Thus, the membership set for a given convention at time $t$ is given by:

$$membership(\phi, t) = \{x \mid x \in Ag, \phi \in \Phi_t, member(x, \phi, t)\} \tag{8}$$

By measuring the size of convention membership sets over time we can monitor how conventions become established and grow without internal observation of agents' decision making. Furthermore, we can distinguish between agents who used a convention due to exploration and those who are truly members.

### 3.2  Intervention Agents

As discussed in Sect. 2, fixed strategy agents can influence convention emergence when introduced at the beginning of a simulation. We call these fixed strategy agents *Intervention Agents* (IAs) and, unlike in previous work, they are introduced to destabilise established conventions. Building on the work of Franks et al. [6, 7] we propose simultaneously introducing IAs to replace nodes from the primary convention (that with the highest membership) to manipulate convention emergence. The duration of IA placement is varied to investigate the extent of intervention required to elicit a lasting change on the primary convention.

There are two types of destabilisation we can attempt using IAs: *aggressive* and *non-aggressive*. In aggressive destabilisation the aim is to *demote* the primary convention and *promote* a specified alternative convention in its place. In our experimentation we select the second most adopted convention as the alternative for promotion. Thus, we use IAs to encourage members of the primary convention to adopt the secondary convention. Non-aggressive destabilisation aims to demote the primary convention without having to select an alternative convention in its place, instead allowing a new convention to emerge. To accomplish this we propose that IAs adopt a uniform distribution of actions selected from those not already established as conventions. Our hypothesis is that this will destabilise the primary convention and allow an alternative to emerge.

## 4  Experimental Setup

We performed experiments with populations of 1000 agents, that use Q-learning (with a learning rate and an exploration rate of 0.25) to evolve their strategies. Unless otherwise stated we use the 10-action coordination game. We explored other sizes of convention space and obtained similar results to those presented here. All results are averaged over 30 runs, unless otherwise stated.

A window size of $\lambda = 30$ is used for adherence approximation, giving sufficient granularity to estimate membership whilst minimising memory overhead. The required action selection probability for an action to be considered a convention, $\gamma$, is 0.5. This enables more strategies to be considered as conventions (whether or not they are established) to give more information on the effects of intervention.

The convention emergence threshold, $\beta$, is set to 0.9 (in line with other work as discussed above). However, due to our method of measuring convention emergence we do not assume knowledge of whether an agent is exploring. As such, the 90 % threshold must be adjusted to take into account the random exploration of agents (noting that when exploring the agent can potentially still choose the "best" action $1/N$ times). This gives: $\beta = 0.9 \times (1 - (p_{explore}(N-1))/N))$, where

$N$ is the number of actions, $p_{explore}$ is the exploration rate, and $(N-1)/N$ represents the ratio of randomly chosen actions that are not the "best".

We used the Java Universal Network/Graph Library (version 2.0.1)[1] to generate interaction topologies. Scale-free topologies were generated using the Barabási-Albert algorithm with parameters $m_0 = 4$, $m = 3$, where $m_0$ is the initial number of vertices and $m \leq m_0$ is the number of edges added from a new node to existing nodes each evolution [1]. Small-world topologies were generated using the Kleinberg model with a lattice size of $10 \times 100$, clustering exponent $\alpha = 5$ and one "long-distance" connection per node [11].

We ran simulations for 5000 timesteps before introducing IAs, since this was found to be sufficient time for convention emergence and stabilisation in all topologies. At timestep 5000 a set of IAs were introduced, replacing nodes within the primary convention selected either randomly or by highest degree. The IAs remain for either a fixed number of timesteps or until the end of the simulation, to investigate the duration required for destabilisation and whether the primary convention can recover when the IAs are removed. Upon removal of the fixed strategy nature agents again use Q-learning to choose actions (with learning continuing during the fixed strategy period). Unless otherwise stated, the simulations were performed for 10000 iterations in total, to enable replacement conventions to emerge after destabilisation.

If there are insufficient members of the primary convention for the target number of IAs to be introduced then additional IAs are placed throughout the rest of the population according to the current placement strategy. Note that this implies the primary convention is immediately destabilised (as all of its members are now IAs) but such settings are included for completeness.

## 5    Results and Discussion

### 5.1    Number of Fixed Strategy Agents

We begin by examining the effect of introducing a varying number of IAs into the population indefinitely. To establish a baseline for the minimum number of IAs required to enact a change, we introduce a set of IAs at time 5000 that remain until the end of the simulation. For these results we use *aggressive destabilisation*, such that IAs use the action of the secondary convention (determined by ranking conventions by membership size and then average adherence). IAs replace the highest degree agents that were members of the primary convention. We also performed experiments using random placement, which confirmed the results of Franks et al. that random placement is inferior to placement by degree [6,7]. Thus, in the remainder of this paper we focus on placement by degree.

Our simulations were performed on scale-free and small-world networks as described in Sect. 4, and on random graphs generated using the Erdös-Rényi generator to provide a baseline. In order to provide similar edge numbers to the scale-free and small-world graphs we used a connection probability of 0.006.

---

[1] http://jung.sourceforge.net/.

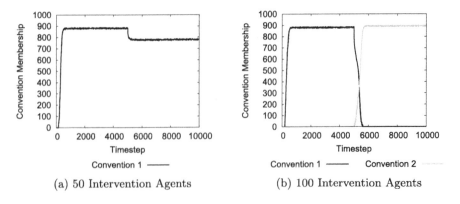

(a) 50 Intervention Agents    (b) 100 Intervention Agents

**Fig. 1.** The effect of Intervention Agents on random graphs

For all figures in this section (excluding Fig. 8), all conventions which have significant non-zero membership during the simulation are plotted. Those with zero or near-zero membership have been excluded from the graphs for clarity.

Figure 1 shows the effect of different numbers of IAs on the random graph topology. With the introduction of 50 IAs the membership of the primary convention (displayed in black) drops (more so than the 50 agents who became IAs would account for) but stabilises again rather than destabilising completely. This is likely due to the IAs being able to influence a local area around themselves but agents further away being too adherent to the primary convention to be affected. We would therefore expect this "dip" to increase in depth as the number of IAs increases and, indeed, this is what was observed. This behaviour continued until around 80–100 IAs after which the primary convention becomes destabilised enough for the secondary convention (displayed in grey) to overtake it. This behaviour is shown in Fig. 1(b). Of particular interest is that the speed with which the changeover happens indicates that, once the critical number of IAs are included, they are only needed for a short period of time.

Figure 2 shows results for scale-free graphs. We see similar behaviour to random graphs, with the decrease in membership of the primary convention increasing proportionally to the number of IAs until a critical number of IAs where the destabilisation is enough to allow the promotion of the secondary convention. Scale-free networks require significantly fewer IAs than random graphs, needing only 40, to achieve destabilisation. This is accounted for by the presence of "hubs" which are able to influence large groups of agents, at least some of which will be chosen as locations for IAs due to their high degree. In both cases however the primary convention is fully destabilised whilst the secondary is promoted to the same membership size as the primary originally had.

Results for small-world networks are shown in Fig. 3. Whilst the overall behaviour is similar, in that there is a critical number of IAs after which destabilisation will occur, the behaviour pre-transition is less well-defined. In particular, the characteristic "dip" that occurs in scale-free and random topologies

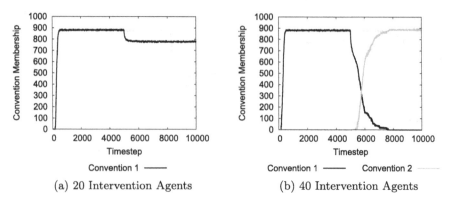

(a) 20 Intervention Agents          (b) 40 Intervention Agents

**Fig. 2.** The effect of Intervention Agents on scale-free graphs

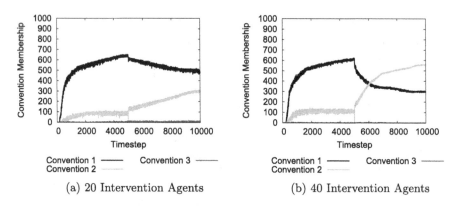

(a) 20 Intervention Agents          (b) 40 Intervention Agents

**Fig. 3.** The effect of Intervention Agents on small-world graphs

is not present to the same extent, and the drop in membership of the primary convention is slower. Additional simulations over longer durations show that the convention does eventually stabilise but takes a large number of iterations (approximately 20000). This likely follows from the clustered nature of small-world graphs, and we hypothesise that the clusters are slow to adapt to the changes in convention. This hypothesis is supported by the number of agents in the primary convention before intervention being substantially lower than in scale-free and random graphs, implying that the clustering slows convention emergence. Previous work by Franks et al. observed similar disparities in convention adoption between scale-free and small-world graphs [7].

Full destabilisation, as seen in Figs. 1 and 2, was found to occur in small-world topologies with 70 or more fixed agents, with 40 the minimum required to replace the primary convention. Additionally, a third convention is present at the bottom of the graphs. The presence of this is unique to small-world graphs and is included to show this difference between topologies.

## 5.2  Length of Intervention

We have shown that destabilisation is possible and have identified the smallest number of IAs needed. In this section we determine the duration needed for a permanent change, by adding IAs temporarily for a fixed duration.

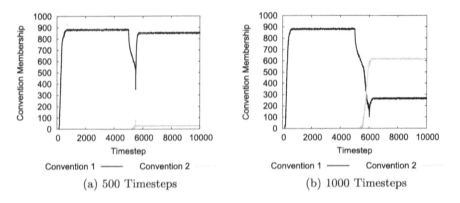

(a) 500 Timesteps                           (b) 1000 Timesteps

**Fig. 4.** The effect on scale-free graphs of 40 IAs when introduced for finite time

Figure 4 shows the effect of varying the duration for which 40 IAs are present on scale-free graphs. In the previous section we demonstrated that 40 IAs is sufficient for destabilisation. In Fig. 4(a) IAs are introduced for 500 timesteps. Whilst the characteristic decrease in numbers we saw previously starts to occur, when IAs are removed the primary convention rapidly recovers. However, we begin to see the effect of IAs since after the intervention a stable secondary convention emerges. The size of this convention is comparable to the difference in the primary convention size before and after intervention, implying that the second convention represents agents who have permanently changed convention.

Increasing the intervention length to 1000 timesteps, as shown in Fig. 4(b), is sufficient for destabilisation, and for the secondary convention to overtake the primary. However, it is not as well established as with permanent interventions, indicating that keeping the IAs for longer would further destabilise the primary convention. This was verified by testing over longer time periods. It is also worth noting that the primary convention manages to recover slightly before stabilising, but that this does not shrink the secondary convention. Therefore, the primary convention is regaining nodes that were no longer strong adherents to the primary but had not yet become strong adherents to the secondary convention.

Figure 5 shows the effect of temporary interventions for small-world graphs. Figure 5(a) shows similar behaviour to its scale-free counterpart as the intervention duration is insufficient for destabilisation. The change in membership is larger than in scale-free networks, in terms of absolute and relative size, which supports our hypothesis regarding the clustered nature of small-world graphs implying that influence internal to a cluster is easier than changing it externally.

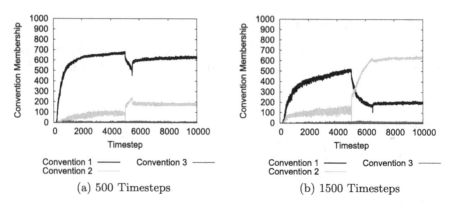

(a) 500 Timesteps          (b) 1500 Timesteps

**Fig. 5.** The effect on small-world graphs of 40 IAs when introduced for finite time

As such, when clusters change from the primary to the secondary convention they are unlikely to change back when IAs are removed.

Figure 5(b) shows that the length of intervention needed for permanent change in small-world networks is longer than for scale-free networks, taking 1500 iterations rather than 1000. This is due to the clustered nature of small-world graphs, and supports the findings of Griffiths and Anand [8] showing that small-world networks converge slower than scale-free and, in this case, take longer to change.

### 5.3  Non-aggressive Destabilisation

Previous simulations have focused on aggressive destabilisation, where the primary convention is demoted whilst promoting the secondary. We now consider *non-aggressive destabilisation* where we attempt to destabilise the primary convention without explicitly promoting another convention in its place.

Figure 6 shows sample runs from inserting 100 IAs that replace the high degree nodes of the primary convention in a scale-free topology. In Fig. 6(a) and (b) the IAs are inserted indefinitely, while in (c) and (d) they are removed after 2000 iterations. Unlike aggressive destabilisation the IA strategies are selected uniformly at random from the bottom 7 ranked strategies at time 5000. Each plot shows a different run, since average results are not appropriate as the final emergent convention differs at random. The runs show the same behaviour, with the primary convention being destabilised around timestep 6000. This is slower than the destabilisation achieved with aggressive IAs, but is expected due to the lack of a coordinated effort to replace the influenced agents' strategies. In each run a new convention emerges around timestep 8500 and since this convention emerges naturally it may differ each time. By destabilising the primary convention, but not explicitly favouring another, a new convention naturally emerges, but we cannot predict what it will be. This contrasts with aggressive destabilisation where the secondary (targeted) convention always emerges.

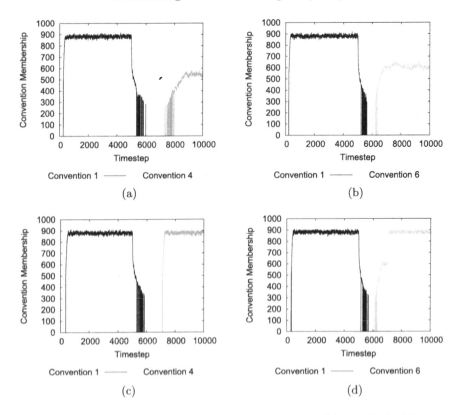

**Fig. 6.** Non-aggressive destabilisation in scale-free graphs. In (a) and (b) the IAs remain indefinitely. In (c) and (d) they remain for 2000 timesteps.

The length of the intervention affects the final membership size attained by the new convention. Where IAs remain indefinitely (the upper two plots) the stable membership size is several hundred less than with a temporary intervention (the lower two plots). This can be explained by the presence of the IAs, which randomly select strategies from the lowest 7 conventions at the time of initial intervention, continuing to hinder the new convention from spreading in much the same way as they destabilised the original primary convention. We would expect that when IAs are removed the new convention will spread to the area that they were occupying, which is seen in Fig. 6 (lower two plots) where the new convention undergoes rapid size increase as soon as the IAs are removed.

Figure 7 shows individual non-aggressive runs on small-world topologies. The length of time the IAs are present is the same as in Fig. 6 but the number of IAs is increased to 200, as 100 agents is insufficient for destabilisation in this setting. This relates to the hypothesis that the clusters in small-world topologies make change slower and more difficult to achieve than in scale-free topologies. The findings are similar to those in scale-free graphs: once destabilisation of the primary convention has occurred another emerges after a small period of time

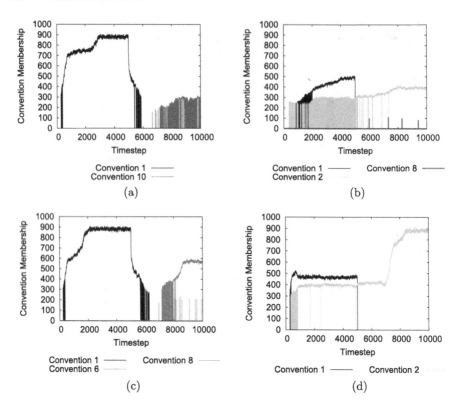

**Fig. 7.** Non-aggressive destabilisation in small-world graphs. In (a) and (b) the IAs remain indefinitely. In (c) and (d) they remain for 2000 timesteps.

and without predictable strategy. Whilst the overall convention membership size is smaller than those in scale-free topologies (as was the case in other simulations) the relationship between the IAs remaining and the lower membership sizes of the replacement convention still holds. Again, removing IAs after destabilisation is conducive to a stronger new convention emerging.

## 5.4    Cost of Intervention vs. Effect

Finally, we consider the relationship between the number of IAs and the duration of intervention needed for destabilisation. We define one unit of cost to be one IA being included for one iteration. Thus, 200 IAs present for one iteration have a cost of 200, while 5 IAs present for 20 iterations have a cost of 100. Since real-world interventions, such as incentives or payments, are likely to have a tangible cost it is useful to measure the expense of a strategy for using IAs.

In this set of experiments we varied the number of IAs from 40 (the minimum number required for destabilisation) to 500, while simultaneously increasing the duration of intervention from 0 in steps of 50 until destabilisation occurred. For numbers of IAs above 200, where more granularity in the length of time was

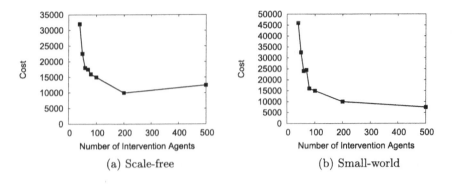

**Fig. 8.** Number of IAs vs. the minimum cost to cause destabilisation

needed, the duration was increased in steps of 5. These values were then used to calculate the minimum cost associated with causing the destabilisation.

For both small-world and scale-free topologies, increasing the number of agents decreased the cost needed for destabilisation, as shown in Fig. 8. This is because, even though the number of IAs increases, the required duration decreases by a higher proportion, resulting in a lower cost. The effect of increasing the number of agents is one of diminishing returns: increasing the number of agents produces smaller reductions in cost each time. In addition, whilst influencing small numbers of agents in a population is likely to be possible, being able to influence half of all agents is, due to the lack of centralised control, unlikely in most domains, and so 500 IAs are included only for completeness.

Whilst the relationship between cost and number of IAs is similar in scale-free and small-world networks it is worth noting that the costs associated with intervening in a small-world topology are substantially higher than those for scale-free topologies. This is due to the need to include IAs for longer periods in small-world topologies, which relates to the decreased speed with which small-world graphs allow conventions to emerge. However, these results show that in general as many IAs as possible should be introduced if they require an ongoing cost. If, instead, placing them only requires a one-off cost, then using the minimum number for destabilisation is preferable as additional agents will increase the cost with little additional benefit (as can be seen in previous sections).

# 6    Conclusions

We have shown that it is possible to destabilise established conventions by introducing a small proportion of IAs. When using aggressive IAs, whose fixed strategy is that of the second most popular convention, to replace the highest degree nodes in the primary convention we found that 40 agents (4 % of the population) is sufficient to destabilise the primary convention and for the secondary convention to be promoted. This occurs in small-world, scale-free and random topologies, with the latter requiring 100 agents for destabilisation to occur.

We also investigated the minimum duration that IAs must remain in order to cause a permanent destabilisation and prevent the primary convention from re-establishing itself. We found that there was a minimum number of agents and a minimum duration needed to cause this effect, and that the minimum duration for small-world graphs is longer than that required for scale-free graphs. Interventions less than this minimum duration cause a temporary decrease in membership of the targeted convention, which disappears when IAs are removed.

A different method of destabilisation was investigated in the form of non-aggressive destabilisation, which attempts to demote the primary convention without explicitly promoting another. We found that the number of IAs required was higher than in aggressive destabilisation, and that small-world topologies required more IAs than scale-free topologies. We showed that the primary convention would be destabilised and that, whilst a new convention would emerge, its strategy was unpredictable.

Finally, we proposed a method of calculating a "cost" for an intervention and showed that increasing the number of agents was beneficial, assuming that the intervention had an ongoing cost per iteration. We also found that performing interventions was more expensive in small-world than in scale-free topologies.

Overall, we have found that the ability to intervene in a system and remove previously established conventions is possible. The ability to do this means that undesirable conventions can be removed even if they are heavily adhered to, allowing the system to replace such conventions either with direction to a particular convention (the aggressive approach) or through natural emergence.

# References

1. Albert, R., Barabási, A.L.: Statistical mechanics of complex networks. Rev. Mod. Phys. **74**(1), 47–95 (2002)
2. Axelrod, R.: An evolutionary approach to norms. Am. Polit. Sci. Rev. **80**, 1095–1111 (1986)
3. Bicchieri, C., Jeffrey, R.C., Skyrms, B.: The Dynamics of Norms. Cambridge University Press, Cambridge (1997)
4. Delgado, J.: Emergence of social conventions in complex networks. Artif. Intell. **141**(1–2), 171–185 (2002)
5. Delgado, J., Pujol, J.M., Sangüesa, R.: Emergence of coordination in scale-free networks. Web Intell. Agent Syst. **1**(2), 131–138 (2003)
6. Franks, H., Griffiths, N., Anand, S.: Learning agent influence in MAS with complex social networks. Auton. Agent. Multi-Agent Syst. **28**(5), 836–866 (2014)
7. Franks, H., Griffiths, N., Jhumka, A.: Manipulating convention emergence using influencer agents. Auton. Agent. Multi-Agent Syst. **26**(3), 315–353 (2013)
8. Griffiths, N., Anand, S.S.: The impact of social placement of non-learning agents on convention emergence. In: 11th International Conference on Autonomous Agents and Multiagent Systems, vol. 3, pp. 1367–1368. International Foundation for Autonomous Agents and Multiagent Systems, Richland, SC (2012)
9. Kandori, M.: Social norms and community enforcement. Rev. Econ. Stud. **59**(1), 63–80 (1992)

10. Kittock, J.: Emergent conventions and the structure of multi-agent systems. In: Lectures in Complex Systems: The Proceedings of the 1993 Complex Systems Summer School, pp. 507–521. Addison-Wesley, Reading, MA (1995)
11. Kleinberg, J.: Navigation in a small world. Nature **406**(6798), 845–845 (2000)
12. Mukherjee, P., Sen, S., Airiau, S.: Norm emergence with biased agents. Int. J. Agent Technol. Syst. **1**(2), 71–84 (2009)
13. Salazar, N., Rodriguez-Aguilar, J.A., Arcos, J.L.: Robust coordination in large convention spaces. AI Commun. **23**(4), 357–372 (2010)
14. Savarimuthu, B.T.R., Arulanandam, R., Purvis, M.: Aspects of active norm learning and the effect of lying on norm emergence in agent societies. In: Kinny, D., Hsu, J.Y., Governatori, G., Ghose, A.K. (eds.) PRIMA 2011. LNCS, vol. 7047, pp. 36–50. Springer, Heidelberg (2011)
15. Sen, S., Airiau, S.: Emergence of norms through social learning. In: 20th International Joint Conference on AI, pp. 1507–1512. Morgan Kaufmann, San Francisco (2007)
16. Shoham, Y., Tennenholtz, M.: On the emergence of social conventions: modeling, analysis, and simulations. Artif. Intell. **94**(1–2), 139–166 (1997)
17. Villatoro, D., Sabater-Mir, J., Sen, S.: Social instruments for robust convention emergence. In: 22nd International Joint Conference on AI, pp. 420–425. AAAI Press (2011)
18. Villatoro, D., Sen, S., Sabater-Mir, J.: Topology and memory effect on convention emergence. In: 2009 IEEE/WIC/ACM International Joint Conference on Web Intelligence and Intelligent Agent Technology, vol. 2, pp. 233–240. IEEE Computer Society, Washington, DC (2009)
19. Walker, A., Wooldridge, M.: Understanding the emergence of conventions in multi-agent systems. In: International Conference on Multi-Agent Systems, pp. 384–389. MIT Press (1995)
20. Young, H.P.: The economics of convention. J. Econ. Perspect. **10**(2), 105–122 (1996)

# Towards a Framework for Socio-Cognitive Technical Systems

Pablo Noriega[1], Julian Padget[2]($\boxtimes$), Harko Verhagen[3], and Mark d'Inverno[4]

[1] IIIA-CSIC, Barcelona, Spain
pablo@iiia.csic.es
[2] Department of Computer Science, University of Bath, Bath, UK
j.a.padget@bath.ac.uk
[3] Stockholm University, Stockholm, Sweden
verhagen@dsv.su.se
[4] Goldsmiths, University of London, London, UK
dinverno@gold.ac.uk

**Abstract.** This paper is an invitation to carry out science and engineering for a class of socio-technical systems where individuals — who may be human or artificial entities — engage in purposeful collective interactions within a shared web-mediated social space. We put forward a characterization of these systems and introduce some conceptual distinctions that may help to plot the work ahead. In particular, we propose a tripartite view (*WIT Trinity*) that highlights the interplay between the institutional models that prescribe the behaviour of participants, the corresponding implementation of these prescriptions and the actual performance of the system. Building on this tripartite view we explore the problem of developing a conceptual framework for modelling this type of systems and how that framework can be supported by technological artefacts that implement the resulting models. The last section of this position paper outlines a list of challenges that we believe are worth facing. This work draws upon the contributions that the MAS community has made to the understanding and realization of the concepts of coordination, norms and institutions from an organisational perspective.

## 1   Introduction

"Social coordination" is a many-faceted phenomenon that has been the subject of attention in a number of scientific communities: from economics to social anthropology, from biology to computer science. The arrival of the internet and the massive adoption of social networks and other web-enabled practices have lead the notion of social coordination to acquire new meaning and, in reference to such on-line situations, an unprecedented and substantial economic and social importance. Hence, we put forward this position paper in order to start a debate about the research agenda (i) by making a first attempt to identify the key features that characterize the space of artificial socio-cognitive technical systems (SCTS) (ii) outlining an intentional architecture for SCTS, and (iii) sketching

© Springer International Publishing Switzerland 2015
A. Ghose et al. (Eds.): COIN 2014, LNAI 9372, pp. 164–181, 2015.
DOI: 10.1007/978-3-319-25420-3_11

some ideas, informed by some possible application domains, for a software engineering approach to help realize SCTS, utilizing the many contributions of the COIN community.

We are witnessing the birth of a new sort of tools that, anchored to human cognitive capabilities, aim to support human-like social interactions in a virtual space where the frontiers between the physical and the artificial are increasingly difficult to determine. There is an opportunity to observe with a scientific eye how this process is taking place and articulate an understanding that gives grounds to a serious assessment of its positive and negative aspects and, perhaps, to its evolution. On the other hand, there is also a technological opportunity to address the creation of those new tools in a principled way. Needless to say that behind those opportunities there are ethical concerns that should be taken into account.

This paper aims to be a step towards realising those two opportunities. Hence, its focus is on social coordination within a particular kind of systems that enable individuals — who may be human or artificial entities — to interact in a shared web-mediated social space in a purposeful fashion. We shall call them *(artificial) socio-cognitive technical systems* (SCTS). Our goal is to provide foundations for an understanding of these systems and in time establish a principled methodology for their construction. The immediate outcome in this paper is the introduction of some conceptual distinctions for that purpose. The ancillary objective of this paper is to point the way towards future actions.

This is a position paper in which our key contributions are:

1. An intentional definition of SCTS (Sect. 2), with two essential distinct components: socio-cognitive agents and the social space where these interact;
2. A "tripartite view" (Sect. 3) that attempts to explain the interplay among the three complementary aspects of an SCTS: the institutional, the technological and the "real-world";
3. An identification of those features that are required to model a social space for SCTS that has at least three properties or *affordances* (see Sect. 4): (i) Awareness, by which participants perceive their context (ii) Coordination, by which collective action is enabled and (iii) Validity which establishes a set of correspondences between the elements of our tripartite description of SCTS;
4. How the relationship between the model of an SCTS and its implementation is mediated by a metamodel and a platform (Sect. 5), and, finally
5. A call to arms (Sect. 6)

## 2   A Superficial Exploration of SCTS

Broadly speaking, our aim is to study systems that involve several rational participants who come together to perform a collective activity that they cannot accomplish on their own and such action does not occur directly between individuals but is mediated by technological artefacts.

This crude characterisation may be clarified by making explicit some underlying assumptions:

**Notion 1.** *A* socio-cognitive technical system (SCTS) *is a multiagent system that satisfies the following assumptions:*

**A.1 System.** *A socio-cognitive technical system is composed by two ("first class") entities: a* social space *and the* agents *who act within that space. The system exists in the real world and there is a boundary that determines what is inside the system and what is out.*

**A.2 Agents.** *Agents are entities who are capable of acting within the social space. They exhibit the following characteristics:*

**A.2.1 Socio-cognitive.** *Agents are presumed to base their actions on some internal decision model. The decision-making behaviour of agents, in principle, takes into account social aspects because the actions of agents may be affected by the social space or other agents and may affect other agents and the space itself [7].*

**A.2.2 Opaque Socio-cognitive Agents.** *The system, in principle, has no access to the decision-making models, or internal states of participating agents.*

**A.2.3 Mixed.** *Agents may be human or software entities (we shall call them all "agents" or "participants" where it is not necessary to distinguish).*

**A.2.4 Heterogeneous.** *Agents may have different decision models, different motivations and respond to different principals.*

**A.2.5 Autonomous.** *Agents are not necessarily competent or benevolent, hence they may fail to act as expected or demanded of them.*

**A.3 Persistence.** *The social space may change either as effect of the actions of the participants, or as effect of events that are caused (or admitted) by the system.*

**A.4 Perceivable.** *All interactions within the shared social space are mediated by technological artefacts — that is, as far as the system is concerned there are no direct interactions between agents outside the system and only those actions that are mediated by a technological artefact that is part of the system may have effects in the system — and although they might be described in terms of the five senses, they can collectively be considered percepts.*

**A.5 Openness.** *Agents may enter and leave the social space and a priori, it is not known (by the system or other agents) which agents may be active at a given time, nor whether new agents will join at some point or not.*

**A.6 Constrained.** *In order to coordinate actions, the space includes (and governs) regulations, obligations, norms or conventions that agents are in principle supposed to follow.*

We may think of these systems as *socio-technical* systems because of the participation of humans and software components [23], although they are better understood in the sense of [18] or even [22] where software agents may be involved. We use the term *artificial* because we want to stress the fact that there is some external design of the system and the term *socio-cognitive* to stress the fact the we glimpse some notion of social intelligence. Because of the assumption of intrinsic constraint on action (**A.6**), in standard multiagent systems terminology, the above assumptions characterize a type of *normative multiagent system* [3].

Jones et al. [16] refer to this type of system as an *intelligent socio-technical system*. While in this characterization, the adjective "intelligent" denotes an assumption of rationality, they also assert that these systems involve entities that *"interact with each other against a social, organisational or legal background"* (as in **A.2** above). Analogously, Castelfranchi calls them *socio-cognitive technical systems* to stress the fact that in order to characterize or deploy them we need to *"'understand' and reproduce features of the human social mind like commitments, norms, mind reading, power, trust, 'institutional effects' and social macrophenomena"* [7]. It is in this spirit that we adopt the term; however, we would like to stress the fact that in this paper we are mostly concerned by the fact that these systems are designed and built with some purpose in mind and occasionally refer to them as *artificial* socio-cognitive systems to capture the essence of these last two interpretations and omit the "technical" label to avoid redundancy.

Although it would be premature to propose a broad taxonomy of artificial socio-cognitive systems, it is nevertheless possible to identify application domains where these systems are or will be paradigmatic. For example, serious on-line games, massive multiplayer on-line role playing games, mixed-level participatory simulation of social systems, open innovation environments as well as other crowd-based applications, on-line electronic markets, policy support systems, or on-line alternative dispute resolution, to name a few. Such an empirical approach would be essential if one aspires to a serious characterization of SCTS. An argument for the need of empirical research on existing SCTS is formulated below (Subsect. 6.2). The pursuit of a proper characterization of SCTS (and its empirical foundations) was articulated in [9].

The research programme for SCTS that we envision should eventually enable us to design new such systems using a principled approach. We propose to address the general problem, first by delimiting the universe to an explicit set of features that may allow us to decide whether a given system — existing or in design — belongs to that universe, and second, developing an abstract understanding of what is common to these systems. These two steps would provide foundations for SCTS formalisms, tools and methodologies.

## 3   The WIT Trinity: A Tripartite View of Artificial Socio-cognitive Systems

Keeping the assumptions **A.1–6** and examples in mind, one may advance an intuitive description of SCTS as systems where it is possible to *govern* the interaction of agents that are situated in a physical or artificial world by means of technological artefacts. The key element in this description is in the "governance" part that mediates between the world and the technological artefacts. It is an aspect worth distinguishing in SCTS because of the need to control the activity of complex individuals that is at the root of SCTS (**A.2** and **A.6**). In order to elucidate how such governance is achieved we propose the following tripartite view of SCTS (the *WIT Trinity*)[1]:

---

[1] We abuse the term "trinity" to stress the fact that every SCTS has these three views, that each of these views has several characteristic features but that the three views are interrelated in an indissoluble way in order to constitute *the* SCTS.

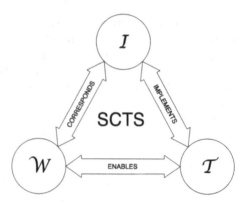

**Fig. 1.** The WIT trinity: The ideal system, $\mathcal{I}$; the technological artefacts that implement it, $\mathcal{T}$, and the actual world where the system is used, $\mathcal{W}$. After [19].

View 1: The *world* system, $\mathcal{W}$, as the agents (both human and software) see it and relate to it.

View 2: An ideal *institutional* system, $\mathcal{I}$, that stipulates the way the system should behave.

View 3: The *technological artefacts*, $\mathcal{T}$, that implement the ideal system and run the applications that enable users to accomplish collective actions in the real world according to the rules set out in $\mathcal{I}$.

These three views are interrelated through three binary relationships (as depicted in Fig. 1). The institutional world corresponds with the real world by a sort of "counts-as" relationship [15, 21] by which (brute) facts and (brute) actions in the real world correspond to institutional facts and actions in the institutional world $\mathcal{I}$ only when these comply with the institutional conventions, in which case the institutional effects of those institutional actions carry over to have effects in the real world.[2]

Secondly, the conventions prescribed in the institutional world have their counterpart in the technological world in the sense that institutional conventions

---

[2] Note that $\mathcal{W}$ is not the *entire* real-world, it is only the fragment of the physical reality that affects and is affected by the SCTS. Thus, if we think of *Amazon* as an SCTS the $\mathcal{W}$ (of *Amazon*) corresponds only to the reality around those online transactions that take place on line between a company call *Amazon.com*, buyers and sellers of books through the system that supports these transactions. In other words, there are events that happen in the word that may or may not be relevant for *Amazon* depending on what $\mathcal{I}$ (of *Amazon*) stipulates, for instance; the real-world event "new dollar / euro exchange rate" is in $\mathcal{W}$ (of *Amazon*) –or "meaningful" or relevant in *Amazon*–only if payments may be made in either of those two currencies. Likewise, a move in an online chess game is part of the game (*is* in $\mathcal{W}$), if and only if it is communicated and acknowledged through the on-line system ($\mathcal{T}$) and complies with the rules of chess defined in $\mathcal{I}$ (it is a proper chess move and is made on time, for example).

constitute a specification of the requirements of the system that is implemented in $T$.

In turn, the system, as implemented in $T$ is what enables interactions (through a proper interface) in $W$, so the agents in $W$ control the artefacts in $T$, but also, we contend, this relationship is symmetric, in that by virtue of the percepts delivered via $T$, the artefacts in $T$ effect some control over the agents in $W$. It should be noted that each of these three binary relationships needs to satisfy certain integrity conditions:

- The *corresponds* relationship needs: (i) to guarantee that the objects and concepts involved in the descriptions and functioning in $\mathcal{I}$ are properly associated with entities in $W$; i.e., that there is a bijection between terms in the languages in $\mathcal{I}$ and objects and actions in $W$. (ii) the identity of agents in $W$ to be properly reflected in their counterparts in $\mathcal{I}$ and preserved as long as the agents are active in the system, (iii) the agents that participate in $W$ to have the proper entitlements to be subject to the conventions that regulate their interactions and in particular to fulfil in $W$ those commitments that they establish in $\mathcal{I}$, and (iv) the commitments that are established according to $\mathcal{I}$, to be properly reflected in $W$.
- The *implements* relationship needs to be a faithful programming of the institutional conventions so that actions and effects are well programmed, norms are properly represented and enforced, etc.
- Finally, the *enables* relationship needs to make sure that: (i) the technological artefacts work properly (communication is not scrambled, data bases are not corrupted, etc.) and (ii) inputs and outputs are properly presented and captured in $W$, according to the implementation of the corresponding processes in $\mathcal{I}$. (iii) Algorithms and data structures in $T$ behave as the conventions in $\mathcal{I}$ prescribe.

### 3.1 The Shared State of an Artificial Socio-Cognitive System

We emphasize that, in the preceding discussion, we are suggesting that the three views correspond to the same SCTS. In other words, when we make reference to an SCTS, we always refer to an entity that exists in the real world, works by means of some technological artefacts and behaves according to some institutional conventions. We also state that the three views are interrelated. However, we may go a step further and establish the actual correspondence between the three views. For that purpose we rely on the notion of *shared state*.

The intuition behind shared state is that at any point in time, what happens in the world and enters the system produces some effects in the computational system that become effective in the world. In other words, that the *state of the world*, as far as the system is concerned, changes if and when an *attempted* action in $W$ is *validated* by $\mathcal{I}$, and then the code in $T$ *processes* the input that happens in $W$ and outputs the effects in $W$.

We may use the WIT Trinity of SCTS to get a clearer picture of how interactions of agents within the system change the shared state. Figure 2 illustrates how interactions among individuals take place within a socio-cognitive system.

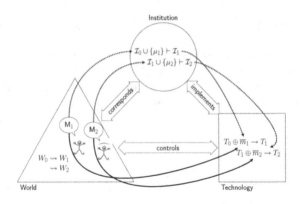

**Fig. 2.** Shared state in a socio-cognitive system

First let us focus on $\mathcal{W}$. Take two agents $a_1$ and $a_2$, in $\mathcal{W}$, who are about to interact within the system, each through its own interface device. Notice that, since these individuals are real — human or software agents — and are present in the part of the real world involved with the system, then the objects that exist, the facts that are true and whatever changes take place *in that part of the real world*, are the same for both agents, and for every other agent that is in the system at that point in time. Technically speaking, the agents *share the state* of $\mathcal{W}$. Now let the first agent ($a_1$) take an action $M_1$ in $\mathcal{W}$. Provided that $M_1$ is a *feasible* action, that action changes some facts in $\mathcal{W}$, and the state of the world changes from $\mathcal{W}_0$ to $\mathcal{W}_1$. Now, if $a_2$ takes a new feasible action $M_2$ the world changes to a new shared state $\mathcal{W}_2$. Second, from a computational perspective, inputs $M_1$ and $M_2$ correspond to messages $\bar{m}_1$ and $\bar{m}_2$ that when *processed* in $\mathcal{T}$, produce changes in the data structures and values of variables in $\mathcal{T}$, hence new successive *shared computational states*, $\mathcal{T}_1$ and $\mathcal{T}_2$. Finally, a similar thing happens in $\mathcal{I}$ when an institutional action $\mu_1$, (that corresponds to action $M_1$ and is implemented as message $\bar{m}_1$) takes the system from an *institutional state* $\mathcal{I}_0$ where certain formulas are admitted, to a new shared institutional state $\mathcal{I}_1$ with new admitted formulas, if and when $\mu_1$ is an institutionally *admissible* action, and likewise for a proper $\mu_2$. In other words, we have now established a more abstract notion of an SCTS by introducing three complementary components:

- A tripartite understanding of artificial socio-cognitive systems.
- The notion of state (of the world, computational, institutional), the use of valid interactions as the sole way of changing that state and the existence of a set of conventions that determine when an interaction is valid and, if so, how it changes the state.
- Three mappings between the three views of the system: (i) mappings between actions, messages and formulas, (ii) mappings between states of the world, system and institution and (iii) mappings between three notions of validity of interactions: feasible, processable and admissible.

These constructs can be made precise, although such task is beyond the scope of this paper, but even this crude description brings to light three crucial features that an SCTS must provide in order to control sophisticated interactions. First, an agent needs to be *aware* of the state of the world in order to decide what to do at some point. Moreover, in order to attempt an action, that agent needs to *coordinate* with other agents with whom it is interacting or would like to interact. Finally, the system needs to support a proper notion of *validity*, so that the "isomorphisms" described above between the evolution of the states of $\mathcal{W}$, $\mathcal{I}$ and $\mathcal{T}$ are operational.

## 4    Designing the Social Space

In Sect. 2, we characterized SCTS as collective processes involving several socio-cognitive agents (human or not) who engage in web-enabled interactions within a shared social space. We now want to move a step ahead and see how an SCTS can be designed or modelled. For that purpose and based on the previous discussion, we need to account for a way of dealing with the evolution of the shared state. Keeping in mind the distinctions between system, participants and social space (**A.1**) and the fact that agents are opaque to the system (**A.2.2**), we may limit our attention to the social space. Moreover, because of the correspondences implicit in the WIT Trinity, we may limit the discussion to the features of the social space in $\mathcal{I}$ and then extend that understanding to $\mathcal{T}$ and $\mathcal{W}$. In other words, if we want to design SCTS, what are the features we need in the social space so one can determine what is a state of the system and what is involved in performing a valid action. We propose to achieve this through what we call "affordances" (in the spirit of Norman [20]) needed to *model* an SCTS.[3]

**Notion 2.** *An* affordance *(of the social space of an SCTS) is a property of the social space that supports effective interactions of agents within an SCTS.*

At the end of the previous section, we postulated three *affordances* of every SCTS:

1. *Awareness*, which provides participating entities access to those elements of the shared state of the world that should enable them to decide what to do
2. *Coordination*, so that the actions of individuals are conducive to the collective endeavour that brings them to participate in the SCTS and
3. *Validity* that preserves the proper correspondences of the tripartite view.

There may be others, but we identify these because they contribute directly firstly, to the establishment of individual perception of (common) social situations, secondly to the realization of the mechanisms for collective action and thirdly to the correctness of the activity as a whole.

---

[3] Recall Norman's barrel. It is a water-tight cylinder with an intended affordance for holding liquids but it also provides affordances of a table or a hiding place. Similarly, the features we enumerate below have an intended affordance but others affordances may be achieved (for free) depending on the way they are specified or implemented.

It is evident that *awareness* and *coordination* — and other affordances as well — may be achieved by a variety of means. Consequently, one could use a way to make explicit the particular means through which these properties are achieved in a given SCTS; first because there may be reasons to choose among different particular means and second because participants — and technological artefacts — need to conform to the particular means used for modelling the given SCTS. For this purpose we, first, take a look at features that are involved in the achievement of the essential affordances. Next we postulate the notion of a *metamodel* as a way of describing the particular means that are used to generate those features.

A glance at some families of SCTS mentioned earlier (games, simulation, crowd-based systems, electronic markets,...) suggest concrete features that appear to be necessary for the modelling of most SCTS:

1. **Ontology.** The point of this feature is to establish the objects that describe and populate the social space. Some objects may be generic to a metamodel (norm, scene, workspace,..) or to a family of SCTS (weapons in first person shooter games, contract in prediction markets, etc.), others are specific to the application domain of the particular SCTS (sword, bid,...).
2. **Primitive Actions and Events.** How percepts are represented. For example, offering a picture for sale in an auction, bidding for it and declaring a bid invalid; reading the room temperature.
3. **Activities.** The possibility of organising atomic actions into repetitive activities through protocols, social semantics, a set of norms, etc. (to represent a bidding round or mapping crisis events of a city).
4. **Subspaces and their Interrelationships.** Constructs to describe (i) activities that involve only part of the participants who share a substate of the system that is not necessarily accessible to other participants, (ii) how these activities are interrelated and (iii) whether or not agents may be active in more than one activity at a given time (e.g., sequential scenes in a play, simultaneous auctions in *eBay*).
5. **Social Structure.** Roles (author and reviewer) and relationships among roles (authors cannot review their papers); groups (ad.hoc: task force; standard: jury; board of directors) and organisational structures (team, department).
6. **Social Devices.** Means for (i) tagging the behaviour of individuals, so that participants may become aware of particular qualities (trust, social standing) or (ii) processes for modifying it (ostracism, whitewashing, fines and incentives).
7. **Regulatory System.** Norms, normative consequence, enforcement mechanisms and procedures, norm life-cycle management, etc. (see [19] for a thorough discussion of normative affordances and features).
8. **Dynamics of the System.** How to measure the performance of the system and the means to make the system change over time.
9. **Types of Agents.** Means to choose the composition of the class of participants and specially to include as part of the system design those agents (or

their roles) whose decision-making model is defined or is in control of the system itself. Two types are most usual: *external* agents that are opaque to the system and *internal* who act on behalf of the system who is responsible for their behaviour. For example, in games: "players" (usually human) and "non-player characters" (software agents deployed by the system designer).

10. **Languages and Information Framework**. Needed to express the specific instantiation of features (for protocols, norms,...) and to store the design and enactment data (local and global states of the system, agent profiles, performance indicators, etc.).

These examples of features are meant to suggest how to make explicit the means required for designing or modelling an SCTS. With the following descriptions we aim to make more precise what we understand by "the means for modelling" and "modelling" an SCTS.[4]

**Notion 3.** *A metamodel (for SCTS) is a collection of languages, data structures and operations that when instantiated produce a model of an SCTS (and its internal agents, if any), through features that achieve the affordances of awareness and coordination in a social space.*

Consequently, a model is simply a "good" description of a socio-cognitive system:

**Notion 4.** *A model of an artificial socio-cognitive system $S$ is the instantiation of a metamodel for SCTS, such that the correspondence between the view of $S$ in $W$ matches the view of $S$ in $\mathcal{I}$.*

Note that this "matching" entails that the integrity requirements of the three relationships are in fact correctly achieved. In particular (i) the *counts-as* relationship is correctly established by participants having the proper entitlements and an appropriate bijection between terms in $\mathcal{I}$ and objects and potential actions in $W$, (ii) the model is faithfully implemented in $\mathcal{T}$ and (iii) the input/output flow between $\mathcal{T}$ and $W$ is not corrupted. Note also that while we have kept the discussion in $\mathcal{I}$, in the next section we connect $\mathcal{I}$ with $\mathcal{T}$ by clarifying the relationship between the ideal model of an SCTS and the actual implementation of that SCTS that is underneath the achievement of (ii).

## 5    Metamodels and Platforms

In our characterization of metamodel (Notion 3) we did not commit to implementation and formalisation although both are desirable properties. As far as

---

[4] We adapt to SCTS the standard use of *model* as an abstract representation of a real entity and *metamodel* as the abstract representation of models. See for example this use in UML: "...[an abstract syntax that defines] modelling concepts, their attributes and their relationships, as well as the rules for combining these concepts to construct partial or complete ... models." (superstructure version 2.2 (2009-02-03), p1).

implementation is concerned, it would be rather convenient to have a cohesive collection of technological artefacts (a platform) that includes a specification language to make a precise definition of the model. Then, other artefacts of the platform would produce a run-time implementation of the model that controls inputs and outputs that preserve the validity conditions of the shared context, as postulated in Sect. 3. Thus, the "implement" relationship depicted in Fig. 1 may be elucidated by the diagram in Fig. 3a.

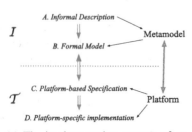

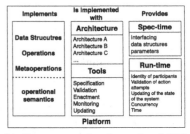

(a) The implementation process of an SCTS.

(b) Contents and functions of an SCTS platform.

**Fig. 3.** Metamodel and platform

In a top-down reading of the diagram, one starts with an informal understanding of the system (A) that will be implemented (D). Ideally, one would expect to have a formal model (B), which corresponds to the exact version of the SCTS that one would like to have in $\mathcal{I}$ so that the effects of the actions on $\mathcal{W}$ have the exact effect $\mathcal{W}$ prescribed in $\mathcal{I}$. However, the transition from an informal representation of an SCTS to a formal model is far from straightforward [16]. One way out is to rely on the metamodel to connect (A) and (B) since, ideally, it provides the abstract constructs to describe (A) in precise terms. The metamodel also provides a bridge between (B) and (D) when it is linked to a *platform* that includes a specification language such that the metamodel instantiations specified with it (C) generate faithful implementations of the formal models (B).[5]

A bottom-up reading of the diagram suggests a symmetric path where one starts with an existing platform and intends to determine formal and computational properties of the models that can be implemented with it (such would be the case of SCTS constructed using, for example the *Amazon Turk* or mash-ups of *Facebook* and *Ushahidi*).

---

[5] This point is aptly made in Jones et al. [16] (Step 1, Step 2. Phase 1, and Step 3) where they argue for a rigorous analysis of the expressiveness of the formalisms and their operationalisation, in order to arrive to a proper specification (C). We acknowledge that those same issues — as well as the computational considerations of their Step 2, Phase2 — are all present in the "top-down" design and the choice of the metamodel.

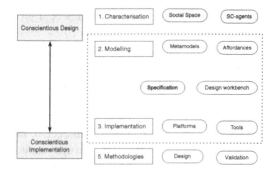

**Fig. 4.** Main research blocks on SCTS

There are some metamodels for social coordination motivated by work on open multiagent systems. The following have been in development for a number of years and have a cohesive collection of technological artefacts that support them and have been used to design or implement SCTS of reasonable complexity: ANTE [6], EI/EIDE [11], InstAL [10], MOISE/JaCaMo [17] OCeaN [13], OperA/ OperettA [2] and THOMAS/ROMAS [14]. It is outside the scope of this paper to make a systematic analysis of these but an illustrative comparison of ANTE, OCeaN and EI/EIDE is available in [12].

# 6   A Call to Arms

This paper looks at artificial socio-cognitive technical systems from a broad and superficial perspective, as an attempt to open a path into a new field. Although it is too early to draft something as precise as a research programme, Fig. 4 maps a rough itinerary suggested by the previous discussion.

## 6.1   Technical Challenges

*Validity as an affordance.* When we introduced the notion of *affordance* (Notion 2), we stated that *validity* is an essential affordance of the social space, in addition to awareness and coordination; an assertion based on the preceding discussion of shared context. In the discussion of the notion of *model* (Notion 4), we stated that a model is *valid* if it preserves the "counts-as" relationship (and by transitivity of the tripartite diagram, its implementation is supposed to uphold that validity in the real world). In other words we wish to sustain the implicit claim that validity is a *supervened affordance* of the social space. A claim that should first be made precise and then made operational. Informally, the argument is as follows: from a top-down perspective, one would need to prove that the normative components of the metamodel define models whose validity can be demonstrated; and from a bottom-up perspective, the kernel of the proof is in the bridge between the *platform* and the *metamodel*, since one may take the position that an action in $\mathcal{W}$ is valid in $\mathcal{T}$ (is accepted as an input), and should be valid in $\mathcal{I}$ only if the *metamodel* is a faithful formalisation of the *platform*.

*Affordances and features.* We also side-stepped – in Sect. 4 – two issues that are central to the notion of metamodel:

1. The first is ontological. It is the problem of determining whether a list of features is a good way to support the affordances of SCTS. On one hand, we have incidental indication that all the features we mentioned are present in one way or another in the families of examples we have mentioned along the paper, and some objective indication that most are needed to implement the type of SCTS that the seven frameworks mentioned in Sect. 5, in as much as most of these features are directly accessible (i.e. features may be expressed and implemented with their basic constructs and artefacts), and may otherwise be paraphrased. However, a serious effort on an extensional description of SCTS is needed to avoid the latent *petitio* of this argument.
2. The second is methodological. Whichever way this "completeness" is achieved or demonstrated, the problem of choosing a collection of features and a good form of description and implementation for those features needs to be resolved for the design of a metamodel (and its corresponding platform), and then the actual instantiation has to be decided when modelling a particular SCTS.

*Metamodel specialisation.* The previous remark directs attention at a significant design challenge: how specialised should a metamodel be? There is no obvious reason that we can find that prevents the creation of a single metamodel for all SCTS but neither is there an obvious reason that we can find to claim that developing such an archetype would be advantageous.

Experience with the seven metamodels listed in Sect. 5 confirm the procrustean curse of formalisms and implementations: every time one models an SCTS with one of those frameworks, the SCTS is "tortured" into the particular features afforded directly by the framework. We presently lack a systematic comparison of frameworks that assesses their advantages and limitations and provides sound guidelines for choosing one or another, or to approach the question of whether a unifying framework would be that ultimate metamodel.

On the other hand, the same reservations about the procrustean curse would suggest the possibility of moving in the opposite direction. That is, develop metamodels (and platforms) that are well-adapted to particular types of SCTS: a metamodel for games, another one for participatory social simulations, yet another one for crowd-based SCTS, and so on. The question then is, where should the specialisation stop? A metamodel for games or a metamodel for first-person shooter games and one for MMORGs and one for serious games? Again, we lack enough empirical analysis of families of SCTS and a robust understanding of affordances, features and metamodels to venture even a tentative answer, but these are open questions that, we believe, may be fruitfully explored.

*Metamodel/platform interplay.* In Sect. 5 we pointed out the *Whorfian* [24] relationship between the conceptual framework that supports the formulation of a model of an SCTS and the artefacts that are used to implement it (i.e., the expressiveness of the conceptual metamodels and the facilities provided by platforms that serve to implement particular SCTS). In some families of SCTS, there is a predominance of the platform over the metamodel fostered by the wealth of cases for which an existing platform is a good match (for example the *Amazon Turk*[6] or MMORG engines, like *RedDwarf server*), or fostered by the versatility of the basic functionalities of a platform (e.g. *Facebook* used as the input for crowd-sourcing the draft of the Moroccan Constitution). On the other hand the experience with current metamodels is that the platform that supports them is not necessarily an integral implementation. Although in many cases the actual features of the metamodels are immediately expressible in the platform, many times they can be achieved only through paraphrases.

The trade-off is not always clear and we believe that it is worth exploring ways to find a balance of platform and metamodel expressiveness by examining the problem from both sides. One possibility (mentioned above) may be to develop a more "generic" metamodel that addresses all properties with a variety of formalisms that may be assembled or instantiated in order to model specific SCTS. Figure 5 is a toy candidate for the type of generic metamodel that involves all the properties we listed in Sect. 4. Another approach to the interplay of metamodel and platform is to construct a sound conceptual model for mashing-up available artefacts and platforms in order to provide proper foundations to those components and, by extension, to the resulting mash-up.

*The dynamics of actual SCTS.* In this paper we have discussed SCTS as if they were static objects that exist in an abstract reality that is limited to those events, facts and actions that are directly relevant to the state of that SCTS. This simplification is wholly inappropriate when observing and designing actual SCTS. In that situation, a framework for SCTS needs to address two significant aspects: First, the social context where the SCTS is designed and operates, and second, how to account for the changes that a given SCTS may undergo beyond the evolution that has been programmed into it at design-time. A first discussion of these issues can be found in [9] but, evidently, these are no minor challenges.

*Separation of concerns.* We hold the assumption (***A.1***) that agents and social space are different components of an SCTS. This separation is useful for a conceptual analysis of SCTS, but it may also be valuable from a design point of view. An illustration of this value is the advantages of designing non-player characters (NPC), or in general BDI agents [5] within a norm-regulated environment. Likewise, the separation of design and implementation — achieved by having a metamodel and platform — gives designers the possibility of choosing the tools that implement their ideas, rather than choosing the problems that are implementable by the tools. The degree and tooling of those types of separation deserve, we believe, a systematic analysis.

*Reinventing the wheel.* Because of the intrinsic interdisciplinary character of social coordination in SCTS, there is a natural propensity to approach the subject from a particular perspective — ours being software development and regulated MAS — without paying due attention to the questions, principles, theories

---

[6] https://www.mturk.com.

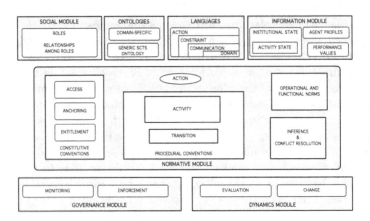

**Fig. 5.** A "generic" metamodel for SCTS. Each feature contains several formalisms and their supporting artefacts that are tailored to the peculiarities of a given SCTS

and artefacts that have been and are being developed in the theoretical fields of the inter-discipline. As Jones et. al. propose in [16], a serious use of the pertinent developments of other converging disciplines is not only useful but essential, if one intends to develop a principled approach to the description and design of SCTS.

*Towards a conscientious design of SCTS.* This meandering of SCTS is motivated by the inevitability of socio-cognitive systems and therefore the need to become aware of the social significance of these systems and the responsibility that scientists and engineers have in the design and deployment of artificial socio-cognitive technical systems. The challenge is to develop precise notions and the associated methodological guidelines and tools to design systems in a conscientious way. This entails, first a clear understanding the inherent values, how to operationalise them and then how to assess that they are properly reflected in the design and the deployed system. A tentative blueprint of the inherent issues may address three dimensions:

1. *Thoroughness.* This is achieved when the system is technically correct, requirements have been properly identified and faithfully implemented. This entails the use of appropriate formalisms, accurate modelling and proper use of tools.
2. *Mindfulness.* This describes supra-functional features that provide the users with awareness of the characteristics of the system and the possibility of selecting a satisfactory tailoring to individual needs or preferences. Thus, features that should be accounted for should include ergonomics, governance, coherence of purpose and means, identification of side-effects, no hidden agency, and the avoidance of unnecessary affordances.
3. *Responsibility.* This is true both towards users and to society in general. It requires a proper empowerment of the principals to honour commitments

and responsiveness to stakeholders legitimate interests. Hence, features like its scrutability, transparency and accountability alongside a proper support of privacy, a "right to forget"; proper handling of identity and ownership, attention to liabilities and proper risk allocation, and support of values like justice, fairness and trustworthiness.

## 6.2    A Wider View

The motivation behind this work is the realisation that the MAS community and the COIN community in particular is well-positioned to address the challenges that SCTS brings and harness the possibilities of developing a principled methodology for the study and development of SCTS. The space for innovation is still to be plotted but it is undoubtedly vast and some milestones are already visible.

*Empirical study of SCTS.* This task should be approached for two kinds of reasons. One is to provide an objective basis for theoretical and technological developments, and (as argued in [9]) formulate a characterization of SCTS in the spirit of Kenneth Arrow's [4] or Alchourron, Gardenfors and Makinson [1]. The other is to understand — from economic, sociological, political and anthropological perspectives — how value is created through SCTS and how that value can be acquired for the benefit of society. This task is, evidently, a rather obvious challenge for interdisciplinary research.

*Technological developments.* Little needs to be argued about the social significance of platforms that are already available for developing SCTS and how some of their original or intended applications have become massive social phenomena and considerable economic successes. This is not likely to cease in the near future and consequently there is a substantial opportunity for innovation in tools, methodologies and applications. Specially if the emphasis on "principled" design is taken to heart.

*Synergies.* A systematic study of SCTS will most likely require the convergence of several disciplines. The topic of social coordination is currently being inspected (within the SINTELNET project) from different standpoints: games, social simulation, analytical sociology, cognitive and social psychology, formalisms for informal phenomena, crowd-based applications, institutional theory and philosophy of law. These activities are already fostering collaborations with a strong synergistic component. This experience points in the direction of new academic communities that are likely to spawn conferences and periodic publications and eventually develop curricula and training.

*An emerging scientific field.* We share the view of Castelfranchi [8], that we are on the threshold of a new society where SCTS will be a pervasive reality. It is one that we do not fully understand and one of which we are becoming citizens through our use of SCTS. It is perhaps not an exaggeration to claim that it may be worth developing a scientific view of this reality and consequently develop the conceptual and theoretical constructs to explain what is happening and to have a crisper view of what comes next. Maybe, in a way not all that dissimilar to the *zeitgeist* of the early fifties that gave birth to artificial intelligence — with its "mind as processor" model for individual rationality, we are witnessing a new *zeitgeist* that may give birth to a new *artificial social intelligence* — with "social coordination" as the core of socio-cognitive rationality.

**Acknowledgements.** The authors wish to acknowledge the support of SINTELNET (FET Open Coordinated Action FP7-ICT-2009-C Project No. 286370) in the writing of this paper. In addition, d'Inverno acknowledges the support of the FP7 Technology Enhanced Learning Program Project: Practice and Performance Analysis Inspiring Social Education (PRAISE).

# References

1. Alchourron, C., GLrdenfors, P., Makinson, D.: On the logic of theory change: partial meet contraction and revision functions. J. Symbolic Logic **50**, 510–530 (1985)
2. Aldewereld, H., Dignum, V.: OperettA: organization-oriented development environment. In: Dastani, M., El Fallah Seghrouchni, A., Hübner, J., Leite, J. (eds.) LADS 2010. LNCS, vol. 6822, pp. 1–18. Springer, Heidelberg (2011)
3. Andrighetto, G., Governatori, G., Noriega, P., van der Torre, L.W.N. (eds.): Normative Multi-Agent Systems. Dagstuhl Follow-Ups, vol. 4. Schloss Dagstuhl - Leibniz-Zentrum fuer Informatik, Wadern (2013)
4. Arrow, K.J.: Social Choice and Individual Values, vol. 12. Yale University Press, New Haven (2012)
5. Balke, T., De Vos, M., Padget, J.: Normative run-time reasoning for institutionally-situated bdi agents. In: Cranefield, S., van Riemsdijk, M.B., Vázquez-Salceda, J., Noriega, P. (eds.) COIN 2011. LNCS, vol. 7254, pp. 129–148. Springer, Heidelberg (2012)
6. Cardoso, H.L., Urbano, J., Brandão, P., Rocha, A.P., Oliveira, E.: ANTE: agreement negotiation in normative and trust-enabled environments. In: Demazeau, Y., Müller, J.P., Rodríguez, J.M.C., Pérez, J.B. (eds.) Advances on PAAMS. AISC, vol. 155, pp. 261–264. Springer, Heidelberg (2012)
7. Castelfranchi, C.: InMind and OutMind; Societal Order Cognition and Self-Organization: The role of MAS. Invited talk for the IFAAMAS "Influential Paper Award". AAMAS 2013. Saint Paul, Minn, US, May 2013. http://www.slideshare.net/sleeplessgreenideas/castelfranchi-aamas13-v2?ref=http
8. Castelfranchi, C.: Making visible "the invisible hand" the mission of social simulation. In: Adamatti, D.F., Dimuro, G.P., Coelho, H. (eds.) Interdisciplinary Applications of Agent-Based Social Simulation and Modeling, pp. 1–314. IGI Global, Hershey (2014)
9. Christiaanse, R., Ghose, A., Noriega, P., Singh, M.P.: Characterizing artificial socio-cognitive technical systems. In: Herzig, A., Lorini, E. (eds.) Proceedings of the European Conference on Social Intelligence (ECSI-2014), Barcelona, Spain, November 3–5, 2014. CEUR Workshop Proceedings, vol. 1283, pp. 336–346. CEUR-WS.org (2014)

10. Cliffe, O., De Vos, M., Padget, J.: Answer set programming for representing and reasoning about virtual institutions. In: Inoue, K., Satoh, K., Toni, F. (eds.) CLIMA 2006. LNCS (LNAI), vol. 4371, pp. 60–79. Springer, Heidelberg (2007)
11. d'Inverno, M., Luck, M., Noriega, P., Rodriguez-Aguilar, J.A., Sierra, C.: Communicating open systems. Artif. Intell. **186**, 38–94 (2012)
12. Fornara, N., Cardoso, H.L., Noriega, P., Oliveira, E., Tampitsikas, C., Schumache, M.I.: Modelling agent institutions. In: Ossowski, S. (ed.) Agreement Technologies. Law, Governance and Technology Series, vol. 8, pp. 277–307. Springer, Dordrecht (2013)
13. Fornara, N., Vigan, F., Verdicchio, M., Colombetti, M.: Artificial institutions: a model of institutional reality for open multiagent systems. Artif. Intell. Law **16**(1), 89–105 (2008)
14. Garcia, E.: Engineering Regulated Open Multiagent Systems. AI Communications (in press)
15. Jones, A.I.J., Sergot, M.: A formal characterization of institutionalized power. Logic J. IGPL **4**(3), 427–446 (1996)
16. Jones, A.I.J., Artikis, A., Pitt, J.: The design of intelligent socio-technical systems. Artif. Intell. Rev. **39**(1), 5–20 (2013)
17. Kitio, R., Boissier, O., Hübner, J.F., Ricci, A.: Organisational artifacts and agents for open multi-agent organisations: "giving the power back to the agents". In: Sichman, J.S., Padget, J., Ossowski, S., Noriega, P. (eds.) COIN 2007. LNCS (LNAI), vol. 4870, pp. 171–186. Springer, Heidelberg (2008)
18. Nikolic, I., Ghorbani, A.: A method for developing agent-based models of socio-technical systems. In: 2011 IEEE International Conference on Networking, Sensing and Control (ICNSC), pp. 44–49. IEEE (2011)
19. Noriega, P., Chopra, A.K., Fornara, N., Cardoso, H.L., Singh, M.P.: Regulated MAS: social perspective. In: Andrighetto, G., Governatori, G., Noriega, P., van der Torre, L.W.N. (eds.) Normative Multi-Agent Systems. Dagstuhl Follow-Ups, vol. 4, pp. 93–133. Schloss Dagstuhl-Leibniz-Zentrum fuer Informatik, Dagstuhl (2013)
20. Norman, D.A.: Affordance, conventions, and design. Interactions **6**(3), 38–43 (1999)
21. Searle, J.R.: What is an institution? J. Inst. Econ. **1**(01), 1–22 (2005)
22. Singh, M.P.: Norms as a basis for governing sociotechnical systems. ACM Trans. Intell. Syst. Technol. (TIST), 1–21 (2013, in press)
23. Trist, E.: The Evolution of Socio-technical Systems. Occasional Paper, vol. 2. Ontario Ministry of Labour, Ontario (1981)
24. Whorf, B.L.: The relation of habitual thought and behavior to language. In: Carroll, J.B. (ed.) Language, Thought, and Reality: Selected Writings of Benjamin Lee Whorf, pp. 134–159. MIT Press (1956). ISBN 0-262-73006-5

# Comparing and Evaluating Organizational Models: A Multi-agent Programming Contest Case Study

Mariana Ramos Franco[✉] and Jaime Simão Sichman

Laboratório de Técnicas Inteligentes (LTI),
Escola Politécnica (EP), Universidade de São Paulo (USP), São Paulo, Brazil
mafranko@usp.br, jaime.sichman@poli.usp.br

**Abstract.** An important subset of multi-agent systems (MAS) are based on *organizational models*. These models try to define pre-defined intended agent interaction patterns. Given an application domain, however, the choice of a particular organizational model that better solves the problem is still an open problem. In order to guide this choice, a MAS developer must have the opportunity to test distinct organizational models easily. In this work, we compare and evaluate different organization models of a MAS, whose goal is to evolve in the "Agents on Mars" scenario proposed in the Multi-Agent Programming Contest (MAPC).

## 1 Introduction

Recently, there have been a movement towards the explicit design and use of organizations in multi-agent systems (MAS). An organization helps to better model the problem being tackled, and it helps to increase the system's efficiency, by defining the MAS structure and the rules which the agents must follow to achieve individual and system level goals. However, in many cases it is difficult to define the organizational model that best solves the problem.

Trying to contribute to this issue, we present in this paper an experimental analysis of the overall result of different organization-oriented MAS, which were created for the "Multi-Agent Programming Contest" scenario.

## 2 Background

### 2.1 Agent Organizational Models

Organization is a complex notion: there are several views, definitions, and approaches to characterize them, addressing different issues: it is a supra-individual phenomena [1], it is defined by the designer or by the actors involved [2], and it is a pattern of predefined [3] or emergent [4] cooperation.

We will adopt here the following definition [5]:

© Springer International Publishing Switzerland 2015
A. Ghose et al. (Eds.): COIN 2014, LNAI 9372, pp. 182–196, 2015.
DOI: 10.1007/978-3-319-25420-3_12

*"An organization is a supra-agent pattern of emergent cooperation or prede-
fined cooperation of the agents in the system, that could be defined by the designer
or by the agents themselves, in order to achieve a purpose."*

One important issue is the relation between organizational constraints and
agents' autonomy, as studied by Castelfranchi [6]. When seen as a predefined
cooperation pattern, an organization aims to constrain the agents' autonomy. In
fact, this limitation aims to guarantee that the global goals are achieved in an
optimized way. If agents strictly follow their organizational constraints, they will
know what to do, when and with whom to interact in crucial problem solving
situations.

Given that an organization constrains the agents' autonomy, a further step
is to investigate how this limitation can be properly engineered and designed.
Coutinho et al. [7] propose some modeling dimensions for organizational design:
*(i)* the *structural dimension*, mainly composed of notions like roles and groups,
as used in the AGR model [8]; *(ii)* the *interactive dimension*, characterized by
dialogical interaction structures, as used in the Electronic Institutions model [9];
*(iii)* the *functional dimension*, formed by goal/task decomposition structures, as
proposed by the TAEMS model [10]; and *(iv)* the *normative dimension*, in which
we find the concepts of norms, rights, rules, like used in the OPERA model [11].

However, the organizational design problem has not been solved so far by
researchers in business and management domains. This problem can be stated
as: how to find an optimal constraint set that could guarantee global efficiency
for a given task scenario? The same problem arises concerning multi-agent organizations [12].

In this paper, we present a comparison and evaluation of different organization models, that were applied to "Agents on Mars" scenario, described next.

## 2.2  MAPC

The "Multi-Agent Programming Contest"[1] (MAPC) is held every year since
2005, and it is an attempt to stimulate research in MAS programming techniques [13]. In the contest, two teams of agents are located in the same environment and compete directly in a scenario set by the organizers. By being a
direct competition, it is an interesting testbed to evaluate and compare different
systems, allowing to identify strengths and weaknesses, and thus promoting the
development of all participants.

Since 2011, a scenario called *"Agents on Mars"* has been used. In this scenario, two teams of 28 agents compete to explore and dominate the best top
wells of the planet. The environment is represented by a weighted graph, where
the vertices denote wells and possible locations for the agents, and the edges
indicate the possibility of crossing from one vertex to another with an energy
cost for the agent. Each vertex has a value corresponding to its water well use-
fulness, and this value is used to calculate the value of the areas occupied by the
agents.

---

[1] http://multiagentcontest.org.

A zone is a subgraph covered by a team according to a coloring algorithm based on the notion of domain [14]. Several agents from different teams can be located in a single vertex, but the team with the highest number of agents dominates this vertex, which receives the dominant team color. An uncolored vertex inherits the color from its neighbourhood dominant team. Hence, if the graph contains a subgraph with a colored border, all the nodes that are within this boundary receive the same color. This means that an agent team may cover a subgraph which has more vertices than the number of its members. Figure 1 shows a map with the colored subgraphs.

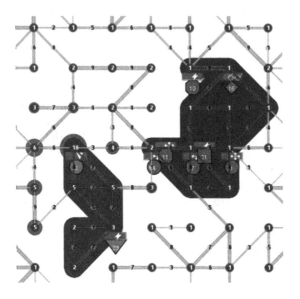

**Fig. 1.** *"Agents on Mars"* scenario.

At the beginning of the simulation, the map is unknown to the agents. Thus, each team needs to explore the graph before starting to conquer areas, since the agents have a limited view of the map and only perceive their neighbour vertices. Additionaly, sometimes a team needs to sabotage the other team to increase its area, or to defend areas in order not to lose them to the opponent.

Each team consists of 28 players, that can play 5 different roles: explorers (Exp), sentinels (Sen), saboteurs (Sab), inspectors (Ins) and repairers (Rep). These roles define the characteristics of each agent, such as life level, maximum energy, strength, and visibility. The roles also limit the possible actions that the agent can perform in the environment, as shown in Table 1. For instance, explorers can find water wells and help to explore the map, while sentinels have long distance sensors and thus can observe larger areas, saboteurs can attack and disable enemies, inspectors can spy opponents, and repairers can repair damaged agents.

**Table 1.** "Agents on Mars" roles and actions.

|  | Explorer | Repairer | Saboteur | Sentinel | Inspector |
|---|---|---|---|---|---|
| Recharge | x | x | x | x | x |
| Attack |  |  | x |  |  |
| Parry |  | x | x | x |  |
| Goto | x | x | x | x | x |
| Probe[a] | x |  |  |  |  |
| Survey[b] | x | x | x | x | x |
| Inspect[c] |  |  |  |  | x |
| Buy | x | x | x | x | x |
| Repair |  | x |  |  |  |
| Skip | x | x | x | x | x |

[a] A priori, the agents have no knowledge about the value of water wells. A team only gets the full value of a vertex after one agent in the team has analyzed the water well.
[b] Initially, the agents do not know the cost of crossing from one vertex to another. An agent needs to survey it to find the value of each edge.
[c] This action collects information about the opponents present in neighboring vertices, such as energy and role.

A team receives a cash reward whenever it reaches a major milestone. This reward can be used to empower the agents, increasing, for instance, their maximum energy or strength. Different milestones can be reached during a competition, such as dominating areas with fixed values (e.g., 10 or 20), having performed a successful number of attacks or successful defenses. If not used, the reward is added to the team's total score.

The goal of each team is to maximize its score, defined as the sum of the values obtained by the occupied zones with the earned (and not yet spent) rewards in each step of the simulation, as shown in Eq. 1:

$$score = \sum_{p=1}^{steps} (zones_p + rewards_p) \qquad (1)$$

We present next a proposal of an agent team, called LTI-USP, based on different organizational models, to solve this problem.

## 3   LTI-USP Agent Team

### 3.1   Architecture

The architecture of the LTI-USP team is shown in Fig. 2. In this architecture, we used BDI agents. Each agent is composed of plans, a belief base and its own

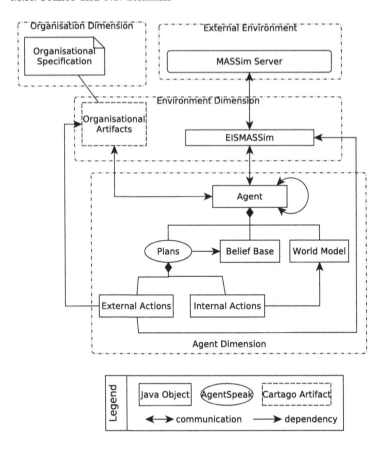

**Fig. 2.** LTI-USP team architecture.

world model. The agent decides which plan will be executed according to its beliefs and the local view of the world.

The world model consists a graph developed in *Java*, using simple data structures and classes. It captures every detail received from the MASSim contest server, such as explored vertices and edges, opponents' position, disabled teammates, etc. At each step, the agent's world model is updated with the percepts received from the MASSim server, and with the information received from the other agents.

Some of the percepts received from the MASSim server are also stored in the agent's belief base, such as the agent's role, energy, position and team's rewards, thus allowing the agent to have a direct access to these information without having to access its world model. Percepts about vertices, edges and other agents were not stored in the belief base so as to not compromise the agent's performance, as it could be very expensive to update and to access the belief base with so much information. Moreover, since we wanted to update a belief whenever a new instance was inserted (instead of adding a second one), we decided to use an indexed belief base in which some beliefs are unique and indexed for faster access.

Our team was developed using $JaCaMo^2$. $JaCaMo$ [15] is a platform for multi-agent programming which supports all levels of abstractions – agent, environment, and organization – that are required for developing sophisticated MAS, by combining three separate technologies: $Jason^3$ [16], for programming autonomous agents; $CArtAgO^4$ [17], for programming environment artifacts; and $Moise^5$ [18], for programming multi-agent organizations.

$Jason$ is a Java-based interpreter for an extended version of the AgentSpeak programming language, suitable for programming BDI agents.

$CArtAgO$ is a framework for environment programming based on the A & A meta-model [19]. In $CArtAgO$, the environment can be designed as a dynamic set of computational entities called artifacts, organized into workspaces, possibly distributed among various nodes of a network [15]. Each artifact represents a resource or a tool that agents can instantiate, share, use, and perceive at runtime. For this project, we did not create any new artifact; we only made use of the organizational artifacts provided in $Moise$.

$Moise$ [18,20] is an organizational model for MAS based on three comple-mentary dimensions: *structural*, *functional* and *normative*. The model enables a MAS designer to explicitly specify its organizational constraints, and it can be also used by the agents to reason about their organization. We used the $Moise$ model to define the agent's roles, groups and missions.

Agents communicate with the MASSim server through the EISMASSim environment-interface included in the contest software-package. EISMASSim is based on $EIS^6$ [21], which is a proposed standard for agent-environment inter-action. It automatically establishes and maintains authenticated connections to the server and abstracts the communication between the MASSim server and the agents to simple Java-method-calls and call-backs. In order to use this interface, we extended the $JaCaMo$ default agent architecture to perceive and to act not only on the $CArtAgO$ artifacts, but also on the EIS environment as well.

## 3.2    Strategies

The main strategy of our team is to divide the agents into two or more subgroups: one in charge of attacking the opponents (infantry), and the others (squads) in charge of occupying the best zones in the graph. Moreover, regarding the agents' roles, we decided not to map the five types specified in the scenario (Exp, Ins, Rep, Sab and Sen) directly to the roles in our team. Instead, we defined additional different roles in our system according to the adopted strategy, as shown in Fig. 3.

---

[2] Available at http://jacamo.sourceforge.net/.
[3] Available at http://jason.sourceforge.net/.
[4] Available at http://cartago.sourceforge.net/.
[5] Available at http://moise.sourceforge.net/.
[6] Available at http://sourceforge.net/projects/apleis/.

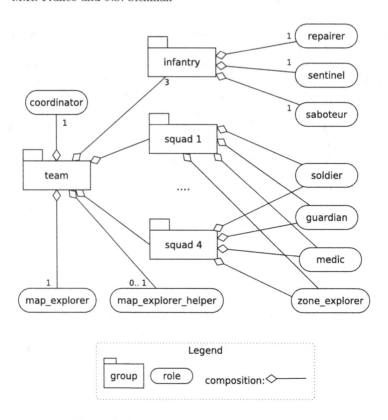

**Fig. 3.** LTI-USP Team *structural specification*.

Each of these roles has a mission associated to it, and can be played by one or more type of agents. For example, the map_explorer role can be played only by the explorer type, while the soldier role can be played by all types of agents. Below we describe the missions related to each role:

– **map_explorer** (Exp): Explores the whole graph by probing every vertex and surveying all edges on its path;
– **map_explorer_helper** (Exp): Helps the map_explorer to explore the graph, but only in the first 250 steps. After that, the agent leaves this role to adopt the soldier role in the best_zone subgroup;
– **soldier** (all types): Tries to occupy one of the best zones indicated by the coordinator agent. When all the vertices of the designated best zone are occupied the soldier starts to look to the neighbour vertices of the team's zone to which he can move to increase the zone size;
– **guardian** (Sab): Defends the subgroup best zone by attacking any opponent that is close to the team's zone, or trying to invade it;
– **medic** (Rep): Occupies the center of the designated best zone and is responsible for repairing the agents in the subgroup, or other agents which eventually

need to be repaired, such as the `map_explorer`. In our team, the damaged agents move to the repairers position in order to be repaired;

- **zone_explorer** (Exp): Explores the team's zone by probing the vertices whose values are unknown. When all vertices are probed, the `zone_explorer` helps the `soldiers` to increase the zone size;
- **saboteur** (Sab): Attacks any close opponent, or the opponent who occupies a good vertex;
- **sentinel** (Sen): Tries to sabotage the opponent by moving inside its zone;
- **repairer** (Rep): Follows the `saboteur`, but always staying two vertices away from it, in order to be prepared to repair the `saboteur` when necessary, but without taking too much risk;
- **coordinator** (none): Agent internal to our system which does not communicate with the MASSim server. It builds its local view of the world through the percepts broadcasted by the other agents. Whenever the world model is updated, it computes which are the best zones in the graph and send this information to the other agents. The `coordinator` is also responsible for creating the organizational artifacts, in the beginning of the simulation, and for distributing the groups, roles and missions among the other agents, in order to eliminate the performance issues caused by two or more agents trying to adopt the same role in a group, or trying to commit to the same mission.

The best zone in the map is obtained by calculating for each vertex the sum of its value with the value of all its direct and second degree neighbours. The vertex with the greatest sum of values is the center of the best zone. Zones with the sum of values below 10 are not considered in the calculation[7]. The same computation is performed again to determine if there is a second, third and fourth best zone, and so on, but this time removing the vertices belonging to the first best zone from the analysis. If the number of best zones is smaller than the number of **squads**, the first best zone is designated to the subgroups without specific best zone.

## 4 Experiments and Results

### 4.1 Experiments

In the MAPC, each team plays against each other team three times, and the team that wins most matches wins the overall tournament. Each match has 750 steps and the map is randomly generated, thus from one match to another the number of vertices, edges and high-valued areas can change.

The fact that the number of high-valued areas may change leads in some cases to situations where to protect a single best area is a better strategy, while in other cases it would be better to divide the team in smaller groups to try to gain control over several areas. Therefore, we have performed some experiments

---

[7] This threshold value was obtained empirically, by analyzing the results of previous editions of the contest.

**Table 2.** LTI-USP team configurations.

| Team | Squad | Soldiers | Guardians | Medics | Zone_explorers | Agents |
|------|-------|----------|-----------|--------|----------------|--------|
| TG1 | 1 | 20 | 1 | 1 | 1 | 23 |
| TG2 | 1 | 10 | 1 | 1 | 1 | 13 |
|     | 2 | 7 | 1 | 1 | 1 | 10 |
| TG3 | 1 | 5 | 1 | 1 | 1 | 8 |
|     | 2 | 5 | 1 | 1 | 1 | 8 |
|     | 3 | 4 | 1 | 1 | 1 | 7 |
| TG4 | 1 | 3 | 1 | 1 | 1 | 6 |
|     | 2 | 3 | 1 | 1 | 1 | 6 |
|     | 3 | 3 | 1 | 1 | 1 | 6 |
|     | 4 | 3 | 0 | 1 | 1 | 5 |

**Table 3.** Scenarios properties.

|     | Vertex | Edges (thinning factor) | Possible zones |
|-----|--------|--------------------------|----------------|
| SC1 | 400 | 1110 (20 %) | 9 |
| SC2 | 500 | 1345 (40 %) | 6 |
| SC3 | 600 | 1234 (10 %) | 6 |

to analyse how the number of squads in our team can impact in its overall performance.

The experiments consisted of four teams (TG1, TG2, TG3 and TG4), all of them with the structure shown in Fig. 3, except with respect to the number of squads as shown in Table 2. These teams competed in three different scenarios/maps (SC1, SC2 and SC3), described in Table 3. In this table, possible zones means areas in the map with high value vertices, that are hence possible candidates for a best zone. These scenarios are also represented in Fig. 4.

The number of vertices and edges shown in Table 3 were chosen according to the parameters set in the MAPC, in which the maps had from 400 to 600 vertices and the thinning factor, i.e., the number of removed edges from a complete connect graph in percent, varies from 10 % to 60 %.

## 4.2 Results

For each scenario previously described, we performed 10 simulations for each of the following matches: TG1 vs TG2, TG1 vs TG3, and TG1 vs TG4. The data collected in all simulation were: (i) the winner, (ii) the teams' final scores and (iii) the score conquered in each step for each of the two competing teams. Table 4 shows a summary of the number of wins for each team by match and scenario.

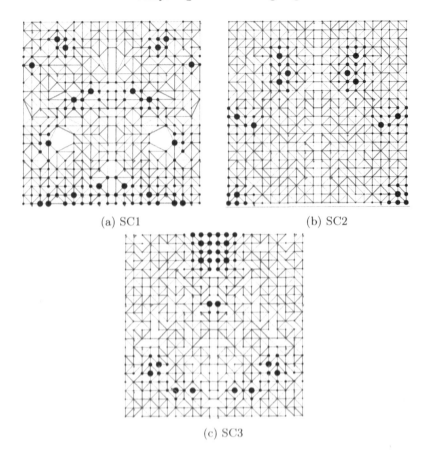

(a) SC1                    (b) SC2

(c) SC3

**Fig. 4.** Experiment scenarios.

Given the results, we used a hypothesis test, the *Wilcoxon T test*, to define for each match if the 10 simulations were sufficient or not to conclude that a team was better than other in a determined scenario. The *Wilcoxon T test* (also called *Wilcoxon signed-rank test*) is a non parametric test for dependent samples that can indicate with some stated confidence level if a particular population tends to have larger values than other.

The results of this analysis are shown in Table 5, where the values correspond to the *p-value* result of the *Wilcoxon T test* applied on the final score of the 10 simulations performed for each match. A *p-value* lower than 0.05 indicates that the results observed in the 10 simulations are enough to conclude that a certain team tends to obtain higher scores than other.

The results obtained for each scenario are analysed in the following subsections.

**Table 4.** Results summary - number of wins.

|      | TG1 × TG2 | TG1 × TG3 | TG1 × TG4 |
|------|-----------|-----------|-----------|
| SC1  | 2 × 8     | 4 × 6     | 1 × 9     |
| SC2  | 0 × 10    | 0 × 10    | 0 × 10    |
| SC3  | 4 × 6     | 1 × 9     | 2 × 8     |

**Table 5.** *Wilcoxon T test*

|      | TG1 x TG2 | TG1 x TG3 | TG1 x TG4 |
|------|-----------|-----------|-----------|
| **SC1** | 0.02881 | 0.5787    | 0.005196  |
| **SC2** | 0.0115  | 0.002879  | 0.0002057 |
| **SC3** | 0.1655  | 0.06301   | 0.02323   |

**Scenario 1.** In the first scenario, the teams with more squads won most of the simulations against TG1 (control team) and, given the *p-values* of the *Wilcoxon T test*, we can conclude that TG2 and TG4 are better than TG1, but for TG3 we can not conclude the same.

Figure 5 shows the final scores of the 10 simulations for the match TG1 vs TG3. Analysing the simulations where TG1 defeats TG3, we were able to identify why we have good results for TG2 against TG1, while this has not occurred when TG3 played against TG1. TG3 divides its agents in three squads to occupy three different zones in the map, while TG1 uses all its agents (apart from those used to attack the opponent and to explore the map) to try to conquer the best zone in the map. In this first scenario, there is a unique huge high valued area in the left bottom of map, which is easily conquered by TG1 since the number of agents from TG3 that will fight for the same zone is not enough to defeat the

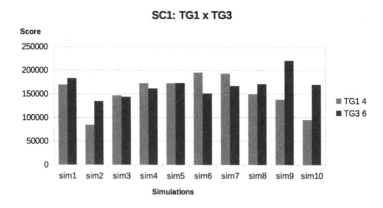

**Fig. 5.** Scenario 1: Final scores for TG1 vs TG3.

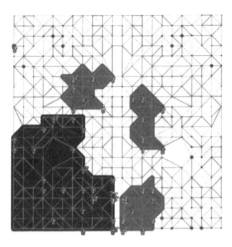

**Fig. 6.** Scenario 1 - TG1 (blue) vs TG3 (green) (Color figure online).

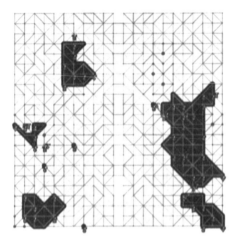

**Fig. 7.** Scenario 2: TG1 (green) vs TG4 (blue) (Color figure online).

opponent (Fig. 6). Besides that, the score summed from the two others TG3's squads was lower than the score obtained by TG1 in the best zone.

**Scenario 2.** In contrast with the first scenario, the second one does not has a huge high valued area, and all possible best zones have almost the same value, which is good for the teams with more squads, as shown in Fig. 7.

**Scenario 3.** The third scenario, as the first one, has an unique huge high valued area which now is located in the top of the map, but in this scenario TG2 did not performed as well as in the first scenario.

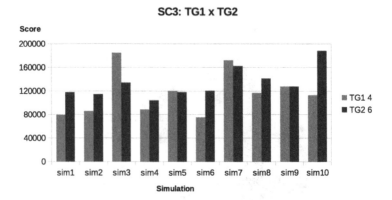

**Fig. 8.** Scenario 3: Final scores for TG1 vs TG2.

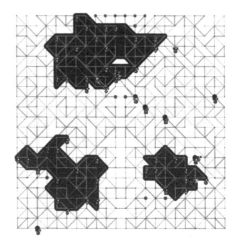

**Fig. 9.** Scenario 3: TG1 (blue) vs TG2 (green) (Color figure online).

Figure 8 shows the results of the 10 simulations for the match TG1 vs TG2, where it is possible to see that TG2 narrowly lost two simulations for TG1.

Comparing the match TG1 vs TG2 in this scenario with the first one, we were able to identify that in this third scenario, TG2 does not find in some simulations the best zone in the map, since the zone is not so spread out as in the first scenario. In these cases, TG1 won when it was able to find the best zone and TG2 not, as depicted in Fig. 9.

## 5    Conclusions

The problem of determining an appropriate or best MAS organization for a given scenario is a key problem in MAS research, and empirical approaches can be very useful in this regard. Aiming to contribute in this issue, we presented an evaluation of different organizations over three distinct scenarios of the Multi-Agent Programming Contest case study. To validate our observations, a statistical test, the *Wilcoxon T test*, was used to detect differences in the performance of the organizations.

The results obtained by confronting the four LTI-USP teams, even though they can suggest that TG4 is the best organizational choice, are not conclusive since the number of scenarios used in our evaluation was relatively small, and the scenario can greatly impact the performance of the team as we showed in Sect. 4.2.

Therefore, in future work we intend to increase the number of different tested scenarios, and also evaluate different structures of organizational models, changing not only the number of **squad** but also other parameters, for instance the number of agents in charge of attacking the opponents.

Another possibility is to use the results obtained in this study to develop a team capable of reorganizing according to the characteristics of the environment. As discussed in [22], the reorganization is an important aspect in MAS, since the environment is most often not static. Therefore, MAS should be able to modify your organization to adapt to changes in the environment.

**Acknowledgements.** Jaime Simão Sichman is partially supported by CNPq and FAPESP/Brazil.

# References

1. Gasser, L.: Organizations in multi-agent systems. In: Pre-proceedings of the 10th European Workshop on Modelling Autonomous Agents in a Multi-Agent World. IMAG, Annecy, France (2001)
2. Malone, T.W.: Modeling coordination in organizations and markets. In: Bond, A.H., Gasser, L. (eds.) Readings in Distributed Artificial Intelligence, pp. 151–158. Morgan Kaufmann Publishers Inc, San Mateo (1987)
3. Bernoux, P.: La Sociologie des Organisations. Seuil, Paris (1985)
4. Morin, E.: La Méthode (1): La Nature de la Nature. Seuil, Paris (1977)
5. Boissier, O., Sichman, J.S.: Organization oriented programming. In: Tutorial Notes, 3rd International Joint Conference on Autonomous Agents and Multiagent Systems (AAMAS 2004), New York, USA, August 2004
6. Castelfranchi, C.: Guarantees for autonomy in cognitive agent architecture. In: Wooldridge, M.J., Jennings, N.R. (eds.) Intelligent Agents. LNCS(LNAI), vol. 890, pp. 56–70. Springer, Heidelberg (1995)
7. Coutinho, L.R., Sichman, J.S., Boissier, O.: Modelling dimensions for agent organizations. In: Dignum, V. (ed.) Handbook of Research on Multi-Agent Systems: Semantics and Dynamics of Organizational Models, pp. 18–50. IGI Global, Hershey (2009)
8. Ferber, J., Gutknecht, O.: A meta-model for the analysis and design of organizations in multi-agents systems. In: Demazeau, Y. (ed.) Proceedings of the 3rd International Conference on Multi-Agent Systems, pp. 128–135. IEEE Computer Society Press, Paris, France (1998)

9. Esteva, M., Rodríguez-Aguilar, J.-A., Sierra, C., Garcia, P., Arcos, J.-L.: On the formal specification of electronic institutions. In: Sierra, C., Dignum, F.P.M. (eds.) AgentLink 2000. LNCS (LNAI), vol. 1991, pp. 126–147. Springer, Heidelberg (2001)

10. Decker, K.S.: TÆMS: a framework for environment centered analysis and design of coordination mechanisms. In: O'Hare, G.M.P., Jennings, N. (eds.) Foundations of Distributed Artificial Intelligence, pp. 429–447. Wiley, Baffins Lane (1996)

11. Dignum, V.: A model for organizational interaction: based on agents, founded in logic. Ph.D. thesis, University of Utrecht, Utrecht, The Netherlands (2004)

12. Horling, B., Lesser, V.R.: A survey of multi-agent organizational paradigms. Knowl. Eng. Rev. **19**(4), 281–316 (2004)

13. Behrens, T., Köster, M., Schlesinger, F., Dix, J., Hübner, J.F.: The multi-agent programming contest 2011: a Résumé. In: Dennis, L., Boissier, O., Bordini, R.H. (eds.) ProMAS 2011. LNCS, vol. 7217, pp. 155–172. Springer, Heidelberg (2012)

14. Behrens, T., Köster, M., Schlesinger, F.: The multi-agent programming contest 2011: a Résumé. Program. Multi-Agent Syst. **2012**, 155–172 (2011)

15. Boissier, O., Bordini, R.H., Hübner, J.F., Ricci, A., Santi, A.: Multi-agent oriented programming with JaCaMo. Sci. Comput. Program. (2011)

16. Bordini, R., Hübner, J., Wooldridge, M.: Programming multi-agent systems in AgentSpeak using Jason. Wiley-Blackwell, Chichester (2007)

17. Ricci, A., Piunti, M., Viroli, M.: Environment programming in multi-agent systems: an artifact-based perspective. Auton. Agent. Multi-Agent Syst. **23**(2), 158–192 (2010)

18. Hübner, J.F., Boissier, O., Kitio, R., Ricci, A.: Instrumenting multi-agent organisations with organisational artifacts and agents. Auton. Agent. Multi-Agent Syst. **20**(3), 369–400 (2009)

19. Omicini, A., Ricci, A., Viroli, M.: Artifacts in the a & a meta-model for multi-agent systems. Auton. Agent. Multi-Agent Syst. **17**(3), 432–456 (2008)

20. Hübner, J., Sichman, J., Boissier, O.: Developing organised multiagent systems using the MOISE+ model: programming issues at the system and agent levels. Int. J. Agent-Orient. Softw. Eng. 1–27 (2007)

21. Behrens, T.M., Dix, J., Hindriks, K.V.: The environment interface standard for agent-oriented programming - platform integration guide and interface implementation guide. Technical report IfI-09-10, Department of Informatics, Clausthal University of Technology (2009)

22. Dignum, V.: Handbook of Research on Multi-agent Systems: Semantics and Dynamics of Organizational Models. Information Science Reference. IGI Global, Hershey (2009)

# Mirror Worlds as Agent Societies Situated in Mixed Reality Environments

Alessandro Ricci[1]([✉]), Luca Tummolini[2], Michele Piunti[3],
Olivier Boissier[4], and Cristiano Castelfranchi[2]

[1] University of Bologna, via Venezia 52, Cesena, Italy
a.ricci@unibo.it
[2] Istituto di Scienze e Tecnologie Della Cognizione - CNR, Rome, Italy
[3] Reply, Rome, Italy
[4] FAYOL- ENS Mines and LHC CNRS:UMR5516, Saint-Étienne, France

**Abstract.** Last years have seen the raise of several contexts such as Ambient Intelligence, Augmented Reality where Artificial Intelligence is combined with other domains such as Ubiquitous Computing, Sensor Network Technologies in order to provide proactive and responsive services to users. However, these systems are most of the times *ad hoc*, lacking a conceptual foundation. In this paper we provide a broad overview of *mirror worlds*, as physically situated agent societies, useful in particular as a framework for investigating inter-disciplinary aspects – from cognition to interaction, cooperation, governance – concerning future smart environments and cities shaped as large-scale mixed-reality systems.

## 1 Introduction

In recent years, the impressive development of hardware technologies related to mobile and embedded computing, Internet and the web is going to make the futuristic scenarios envisioned by Ambient Intelligence (AmI) and Smart Environments [32] an every-day reality, integrating research contributions from Ubiquitous Computing, Sensor Network Technology and Artificial Intelligence (AI). Following the ubiquitous computing vision [35], AmI environments are characterized by the pervasive use of information processing devices thoroughly fused into "the fabric of everyday life until they are indistinguishable from it" [36], and integrated with other key enabling technologies such as sensors and wireless networks. On this fabric, the software layer exploits AI techniques to create environments that are sensitive and responsive to inhabitants' needs and capable of anticipating their needs and behaviors as well. Moreover, Augmented Reality (AR), Mobile AR and mixed reality [12, 21] are going to strongly impact on how we interact with these systems, by exploiting wearable devices such as AR glasses.

In spite of this convergence of technologies and the availability of formidable but *ad hoc* solutions, we lack a conceptual foundation, effective enough to model open, possibly-large scale smart environments and their interaction with aspects related to human cognition, psychology, sociality. We argue that

© Springer International Publishing Switzerland 2015
A. Ghose et al. (Eds.): COIN 2014, LNAI 9372, pp. 197–212, 2015.
DOI: 10.1007/978-3-319-25420-3_13

such foundation is essential to understand things that concern systems where the digital/computational layer is strongly intertwined with the social and physical one—impacting on aspects that concern the organization and governance of such systems.

To this purpose, we introduce the notion of *mirror worlds* (Sect. 2), extending the original idea exposed by Gelernter [17] with concepts and visions based on the research on agents and multi-agent systems. Mirror worlds (MW[1]) bring together research contributions from different fields apart agents and MAS, from Ambient Intelligence and smart environments, Internet-of-Things down to mixed/augmented reality. A MW can be abstractly conceived as a digital world shaped in terms of a multi-agent system, situated into some virtual environment which is *coupled* to some physical environment, *augmenting* its functionalities and the capabilities of the people that live or work inside it [9, 28].

Mirror worlds aim at being an interesting framework in which to investigate the integration of various technologies – for instance, multi-agent systems and mobile augmented reality – but, above all, the definition of open computer-supported cooperative environments where human and software agents interact and cooperate – typically implicitly. Furthermore, MW aim at being *laboratories* in which to explore together inter-disciplinary aspects, ranging from how human/agent action, perception, cognition is enhanced and supported by MW, to how to think about the co-design of physical objects and environments and related digital counterpart, down to the definition of proper models for interaction, coordination, organization, and governance of these agent-based mixed-reality systems. The idea is related to existing works exploring the application of agent technologies to develop mixed-reality systems [18], agent-based intelligent virtual environments [2, 20], context-aware systems [1] as well as embodied organisations [26] and situated electronic institutions [6].

The remainder of the paper is organized as follows: In Sect. 2 we provide a general overview about mirror worlds, and in Sect. 3 we discuss in more detail the main kinds of *augmentation* that the idea promotes. Then, in Sect. 4 we focus on the design and programming of mirror worlds, providing an overview of a first approach based on the A&A conceptual model [23] and a platform based existing agent technologies (i.e. JaCaMo [4]). Finally, in Sect. 5 we discuss a main open issue, which is the definition of organisation and institution models for MW. In Sect. 6 we conclude the paper some final remarks and ideas for future works.

## 2    Mirror Worlds – Overview

In Gelernter's view, Mirror Worlds are software models of some chunk of reality, "some pieces of the real world going on outside your windows", endlessly fed by oceans of information through hardware and software pipes [17]. Using Gelernter's words, they represent a true-to-life mirror image trapped inside a computer, which can be then viewed, zoomed, analyzed by citizens living in the

---

[1] in the remainder of the paper, we will use the acronym MW to refer either the singular (mirror world) or the plural (mirror worlds), depending on the context.

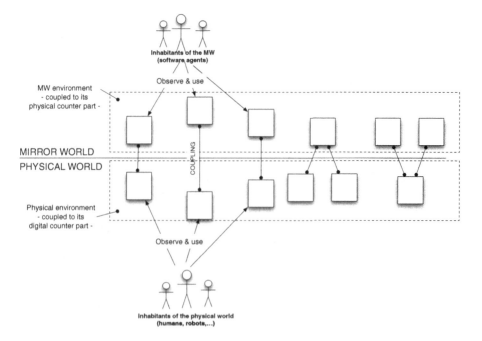

**Fig. 1.** A Vision of mirror worlds as situated agent societies.

real-world with the help of proper *software assistant agents*. They are meant to be like scientific viewing tools – like microscopes, telescopes – focused not on hugely large or small items, but on the human-scale social world of organizations, institutions and machines. The final objective is to strongly impact on the life of the citizens of the real-world, who can exploit such tools to tackle the increasing perilous complexity of their government, business, transportation, health, school, university and legal systems.

In Gelernter's vision *tuple spaces* [16] are the coordination media where information from the physical world are stored and then queried by software agents by means of Linda's coordination primitives. From an agent point of view, tuples spaces represent their environment. In the context of multi-agent systems, tuples spaces and coordination media have been the starting point to define the more general concept of *coordination artifact* [24] and *artifact* [23, 31]. Such an abstraction aims at being used for modelling any environmental object – possibly encapsulating some kind of functionality and behaviour – which can be shared, observed and used by agents to do their job. So if agents are useful to model autonomous pro-active and reactive task/goal-oriented entities, artifacts are useful to model basic non-autonomous environmental bricks, to be composed to design complex and possibly distributed environments. At a metaphor level, if agents are like people in an organization, artifacts represent the things and tools, that is the environment that people use.

This concept makes it possible to go back to the mirror world idea and conceive an extension in which the environment based on information spaces is re-shaped in terms of an open set of artifacts, part of them directly *mirroring* artifacts in the real world (see Fig. 1). Mirroring in this case means a form of *coupling*, such that an action on artifacts in the physical world causes some kind of changes in artifacts in the mirror, perceivable then by software agents. Vice versa an action by agents on artifacts in the MW can have an effect on artifacts in the physical world, perceivable by people. In that view the MW becomes an open computational layer, strongly coupled with the physical one, structured and organized as an open digital city whose inhabitants are software agents [28]. It can be understood then as a kind of *situated agent society*, built upon agents and artifacts as basic computational first-class bricks and where *stigmergy* plays an important role to bridge the human and the agent layer [9]. From an hardware perspective, the bridge between the physical and the digital layers is given by a multitude of heterogeneous networked (invisible or not) devices, sensors and actuators, making it possible to keep a continuous and consistent coupling. So, Internet-of-Things is an enabling technology for mirror worlds.

Another enabling technology is given by (mobile) augmented reality. In fact, objects of the physical world may have – explicitly or implicitly – a digital/computational extension in the mirror world representing the object itself, in terms of a software agent or as part of the agents' environment. Such an extension can include also an *augmentation* as in the case of (mobile) augmented reality, that is some *manifestation* – either static or dynamic – that can be perceived by inhabitants of the physical world through devices like glasses or smartphones, superimposed on the physical image. Purely virtual entities of MW can also have a manifestation in the real world, either in some specific location or anchored to some physical object. Differently from augmented reality, here the augmentation would not be only about visual information: artifacts (and agents) in the mirror world could augment artifacts of the physical world in terms of capabilities, services and functionalities.

### 2.1    A Toy Example: Ghosts-in-the-City Game as a MW

Here we consider a classic mobile AR game [33] modelled as a MW, to clarify some aspects (see Fig. 2). The MW is composed by a collection of treasures and ghosts distributed in some part of a city. There are two teams of human players. Their objective is to collect as many treasures as possible – walking around – without being caught by the ghosts. Players have AR glasses and a smart-phone, used as a magic wand. Ghosts are agents autonomously moving in the MW – and in the city. Players perceive ghosts by means of their AR glasses – as soon as they are in the same location. Ghosts as well can perceive the players, as soon as they are within some distance. Ghosts' objective is to catch human players: so they follow them as soon as they can perceive them. A ghost catches a human player by grabbing her body in the MW—this can be physically perceived by humans by means of the magic wand (trembling). Different kinds of ghosts may prefer different kinds of zones, according to some physical parameter of the zone—e.g.,

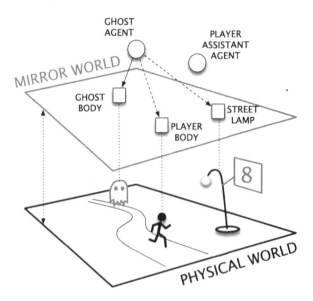

**Fig. 2.** An abstract representation of a mirror world, using the Ghosts-in-the-City game example.

humidity, light, temperature. So ghosts can perceive the physical world too, by means of proper artifacts in the MW. This fact can be exploited also by players: a player chased by a ghost which is known to be intolerant to light can run under a street lamp (in the case of a night setting of the game...). However a ghost can have the power to switch off the physical lights (by acting on its counterpart in the MW), supposing to include also physical places that can be controlled by the MW. A player with enough power can create temporary holes in the ground by means of the magic wand, which can absorb ghosts. Ghosts can set up team strategies to catch players exploiting their knowledge about the physical world, e.g. for doing encirclements. And so on.

In spite of being a game, this example shows a number of features that may be found in a MW concerning the action/perception of human actor players and agents in the augmented/mixed environment.

## 3   Augmenting Human Cognition and Sociality in MW – Perspectives

Given the tight coupling between the physical world and its mirror, the vision of MW will have a profound impact also on our human cognitive systems and on the way human societies function. Below we discuss some of these consequences.

## 3.1  Social Augmentation

The hybrid reality that we will inhabit according to the MW vision will be entrenched with core human cognitive abilities and with a specific sociality.

On the one hand, the environment in MW will not *just* support the physical actor (be that a human or a robot) in her autonomous intentions: the artificial intelligences living in the MW will go beyond "reading" the actor's behavior and her mind in order to anticipate needs and behaviors and to help or over-help, but will read behavior and ascribe beliefs and goals in order to *change the mind* of the actor, to *influence/manipulate* her, by means of explicit advice and explanations or by practically modifying the world in order to block or promote the actor's intentions [34]. This interference is a pre-requisite for a fully *social* interaction and psychology.

On the other hand, physical actors as well need not be passive; beyond being simply assisted by the environment, they will also try to influence it or, even, *communicate* with it. That is, the actor will practically act and physically inter-act also in a virtual and in a mixed (real and virtual) environment with the other artificial agents: via explicit communication and message but also by means of behavioral communication and stigmergy. In fact, since the physical actor will realize that the MW is intelligently reading her behavior and interpreting her mind, she will act also on purpose in order to make the environment understand what she has in mind. Since sociality does not consist (just) in communication, the interaction will be more socially significant: the environment and the actors will practically interact, by cooperation, conflict, or independent activities in just one and the same mixed world. They will interact with each other by moving objects, building or eliminating things, that is by changing the common *augmented world*. In other words, the physical inhabitants of MW will act feeling the *presence* (visible or invisible) of this floating intelligence, of this observing "eyes", of these protective "spirits".

Indeed, such a *feeling of presence*, the idea that someone or something is actu-ally present though cannot be seen, is common to possibly all humans cultures as it is suggested by the wide variety of tales of ghosts and other apparitions reported in many societies. Moreover, in all human cultures we have in fact coex-isted with some *presence* that was *super-natural* or magic, that is, in or from another world (visible only in some circumstances: dreaming, drugs, trance, ...) either favoring and protecting us (angels, spirits of our ancestors, gods ...) or dangerous and hostile (ghosts, devils and such), or just catty (elves).

Moreover, we have always also needed to read the physical or biological world with an *intentional stance* [13], that is, by ascribing to these entities some *mind* and intentionality; we were socially relating us with nature. While such feeling of presence is sometimes the product of neurological or psychiatric disorders [3], it has been experienced by healthy individuals in a variety of conditions, especially by individuals under extreme physical distress [15]. Recently, moreover, it has been shown that an appropriate coupled physical and robotic system can even generate such experiences in controlled settings, thus uncovering the neural and psychological mechanisms responsible for these illusions [3].

What we suggest is that MW, as we conceive them, will enable the design of new environments that will take advantage of these basic cognitive phenomena to provide new functionalities. For instance, such apparitions might play several roles, like the teacher of a given tool or technique, explaining and monitoring our learning, or like a surveillant monitoring our conformity to rules and tasks. They may act like a parent protecting us from possible unrealized dangers or interferences, or like a mother enlightening us about the effects of our behaviors or the emotions of others. They can be a super-ego remembering us our duties, moral binds, or objectives, or a friend supporting and comforting us or congratulating, or spontaneously and immediately helping us in some wrong action, etc. In MW we can *design the spirits* (angels and elves) monitoring us and interfering with our life and actions. They can learn, evolve, negotiate, be eliminated. And we will perceive them either as *another part of us*, other instances of the self and even other personalities, or as *other entities* interacting and communicating with us.

### 3.2    Cognitive Augmentation

The augmented reality of MW will be augmented also in terms of object affordances ("What is that for?" and "How to approach/use that?"), of understanding, explanations, and of an intentional stance applied to objects: we will perceive things by reading their *mind*; we will be able to *see* what is hidden in general in the object: not only the internal body and mechanisms, but its history, working, mind, rules. At the same time, reality will not be augmented in a static way but in a context-dependent and intelligent way making us see different things in different moments according to the relevant purposes and contexts. Cognition already selects the information and we see what is *relevant* for our goals or for our survival or learning; but this selection and attention focus will be enormous and projected on the world. Our augmented, mirror, *niche* will be continuously adjusted to what is relevant for us.

Once MW will be in place, we will behave in this augmented reality with the assistance and in interaction with (more or less hidden) artificial intelligences. However, more importantly, what will actually emerge and be technically and culturally built is a *new extended mind* [11], with intelligent functions out of our brain, not only actively *consulted* by us (like our agenda, calculators, books, search engines...) but just spontaneously provided, emerging, like when we have a memory retrieval or an intuition. A mixed artificial and natural brain, which will be at the same time individual and social: a collective cooperative intelligence, that I will experience in several cases as *my* intelligence/mind; such hybrid mind/brain will be necessary for dealing with the new augmented and mixed (mirror) world, where other eyes, senses, actions, data, reasoning, are needed.

In other words, there will also be an explosion of the *augmenting* function of our brain. One of the most significant functions of having a brain is to augment reality. By creating a virtual world in imagination we are able to explore – with less costs, risks and non-reversibility – possible actions and their effects, in order to mentally solve problems (intelligence), or in order to make predictions on real world and to have expectations about possible outcomes (the non perceivable future interfering with the perceived present). More importantly, however, a brain serves to integrate current perception of the physical world. We *see* much more than what impinges on our retina because we integrate and interpret the stimuli with our top down memory-based predictions [14]: we see balls and spheres even if we just receive the stimuli of a semi-sphere or we perceive that an ambulance is coming even if we just half hear a siren. Now, even if natural cognition is already a form of *augmented reality*, it will multiply because we will have infinite memory, data, elaboration, simulation of relevant information during our action in the world from the parallel and integrated computational world. Our intelligence of the world will mainly be artificial, but in real time, changing here and now what we see, what we imagine, what we can and in fact do.

Another possible consequence involves the feeling of agency, that is, the feeling to be the author of one's own action or to participate to a joint endeavor, which is crucial to sustain our sense of being in control and, ultimately, morally responsible for what we do. Recent research in the cognitive sciences have revealed that such feeling of agency depends on the perceived congruence between predicted and actual outcomes both in individual and in joint action contexts [25]. In order not to disrupt this core cognitive process, the extended range of agency of individuals and groups that will be available in mirror worlds should match this requirement by design. In particular it should be possible to support the simulation of individual and combined effects in the MW in a way that is shared and observable both by human and artificial agents, that is updated in runtime and that can be matched to perceived results in the physical world.

### 3.3   Temporal Augmentation

As a basic functionality, a MW can keep track of the history of things and events happening inside. Thus, given a physical thing which is coupled in the mirror, users – by means of augmented reality – can perceive not only how the (augmented) thing is *now*, but in principle how it was e.g. 5 min ago or yesterday, *browsing/querying in real-time* its history—which may imply traveling not only in time but also through the space. Users can perceive the time-lapse animation showing the chains of state changes that brought the thing to its current state. Travelling can happen then also in the future, in terms of *simulation* and *prediction*, supposing that the thing has been equipped with some kind of model that allows for computing predictions [8].

This functionality brings the temporal dimension in to the augmentation, allowing the users being in a specific place or using some specific things to perceive and reason about what they were and what they will be. It is not (only) like retrieving a piece of information from an archive; it is about enhancing the context about the things that I'm perceiving and using *here and now* including also the past and the future. Both simulating the possibilities of future interaction as well as remembering the past are again basic functions of human cognitive systems. Still, offloading these cognitive functions to MW will uncap new possibilities. What will happen if such time traveling will be enabled by MW? Such simulations will not be entirely up to the human actors, and it will not be up to them to decide to simulate what it will happen in the future, or what could have happened in the past. If the MW is monitoring its inhabitants and offer feedbacks, the anticipation of what will happen to its inhabitants will become a constitutive feature of the user assistant agents living in the MW. At the same time, such past and future will be here and now making it possible for us to literally see with our eyes what has happened and is just going to. Hypothetical worlds will be perceived as co-occurring with the actual and *real* one.

After providing the main concepts and visions about mirror worlds, in next section we focus on the first explorations done about methods and technologies for developing mirror worlds.

## 4 Designing and Programming Mirror Worlds – First Explorations Using Existing Agent Technologies

In order to experiment in practice the idea of mirror worlds, a first platform based on existing agent technologies and frameworks has been developed [29]. It is based on the A&A (Agents and Artifacts) meta-model [23], which provides first-class abstractions to model the environment where agents are situated, and the JaCaMo platform [4], where the A&A meta-model is integrated with BDI agents, implemented using the Jason programming language [5], and organization programming, based on MOISE [19].

### 4.1  A&A: Agents, Artifacts, Workspaces

A&A introduces *artifacts* as first-class abstractions to model and design the application environments where agents are logically situated. An artifact can be used to model and design any kind of (non-autonomous) resources and tools used and possibly shared by agents to do their job [31]. Artifacts are collected in *workspaces*, which represent logical containers possibly distributed over the network.

In A&A artifacts are then the basic blocks to modularize in a uniform way the agent environment, which can be distributed across multiple network nodes and that eventually function also as the interface to the physical environment. As described in the literature about environments for MAS [37], such environments can be useful at different levels in engineering MAS, not only for interfacing with the external environment but also as an abstraction layer for shaping mediated interaction and coordination among agents.

From the agent viewpoint, an artifact is characterised by two main aspects: an observable state, represented by a set of *observable properties*, whose changes can be perceived by agents as observable events; a set of *operations*, which represent the actions that an agent can do upon that piece of environment. When used by BDI agents, like in the case of the JaCaMo framework, artifacts observable properties are mapped into beliefs that agents have about the environment that they are perceiving, while operations become the external actions that agents can perform.

Originally, the artifact meta-model has been conceived by taking inspiration from Activity Theory [30] and human environments, mimicking the artifacts that are designed, shared and used by humans (as cognitive agents) to work, to live. So it is not surprising that we found such an abstraction quite natural to model mirror words, where the coupling with human physical artifacts is an essential aspect.

### 4.2    Modelling MW with A&A

A MW is modelled in term of a set of *mirror workspaces*. A mirror workspace extends the concept of workspace defined in A&A with an explicit coupling with the physical world. In particular, for each mirror workspace a *map* is defined, specifying which part of the physical world is coupled by the MW. It could be a part of a city, a building, a room. Each point belonging to the map has a geolocation, which can be defined in terms of latitude and longitude, or using local reference systems.

Figure 3 shows an abstract representation of the elements composing a MW, including the infrastructure levels based on JaCaMo platform. A mirror workspace contains a dynamic set of *mirror artifacts* — besides the normal artifacts. Mirror artifacts are artifacts anchored to some specific location inside the physical world, as defined by the map. Such location could be either a geo-location, or some trackable physical marker/object. Such a physical location/position is reified into an observable property. The position can change dynamically and can be perceived then by agents observing the artifact.

As depicted in Fig. 3, a MW can include multiple mirror workspaces spread over different computational nodes, used to run the infrastructure.

**Mirror Agents.** An agent can perceive/continuously observe a mirror artifact in two basic ways. One is exactly the same as for normal artifacts, that is explicitly *focusing* on the artifact, given its identifier [31]. The second one instead is peculiar to mirror workspace and is the core feature of agents living in mirror workspaces, that is: perceiving an artifact depending on its position inside the situated workspace. To that purpose, an agent joining a mirror workspace can create a *body* artifact, which is a builtin mirror artifact useful to situate the agent in a specific location of the workspace. We call *mirror agent* an agent with a body in a mirror workspace. A body artifact enables an agent in a mirror workspace to observe all the mirror artifacts that satisfy some observability criteria – such as being at a physical distance less than some radius. These criteria can be controlled by the agent by acting on its body. An agent can have multiple bodies, one for each joined mirror workspace.

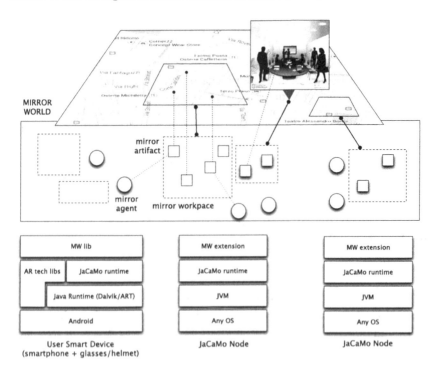

**Fig. 3.** Abstract view of organization of a mirror word and of the layers that characterise the MW infrastructure.

**Coupling.** Mirror artifacts can be of two different kinds: either completely virtual, i.e. situated in some physical location but uncoupled from any physical device, or coupled to some physical artifact. In the first case, the geo-position inside the mirror (and the physical environment) is specified when instantiating the artifact, and it can be updated then by operations provided by the artifact. In the second case, at the infrastructure level, the artifact is meant to be periodically *synched* by some device which is responsible to establish the coupling between the two levels, the mirror and the physical. It can be e.g. a smartphone device with a GPS sensor, or some other localization device. So, for instance, the body of a mirror agent can be bound to the position of the smartphone of a user, and then change as soon as the user moves.

The location of a mirror artifact in the physical world is not necessarily expressed as an absolute geo-position, but could be a relative position with respect to some physical object, such as a *marker* or an existing physical object. In that case AR technologies – hardware (cameras and other sensors mounted on the smartglasses) and software (computer vision algorithms, pattern recognition) – are essential to realize the coupling between the two layers.

Coupling is not limited to the physical location: it could concern any property of the physical world, of some physical entity, that we want to make it observable to agents living in the MW. An examples could be the temperature of a room or the luminosity of a lamp or the force on some object.

**Humans in the Loop.** A main ingredient of mirror worlds is the capability of human situated in such environments to perceive the augment layer, by adopting devices such as smart glasses or AR helmets. This can be modelled by adopting user assistant mirror agents with a body coupled to the physical location of the human user, by means of a smart device—glass, phone, whatever. Such agents can exploit the device to communicate with the user, in terms of messages, cues, etc. In more sophisticated scenario, the user assistant agent can superimpose to the image of the physical reality perceived by the user information or objects that represent some kind of extension of the reality, given the set of mirror artifacts perceived. Existing (mobile) AR frameworks – e.g. Metaio[2] – can be exploited inside the mirror world middleware to implement these functionalities.

### 4.3   Programming MW in JaCaMo

A first framework for programming and running simple mirror worlds based on the meta-model described above has been developed on top JaCaMo [4], which natively supports the development of multi-agent systems based on BDI agents living in artifact-based environments. In particular, JaCaMo is based on the synergistic integration of three different dimensions (and technologies):

– the *agent* dimension — agents are programmed using the Jason agent programming language [5], which is an practical extension and implementation of AgentSpeak(L) [27];
– the *environment* dimension – artifact-based environments are programmed using the CArtAgO framework [31], which provides a Java API for that purpose;
– the organization dimension – organizations can be specified using the MOISE organization model and language.

JaCaMo – and in particular CArtAgO – has been recently extended so as to support *situated* workspaces and *situated* artifacts as an extension of normal workspaces and artifacts, as described in previous section. Mirror words are realized by situated workspaces equipped by specific maps, establishing a coupling with physical environments such as city zones, buildings, rooms.

   More details about MW programming in JaCaMo can be found in [29], including some concrete programming examples.

## 5   The Road Ahead – Organizations and Institutions in Mirror Worlds

The definition of proper organizational models appears an important aspect of MW, in order to deal with aspects such as the openness, the autonomy of the

---

[2] http://www.metaio.com/.

agents living in the MW, the size in terms of number of entities composing the MW, and so on. So natural questions are: are current organization meta-models proposed by open Multi-Agent System effective for modelling MW organization? Is it useful to support some explicit coupling between organization models adopted in the physical/social layer and the ones to be adopted in the digital one, in the MW? Can we exploit the coupling between the two levels for effectively defining a notion of institutional actions and institutional facts inside MW? We believe that a good starting point for investigating these issues could be understanding the relationships between MW and Artificial Socio-Cognitive Systems (ASCS).

The notion of ASCS has been recently introduced in [10,22], inspired by [7], to foster the study of the science and engineering of *that class of socio-technical systems where individuals – who may be human or artificial entities – engage in a purposeful collective interactions within a shared web-mediated social space*. Indeed MW are socio-cognitive technical systems, because in order to characterise or deploy them we may need to "understand and reproduce features of the human social mind like commitments, norms, mind reading, power, trust, institutional effects and social macrophenomena" [7].

Like ASCS, MW aim to "support human-like social interactions in a virtual space where the frontiers between the physical and artificial are increasingly difficult to determine" [10]. In the case of MW such frontiers can be further refined as being between the physical and the *digital*. In fact, mirror worlds are real-worlds that can be perceived either by means of suitable devices, or by the effects that they produce on the physical (and social) world.

The notion of *shared space* is a key notion for MW, as for ASCS. It is interesting to notice that if ASCS take the *web* as the context of interaction and then web-mediated social space as reference environment, MW take the physical world, augmented with the digital layer. We can say then that MW in an ASCS perspective enable individuals – who maybe humans or artificial entities – to interact in a shared social space *bound to some augmented physical environment* in a purposeful fashion. So, from this point of view, MW could be conceived as a kind of *augmented* ASCS.

Related to the common notion of shared space, an important key point linking MW and ASCS is the notion of *validity* as defined in ASCS, which corresponds to the notion of *coupling* in MW. To understand the notion of validity, the *tripartite view* of ASCS (W, I, T) is introduced in [10,22], composed by:

– The world system W - as the agents (human, software) see it and relate to it;
– The institutional system I - that stipulates the way the system should behave;
– The technological artefacts T - that implement the ideal system and run applications that enable users to accomplish collective actions in real word according to the rules set out in I.

The notion of validity expresses an *isomorphism* between the evolution of the states of W, I, T, so that: "at any point in time, what happens in the world W and enters the system produces some effects in the computational system that become effective in the world; that is, the *state of the world*, as far as the system is concerned, changes if and when *attempted* action in W is *validated* by I, and the code in T *processes* the input that happens in W and outputs the effects in W." The notion of *coupling* in MW is related, in that for those entities of the physical world that are mirrored in MW, the shared state perceived by agents living in the mirror must be coherent and consistent to the physical one, according to some kind of *isomorphism* defined by the coupling itself, and more generally with the one perceived by human agents. Moreover, in MW we can distinguish two levels of validity/coupling in this case, *horizontal* and *vertical*. Horizontal is related to agents at the same level (physical or digital), sharing the state of the environment at that level; vertical is related to the state of mirror entities that cross the physical and digital level, being physical with a digital augmentation and/or being digital with a physical position and appearance.

Besides these initial notes, we believe that future investigations about MW will be useful for deepening the knowledge about *situated* ASCS out of the web, that is ASCS where the shared social space is given by mixed realities and hybrid collections of augmented worlds. Or, where the web is merged with the physical world, like in the case of Internet of Things and Web of Things scenarios.

## 6    Concluding Remarks

In this paper we gave a broad discussion about mirror words, as a blueprint to model, understand and design *augmented worlds* inhabited by both human and software agents. The research on mirror worlds is still in its infancy, and there are several inter-disciplinary issues and questions that we believe are worth to be explored in the future, besides further developing the ones sketched in this paper. A main one is about finding a proper *formalization* of mirror worlds, to describe more rigorously the concepts that have been presented in this paper. To that purpose, the similarities and link with Artificial Socio-Cognitive Systems, to be further explored, can be helpful. A further one is about investigating how the exploit mirror worlds to enhance the strategies that can be adopted to support human interaction, cooperation, collaboration.

Beside specific issues, it is clear that broad aspects such as *security, privacy,* and *ethics* – that are more and more critical in current Internet/social-network based society – will be even more delicate and challenging in MW, where the coupling with the physical world is a primary aspect—like in scenarios based on Internet-of-Things, smart environments. In the MW case, the discussion of such aspects cannot be fully developed independently from another long-standing discussion about living within systems with some significant degree of autonomy—which in MW is explicitly modelled in terms of the mirror agents. In MW, such autonomy is useful not only to increase automation, but to *human augmentation* (individual and social) – which is strongly related to the augmentation of the physical reality [38]. The idea of human augmentation puts forth interesting questions, which are more and more important as soon as such augmentation becomes essential for people in their everyday life.

# References

1. Baldauf, M., Dustdar, S., Rosenberg, F.: A survey on context-aware systems. Int. J. Ad Hoc Ubiquitous Comput. **2**(4), 263–277 (2007)
2. Barella, A., Ricci, A., Boissier, O., Carrascosa, C.: MAM5: multi-agent model for intelligent virtual environments. In: 10th European Workshop on Multi-Agent Systems (EUMAS 2012), pp. 16–30 (2012)
3. Blanke, O., et al.: Neurological and robot-controlled induction of an apparition. Curr. Biol. **24**(22), 2681–2686 (2014)
4. Boissier, O., Bordini, R.H., Hübner, J.F., Ricci, A., Santi, A.: Multi-agent oriented programming with JaCaMo. Sci. Comput. Program. **78**(6), 747–761 (2013)
5. Bordini, R.H., Hübner, J.F., Wooldrige, M.: Programming Multi-Agent Systems in AgentSpeak using Jason. John Wiley & Sons, New York (2007)
6. Campos, J., López-Sánchez, M., Rodríguez-Aguilar, J.A., Esteva, M.: Formalising situatedness and adaptation in electronic institutions. In: Hübner, J.F., Matson, E., Boissier, O., Dignum, V. (eds.) COIN@AAMAS 2008. LNCS, vol. 5428, pp. 126–139. Springer, Heidelberg (2009)
7. Castelfranchi, C.: InMind and OutMind: societal order cognition and self-organization: the role of MAS. In: AAMAS 2013, Saint Paul, Minnesota (2013). invited Talk for the IFAAMAS Influential Paper Award
8. Castelfranchi, C.: Making visible the invisible hand: the mission of social simulation. In: Adamatti, D.F., Dimuro, G.P., Coelho, H. (eds.) Interdisciplinary Applications of Agent-Based Social Simulation and Modeling. IGI Global (2014)
9. Castelfranchi, C., Piunti, M., Ricci, A., Tummolini, L.: Am I systems as agent-based mirror worlds: bridging humans and agents through stigmergy. In: Bosse, T. (ed.) Agents and Ambient Intelligence, Ambient Intelligence and Smart Environments, vol. 12, pp. 17–31. IOS Press (2012)
10. Christiaanse, R., Ghose, A., Noriega, P., Singh, M.: Characterizing artificial socio-cognitive technical systems. CEUR Workshop Proceedings, vol. 1283, pp. 336–346. Barcelona 03 November 2014
11. Clark, A.: Supersizing the Mind: Embodiment, Action and Cognitive Extension. Oxford University Press, New York (2008)
12. Costanza, E., Kunz, A., Fjeld, M.: Mixed reality: a survey. In: Lalanne, D., Kohlas, J. (eds.) Human Machine Interaction. LNCS, vol. 5440, pp. 47–68. Springer, Heidelberg (2009)
13. Dennett, D.: The Intentional Stance. MIT Press, Cambridge (1987)
14. Frith, C.: Making up the Mind: How the Brain Creates Our Mental World. Wiley-Blackwell Publishing, Massachusetts (2007)
15. Geiger, J.: The Third Man Factor: Surviving the Impossible. Weinstein Books, New York (2009)
16. Gelernter, D.: Generative communication in Linda. ACM Trans. Program. Lang. Syst. **7**(1), 80–112 (1985)
17. Gelernter, D.H.: Mirror Worlds: or the Day Software Puts the Universe in a Shoebox...How It Will Happen and What It Will Mean. Oxford University Press, UK (1992)
18. Holz, T., Campbell, A.G., O'Hare, G.M., Stafford, J.W., Martin, A., Dragone, M.: MiRA - mixed reality agents. Int. J. Hum.-Comput. Stud. **69**(4), 251–268 (2011)
19. Hübner, J.F., Sichman, J.S., Boissier, O.: Developing organised multi-agent systems using the MOISE+ model: programming issues at the system and agent levels. Agent-Oriented Softw. Eng. **1**(3/4), 370–395 (2007)

20. Luck, M., Aylett, R.: Applying artificial intelligence to virtual reality: intelligent virtual environments. Appl. Artif. Intell. **14**(1), 3–32 (2000)

21. Milgram, P., Kishino, F.: A taxonomy of mixed reality visual displays. IEICE Trans. Inf. Syst. **E77–D**(12), 1321–1329 (1994)

22. Noriega, P., Padget, J., Verhagen, H., d'Inverno, M.: The challenge of artificial socio-cognitive systems. In: COIN@AAMAS2014, Paris May 2014

23. Omicini, A., Ricci, A., Viroli, M.: Artifacts in the A&A meta-model for multi-agent systems. Auton. Agent. Multi-Agent Syst. **17**(3), 432–456 (2008)

24. Omicini, A., Ricci, A., Viroli, M., Castelfranchi, C., Tummolini, L.: Coordination artifacts: environment-based coordination for intelligent agents. In: Jennings, N.R., Sierra, C., Sonenberg, L., Tambe, M. (eds.) Proceedings of AAMAS 2004, vol. 1, pp. 286–293. ACM, New York 19–23 July 2004

25. Pacherie, E.: Sense of agency: many facets, multiple sources. In: Terrace, H.S., Metcalfe, J. (eds.) Agency and Joint Attention, pp. 321–345. Oxford University Press, New York (2013)

26. Piunti, M., Boissier, O., Hübner, J.F., Ricci, A.: Embodied organizations: a unifying perspective in programming agents, organizations and environments. In: Boissier, O., Fallah-Seghrouchni, A.E., Hassas, S., Maudet, N. (eds.) MALLOW. CEUR Workshop Proceedings, vol. 627 (2010). http://www.ceur-ws.org

27. Rao, A.S.: AgentSpeak(L): BDI agents speak out in a logical computable language. In: Perram, J., Van de Velde, W. (eds.) MAAMAW 1996. LNCS, vol. 1038. Springer, Heidelberg (1996)

28. Ricci, A., Piunti, M., Tummolini, L., Castelfranchi, C.: The mirror world: preparing for mixed-reality living. IEEE Pervasive Comput. **14**(2), 60–63 (2015)

29. Ricci, A., Croatti, A., Brunetti, P., Viroli, M.: Programming mirror-worlds: an agent-oriented programming perspective. In: Proceedings of the EMAS 2015 (2015)

30. Ricci, A., Omicini, A., Denti, E.: Activity theory as a framework for MAS coordination. In: Petta, P., Tolksdorf, R., Zambonelli, F. (eds.) ESAW 2002. LNCS (LNAI), vol. 2577, pp. 96–110. Springer, Heidelberg (2003)

31. Ricci, A., Piunti, M., Viroli, M.: Environment programming in multi-agent systems: an artifact-based perspective. Auton. Agent. Multi-Agent Syst. **23**(2), 158–192 (2011)

32. Sadri, F.: Ambient intelligence: a survey. ACM Comput. Surv. **43**(4), 36 (2011)

33. Thomas, B.H.: A survey of visual, mixed, and augmented reality gaming. Comput. Entertain. **10**(3), 1–33 (2012)

34. Tummolini, L., Mirolli, M., Castelfranchi, C.: Stigmergic cues and their uses in coordination: An evolutionary approach. In: Uhrmacher, A., Weyns, D. (eds.) Agents, Simulation and Applications, pp. 243–265. CRC Press (2009)

35. Weiser, M.: Some computer science issues in ubiquitous computing. Commun. ACM **36**, 75–84 (1993)

36. Weiser, M.: The computer for the 21st century. SIGMOBILE Mob. Comput. Commun. Rev. **3**, 3–11 (1999)

37. Weyns, D., Omicini, A., Odell, J.: Environment as a first class abstraction in multiagent systems. Auton. Agent. Multi-Agent Syst. **14**(1), 5–30 (2007)

38. Xia, C., Maes, P.: The design of artifacts for augmenting intellect. In: Proceedings of the 4th Augmented Human International Conference AH 2013, pp. 154–161. ACM, New York (2013)

# The Power of Teams that Disagree: Team Formation in Large Action Spaces

Leandro Soriano Marcolino[1]($\boxtimes$), Haifeng Xu[1], Albert Xin Jiang[1],
Milind Tambe[1], and Emma Bowring[2]

[1] University of Southern California, Los Angeles, CA 90089, USA
{sorianom,haifengx,jiangx,tambe}@usc.edu
[2] University of the Pacific, Stockton, CA 95211, USA
ebowring@pacific.edu

**Abstract.** Recent work has shown that diverse teams can outperform a uniform team made of copies of the best agent. However, there are fundamental questions that were never asked before. When should we use diverse or uniform teams? How does the performance change as the action space or the teams get larger? Hence, we present a new model of diversity, where we prove that the performance of a diverse team improves as the size of the action space increases. Moreover, we show that the performance converges exponentially fast to the optimal one as we increase the number of agents. We present synthetic experiments that give further insights: even though a diverse team outperforms a uniform team when the size of the action space increases, the uniform team will eventually again play better than the diverse team for a large enough action space. We verify our predictions in a system of Go playing agents, where a diverse team improves in performance as the board size increases, and eventually overcomes a uniform team.

**Keywords:** Coordination & Collaboration · Distributed AI · Team formation

## 1 Introduction

Team formation is crucial when deploying a multi-agent system [7,12,15,16]. Many researchers emphasize the importance of diversity when forming teams [8,10,11,14]. However, there are many important questions about diversity that were not asked before, and are not explored in such models. LiCalzi and Surucu (2012) [11] and Hong and Page (2004) [8] propose models where the agents know the utility of the solutions, and the team converges to the best solution found by one of its members. In complex problems the utility of solutions would not be

---

This paper is the full version of our AAAI'2014 paper "Give a Hard Problem to a Diverse Team: Exploring Large Action Spaces", containing: (i) The full proof of all theorems; (ii) Additional details about the experiments and the experimental analysis; (iii) Extended related work section and discussions.

© Springer International Publishing Switzerland 2015
A. Ghose et al. (Eds.): COIN 2014, LNAI 9372, pp. 213–232, 2015.
DOI: 10.1007/978-3-319-25420-3_14

available, and agents would have to resort to other methods, such as voting, to take a common decision. Lamberson and Page (2012) [10] study diversity in the context of forecasts, where the solutions are represented by real numbers and the team takes the average of the opinion of its members. Domains where the possible solutions are discrete, however, are not captured by such a model.

Marcolino, Jiang, and Tambe (2013) [14] study teams of agents that vote in discrete solution spaces. They show that a diverse team of weaker agents can overcome a uniform team made of copies of the best agent. However, this does not always occur, and they do not present ways to know when we should use diverse teams. Moreover, they lack a formal study of how the performance of diverse teams change as the number of agents and/or actions increases.

In this paper we shed new light on this problem, by presenting a new, more general model of diversity for teams of voting agents. Our model captures, better than the previous ones, the notion of a diverse team as a team of agents that tend to not agree on the same actions, and allows us to make new predictions. Our main insight is based on the notion of *spreading tail* ($ST$) and *non-spreading tail* ($NST$) agents. As we will show, a team of $ST$ agents has a diverse behavior, i.e., they tend to not agree on the same actions. Hence, we can model a diverse team as a team of $ST$ agents, and show that the performance improves as the size of the action space gets larger. We also prove upper and lower bounds on how fast different teams converge. The improvement can be large enough to overcome a uniform team of $NST$ agents, even if individually the $ST$ agents are weaker. As it is generally hard to find good solutions for problems with a large number of actions, it is important to know which teams to use in order to tackle such problems. Moreover, we show that the performance of a diverse team converges to the optimal one exponentially fast as the team grows. Our synthetic experiments provide even further insights about our model: even though the diverse team overcomes the uniform team in a large action space, the uniform team eventually will again play better than the diverse team as the action space keeps increasing if the best agent does not behave exactly like an $NST$ agent.

Finally, we test our predictions by studying a system of voting agents, in the Go domain. We show that a uniform team made of copies of the best agent plays better in smaller boards, but is overcome by a diverse team as the board gets larger. We analyze the agents and verify that weak agents have a behavior closer to $ST$ agents, while the best agent is closer to an $NST$ agent. Therefore, we show that our predictions are verified in a real system, and can effectively be used while forming a multi-agent team.

## 2   Related Work

This paper is mainly related to team formation, but we also find related work in social choice and machine learning. We start by focusing on team formation research. Such study goes beyond computer science, and several works can be found in the economics literature. Hong and Page (2004) [8] is an impactful work showing the importance of diversity when forming (human) teams. Even though recently some of the mathematical arguments were put into question [19], it remains as a mile-stone on the study of the importance of diversity, as many researchers were influenced by their work. For example, LiCalzi and Surucu (2012) [11] present another model, that focuses on the importance of diversity when teams solve problems in large action spaces. However, both Hong and Page (2004) [8] and LiCalzi and Surucu (2012) [11] assume that the agents are able to know the utility of the solutions, and hence the team can pick the best solution found by one of its members. Therefore, their models do not apply for a team of voting agents. Lamberson and Page (2012) [10] study diversity in the context of forecasts. They assume that solutions are represented by real numbers, and a team converges to the average of the opinion of its members. Hence, they do not capture domains with discrete solutions, and the model also does not cover teams of voting agents.

In the multi-agent system literature, team formation is classically seen as selecting the team with maximum expected utility for a task, based on a model of the capabilities of each agent [7,16]. However, in many domains we do not have such a model. The study of "ad-hoc" teamwork deals with multi-agent teams with absence of information [1,2]. They focus, however, on how a new agent must decide its behavior in order to cooperate with agents of unknown types, not on picking the best team.

Recently, Marcolino, Jiang, and Tambe (2013) [14] showed the importance of diversity when forming teams of voting agents. They show that it is possible for a diverse team of weaker agents to overcome a uniform team of copies of the best agent, if the weaker agents are able to play better than the best agent at some world states. This is only a necessary condition, however, so it still does not provide ways to know when diverse or uniform teams should be used. Jiang et al. [9] propose a novel model to study diverse teams, where the agents' votes are modeled as two samples from distributions: one that fixes the algorithm (or the biases) of the agent, and a second that models the actual voting process. Moreover, they experimentally study the performance of different voting rules in the Computer Go domain. However, the effects of changing the action space size are not studied, neither theoretically nor experimentally.

Concerning social choice, this paper is related to the view of voting as a way to discover an optimal choice (or ranking). Classical models study this view of voting for teams of identical agents [5,13]. However, more recent works are also considering agents with different probability distribution functions. Caragiannis, Procaccia, and Shah (2013) [3] study which voting rules converge to the true ranking as the number of agents goes to infinity.

In Soufiani, Parkes, and Xia (2012) [18] the problem of inferring the true ranking is studied, assuming agents with different pdfs, but drawn from the same family. However, even though recent works on social choice are not assuming identical agents, they still do not provide a way to find the best teams of voting agents.

More related works can be found in machine learning. Ensemble systems are very common in machine learning, where a strong classifier is built by combining multiple weak classifiers, for example by voting [17]. Diversity is known to be important when forming an ensemble, and some systems try to minimize the correlation between the classifiers [4]. Still, an important problem is how to form the ensemble system, i.e., how to pick the classifiers that lead to the best predictions [6]. Our model, based on the notion of *spreading tail* and *non-spreading tail* agents, allows us to make predictions about teams as the action space and/or number of agents changes, and also compare the rate of change of the performance of different teams. To the best of our knowledge, there is no model similar to ours in the machine learning literature.

## 3   Model for Analysis of Diversity in Teams

Consider a problem defined by choosing an action $a$ from a set of possible actions $\mathbf{A}$. Each $a$ has an utility $U(a)$, and our goal is to maximize the utility. We always list the actions in order from best to worst, therefore $U(a_j) > U(a_{j+1}) \; \forall j$ ($a_0$ is the best action). In some tasks (like in Sect. 4), a series of actions are chosen across different states, but here we focus on the decision process in a given state.

Consider a set of agents, voting to decide over actions. The agents do not know the utility of the actions, and vote for the action they believe to be the best according to their own decision procedure, characterized by a probability distribution (pdf). We write as $p_{i,j}$ the probability of agent $i$ voting for action $a_j$. We denote by $p_{i,j}(m)$, when we explicitly talk about $p_{i,j}$ for an action space of size $m$. If the pdf of one agent is identical to the pdf of another agent, they will be referred to as copies of the same agent. The action that wins by plurality voting is taken by the team. Ties are broken randomly, except when we explicitly talk about a tie breaking rule. Let $\mathbf{D_m}$ be the set of suboptimal actions ($a_j, j \neq 0$) assigned with a nonzero probability in the pdf of an agent $i$, and $d_m = |\mathbf{D_m}|$. We assume that there is a bound in the ratio of the suboptimal action with highest probability and the one with lowest nonzero probability, i.e., let $p_{i,min} = \min_{j \in \mathbf{D_m}} p_{i,j}$ and $p_{i,max} = \max_{j \in \mathbf{D_m}} p_{i,j}$; there is a constant $\alpha$ such that $p_{i,max} \leq \alpha p_{i,min} \; \forall$ agents $i$.

We define strength as the expected utility of an agent and/or a team. The probability of a team playing the best action will be called $p_{best}$. We first consider a setting where $U(a_0) \gg U(a_j) \forall j \neq 0$, hence we can use $p_{best}$ as our measure of performance. We will later consider more general settings, where the first $r$ actions have a high utility.

We define team formation as selecting from the space of all agents a limited number of agents that has the maximum strength by voting together to decide on actions. We study the effect of increasing the size $m$ of the set of possible actions on the team formation problem. Intuitively, the change in team performance as $m$ increases will be affected by how the pdf of the individual agents $i$ change when $m$ gets higher. As we increase $m$, $d_m$ can increase or not change. Hence, we classify the agents as *spreading tail* ($ST$) agents or *non-spreading tail* agents ($NST$).

We define $ST$ agents as agents whose $d_m$ is non-decreasing on $m$ and $d_m \to \infty$ as $m \to \infty$. We consider that there is a constant $\epsilon > 0$, such that for all $ST$ agents

$i$, $\forall m$, $p_{i,0} \geq \epsilon$. We assume that $p_{i,0}$ does not change with $m$, although later we discuss what happens when $p_{i,0}$ changes.

We define $NST$ agents as agents whose pdf does not change as the number of actions $m$ increases. Hence, let $m_{i0}$ be the minimum number of actions necessary to define the pdf of an $NST$ agent $i$. We have that $\forall m, m' \geq m_{i0}$, $\forall j \leq m_{i0}$ $p_{i,j}(m) = p_{i,j}(m')$, $\forall j > m_{i0}$ $p_{i,j}(m) = 0$.

We first give an intuitive description of the concept of diversity, then define formally diverse teams. By diversity, we mean agents that tend to disagree. In Marcolino, Jiang, and Tambe (2013) [14], a diverse team is defined as a set of agents with different pdfs. Hence, they disagree because of having different probabilities of playing certain actions. Here, we generalize their definition to capture cases where agents disagree on actions, regardless of whether their pdfs are the same or not. Formally, we define a diverse team to be one consisting of a set of $ST$ agents (either different $ST$ agents or copies of the same $ST$ agent). In our theoretical development we will show that this definition captures the notion of diversity: a team of $ST$ agents will tend to not agree on the same suboptimal actions. We call uniform team as the team composed by copies of an $NST$ agent. This is an idealization to perform our initial analysis. We will later discuss more complex domains, where the agents of the uniform team also behave like $ST$ agents.

We start with an example, to give an intuition about our model. Consider the agents in Table 1(a), where we show the pdf of the agents, and $p_{best}$ of the uniform team (three copies of agent 1) and the diverse team (one copy of each agent). We assume agent 1 is an $NST$ agent, while agent 2 and 3 are $ST$ agents. In this situation the uniform team plays better than the diverse team. Now let's add one more action to the problem. Because agent 2 and 3 are $ST$ agents, the probability mass on action 2 scatters to the newly added action (Table 1(b)). Hence, while before the $ST$ agents would always agree on the same suboptimal action if they both did not vote for the optimal action, now they might vote for different suboptimal actions, creating a tie between each suboptimal action and the optimal one. Because ties are broken randomly, when this happens there will be a $1/3$ chance that the tie will be broken in favor of the optimal action. Hence, $p_{best}$ increases when the probability of the $ST$ agents agreeing on the same suboptimal actions decreases, and the diverse team now plays better than the uniform team, even though individually agents 2 and 3 are weaker than agent 1.

We now present our theoretical work. First we show that the performance of a diverse team converges when $m \to \infty$, to a value that is higher than the performance for any other $m$.

**Theorem 1.** $p_{best}(m)$ of a diverse team of $n$ agents converges to a certain value $\tilde{p}_{best}$ as $m \to \infty$. Furthermore, $\tilde{p}_{best} \geq p_{best}(m)$, $\forall m$.

*Proof.* Let $p_{i,min} = \min_{j \in \mathbf{D_m}} p_{i,j}$, $p_{i,max} = \max_{j \in \mathbf{D_m}} p_{i,j}$ and $\mathbf{T}$ be the set of agents in the team. By our assumptions, there is a constant $\alpha$ such that $p_{i,max} \leq \alpha p_{i,min}$ for all agents $i$. Then, we have that $1 \geq 1 - p_{i,0} = \sum_{j \in \mathbf{D_m}} p_{i,j} \geq d_m p_{i,min}$.

**Table 1.** Performance of diverse team increases when the number of actions increases.

(a) With 2 actions, uniform team plays better than diverse team.

| Agents | Action 1 | Action 2 |
|---|---|---|
| Agent 1 | 0.6 | 0.4 |
| Agent 2 | 0.55 | 0.45 |
| Agent 3 | 0.55 | 0.45 |
| Uniform $p_{best}$: | 0.648 | |
| Diverse $p_{best}$: | 0.599 | |

(b) When we add one more action, diverse team plays better than uniform team.

| Agents | Action 1 | Action 2 | Action 3 |
|---|---|---|---|
| Agent 1 | 0.6 | 0.4 | 0 |
| Agent 2 | 0.55 | 0.25 | 0.2 |
| Agent 3 | 0.55 | 0.15 | 0.3 |
| Uniform $p_{best}$: | 0.648 | | |
| Diverse $p_{best}$: | 0.657 | | |

Therefore, $p_{i,min} \leq \frac{1}{d_m} \to 0$ as $d_m$ tends to $\infty$ with $m$. Similarly, $\alpha p_{i,min} \to 0$ as $d_m \to \infty$. As $p_{i,j} \leq \alpha p_{i,min}$ we have that $\forall j \ p_{i,j} \to 0$ as $d_m \to \infty$. We show that this implies that when $m \to \infty$, weak agents never agree on the same suboptimal action. Let $i_1$ and $i_2$ be two arbitrary agents. Without loss of generality, assume $i_2$'s $d_m$ ($d_m^{(i_2)}$) is greater than or equal $i_1$'s $d_m$ ($d_m^{(i_1)}$). The probability ($\sigma_{i_1,i_2}$) of $i_1$ and $i_2$ agreeing on the same suboptimal action is upper bounded by $\sigma_{i_1,i_2} = \sum_{a_j \in \mathbf{A} \backslash a_0} p_{i_1,j} p_{i_2,j} \leq d_m^{(i_2)} p_{i_1,max} p_{i_2,max} \leq d_m^{(i_2)} \alpha p_{i_2,min} p_{i_1,max} \leq \alpha p_{i_1,max}$ (as $d_m^{(i_2)} p_{i_2,min} \leq 1$). We have that $\alpha p_{i_1,max} \to 0$ as $p_{i_1,max} \to 0$, because $\alpha$ is a constant. Hence the probability of any two agents agreeing on a suboptimal action is $\frac{\sum_{i_1 \in T} \sum_{i_2 \in T, i_2 \neq i_1} \sigma_{i_1,i_2}}{2} \leq \frac{n(n-1)}{2} \max_{i_1,i_2} \sigma_{i_1,i_2} \to 0$, as $n$ is a constant.

Hence, when $m \to \infty$, the diverse team only chooses a suboptimal action if all agents vote for a different suboptimal action or in a tie between the optimal action and suboptimal actions (because ties are broken randomly). Therefore, $p_{best}$ converges to:

$$\tilde{p}_{best} = 1 - \prod_{i=1}^{n}(1 - p_{i,0}) - \sum_{i=1}^{n}(p_{i,0} \prod_{j=1,j\neq i}^{n}(1 - p_{j,0}))\frac{n-1}{n}, \tag{1}$$

that is, the total probability minus the cases where the best action is not chosen: the second term covers the case where all agents vote for a suboptimal action and the third term covers the case where one agent votes for the optimal action and all other agents vote for suboptimal actions.

When $m$ is finite, the agents might choose a suboptimal action by agreeing over that suboptimal action. Therefore, we have that $p_{best}(m) \leq \tilde{p}_{best} \ \forall m$. □

Let $p_{best}^{uniform}(m)$ be $p_{best}$ of the uniform team, with $m$ actions. A uniform team is not affected by increasing $m$, as the pdf of an $NST$ agent will not change. Hence, $p_{best}^{uniform}(m)$ is the same, $\forall m$. If $\tilde{p}_{best}$ is high enough so that $\tilde{p}_{best} \geq p_{best}^{uniform}(m)$, the diverse team will overcome the uniform team, when $m \to \infty$. Therefore, the diverse team will be better than the uniform team when $m$ is large enough.

In practice, a uniform team made of copies of the best agent might not behave exactly like a team of $NST$ agents, as the best agent could also increase its $d_m$ as $m$ gets larger. We discuss this situation in Sect. 4. In order to perform that study, we derive in the following corollary how fast $p_{best}$ converges to $\tilde{p}_{best}$, as a function of $d_m$.

**Corollary 1.** $p_{best}(m)$ of a diverse team increases to $\tilde{p}_{best}$ in the order of $O\left(\frac{1}{d_m^{min}}\right)$ and $\Omega\left(\frac{1}{d_m^{max}}\right)$, where $d_m^{max}$ is the highest and $d_m^{min}$ the lowest $d_m$ of the team.

*Proof.* We assume here the notation that was used in the previous proof. First we show a lowerbound on $p_{best}(m)$. We have that $p_{best}(m) = 1 - \psi_1$, where $\psi_1$ is the probability of the team picking a suboptimal action. $\psi_1 = \psi_2 + \psi_3$, where $\psi_2$ is the probability of no agent agreeing and the team picks a suboptimal action and $\psi_3$ is the probability of at least two agents agreeing and the team picks a suboptimal action. Hence, $p_{best}(m) = 1 - \psi_2 - \psi_3 = \tilde{p}_{best} - \psi_3 \geq \tilde{p}_{best} - \psi_4$, where $\psi_4$ is the probability of at least two agents agreeing. Let $\sigma^{max} = \max_{i_1,i_2} \sigma_{i_1,i_2}$, and $i_1^*$ and $i_2^*$ are the agents whose $\sigma_{i_1^*,i_2^*} = \sigma^{max}$. We have that:

$$p_{best}(m) \geq \tilde{p}_{best} - \frac{n(n-1)}{2}\sigma^{max} \geq \tilde{p}_{best} - \frac{n(n-1)}{2}d_m^{(i_2^*)}p_{i_1^*,max}p_{i_2^*,max}$$

$$\geq \tilde{p}_{best} - \frac{n(n-1)}{2}d_m^{(i_2^*)}\alpha p_{i_1^*,min}\alpha p_{i_2^*,min} \geq \tilde{p}_{best} - \frac{n(n-1)}{2}\alpha^2\frac{1}{d_m^{(i_1^*)}},$$

where the last inequality holds since $p_{i,min} \leq \frac{1}{d_m}$. Hence, $p_{best}(m) \geq \tilde{p}_{best} - \frac{n(n-1)}{2}\alpha^2\frac{1}{d_m^{min}} \rightsquigarrow \tilde{p}_{best} - p_{best}(m) \leq O\left(\frac{1}{d_m^{min}}\right)$.

Now we show an upper bound: $p_{best}(m) = \tilde{p}_{best} - \psi_3 \leq \tilde{p}_{best} - \psi_5$, where $\psi_5$ is the probability of at least two agents agreeing and no agents vote for the optimal action. Let $\sigma^{min} = \min_{i_1,i_2} \sigma_{i_1,i_2}$; $i_1^*$ and $i_2^*$ are the agents whose $\sigma_{i_1^*,i_2^*} = \sigma^{min}$; and $p_{max,0} = \max_{i\in T} p_{i,0}$. Without loss of generality, we assume that $d_m^{(i_2^*)} \geq d_m^{(i_1^*)}$. Therefore:

$$p_{best}(m) \leq \tilde{p}_{best} - \frac{n(n-1)}{2}\sigma^{min}(1 - p_{max,0})^{n-2}$$

$$\leq \tilde{p}_{best} - \frac{n(n-1)}{2}d_m^{(i_1^*)}p_{i_1^*,min}p_{i_2^*,min}(1 - p_{max,0})^{n-2}$$

$$\leq \tilde{p}_{best} - \frac{n(n-1)}{2}d_m^{(i_1^*)}\frac{p_{i_1^*,max}p_{i_2^*,max}}{\alpha^2}(1 - p_{max,0})^{n-2}$$

$$\leq \tilde{p}_{best} - \frac{n(n-1)}{2}\alpha^{-2}\frac{1}{d_m^{i_2^*}}(1 - p_{max,0})^{n-2}$$

$$\leq \tilde{p}_{best} - \frac{n(n-1)}{2}\alpha^{-2}\frac{1}{d_m^{max}}(1 - p_{max,0})^{n-2}$$

$$\rightsquigarrow \tilde{p}_{best} - p_{best}(m) \geq \Omega\left(\frac{1}{d_m^{max}}\right).$$

$\square$

Hence, agents that change their $d_m$ faster will converge faster to $\tilde{p}_{best}$. This is an important result when we consider later more complex scenarios where the $d_m$ of the agents of the uniform team also change.

Note that $\tilde{p}_{best}$ depends on the number of agents $n$ (Eq. 1). Now we show that the diverse team tends to always play the optimal action, as $n \rightarrow \infty$.

**Theorem 2.** $\tilde{p}_{best}$ *converges to 1, as* $n \to \infty$. *Furthermore,* $1 - \tilde{p}_{best}$ *converges exponentially to 0, that is,* $\exists$ *constant* $c$, *such that* $1 - \tilde{p}_{best} \leq c(1 - \frac{\epsilon}{2})^n$, $\forall n \geq \frac{2}{\epsilon}$. *However, the performance of the uniform team improves as* $n \to \infty$ *only if* $p_{s,0} = \max_j p_{s,j}$, *where* $s$ *is the best agent.*

*Proof.* By the previous proof, we know that when $m \to \infty$ the diverse team plays the optimal action with probability given by $\tilde{p}_{best}$. We show that $1 - \tilde{p}_{best} \to 0$ exponentially as $n \to \infty$ (this naturally induces $\tilde{p}_{best} \to 1$). We first compute an upper bound for $\sum_{i=1}^{n}(p_{i,0}\prod_{j=1,j\neq i}^{n}(1 - p_{j,0}))$:

$$\sum_{i=1}^{n} p_{i,0}\prod_{j=1,j\neq i}^{n}(1 - p_{j,0}) \leq \sum_{i=1}^{n} p_{i,0}(1 - p_{min,0})^{n-1} \leq np_{max,0}(1 - p_{min,0})^{n-1}$$

$$\leq n(1 - \epsilon)^{n-1} \text{ for } p_{max,0} = \max_i p_{i,0}, p_{min,0} = \min_j p_{j,0}$$

Since $\prod_{i=1}^{n}(1 - p_{i,0}) \leq (1 - \epsilon)^n$, thus we have that $1 - \tilde{p}_{best} \leq (1 - \epsilon)^n + n(1 - \epsilon)^{n-1}$. So we only need to prove that there exists a constant $c$ such that $(1 - \epsilon)^n + n(1 - \epsilon)^{n-1} \leq c(1 - \frac{\epsilon}{2})^n$, as follows:

$$\frac{(1-\epsilon)^{n+1}+(n+1)(1-\epsilon)^n}{(1-\epsilon)^n+n(1-\epsilon)^{n-1}} = (1 - \epsilon)\frac{1-\epsilon+n+1}{1-\epsilon+n} = 1 - \epsilon + \frac{1-\epsilon}{1-\epsilon+n}$$

$$\leq 1 - \tfrac{1}{2}\epsilon, \text{ if } n \geq \tfrac{2}{\epsilon} \text{ (by setting } \tfrac{1-\epsilon}{1-\epsilon+n} \leq \tfrac{\epsilon}{2}).$$

Hence, $\exists c$, such that $(1-\epsilon)^n+n(1-\epsilon)^{n-1} \leq c(1-\frac{\epsilon}{2})^n$ when $n \geq \frac{2}{\epsilon}$. Therefore, the performance converges exponentially.

For the uniform team, the probability of playing the action that has the highest probability in the pdf of the best agent converges to 1 as $n \to \infty$ [13]. Therefore, the performance only increases as $n \to \infty$ if the optimal action is the one that has the highest probability.  □

Now we show that we can achieve further improvement in a diverse team by breaking ties in favor of the strongest agent.

**Theorem 3.** *When* $m \to \infty$, *breaking ties in favor of the strongest agent is the optimal tie-breaking rule for a diverse team.*

*Proof.* Let $s$ be one of the agents. If we break ties in favor of $s$, the probability of voting for the optimal choice will be given by:

$$\tilde{p}_{best} = 1 - \prod_{i=1}^{n}(1 - p_{i,0}) - (1 - p_{s,0})\left(\sum_{i=1,i\neq s}^{n} p_{i,0} \prod_{j=1,j\neq i,j\neq s}^{n}(1 - p_{j,0})\right) \quad (2)$$

It is clear that Eq. 2 is maximized by choosing agent $s$ with the highest $p_{s,0}$. However, we still have to show that it is better to break ties in favor of the strongest agent than breaking ties randomly. That is, we have to show that Eq. 2 is always higher than Eq. 1.

Equation 2 differs from Eq. 1 only on the last term. Therefore, we have to show that the last term of Eq. 2 is smaller than the last term of Eq. 1. Let's begin by rewriting the last term of Eq. 1 as:

$$\frac{n-1}{n}\sum_{i=1}^{n} p_{i,0}\prod_{j=1,j\neq i}^{n}(1-p_{j,0}) =$$
$$\frac{n-1}{n}(1-p_{s,0})\sum_{i=1,i\neq s}^{n} p_{i,0}\prod_{j=1,j\neq i,j\neq s}^{n}(1-p_{j,0}) + \frac{n-1}{n}p_{s,0}\prod_{j=1,j\neq s}^{n}(1-p_{j,0})$$

This implies that:

$$\frac{n-1}{n}\sum_{i=1}^{n} p_{i,0}\prod_{j=1,j\neq i}^{n}(1-p_{j,0}) \geq \frac{n-1}{n}(1-p_{s,0})\sum_{i=1,i\neq s}^{n} p_{i,0}\prod_{j=1,j\neq i,j\neq s}^{n}(1-p_{j,0}).$$

We know that:

$$(1-p_{s,0})\sum_{i=1,i\neq s}^{n} p_{i,0}\prod_{j=1,j\neq i,j\neq s}^{n}(1-p_{j,0}) =$$
$$\frac{n-1}{n}(1-p_{s,0})\sum_{i=1,i\neq s}^{n} p_{i,0}\prod_{j=1,j\neq i,j\neq s}^{n}(1-p_{j,0})+$$
$$\frac{1}{n}(1-p_{s,0})\sum_{i=1,i\neq s}^{n} p_{i,0}\prod_{j=1,j\neq i,j\neq s}^{n}(1-p_{j,0})$$

Therefore, for the last term of Eq. 2 to be smaller than the last term of Eq. 1 we have to show that:

$$\frac{n-1}{n}p_{s,0}\prod_{j=1,j\neq s}^{n}(1-p_{j,0}) \geq \frac{1}{n}(1-p_{s,0})\sum_{i=1,i\neq s}^{n} p_{i,0}\prod_{j=1,j\neq s,j\neq i}^{n}(1-p_{j,0})$$

It follows that the previous equation will be true if:

$$p_{s,0} \geq (1-p_{s,0})\frac{\sum_{i=1,i\neq s}^{n} p_{i,0}\prod_{j=1,j\neq i,j\neq s}^{n}(1-p_{j,0})}{(n-1)\prod_{j=1,j\neq s}^{n}(1-p_{j,0})}$$

$$p_{s,0} \geq (1-p_{s,0})\frac{1}{n-1}\sum_{i=1,i\neq s}^{n} \frac{p_{i,0}}{(1-p_{i,0})}$$

$$\frac{p_{s,0}}{(1-p_{s,0})} \geq \frac{\sum_{i=1,i\neq s}^{n} \frac{p_{i,0}}{(1-p_{i,0})}}{n-1}$$

As $s$ is the strongest agent the previous inequality is always true. This is because $\frac{p_{s,0}}{1-p_{s,0}} = \frac{\sum_{i=1,i\neq s}^{n}\frac{p_{s,0}}{(1-p_{s,0})}}{n-1}$ and $\frac{p_{s,0}}{1-p_{s,0}} \geq \frac{p_{i,0}}{(1-p_{i,0})}\forall i \neq s$. Therefore, it is always better to break ties in favor of the strongest agent than breaking ties randomly.                                                    □

Next we show that with one additional assumption, not only the diverse team converges to $\tilde{p}_{best}$, but also $p_{best}$ monotonically increases with $m$. Our additional assumption is that higher utility actions have higher probabilities, i.e., if $U(a_j) \geq U(a_{j'})$, then $p_{i,j} \geq p_{i,j'}$.

**Theorem 4.** *The performance of a diverse team monotonically increases with* $m$, *if* $U(a_j) \geq U(a_{j'})$ *implies that* $p_{i,j} \geq p_{i,j'}$.

*Proof.* Let an event be one voting iteration, where each agent from a set votes for an action. We denote by $P(\mathbf{V})$ the probability of occurrence of any event in $\mathbf{V}$ (hence, $P(\mathbf{V}) = \sum_{v \in \mathbf{V}} p(v)$). We call it a winning event if in the event the action chosen by plurality is the best action $a_0$ (including ties). We assume that for all agents $i$, if $U(a_j) \geq U(a_{j'})$, then $p_{i,j} \geq p_{i,j'}$.

We show by mathematical induction that we can divide the probability of multiple suboptimal actions into a new action and $p_{best}(m+1) \geq p_{best}(m)$. Let $\lambda$ be the number of actions whose probability is being divided. The base case holds trivially when $\lambda = 0$. That is, there is a new action, but all agents have a 0 probability of voting for that new action. In this case we have that $p_{best}$ does not change, therefore $p_{best}(m+1) \geq p_{best}(m)$.

Now assume that we divided the probability of $\lambda$ actions and it is true that $p_{best}(m+1) \geq p_{best}(m)$. We show that it is also true for $\lambda + 1$. Hence, let's pick one more action to divide the probability. Without loss of generality, assume it is action $a_{d_m}$, for agent $c$, and its probability is being divided into action $a_{d_m+1}$. Therefore, $p'_{c,d_m} = p_{c,d_m} - \beta$ and $p'_{c,d_m+1} = p_{c,d_m+1} + \beta$, for $0 \leq \beta \leq p_{c,d_m}$. Let $p_{best}^{after}(m+1)$ be the probability of voting for the best action after this new division, and $p_{best}^{before}(m+1)$ the probability before this new division. We show that $p_{best}^{after}(m+1) \geq p_{best}^{before}(m+1)$.

Let $\Gamma$ be the set of all events where all agents voted, except for agent $c$ (the order does not matter, so we can consider agent $c$ is the last one to post its vote). If $\gamma \in \Gamma$ will be a winning event no matter if agent $c$ votes for $a_{d_m}$ or $a_{d_m+1}$, then changing agent $c$'s pdf will not affect the probability of these winning events. Hence, let $\Gamma' \subset \Gamma$ be the set of all events that will become a winning event depending if agent $c$ does not vote for $a_{d_m}$ or $a_{d_m+1}$. Given that $\gamma \in \Gamma'$ already happened, the probability of winning or losing is equal to the probability of agent $c$ not voting for $a_{d_m}$ or $a_{d_m+1}$.

Now let's divide $\Gamma'$ in two exclusive subsets: $\Gamma_{d_m+1} \subset \Gamma'$, where for each $\gamma \in \Gamma_{d_m+1}$ action $a_{d_m+1}$ is in tie with action $a_0$, so if agent $c$ does not vote for $a_{d_m+1}$, $\gamma$ will be a winning event; $\Gamma_{d_m} \subset \Gamma'$, where for each $\gamma \in \Gamma_{d_m}$ action $a_{d_m}$ is in tie with action $a_0$, so if agent $c$ does not votes for $a_{d_m}$, $\gamma$ will be a winning event. We do not consider events where both $a_{d_m+1}$ and $a_{d_m}$ are in tie with $a_0$, as in that case the probability of a winning event does not change (it is given by $1 - p'_{c,d_m} - p'_{c,d_m+1} = 1 - p_{c,d_m} - p_{c,d_m+1}$).

Note that for each $\gamma \in \Gamma_{d_m+1}$, the probability of a winning event equals $1 - p'_{c,d_m+1}$. Therefore, after changing the pdf of agent $c$, for each $\gamma \in \Gamma_{d_m+1}$, the probability of a wining event decreases by $\beta$. Similarly, for each $\gamma \in \Gamma_{d_m}$, the probability of a winning event equals $1 - p'_{c,d_m}$. Therefore, after changing the pdf of agent $c$, for each $\gamma \in \Gamma_{d_m}$, the probability of a winning event increases by $\beta$.

Therefore, $p_{best}^{after}(m+1) \geq p_{best}^{before}(m+1)$ if and only if $P(\Gamma_{d_m}) \geq P(\Gamma_{d_m+1})$. Note that $\forall \gamma \in \Gamma_{d_m+1}$ there are more agents that voted for $a_{d_m+1}$ than for $a_{d_m}$. Also, $\forall \gamma \in \Gamma_{d_m}$ there are more agents that voted for $a_{d_m}$ than for $a_{d_m+1}$. If, for all agents $i$, $p_{i,d_m} \geq p_{i,d_m+1}$, we have that $P(\Gamma_{d_m}) \geq P(\Gamma_{d_m+1})$. Therefore, $p_{best}^{after}(m+1) \geq p_{best}^{before}(m+1)$, so we still have that $p_{best}(m+1) \geq p_{best}(m)$. Also note that in order for the next step of the induction to still be valid, so that we can still divide the probability of one more action, it is necessary that $p'_{c,d_m} \geq p'_{c,d_m+1}$. $\square$

In the previous theorems we focused on the probability of playing the best action, assuming that $U(a_0) \gg U(a_j) \ \forall j \neq 0$. We show now that the theorems still hold in more general domains where $r$ actions $(\mathbf{A_r} \subset \mathbf{A})$ have a significant high utility, i.e., $U(a_{j_1}) \gg U(a_{j_2}) \ \forall j_1 < r, j_2 \geq r$. Hence, we now focus on the probability of playing any action in $\mathbf{A_r}$. We assume that our assumptions are also generalized, i.e., $p_{i,j} > \epsilon \ \forall j < r$, and the number $d_m$ of suboptimal actions $(a_j, j \geq r)$ in the $\mathbf{D_m}$ set increases with $m$ for $ST$ agents.

**Theorem 5.** *The previous theorems generalize to settings where* $U(a_{j_1}) \gg U(a_{j_2}) \ \forall j_1 < r, j_2 \geq r.$

*Proof Sketch.* We give here a proof sketch. We just have to generate new pdfs $p'_{i,j}$, such that $p'_{i0} = \sum_{j=0}^{r-1} p_{i,j}$, and $p'_{i,b} = p_{i,b+r-1}, \forall b \neq 0$. We can then reapply the proofs of the previous theorems, but replacing $p_{i,j}$ by $p'_{i,j}$. Note that this does not guarantee that all agents will tend to agree on the same action in $\mathbf{A_r}$; but the team will still tend to pick any action in $\mathbf{A_r}$, since the agents are more likely to agree on actions in $\mathbf{A_r}$ than on actions in $\mathbf{A} \backslash \mathbf{A_r}$. □

Now we discuss a different generalization: what happens when $p_{i,0}$ decreases as $m$ increases ($\forall$ agents $i$). If $p_{i,0} \rightarrow \tilde{p}_{i,0}$ as $m \rightarrow \infty$, the performance in the limit for a diverse team will be $\tilde{p}_{best}$ evaluated at $\tilde{p}_{i,0}$. Moreover, even if $p_{i,0} \rightarrow 0$, our conclusions about relative team performance are not affected as long as we are comparing two $ST$ teams that have similar $p_{i,0}$: the same argument as in Corollary 1 implies that the team with faster growing $d_m$ will perform better.

# 4    Experimental Analysis

## 4.1    Synthetic Experiments

We present synthetic experiments, in order to better understand what happens in real systems. We generate agents by randomly creating pdfs and calculate the probability of playing the best action $(p_{best})$ of the generated teams. We use a uniform distribution to generate all random numbers. When creating a pdf, we rescale the values assigned randomly, so that the overall sum of the pdf is equal to 1.

As we said earlier, uniform teams composed by $NST$ agents is an idealization. In more complex domains, the best agent will not behave exactly like an $NST$ agent; the number of suboptimal actions with a non-zero probability $(d_m)$ will also increase as the action space gets larger. We perform synthetic experiments to study this situation. We consider that the best agent is still closer to an $NST$ agent, therefore it increases its $d_m$ at a slower rate than the agents of the diverse team.

In our first experiment, we use teams of 4 agents. For each agent of the diverse team, $p_{i,0}$ is chosen randomly between 0.6 and 0.7. The remaining is distributed randomly from 10 % to 20 % of the next best actions (the number of actions that will receive a positive probability is also decided randomly). For the uniform team, we make copies of the best agent (with highest $p_{i,0}$) of the diverse

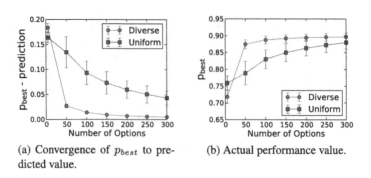

(a) Convergence of $p_{best}$ to predicted value.

(b) Actual performance value.

**Fig. 1.** Comparing diverse and uniform when uniform also increases $d_m$.

team, but distribute the remaining probability randomly from 1 % to 3 % of the next best actions.

We can see the average result for 200 random teams in Fig. 1, where in Fig. 1(a) we show the difference between the performance in the limit ($\tilde{p}_{best}$) and the actual $p_{best}(m)$ for the diverse and the uniform teams; in Fig. 1(b) we show the average $p_{best}(m)$ of the teams. As can be seen, when the best agents increase their $d_m$ at a slower rate than the agents of the diverse team, the uniform teams converge slower to $\tilde{p}_{best}$. Even though they play better than the diverse teams for a small $m$, they are surpassed by the diverse teams as $m$ increases. However, because $\tilde{p}_{best}$ of the uniform teams is actually higher than the one of the diverse teams, eventually the performance of the uniform teams get closer to the performance of the diverse teams, and will be better than the one of the diverse teams again for a large enough $m$.

This situation is expected according to Theorem 1. If the $d_m$ of the best agent also increases as $m$ gets larger, the uniform team will actually behave like a diverse team and also converge to $\tilde{p}_{best}$. $\tilde{p}_{best}^{uniform} \geq \tilde{p}_{best}^{diverse}$, as the best agent has a higher probability of playing the optimal action. Hence, in the limit the uniform team will play better than the diverse team. However, as we saw in Corollary 1, the speed of convergence is in the order of $1/d_m$. Therefore, the diverse team will converge faster, and can overcome the uniform team for moderately large $m$.

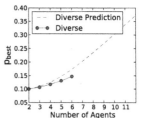

**Fig. 2.** $p_{best}$ of a diverse team as the number of agents increases.

As Theorem 2 only holds when $m \to \infty$, we also explore the effect of increasing the number of agents for a large $m$. The $\tilde{p}_{best}$ of a team of agents is shown as the dashed line in Fig. 2. We are plotting for agents that have a probability of playing the best action of only 0.1, but as we can see the probability quickly grows as the number of agents increases. We also calculate $p_{best}$ for random teams from 2 to 6 agents (shown as the continuous line), when there are 300 available actions. Each agent has a probability of playing the best action of 0.1, and the remaining probability is randomly distributed over the

10 % next best actions. As can be seen, the teams have a close performance to the expected. We only show up to 6 agents because it is too computationally expensive to calculate the pdfs of larger teams.

### 4.2    Computer Go

We present now results in a real system. We use in our experiments 4 different Go software: Fuego 1.1, GnuGo 3.8, Pachi 9.01, MoGo 4, and two (weaker) variants of Fuego (Fuego$\Delta$ and Fuego$\Theta$), in a total of 6 different, publicly available, agents. Fuego is considered the strongest agent among all of them. Fuego is an implementation of the UCT Monte Carlo Go algorithm, therefore it uses heuristics to simulate games in order to evaluate board configurations. Fuego uses mainly 5 heuristics during these simulations, and they are executed in a hierarchical order. The original Fuego agent follows the order <Atari Capture, Atari Defend, Lowlib, Pattern> (the heuristic called Nakade is not enabled by default). Our variation called Fuego$\Delta$ follows the order <Atari Defend, Atari Capture, Pattern, Nakade, Lowlib>, while Fuego$\Theta$ follows the order <Atari Defend, Nakade, Pattern, Atari Capture, Lowlib>. Also, Fuego$\Delta$ and Fuego$\Theta$ have half of the memory available when compared with the original Fuego.

All our results are obtained by playing either 1000 games (to evaluate individual agents) or 2000 games (to evaluate teams), in a HP dl165 with dual dodeca core, 2.33 GHz processors and 48 GB of RAM. We compare results obtained by playing against a fixed opponent. Therefore, we evaluate systems playing as white, against the original Fuego playing as black. We removed all databases and specific board size knowledge of the agents, including the opponent. We call Diverse as the team composed of all 6 agents, and Uniform as the team composed of 6 copies of Fuego. Each agent is initialized with a different random seed, therefore they will not vote for the same action all the time in a given world state, due to the characteristics of the search algorithms. In all the graphs we present in this section, the error bars show the confidence interval, with 99 % of confidence ($p = 0.01$).

We evaluate the performance of the teams over 7 different board sizes. We changed the time settings of individual agents as we increased the board size, in order to keep their strength as constant as possible. The average winning rates of the team members is shown in Table 2, while Table 3 show the winning rates of the individual agents.[1]

We can see our results in Fig. 4(a). Diverse improves from 58.1 % on $9 \times 9$ to 72.1 % on $21 \times 21$, an increase in winning rate that is statistically significant with $p < 2.2 \times 10^{-16}$. This result is expected according to Theorem 1. Uniform changes from 61.0 % to 65.8 %, a statistically significant improvement with

---

[1] In our first experiment, Diverse improved from 56.1 % on $9 \times 9$ to 85.9 % on $19 \times 19$. We noted, however, that some of the diverse agents were getting stronger in relation to the opponent as the board size increased. Hence, by changing the time setting to keep the strength constant, we are actually making our claims harder to show, not easier.

**Table 2.** Average winning rates of the team members across different board sizes. Note that these are not the winning rates of the teams.

| Team | $9 \times 9$ | $11 \times 11$ | $13 \times 13$ | $15 \times 15$ | $17 \times 17$ | $19 \times 19$ | $21 \times 21$ |
|---|---|---|---|---|---|---|---|
| Diverse | 32.2 % | 30.8 % | 29.6 % | 29.4 % | 31.5 % | 31.9 % | 30.3 % |
| Uniform | 48.1 % | 48.6 % | 46.1 % | 48.0 % | 49.3 % | 46.9 % | 46.6 % |

**Table 3.** Winning rates of each one of the agents across different board sizes.

| Agent | $9 \times 9$ | $11 \times 11$ | $13 \times 13$ | $15 \times 15$ | $17 \times 17$ | $19 \times 19$ | $21 \times 21$ |
|---|---|---|---|---|---|---|---|
| Fuego | 48.1 % | 48.6 % | 46.1 % | 48.0 % | 49.3 % | 46.9 % | 46.6 % |
| GnuGo | 1.1 % | 1.1 % | 1.9 % | 1.9 % | 4.5 % | 6.8 % | 6.1 % |
| Pachi | 25.7 % | 22.9 % | 25.8 % | 26.9 % | 23.5 % | 20.8 % | 11.0 % |
| MoGo | 27.6 % | 26.4 % | 22.7 % | 22.0 % | 27.1 % | 30.1 % | 27.1 % |
| Fuego$\Delta$ | 45.7 % | 45.8 % | 42.2 % | 40.4 % | 43.0 % | 44.5 % | 47.4 % |
| Fuego$\Theta$ | 45.5 % | 40.2 % | 39.2 % | 37.6 % | 41.8 % | 42.3 % | 43.6 % |

$p = 0.0018$. As we saw before, an increase in the performance of Uniform can also be expected, as the best agent might not be a perfect *NST* agent. A linear regression of the results of both teams gives a slope of 0.010 for the diverse team (adjusted $R^2$: 0.808, $p = 0.0036$) and 0.005 for the uniform team (adjusted $R^2$: 0.5695, $p = 0.0305$). Therefore, the diverse team improves its winning rate faster than the uniform team. To check if this is a significant difference, we evaluate the interaction term in a linear regression with multiple variables. We find that the influence of board size is higher on Diverse than on Uniform with $p = 0.0797$ (estimated coefficient of "size of the board $\times$ group type": $-10.321$, adjusted $R^2$: 0.7437). Moreover, on the $9 \times 9$ board Diverse is worse than Uniform ($p = 0.0663$), while on the $21 \times 21$ board Diverse is better with high statistical significance ($p = 1.941 \times 10^{-5}$). We also analyze the performance of the teams subtracted by the average strength of their members (Fig. 4(b)), in order to calculate the increase in winning rate achieved by "teamwork" and compensate fluctuations on the winning rate of the agents as we change the board size. Again, the diverse team improves faster than the uniform team. A linear regression results in a slope of 0.0104 for Diverse (adjusted $R^2$: 0.5549, $p = 0.0546$) and 0.0043 for Uniform (adjusted $R^2$: 0.1283, $p = 0.258$).

We also evaluate the performance of teams of 4 agents (Diverse 4 and Uniform 4). For Diverse 4, we removed Fuego$\Delta$ and Fuego$\Theta$ from the Diverse team. As can be seen in Fig. 3, the impact of adding more agents is higher for the diverse team in a larger board size ($21 \times 21$). In the $9 \times 9$ board, the difference between Diverse 4 and Diverse 6 is only 4.4 %; while in $21 \times 21$ it is 14 %. Moreover, we can

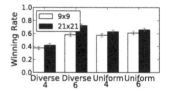

**Fig. 3.** Winning rates for 4 and 6 agents teams.

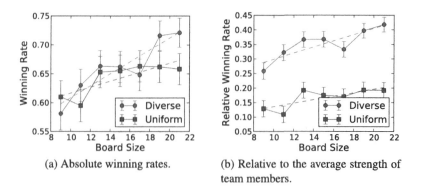

(a) Absolute winning rates.

(b) Relative to the average strength of team members.

**Fig. 4.** Winning rate in the real Computer Go system.

see a higher impact of adding agents for the diverse team, than for the uniform team. These results would be expected according to Theorem 2.

As can be seen, the predictions of our theory holds: the diverse team improves significantly as we increase the action space. The improvement is enough to make it change from playing worse than the uniform team on $9 \times 9$ to playing better than the uniform team with statistical significance on the $21 \times 21$ board. Furthermore, we show a higher impact of adding more agents when the size of the board is larger.

### 4.3  Analysis

To test the assumptions of our model, we estimate a pdf for each one of the agents. For each board size, and for each one of 1000 games from our experiments, we randomly choose a board state between the first and the last movement. We make Fuego evaluate the chosen board, but with a time limit 50x higher than the default one. Therefore, we use this much stronger version of Fuego to approximate the true ranking of all actions. For each board size, we run all agents in each board sample and check in which position of the approximated true ranking they play. This allow us to build a histogram for each agent and board size combination. Some examples can be seen in Fig. 5. We can see that a strong agent, like Fuego, has most of its probability mass on the higher ranked actions, while weaker agents, like GnuGo, has the mass of its pdf distributed over a larger set of actions, creating a larger tail. Moreover, the probability mass of GnuGo is spread over a larger number of actions when we increase the size of the board.

We study how the pdfs of the agents change as we increase the action space. Our hypothesis is that weaker agents will have a behavior closer to $ST$ agents, while stronger agents to $NST$ agents. In Fig. 6(a) we show how many actions receive a probability higher than 0. As can be seen, Fuego does not behave exactly like an $NST$ agent. However, it does have a slower growth rate than the other agents. A linear regression gives the following slopes: 13.08, 19.82, 19.05, 15.82,

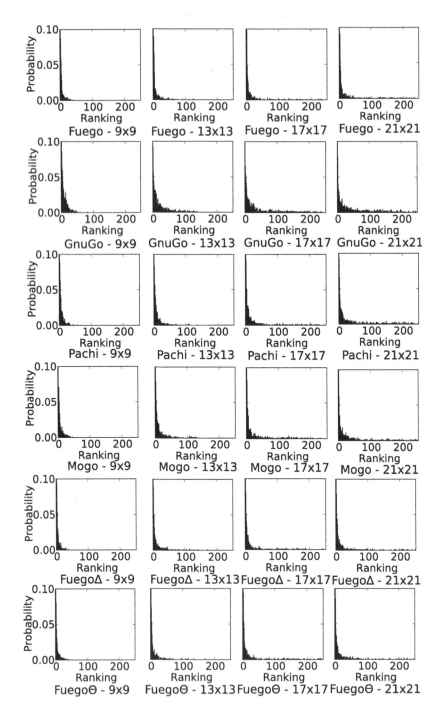

**Fig. 5.** Histograms of agents for different board sizes.

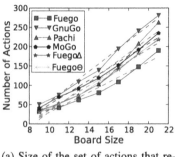

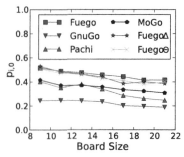

(a) Size of the set of actions that receive a nonzero probability.

(b) $p_{i,0}$ as the size of the board grows.

**Fig. 6.** Verifying the assumptions in the real system.

15.69, 16.03 for Fuego, Gnugo, Pachi, Mogo, Fuego$\Delta$ and Fuego$\Theta$, respectively ($R^2$: 0.95, 0.98, 0.94, 0.98, 0.98, 0.98, respectively). It is clear, therefore, that the probability mass of weak agents is distributed into bigger sets of actions as we increase the action space, and even though the strongest agent does not behave in the idealized way it does have a slower growth rate.

We also verify how the probability of playing the best action changes for each one of the agents as the number of actions increases. Figure 6(b) shows that even though all agents experience a decrease in $p_{i,0}$, it does not decrease much. From $9 \times 9$, all the way to $21 \times 21$, we measure the following decrease: 20 %, 23 %, 39 %, 26 %, 28 %, 22 %, for Fuego, Gnugo, Pachi, Mogo, Fuego$\Delta$ and Fuego$\Theta$, respectively. Hence, on average, they decreased about 25 % from $9 \times 9$ to $21 \times 21$. Even though our assumption about $p_{i,0}$ does not hold perfectly, the predictions of our model are still verified. Therefore, the amount of decrease experienced is not enough to avoid that the diverse team increases in performance as the action space grows.

## 5    Conclusion and Discussions

Diversity is an important point to consider when forming teams. In this paper we present a new model that captures better than previous ones the intuitive notion of diverse agents as agents that tend to disagree. This model allows us to make new predictions. We show that the performance of diverse teams increases as the size of the action space gets larger. Uniform teams may also increase in performance, but at a slower pace than diverse teams. Therefore, even though a diverse team may start playing worse than a uniform team, it can eventually outperform the uniform team as the action space increases. Besides, we show that in large action spaces the performance of a diverse team converges exponentially fast to the optimal one as the number of agents increases.

We start our model with the notion of *spreading tail* (*ST*) and *non-spreading tail* (*NST*) agents. *ST* agents are agents that have a non-zero probability over a larger set of actions as the action space increases, while $NST$ agents always have a constant number of actions with non-zero probability. We define a diverse team as a team of $ST$ agents, and a uniform team as a team of $NST$ agents. Therefore, our focus changes from modeling diverse teams as teams with different agents (as in models such as Marcolino, Jiang, and Tambe (2013) [14]), to focusing on diverse teams as teams where the agents tend to disagree. This change allows us to make new predictions that were not possible before.

Note that our model does *not* say that an $NST$ agent will never vote for a new action. We define the pdfs of the agents by the rankings of the actions. Hence, when the number of actions increases from a certain number $x_0$ to a new number $x_1$, a new action $a*$ may be the action with highest utility. Therefore, an agent will have the same probability of voting for $a*$ that it had for voting for the previously best action when the number of actions was only $x_0$. A uniform team made of copies of the best agent also does *not* mean that the agents always vote for the same actions. The vote of each agent is a sample from a pdf, so copies of a single agent may or may not vote for the same action. In fact, we observe an increase in performance by voting among multiple copies of a single agent, both theoretically and experimentally.

The division of agents into two types ($ST$ and $NST$) is, however, only an idealization, that allows us to isolate and study in detail the effect of diversity. A very strong agent will normally have most of its probability mass on the actions with the highest utility, so in the extreme its pdf would never change by adding new actions. In reality, however, it may also consider a larger set of actions as the action space grows. Therefore, we relax our model, and introduce the hypothesis that the best agent spreads the tail of its pdf at a slower pace than weaker agents. We show that because of this effect, a diverse team increases in performance faster than uniform teams, and we illustrate this phenomenon with synthetic experiments. Hence, even in a relaxed model where both diverse and uniform teams are composed of $ST$ agents, a diverse team still outperforms a uniform team as the action space grows. The effect, however, is transient, as a uniform team may still have a higher convergence point than a diverse team, so in extreme large action spaces it would again outperform the diverse team. If the agents have the same probability of playing the best action, however, then it is clear that in the limit the diverse team will always be better than the uniform team.

Our model needs one strong assumption: that the probability of the individual agents voting for the best action does not change as the action space increases. This assumption allows our analysis to be cleaner, although it may not hold perfectly in a real system. In fact, in our Computer Go experiments we did observe a decrease in the probability of the agents voting for the best action. However, even though the assumption did not hold perfectly, the predictions of our theory holds: a diverse team significantly increased in performance as the action space got larger. Clearly, a decrease in the probability of the individual agents voting for the best action will decrease the performance of a team, while the effects studied in this paper will increase the performance. Therefore, as long as the decrease is not large enough to counter-balance the effect under study, we are still going to observe an increase in performance as the action space gets larger. Moreover, as we discuss in our generalizations, the argument that teams that spread the tail faster converge faster is still valid when the assumption does not hold; hence if the agents are equally strong (i.e., the individual agents have the same probability of voting for the best action) the team with faster growing tail will always perform better.

As mentioned, we verified our theory in a real system of Computer Go playing agents. Not only a real diverse team of agents effectively increased in performance as the board size increased, but we also verified that the strongest agent indeed spreads the tail of its pdf at a slower rate than other weaker agents. We also verified that both diverse and uniform teams increase in performance, but the diverse team increased two times faster. This is explained by the relaxed version of our model, when we predict diverse teams to converge faster than uniform teams, as illustrated by our synthetic experiments.

**Acknowledgments.** This research was supported by MURI grant W911NF-11-1-0332.

# References

1. Agmon, N., Stone, P.: Leading ad hoc agents in joint action settings with multiple teammates. In: AAMAS, Richland, SC, pp. 341–348 (2012)
2. Barrett, S., Stone, P., Kraus, S., Rosenfeld, A.: Teamwork with limited knowledge of teammates. In: AAAI (2013)
3. Caragiannis, I., Procaccia, A.D., Shah, N.: When do noisy votes reveal the truth? In: EC, pp. 143–160 (2013)
4. Chen, H., Yao, X.: Regularized negative correlation learning for neural network ensembles. IEEE Trans. Neural Netw. **20**(12), 1962–1979 (2009)
5. Conitzer, V., Sandholm, T.: Common voting rules as maximum likelihood estimators. In: UAI (2005)
6. Fu, B., Wang, Z., Pan, R., Xu, G., Dolog, P.: An integrated pruning criterion for ensemble learning based on classification accuracy and diversity. In: Uden, L., Herrera, F., Pérez, J.B., Manuel, J., Rodríguez, C. (eds.) Proceedings of the 7th International Conference on Knowledge Management in Organizations. AISC, vol. 172, pp. 47–58. Springer, Heidelberg (2012)
7. Guttmann, C.: Making allocations collectively: iterative group decision making under uncertainty. In: Bergmann, R., Lindemann, G., Kirn, S., Pěchouček, M. (eds.) MATES 2008. LNCS (LNAI), vol. 5244, pp. 73–85. Springer, Heidelberg (2008)
8. Hong, L., Page, S.E.: Groups of diverse problem solvers can outperform groups of high-ability problem solvers. Proc. Natl. Acad. Sci. USA **101**(46), 16385–16389 (2004)
9. Jiang, A.X., Marcolino, L.S., Procaccia, A.D., Sandholm, T., Shah, N., Tambe, M.: Diverse randomized agents vote to win. In: NIPS (2014)
10. Lamberson, P.J., Page, S.E.: Optimal forecasting groups. Manag. Sci. **58**(4), 805–810 (2012)

11. LiCalzi, M., Surucu, O.: The power of diversity over large solution spaces. Manag. Sci. **58**(7), 1408–1421 (2012)
12. Liemhetcharat, S., Veloso, M.: Modeling and learning synergy for team formation with heterogeneous agents. In: AAMAS, Richland, SC, pp. 365–374 (2012)
13. List, C., Goodin, R.E.: Epistemic democracy: generalizing the Condorcet Jury theorem. J. Polit. Philos. **9**, 277–306 (2001)
14. Marcolino, L.S., Jiang, A.X., Tambe, M.: Multi-agent team formation: diversity beats strength? In: IJCAI (2013)
15. Matthews, T., Ramchurn, S.D., Chalkiadakis, G.: Competing with humans at fantasy football: team formation in large partially-observable domains. In: AAAI, pp. 1394–1400 (2012)
16. Nair, R., Tambe, M.: Hybrid BDI-POMDP framework for multiagent teaming. J. Artif. Intell. Res. **23**(1), 367–420 (2005)
17. Polikar, R.: Ensemble learning. In: Zhang, C., Ma, Y. (eds.) Ensemble Machine Learning: Methods and Application, pp. 1–34. Springer, New York (2012)
18. Soufiani, H.A., Parkes, D.C., Xia, L.: Random utility theory for social choice. In: NIPS, pp. 126–134 (2012)
19. Thompson, A.: Does diversity trump ability? an example of the misuse of mathematics in the social sciences. Not. AMS **61**(9), 1024–1030 (2014)

# Towards the Disruption of Plans

Andrada Voinitchi[(⊠)], Elizabeth Black, and Michael Luck

Department of Informatics, King's College London, London, UK
andrada.voinitchi@kcl.ac.uk

**Abstract.** In order for an agent or a group of agents (such as a team) to achieve a goal, a sequence of actions have to be performed. These actions bring about state transitions that constitute a plan. Multiple ways of achieving the goal may exist. In some situations, one may want to prevent or delay an agent or group of agents from achieving a goal. We argue that plans can be disrupted by preventing particular state transitions from happening. We propose four algorithms to identify which state transitions should be thwarted such that the achievement of the goal is prevented (total disruption) or delayed (partial disruption). In order to evaluate the performance of our algorithms we define disruption (partial and total) and also provide metrics for its measurement. We do acknowledge that the disruptor may not always have an accurate representation of the disruptee's plans. Thus, we perform an experimental analysis to examine the performance of the algorithms when some of the state transitions available to the disruptee are unknown to the disruptor.

## 1 Introduction

In order to expose and motivate the issue of plan disruption we consider a real-life scenario: a team of terrorists is planning to place and detonate a bomb in a tube station. The bomb needs to be smuggled in part by part in order for the station staff not to become suspicious. There is more than one way that the team can achieve its target: the bomb can be smuggled a part at a time, while keeping the parts hidden in the tube station or it can be smuggled in different combinations of two or three parts. Then it needs to be assembled and detonated. The terrorists must coordinate in order to assemble the bomb on the premises, and leave the station before the bomb is detonated. In order to ease coordination the terrorists can act according to a common plan, a sequence of state transitions brought about in order to achieve a desired outcome. The terrorists have more than one way of achieving their goal (i.e. smuggling the bomb in different ways, either part by part or in combination), hence, they have a set of plans to achieve the goal. We will refer to the set of all possible plans to achieve the goal as the plan base.

The terrorists do not know that the security services have discovered their intentions. The security services want to prevent achievement of the goal of detonating the bomb and destroying the tube station, but only have partial information about the terrorists' plan base. A question of particular interest

© Springer International Publishing Switzerland 2015
A. Ghose et al. (Eds.): COIN 2014, LNAI 9372, pp. 233–250, 2015.
DOI: 10.1007/978-3-319-25420-3_15

to us arises from this example: is there a way to prevent the terrorists from detonating the bomb? If so, how can it be done?

We believe that the disruption of plans plays an important role in both defensive and competitive settings such as the terrorist attack scenario, where the security services have to work in a time race against the terrorists in order to prevent a disaster. We also believe that the disruption of plans is applicable both in the context of teamwork (teams use plans [1]) as well as the context of single agents [2,3]. If we analyze our scenario (where the terrorists act as a team with a goal and a plan base), we can identify the state transitions that need to be prevented in order to make the attacks fail, providing valuable information about counter-acting malicious behavior. With this motivation, we address the question of disrupting a plan base by determining sets of state transitions that, if prevented, render a goal unachievable. In order to determine such sets, we propose four algorithms that identify state transitions in a plan base, to be prevented in order to make the goal unachievable. We also provide an experimental analysis of the performance of the proposed algorithms given different plan bases, varying parameters such as a plan base's number of states, number of goal states, the number of state transitions that are unknown to the disruptor and the number of state transitions existing as part of the plan base. Our general research focuses on identifying agents, abilities of agents, communication links between agents and resources required for these transitions to happen and finding ways of severing each of these aspects in order to prevent a set of transitions, but this is outside the scope of this paper. This paper presents a first step towards achieving such disruption: it provides a way to identify which transitions in a plan base should be thwarted in order to prevent the achievement of the goal.

The main contribution of this paper consists of the four algorithms that can be used to determine state transitions that must be disrupted in a plan base in order to render its goal unachievable. We also provide an experimental analysis of our algorithms' performance, discussing how the disruption value obtained from each algorithm is influenced by the number of states, goals, the density and the number of transitions unknown to the disruptor in a plan base.

We start by defining the plan base (a graph that captures all possible plans to achieve a goal) in Sect. 3. We further define a metric to measure disruption of a plan base and discuss two types of disruption: full and partial disruption in Sect. 4. Section 5 presents four algorithms that each identify from a plan base, a set of state transitions for which, once prevented, there is no longer a plan to achieve the goal. Since a disruptor may not always have an accurate representation of the plan base it wishes to disrupt, in Sect. 6 we discuss disruption under uncertainty. Sections 7 and 8 present an experiment: set-up and analysis of experimental data for the performance of the proposed algorithms on different plan bases and under uncertainty.

## 2   Related Work

Existing research places the disruption of plans discussed in this paper in the context of disrupting agents or teams of agents. Voinitchi et al. propose that a team's plans are disrupted in order to prevent the team from achieving its goal. They suggest the use of norms and incentives in order to prevent agents from performing state transitions in team's plans, thus causing disruption [4]. This work is preliminary and does not provide a way of identifying state transitions that should be prevented. We address this issue here, starting from the initial idea of finding critical state transitions in a plan.

When considering how a disruptor can determine a set of state transitions that, if prevented, would mean that there is no longer a plan to achieve the goal, we need to be able to represent plans. Work has been done specifying how single agents represent, reason and act about their plans, in order to achieve goals [5,6], and agent architectures such as PRS and dMARS rely on plan libraries in order for such agents to function [2,3]. We use concepts such as sets of plans, plans, states, state transitions and goals as referred to in existing work. We also use the idea of identifying state transitions that are part of more than one plan in a plan base as a way of minimizing the set of state transitions that need to be thwarted in order to obtain disruption of the said plan base. This idea is inspired by work to identify and order landmarks [7] in which, a landmark is a variable (fact) that is true at one point in all of the solution plans for reaching a goal. We do not use landmarks or state variables in our algorithms, but we adopted the idea of finding shared features (in our case, state transitions) among plans and using them to identify sets of state transitions we call critical for disruption.

The concept of representing plans, in the form of malicious attack plans, is also encountered in the context of systems security. Attack trees are used in order to model threats against a computer system. An attack tree is a tree with the malicious goal as the root node and, each of its leaves representing a starting state from which a malicious entity can act in order to bring about the goal [8,9]. A path from a leaf to the root node describes a way of performing a successful attack. While relying on a similar idea, our approach is different as we assume a unique start state for all plans (the state where disruption starts). We acknowledge that there may be more than one goal state and account for this in our model. Each single plan in our model could be represented as a plan in an attack tree with the start state of the plan being a leaf node and the goal state of the plan being the root node. However, due to the fact that our model allows for multiple different goal states to be represented and an attack tree only has one root, all plans of an agent or team of agents can not be represented by a single attack tree. Furthermore, we also study the possibility of not having complete and accurate information about the plans we want to disrupt.

Kordy et al. offers another perspective on modeling and protection against malicious attacks using attack-defense trees in [10,11]. An attack-defense tree is a graphical representation of actions that an attacker can perform in order to attack a computer system and actions that a defender can perform in order to protect the system from the attack. These trees are used in the analysis of security threats in the context of information security [12]. Both this approach and our approach use graph structures to model a collection of plans. However, attack-defense trees model the steps of an attack and the possible response from the part of whoever is disrupting an attack to any of those steps. The perspective implied is one of disruption during an attack. In the same context, our approach is focused on preventing such an attack before it happens. Work on attack-defense trees presented in [10–12] is part of a larger effort to understand and prevent information security threats: the TRESsPASS project[1]. The TRESsPASS project studies information security threats and attacks from multiple perspectives, ranging from technical to social sciences (social engineering) [13]. The project aims to provide tools to analyze information security risks, attacks and ways of preventing or minimizing the occurrence of such attacks.

The idea of representing an opponent's plans has also been presented in the context of adversarial planning [14,15]. The perspective often invoked is that of an actor in a scenario (for example in Go [16] and Capture the Flag [17] game settings) that plans the sequence of actions to achieve a goal in response to the actions that it believes its adversary, or adversaries [15], are likely to perform. Our work is different as we focus on disrupting all possible plans an adversary may have to reach their goal, rather than plan our actions to reach our goal based on what an adversary might do. Furthermore, we view disruption from a global perspective rather than the perspective of an actor in a scenario. We assume a partial representation of a plan base and identify the state transitions to be disrupted in order to prevent or delay the achievement of goals, as a starting step in the disruption of plans.

Teams of agents also use plans to achieve a shared goal. A team of agents is a group of agents that have a joint goal [18,19]. Currently existing teamwork theories all share a common feature: agents in teams use plans in order to achieve the goal. However, the way that the teams' plans are constructed differs from theory to theory. For example, Shared Plans specifies the use of complete plans in which agents know the steps that need to be taken to achieve the goal: plans in which agents are assigned to actions (an agent causes a state transition by performing an action) [1]. Shared Plans also allows partial shared plans which represent a specification of the minimal requirements that agents need to have in order to take part in the collaboration [1]. Joint Intentions differs in that a plan is built as agents commit to performing actions towards achieving the goal: if one agent performs an action, another agent is also committed to doing its share [20]. Joint Responsibility theory involves a joint commitment to a common plan, once it is established that the agents involved fulfill a set of pre-imposed collaboration requirements. A plan specifies how agents should behave in order to achieve a goal, thus answering the question of how the joint goal will be achieved [21]. The fact that agent teams also use plans in order to achieve their goals extends the applicability of our proposed algorithms to disrupting teams' plans.

We choose to represent a plan base as a set of sequences of states that are brought about by uni-directional state transitions. Each plan has one starting state and one goal state. The starting state is unique in a plan base, but, multiple different goal states are allowed. Based on this description, a plan base can be

---

[1] http://www.trespass-project.eu/.

represented as a set of paths in a directed, acyclic graph. Thus, the problem of finding a set of state transitions that need to be disrupted such that no plans to achieve a goal remain, is translated into the problem of finding a set of edges to cut in a graph such that one node (the start state) is part of a different sub-graph to a set of other nodes (the goal states).

One approach to finding cuts that ensure a disconnection between two nodes in a graph is using the Maximum Flow Minimum Cut theorem in conjunction with a maximum flow algorithm such as Ford-Fulkerson [22] or Goldberg and Tarjan's [23] approaches. The Maximum Flow Minimum Cut theorem specifies that the maximum flow directed from a source node to a sink node in a flow network (a directed, weighted graph) is equal to the minimum capacity that, if removed in a specific way from the network, results in a situation where no flow can be directed from the source node to the sink node. In other words, if we find the edges that can no longer be used to direct flows, those edges constitute the minimum cut. Ford-Fulkerson and Goldberg-Tarjan algorithms can be used to determine the maximum flow in a network and proceed towards finding a minimum cut. However, currently our model does not use any edge weights for the graph used to represent a plan base. Using this approach and assigning flow values for each edge ends up indirectly prioritizing state transitions to be cut based on the values assigned. To avoid this, we leave this approach for further work, once edge weights are introduced to account for resources needed to prevent transitions.

A second approach to get the minimum cut in a graph is the non-flow based approach. Algorithms such as Stoer-Wagner [24] and Karger's [25] algorithm can be used to determine cuts of edges between a start node and an end node such that no path between the nodes is available. These algorithms are meant to provide the cut of minimum weight from a graph and work on weighted graphs. We devise our own approach inspired by Karger's algorithm and adapted for unweighted graphs because our model does not involve edge weights at this time. Furthermore, rather than obtaining just one cut, we aim to provide more options, to address scenarios where a specific cut cannot be applied (i.e. one of the state transitions cannot be prevented for whatever reason).

## 3   Representing Plans

We represent a plan as a sequence of transitions between states. We denote the set of all states as $S$ and assume a set of possible state transitions, where a state transition is simply a pair of states. A *plan* is then a sequence of state transitions, the application of which causes the overall transition from the start state to the goal state of the plan.

**Definition 1.** *A* **plan** *with* **start state** $s_0 \in S$ *to achieve* **goal state** $s_g \in S$ *given* **possible state transitions** $T \subseteq S \times S$ *is a sequence of state transitions*

$$[(s_0, s_1), (s_1, s_2), \ldots, (s_{n-1}, s_n), (s_n, s_g)]$$

*where $n \geq 1$ and for all $i$ such that $0 \leq i \leq n-1$, $(s_i, s_{i+1})$ and $(s_n, s_g) \in T$. The set of all plans with start state $s_0$ to achieve goal state $s_g$ given possible state transitions $T$ is denoted* $\mathsf{Plans}(s_0, s_g, T)$.

We are interested in preventing a goal from being achieved; if there were only one state that achieves the goal and only one plan to achieve that goal state, it would be sufficient to prevent a state transition from that plan. However, often there are several states in which the goal is achieved and multiple plans to achieve those goal states from a particular start state. We define a *plan base* for a particular start state, set of goal states and set of possible state transitions as a graph that captures all possible plans that can be used to achieve one of the goal states.

**Definition 2.** *The* **plan base** *with* **start state** $s_0 \in \mathcal{S}$, **goal states** $G \neq \emptyset \subseteq \mathcal{S}$ *and* **possible state transitions** $T \subseteq \mathcal{S} \times \mathcal{S}$, *denoted* $\mathsf{PlanBase}(s_0, G, T)$, *is the graph* $(N, E)$ *such that* $N \subseteq \mathcal{S}$, $E \subseteq T$ *and the following conditions hold.*

1. *For all* $s_g \in G$, *if there exists* $[(s_0, s_1), \ldots, (s_{n-1}, s_n), (s_n, s_g)] \in \mathsf{Plans}(s_0, s_g, T)$, *then for all $i$ such that* $0 \leq i \leq n$, $(s_i, s_{i+1}) \in E$ *and* $\{s_i, s_{i+1}\} \subseteq N$.
2. *If there exists* $(s_x, s_y) \in E$, *then there exists* $s_g \in G$ *such that* $[(s_0, s_1), \ldots, (s_{n-1}, s_n), (s_n, s_g)] \in \mathsf{Plans}(s_0, s_g, T)$ *and there exists $i$ such that* $0 \leq i \leq n$, $s_x = s_i$ *and* $s_y = s_{i+1}$.
3. *If there exists* $s_x \in N$, *then there exists* $s_g \in G$ *such that* $[(s_0, s_1), \ldots, (s_{n-1}, s_n), (s_n, s_g)] \in \mathsf{Plans}(s_0, s_g, T)$ *and either* $s_x = s_g$ *or there exists $i$ such that* $0 \leq i \leq n$ *and* $s_x = s_i$.

Given a particular plan base, in order to try to prevent the achievement of a goal, a disruptor can make certain state transitions impossible. This results in a *disrupted plan base*. If the disrupted plan base is empty, *full disruption* has been achieved. Otherwise, if there does not exist a plan of shorter or equal length than the shortest plan pre-disruption, *partial disruption* has been achieved. *Partial disruption* translates into a delay in the achievement of the goal.

**Definition 3.** *The* **disrupted plan base** *that results from* **applying the prevention of state transitions** $T' \subseteq \mathcal{S} \times \mathcal{S}$ *with regard to* **start state** $s_0 \in \mathcal{S}$, **goal states** $G \subseteq \mathcal{S}$ *and* **possible state transitions** $T \subseteq \mathcal{S} \times \mathcal{S}$, *is denoted* $\mathsf{DisruptedPlanBase}(s_0, G, T, T')$ *such that* $\mathsf{DisruptedPlanBase}(s_0, G, T, T')$ $=$ $\mathsf{PlanBase}(s_0, G, T \backslash T')$. *A disrupted plan base* $\mathsf{DisruptedPlanBase}(s_0, G, T, T')$ *can then be said to be* **fully disrupted** *iff* $\mathsf{DisruptedPlanBase}(s_0, G, T, T') = (\emptyset, \emptyset)$.

In order to try to bring about a fully disrupted plan base, a disruptor must identify which state transitions it could prevent. If preventing a particular set of state transitions produces a fully disrupted plan base, that set of state transitions is a *critical set*.

**Definition 4.** *Let* $s_0 \in \mathcal{S}$, $G \neq \emptyset \subseteq \mathcal{S}$ *and* $T' \subseteq T \subseteq \mathcal{S} \times \mathcal{S}$. *The set of state transitions* $T'$ *is a* **critical set** *with regards to* **start state** $s_0$, **goal states** $G$ *and* **possible state transitions** $T$, *denoted* $T' \in \mathsf{CriticalSets}(s_0, G, T)$, *iff* $\mathsf{DisruptedPlanBase}(s_0, G, T, T')$ *is fully disrupted.*

Preventing a critical set of transitions of a plan base results in full disruption; however, in some cases this may not be possible, either because some of the critical transitions cannot be successfully prevented or because there are some possible state transitions that are unknown to the disruptor. Nevertheless, some disruption may occur if certain plans to reach the goal are no longer possible. In the following section we define a metric for measuring disruption.

## 4   Measuring Disruption

In order to fully disrupt a plan base, it is not enough to disrupt only one of its plans. All plans need to be disrupted such that there is no possibility of bringing about any of the goal states. However, a plan base can also be considered disrupted if the length (i.e. the number of transitions) of the shortest plan post-disruption is larger than the length of the shortest plan pre-disruption (we call this *partial disruption*). We define a *disruption metric* (DM) to measure the disruption of a plan base. DM is calculated as a function of the shortest plan lengths in a plan base pre and post-disruption.

**Definition 5.** *We denote the* **length** *of a plan* $p = [(s_0, s_1), \ldots, (s_n, s_g)]$ *as* $\mathsf{Length}(p)$ *such that* $\mathsf{Length}(p) = n$.
*We denote the* **minimum length** *of a plan base* $P = \mathsf{PlanBase}(s_0, G, T)$ *as* $\mathsf{Min}(P)$ *such that* $\mathsf{Min}(P) = \mathsf{Length}(p)$ *where* $p = \underset{p \in \{\mathsf{Plans}(s_0, s_g, T) \mid s_g \in G\}}{\mathrm{argmin}} \mathsf{Length}(p)$.
*The* **disruption metric** *that results from* **applying the prevention of state transitions** $T'$ *with regards to* **start state** $s_0$, *goal states* $G$ *and* **possible state transitions** $T$ *is denoted* $\mathsf{DM}(s_0, G, T, T') \in [0, 1]$ *such that:*

- $\mathsf{DM}(s_0, G, T, T') = 1$ *iff* $\mathsf{Plans}(s_0, G, T \setminus T') = \emptyset$, *else*
- $\mathsf{DM}(s_0, G, T, T') = \frac{\mathsf{Min}(P') - \mathsf{Min}(P)}{\mathsf{Min}(P')}$ *where* $P' = \mathsf{PlanBase}(s_0, G, T \setminus T')$ *and* $P = \mathsf{PlanBase}(s_0, G, T)$.

As mentioned in Definition 5, DM is a value in the interval $[0, 1]$. A DM value of 0 indicates no disruption of the plan base, while a DM value of 1 indicates full disruption. A DM value in the interval $(0, 1)$ indicates partial disruption of the plan base: there exists a longer plan from the start state to a goal, post-disruption.

Both partial and full disruption can be measured using DM. In the next section we propose four algorithms that each determine a critical set of state transitions to be prevented in order to cause the disruption of a plan base.

## 5   Algorithms for the Disruption of Plans

Identifying a set of critical state transitions in a plan base $PlanBase(s_0, G, T)$ can be abstracted to finding one cut of edges in a directed, acyclical graph such that there is no path between a node $s_0$ and any nodes in the set $G$.

Cutting algorithms such as Ford-Fulkerson [22], Stoer-Wagner [24], Karger's [25] or Goldberg and Tarjan's approach [23] have been considered as a starting point for developing a solution. In the case where one always needs to determine the minimum set of state transitions that need to be prevented (the minimum cut) in order to cause disruption, adapted versions of these algorithms can be used. However, as previously mentioned, we do not always need to find the minimum set of state transitions to be prevented and because using some of the above-mentioned algorithms adds unnecessary complexity to our problem, we have chosen to determine any cut that may cause disruption rather than finding just the minimum cut, for the time being. We propose four algorithms that can be used to obtain cuts: the *Start Cut*, *Goal Cut*, *Random Cut* and *Approximate Minimum Cut*. The performance comparison for all algorithms with regard to DM is presented in detail in Sect. 8.

### 5.1    Start Cut

The *Start Cut* algorithm can be used to determine the set of all edges that are directed out of a given start node of a directed unweighted acyclical graph representing a plan base. It takes a directed unweighted acyclical graph $PlanBase(s_0, G, T) = (N, E)$ as an input and adds all of the edges directed out of the start node to the cut set, as shown in Algorithm 1. It then returns a set of edges that can be cut out of the graph (the cut set) such that the start node and goal nodes are always part of two different sub-graphs.

---

**Algorithm 1.** StartCut: returns the set of all edges directed out of a start node in a graph (a start node has no inward edges)

---

**Data**: $PlanBase(s_0,\ G,\ T) = (N, E)$
**Result**: startCut

startCut $= \emptyset$;
**for** $i \in$ *0,..,(size of N)-1* **do**
   **if** *$(s_0, si) \in E$* **then**
      | startCut $=$ startCut $\bigcup \{(s_0, si)\}$;
   **end**
**end**
return startCut;

---

### 5.2    Goal Cut

The *Goal Cut* algorithm can be used to determine the set of all edges that are directed into any node of a given set of goal nodes of a directed unweighted acyclical graph representing a plan base. It takes a directed unweighted acyclical graph $PlanBase(s_0, G, T) = (N, E)$ as an input and adds all of the edges that are directed into any of the goal nodes to the cut set, as shown in Algorithm 2. It then returns a set of edges that can be cut out of the graph (the cut set) such that the start node and goal nodes are always part of two different sub-graphs.

---

**Algorithm 2.** GoalCut: returns the set of all edges directed into the goal nodes of a graph (a goal node has no outward edges).

**Data**: $PlanBase(s_0, G, T) = (N, E)$
**Result**: goalCut

goalCut = $\emptyset$;
**for** $i \in 0,..,(size\ of\ N)-1$ **do**
 **for** $every\ s_j \in G$ **do**
  **if** $(s_i,s_j) \in E$ **then**
   | goalCut = goalCut $\cup$ {$(s_i,s_j)$}};
  **end**
 **end**
**end**
return goalCut;

---

## 5.3 Random Cut

The *Random Cut* algorithm is used to determine a random set of edges to be removed from a directed, unweighted, acyclical graph (representing a plan base) such that no path exists between a start node and a set of goal nodes. As shown in Algorithm 3, it takes an input consisting of a directed, unweighted, acyclical graph (the $PlanBase(s_0, G, T) = (N, E)$), and is inspired by Karger's algorithm, where a single edge is randomly chosen for contraction at every step, until only one edge is left in the graph. However, our method does not use edge contraction. Instead, we split the nodes in the graph into two sets. The first set, $S_1$ initially contains the start node and the second set, $S_2$, initially contains all of the goal nodes. At every step a node (that is not part of any set) is chosen at random and added to one of the sets (randomly chosen). When there are no more nodes to be added to a set, all of the edges $(s_i, s_j)$, where $s_i \in S_1$ and $s_j \in S_2$ are added to the Random Cut set. The algorithm returns the set of edges representing the Random Cut, as shown in Algorithm 3.

## 5.4 Approximate Minimum Cut

The *Approximate Minimum Cut* algorithm is an alternative to the *Random Cut* algorithm. It can be used to determine an approximation of the minimum set of edges to be removed from a directed, unweighted, acyclical graph (representing a plan base) such that no path exists between a start node and a set of goal nodes. As shown in Algorithm 4, it is inspired by Karger's algorithm and makes use of

**Algorithm 3.** RandomCut: finds a cut of randomly chosen edges so that there is no path between a start node $s_0$ and any of the end nodes $G$ in a graph.

---

**Data:** $PlanBase(s_0, G, T) = (N, E)$
**Result:** randomCut

randomCut $= \emptyset$; $S_1 = \emptyset$; $S_2 = \emptyset$; $S_1 = S_1 \bigcup \{s_0\}$;
**for** $s_g \in G$ **do**
|   $S_2 = S_2 \bigcup \{s_g\}$;
**end**
stateSet $= N \setminus (G \bigcup \{s_0\})$;
**while** $stateSet \neq \emptyset$ **do**
|   index $=$ random of $\{1, 2\}$;
|   randomly select $s_j$ from stateSet;
|   $S_{index} = S_{index} \bigcup \{s_j\}$;
|   stateSet $=$ stateSet $\setminus \{s_j\}$;
**end**
**for** $(s_i, s_j) \in E$ **do**
|   **if** $s_i \in S_1$ *and* $s_j \in S_2$ **then**
|   |   randomCut $=$ randomCut $\bigcup \{(s_i, s_j)\}$;
|   **end**
**end**
return randomCut;

---

the fact that, by generating multiple random cuts of a graph, the minimum cut is eventually obtained [25]. The method is named *ApproximateMinimumCut* as we do not implement Karger's approach regarding the estimated number of iterations of random cutting before a minimum is obtained. We stop after 1000 iterations of the random cut. The method can be improved by adding a convergence test in order to get a more accurate approximation of the minimum cut. The input consists of a directed, unweighted, acyclical graph representing the $PlanBase(s_0, G, T) = (N, E)$. It then runs 1000 iterations of the Random Cut algorithm and determines the minimum cut obtained this way. Upon termination, the algorithm returns a set of edges representing the approximate minimum cut.

The four algorithms presented in this section return a set of edges that represent state transitions to be prevented in order to obtain full disruption of a plan base. Full disruption is guaranteed under the assumption that the disruptor has an accurate representation of the plan base they want to disrupt. In the following sections we investigate the performance of the proposed algorithms when this is not the case.

## 6    Disruption Under Uncertainty

A disruptor may not always have an accurate view of the plan base it is aiming to disrupt. We consider a particular type of uncertainty, where the disruptor has

**Algorithm 4.** ApproximateMinimumCut: finds an approximate minimum set of edges so that no path exists between a start node $s_0$ and any of the end nodes $G$ in a graph.

**Data**: $PlanBase(s_0, G, T) = (N, E)$
**Result**: approximateMinimumCut

approximateMinimumCut = randomCut($PlanBase(s_0, G, T)$);
minCutSize = $|$ $approximateMinimumCut$ $|$;
**for** $i \in 1..1000$ **do**
    temp = randomCut($PlanBase(s_0, G, T)$);
    **if** $|$ temp $|<$ minCutSize **then**
        minCutSize $=|$ temp $|$;
        approximateMinimumCut = temp;
    **end**
**end**
return approximateMinimumCut;

an accurate view of the states that appear in a plan base but may be unaware of the existence of some state transitions. We acknowledge that there may exist false positive state transitions, that are present in the disruptor's view of the plan base they wish to disrupt but are not part of the disruptee's plan base. Even if included in the set to be prevented, these will not affect the disruption produced, only increasing the number of paths in the graph and as a consequence, the size of the sets of cuts returned by the algorithms. False positive state transitions are not discussed further.

A *disruption scenario* is defined by its start state, the goal states, the possible state transitions, and the possible state transitions that are unknown to the disruptor.

**Definition 6.** *A* **disruption scenario** *is a tuple* $(s_0, G, T, T')$ *where* $s_0 \in S$ *is the* **start state**, $G \neq \emptyset \subseteq S$ *is the set of* **goal states**, $T \subseteq S \times S$ *are the* **possible state transitions**, *and* $T' \subseteq T$ *is the set of* **unknown state transitions**.

For a particular disruption scenario, we can consider the *true plan base* the disruptor wishes to disrupt and the (possibly inaccurate) *view of the plan base* the disruptor holds.

**Definition 7.** *Let* $ds = (s_0, G, T, T')$ *be a disruption scenario. The* **true plan base** *of ds, denoted* TruePlanBase(ds), *is the plan base* PlanBase($s_0, G, T$). *The* **disruptor's view of the plan base** *of ds, denoted* DisruptorView(ds), *is a plan base* PlanBase($s_0, G, T \setminus T'$).

In order to evaluate the performance of our proposed algorithms under uncertainty, we have run a set of experiments, which we describe in the following section.

## 7   Experimental Set-Up

In order to find a set of state transitions to prevent, the disruptor uses the proposed algorithms, passing its view of the plan base as a parameter. In order to determine the effectiveness of each algorithm, we measure the disruption caused when preventing the state transitions returned by the algorithm in the true plan base.

To investigate performance under uncertainty, we also vary the following parameters: number of states $nr^s$, number of goal states $nr^g$, percentage of unknown state transitions $perc^{ukn}$ and density of the plan base $density$. For each run of the experiment, we first generate a true plan base with $nr^s$ states and $nr^g$ goal states. A true plan base is generated in two steps, as described below.

First, we generate a graph $(N, E)$ where $|N| = nr^s$, $G \subset N$ and $|G| = nr^g$ and all the following properties hold: there are no cycles: $\nexists (s_i, s_j) \in E$ such that $i \geq j$, $0 \leq i, j \leq nr^s$, there are no edges leaving goal nodes: $\nexists (s_i, s_j) \in E$ such that $s_i \in G$ and the total number of edges is $|E| = \frac{(nr^g - 1)(2nr^s - 1)}{2}$ because each non-goal node $s_i$ has $nr^s - i - 1$ edges leaving it. The formula for the number of edges is derived through an addition of the number of edges leaving each node in the graph that is not a goal node: $(nr^s - 1) + (nr^s - 2) + \ldots + (nr^s - nr^g + 1)$. In order to obtain a graph with these properties, we start with a set of nodes N. For each $s_i \in N$ $i \in [0, nr^s - nr^g - 1]$ we add outgoing edges $(s_i, s_j)$, where $j \in [i + 1, nr^s]$ and $s_j \in N$.

The second step derives a random true plan base from the graph generated in the previous step by removing a number of edges determined by the parameter $density$, where $|E'| = \frac{|E| \times (100 - density)}{100}$. Each edge to be removed $(s_i, s_j) \in E'$ is picked out randomly. If upon removal $\exists (s_i, s_{j'}) \in E$ and $\exists (s_{i'}, s_j) \in E$, where $s_{i'}$ and $s_{j'} \in N$ the edge is removed. If not, then a new edge is picked randomly to be removed. This process continues until $|E'|$ edges are removed from the graph. The true plan base generated this way has $nr^s$ nodes, $nr^g$ goals and each of the nodes in the graph is on a path from a starting node to a goal node.

From the resulting true plan base $(N, E \setminus E')$, we then generate a disruptor view of the plan base. The following conditions hold for the disruptor's view $(N', E'')$: $E'' \subseteq E$, $\frac{|E''|}{|E|} = perc^{ukn}$ and $N = N'$. The disruptor view is generated through edge elimination, in the same way that the random true plan base is derived from the complete plan base.

We apply each of the four algorithms to determine $T'$, the set of state transitions to prevent. We then remove these state transitions from the true plan base and compute $\mathsf{DM}(s_0, G, T, T')$.

We consider the following set of parameter combinations and perform 100 runs of the experiment for each combination in the set. Each run is the equivalent of a disruption scenario.

$nr^s \in \{10, 60, \ldots, 200\}$
$nr^g \in \{1, 2, \ldots, 0.3 \times nr^s\}$
$perc^{ukn} \in \{0, 10, \ldots, 80\}$
$density \in \{10, 20, 30, 40, 50, 60, 70, 79, 89, 99\}$.

For each combination of parameters we return an average of DM over the 100 runs. Experimental results are discussed in the following section.

# 8    Performance Analysis for Plan Disruption

In order to analyze the performance under uncertainty of the four algorithms for identifying state transitions to disrupt in a plan base we performed the experiment described in Sect. 7. In this section we present and discuss the results obtained.

## 8.1    DM Decreases as Number of States in a Plan Base Increases

We averaged the data obtained for each set of plan bases of sizes from 10 to 200 nodes. Thus, one DM value in the plot symbolizes the average of all DM values obtained using a specific cut for all plan bases of a specific number of states and number of goals for all combinations of $perc^{ukn}$ and density covered in the parameter space. The same method applies for all of the following plots as well. For smaller plan bases of sizes 10 to 30 nodes, it can be observed in Fig. 1 that the disruption obtained (DM) is slightly higher than for 30 to 200 nodes. However, DM stabilizes and becomes constant starting at 30 nodes. We conclude that the number of states in a plan base influences the performance of the proposed cutting algorithms. As can be observed, the higher the number of states, the lower the performance. However, the peak in disruption for smaller plan bases (up to 30 nodes) may have also been the result of an experimental bias due to the fact that, sometimes, for smaller plan bases the number of edges removed to create the disruptor's version may have been decreased, in order to avoid graph disconnection that would have resulted in new start states or new goal states in a plan base.

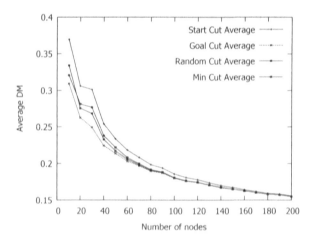

**Fig. 1.** Disruption (DM) vs. number of states (nodes) in a plan base ($nr^s$).

## 8.2    DM Decreases as Unknown State Transitions Increase

We averaged the data obtained for each set of plan bases grouped by the percentage of unknown state transitions, varied from 10 to 90 percent. An almost exponential decrease of DM can be observed in Fig. 2 as the $perc^{ukn}$ increases. As expected, when there are no unknown state transitions in the disruptor's plan base ($perc^{ukn} = 0$), all four algorithms guarantee full disruption (DM = 1). As the percentage of unknown state transitions increases, DM decreases. Some disruption is still obtained as $perc^{ukn}$ approaches 20. However, disruption becomes negligible as $perc^{ukn}$ approaches 70–80. The dramatic decrease of 80 % caused by an increase in unknown state transitions by 20 % shows that the disruption of a plan base is heavily influenced by this. The data also suggests that the algorithms for plan disruption yield significant results when the unknown state transitions in a disruptor's plan base is not higher than 20 %.

## 8.3    DM Decreases as the Number of Goals in a Plan Base Increases

We averaged the data obtained for each set of plan bases grouped by the number of goals, varied from 1 to 60. A decrease of DM can be seen in Fig. 3 as the $nr^g$ increases. As expected, when there are fewer goals in the plan base, a higher value of disruption is obtained. This may be explained by the fact that, when a single goal exists more state transitions in the plan base are shared by plans that lead to the goal, than in the case of multiple goals. In such cases, the removal of one transition does cause disruption of multiple plans. Based on the experimental data, we conclude that the probability of disruption decreases as the number of goals in a plan base increases.

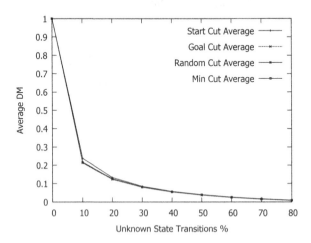

**Fig. 2.** Disruption vs. % of unknown state transitions in a plan base ($perc^{ukn}$).

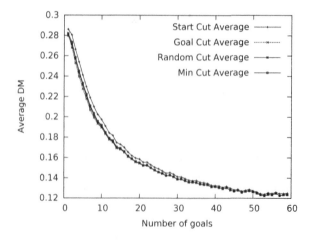

**Fig. 3.** Disruption vs. number of goals in a plan base ($nr^g$).

## 8.4 DM Decreases as the Density of a Plan Base Increases

We averaged the data obtained for each set of plan bases varying from 10 to 99 percent density. The density of a plan base is represented by the percentage of the state transitions that can be performed in a plan base out of all possible state transitions that could be performed in a plan base. A significant decrease of DM can be observed in Fig. 4 as the density of plan bases increases. Some disruption may still be obtained for denser plan bases, however, we notice a significant decrease in disruption around the density of 80 percent. This may be explained by the fact that, as the plan base density increases, the number

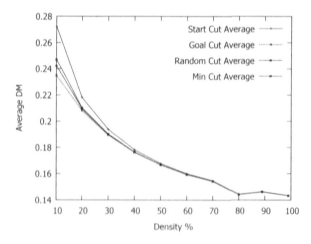

**Fig. 4.** Disruption vs. density of a plan base (density).

of possible state transitions available also experiences an increase (the number of state transitions available in a plan base of size $nr^s$ that has $nr^g$ goals is $2^{(nr^s - nr^g)}$).

## 9   Conclusion and Future Work

In this paper we have discussed the concept of disruption of plans as a way to prevent agents from achieving a goal. We argue that a plan base can be disrupted by preventing particular state transitions. We have discussed two kinds of disruption (partial and total), provided metrics for the disruption of plans and proposed four algorithms to identify which state transitions should be stopped such that the achievement of goals is prevented. We have also considered the fact that the disruptor may not always have an accurate representation of the disruptee's plan base and provided an experimental analysis of algorithm performance under uncertainty.

Based on the experimental data we make the following observations.

1. The number of states in a plan base affects algorithm performance: DM decreases as the number of states increases.
2. The number of unknown state transitions in a plan base impacts algorithm performance: DM decreases as these unknown state transitions increase.
3. The number of goals in a plan base exhibits patterns of inverse exponential dependency: DM decreases as the number of goal states in the base increases.
4. DM obtained using the algorithms decreases as plan base density increases.
5. As observed in Figs. 1, 2, 3 and 4, all four proposed cutting algorithms perform similarly, overall, apart from *Start Cut* which seems to have a slight advantage.
6. All of the proposed algorithms have a chance to cause disruption in any scenario covered in our experiment. This is increased as the number of goals decreases, the percentage of unknown state transitions decreases and the density of a plan base decreases, as stated previously.

The time performance of the algorithms depends on the number of states $(N)$, transitions $(E)$ and goals $(G)$ of a plan base. The Start Cut algorithm has a worst case performance of $O(N)$. The Goal Cut performs in $O(N \times G)$ worst case while the Random Cut's worst case performance is $O(max(N, E))$ and the Approximate Minimum Cut worst case performance is $1000 \times O(max(N, E))$ because the algorithm iterates Random Cut 1000 times. Depending on the known values of parameters $N, E$ and $G$ for a specific disruption scenario, a best performing algorithm in terms of execution time can be determined for the scenario.

The time performance discussion and observations of algorithm performance measured through DM are ultimately to help a disruptor decide whether using any of the proposed algorithms to identify a set of transitions to be prevented in order to disrupt a plan base is sensible. For example, it would be pointless to use our algorithms when 90 % of the transitions in a plan base are unknown to the disruptor; also, if a minimum cut is needed and time constraints on obtaining such a result are loose, then the disruptor can use the Approximate Minimum

Cut algorithm, which yields a more accurate minimum cut than the Random Cut algorithm but at a higher time cost.

Future work aims to study the impact of preventing transitions (returned by our algorithms) on the activity of other agents that are part of the multi-agent system that agents whose plans are disrupted operate in. Such agents are referred to as external agents. Specifically, we aim to answer questions such as: will preventing these transitions cause disruption to the plans of external agents and is it possible to modify the proposed algorithms in order to minimize unintended disruption but still disrupt the plan base? Another idea to explore in future research is the possibility of extending the algorithms proposed in this paper for the scenario where the states in the plan base to be disrupted are partially observable.

Having determined what state transitions can be disrupted in a plan base, we also need to address the question of how these state transitions can be disrupted. We propose the study of disruption using norms as a following step in our work. We also plan to address other ways of preventing state transitions in further research. These include hindering communication links between agents in a team and depleting resources required for specific transitions identified using the algorithms proposed in this paper.

# References

1. Grosz, B.J., Hunsberger, L., Kraus, S.: Planning and acting together. AI Mag. **20**(4), 23–34 (1999)
2. Georgeff, M.P., Lansky, A.L.: Reactive reasoning and planning. In: Proceedings of the 6th National Conference on Artificial Intelligence, pp. 677–682 (1987)
3. d'Inverno, M., Kinny, D., Luck, M., Wooldridge, M.: A formal specification of dMARS. In: Rao, A., Singh, M.P., Wooldridge, M.J. (eds.) ATAL 1997. LNCS, vol. 1365, pp. 155–176. Springer, Heidelberg (1998)
4. Voinitchi, A., Black, E., Luck, M.: Introduction to team disruption mechanisms. In: Proceedings of the 2012 Imperial College Computing Student Workshop, pp. 149–155 (2012)
5. McDermott, D.: Robot planning. AI Mag. **13**(2), 55–79 (1992)
6. Hanks, S., McDermott, D.: Modeling a dynamic and uncertain world: symbolic and probabilistic reasoning about change. Artif. Intell. **66**(1), 1–55 (1994)
7. Porteous, J., Sebastia, L.: Extracting and ordering landmarks for planning. J. Artif. Intell. Res. **22**(1), 215–278 (2004)
8. Schneier, B.: Attack trees: modeling security threats. Dr. Dobbs J. Softw. Tools **24**(12), 21–29 (1999)
9. Mauw, S., Oostdijk, M.: Foundations of attack trees. In: Won, D.H., Kim, S. (eds.) ICISC 2005. LNCS, vol. 3935, pp. 186–198. Springer, Heidelberg (2006)
10. Kordy, B., Mauw, S., Radomirović, S., Schweitzer, P.: Foundations of attack-defense trees. In: Degano, P., Etalle, S., Guttman, J. (eds.) FAST 2010. LNCS, vol. 6561, pp. 80–95. Springer, Heidelberg (2011)
11. Kordy, B., Kordy, P., Mauw, S., Schweitzer, P.: ADTool: security analysis with attack-defense trees. In: Joshi, K., Siegle, M., Stoelinga, M., D'Argenio, P.R. (eds.) QEST 2013. LNCS, vol. 8054, pp. 173–176. Springer, Heidelberg (2013)

12. Kordy, B., Mauw, S., Schweitzer, P.: Quantitative questions on attack–defense trees. In: Kwon, T., Lee, M.-K., Kwon, D. (eds.) ICISC 2012. LNCS, vol. 7839, pp. 49–64. Springer, Heidelberg (2013)
13. TRESsPASS: The tresspass project (2015)
14. Carbonell, J.G.: Counterplanning: a strategy-based model of adversary planning in real-world situations. Artif. Intell. **16**(3), 295–329 (1981)
15. de Cote, E.M., Chapman, A., Sykulski, A.M., Jennings, N.: Automated planning in repeated adversarial games. In: Proceedings of the 26th Conference on Uncertainty in Artificial Intelligence, pp. 376–383 (2010)
16. Willmott, S., Richardson, J., Bundy, A., Levine, J.: Applying adversarial planning techniques to go. Theor. Comput. Sci. **252**(12), 45–82 (2001)
17. Huang, H., Ding, J., Zhang, W., Tomlin, C.J.: A differential game approach to planning in adversarial scenarios: a case study on capture the flag. In: Proceedings of the 2011 IEEE International Conference on Robotics and Automation, pp. 1451–1456 (2011)
18. Tambe, M.: Towards flexible teamwork. J. Artif. Intell. Res. **7**(1), 83–124 (1997)
19. Pynadath, D.V., Tambe, M.: Multiagent teamwork: analyzing the optimality and complexity of key theories and models. In: Proceedings of the 1st International Joint Conference on Autonomous Agents and Multiagent Systems, pp. 873–880 (2002)
20. Jennings, N.R.: Controlling cooperative problem solving in industrial multi-agent systems using joint intentions. Artif. Intell. **75**(2), 195–240 (1995)
21. Jennings, N.R., Mamdani, E.H.: Using joint responsibility to coordinate collaborative problem solving in dynamic environments. In: Proceedings of the 10th National Conference on Artificial Intelligence, pp. 269–275 (1992)
22. Fulkerson, D.R., Ford, L.R.: Maximal flow through a network. Can. J. Math. **8**(1), 399–404 (1956)
23. Goldberg, A.V., Tarjan, R.E.: A new approach to the maximum-flow problem. J. ACM **25**(4), 921–940 (1988)
24. Stoer, M., Wagner, F.: A simple min-cut algorithm. J. ACM **44**(4), 585–591 (1997)
25. Karger, D.R., Stein, C.: A new approach to the minimum cut problem. J. ACM **43**(4), 601–640 (1996)

# Improving Energy Outcomes in Dynamically Formed Micro-grid Coalitions

Muhammad Yasir$^{(\boxtimes)}$, Martin Purvis, Maryam Purvis,
and Bastin Tony Roy Savarimuthu

Department of Information Science, University of Otago, Dunedin, New Zealand
{muhammad.yasir,martin.purvis,maryam.purvis,tony.savarimuthu}@otago.ac.nz

**Abstract.** The energy micro-grid, which is a local energy network that generates and consumes its own electricity, has become an effective method for the rural electrification. Typically a micro-grid is also connected to the nearby external utility grid to sell and buy power. Any failures of the utility grid usually have negative implications on the micro-grid. Whenever there is a deficit of generation, a micro-grid is not able to meet its local demand, and as a result, the community that it serves suffers from the discomfort ("pain") of not meeting its demand. To address this problem, we present in this paper the idea of forming coalitions among micro-grids in order to reduce the pain level of the communities in the coalition. We describe how sharing among the communities in the coalition works and how membership in such communities can be changed dynamically. Based on our simulation experiments, we observe that a dynamic coalition formation approach can provide improved energy outcomes in a straightforward manner.

**Keywords:** Renewable energy · Multi-agent systems · Coalition formation · Micro-grids

## 1 Introduction

A micro-grid (MG) is a local energy system that provides for the generation, storage and consumption of electrical power within a community [6]. The function of a micro-grid is to utilize the distributed local renewable energy resources (such as wind and sun) and to satisfy power needs locally without reliance on nearby utility grids. As a result, the power losses during transmission are reduced and in turn, the quality of the power is improved causing the system to become more robust and resilient. Typically, MG is connected to the nearby utility grid. So, it can sell (during surplus generation) or buy (during deficient generation) power from an energy utility company. However, renewable energy sources (wind, sun) are intermittent in nature and vary hour to hour, even minute to minute, depending upon local conditions [6]. This means that at any time, a MG may have an excess or shortage of power generation. Different energy management strategies are used to mitigate the impact of supply variations, such as storage

© Springer International Publishing Switzerland 2015
A. Ghose et al. (Eds.): COIN 2014, LNAI 9372, pp. 251–267, 2015.
DOI: 10.1007/978-3-319-25420-3_16

devices (batteries, fly wheels, capacitors, etc.), forecasting techniques, demand load management, and backup generators. One of the approaches to address this issue is the interconnection of nearby micro-grids which, by trading among the communities, can reduce the impact of irregularity with respect of renewable energy sources [6]. An agent-based architecture for local energy distribution among micro-grids has been presented in Yasir *et al* [18], where each micro-grid represents a community which has its own power generation based on renewable energy sources and also has its own electric energy demand which varies hourly. Every community has a coordinator agent which, when it has a power surplus or deficit, is responsible for power trading to other interconnected communities or to the utility grid.

Due to the centralized nature of existing electric generation and distribution systems, any technical fault or natural disaster can cause a wide-area blackout. Such power outages from the utility grid will also affect communities having MGs (hereafter interchangeably refereed to simply as "communities"). Ordinarily MGs are not able to fulfill all their power needs by themselves all the time. So when a MG does not meet its demand, then the community will suffer hardship from having to cope with an insufficient energy supply. For brevity, we will refer to this hardship as "pain", and we note that the pain level (as discussed further below) is a nonlinear function of the energy deficit. So if the energy deficit is doubled, then the pain level is more than doubled. In order to address this problem, we believe that a useful approach is the formation of coalitions among the communities. A coalition here is considered to be a group of MGs that can distribute their electric power among each other. By operating in coalitions, communities can reduce their overall pain level, even when there is no additional supply of energy.

In multi-agent systems, a coalition can be defined as a group of agents who decide to cooperate in order to achieve joint goals [10]. According to [15], coalition formation includes three activities: coalition structure generation, solving the optimization problem of each coalition, and dividing the obtained value among the agents. In this paper, our work is focused on the first activity of the coalition formation. We introduce a cooperation mechanism for dynamic coalition formation to reduce the overall pain level of the communities present in the system over time. The goal of our algorithm is not to find the optimal solution but to find a satisfactory coalition match for the community in a non-deterministic environment (where community demand and generation vary hourly without advance knowledge) by relying on recent power and generation data.

The rest of the paper is organized as follows. In Sect. 2 we present the modelling of the problem addressed in this work. Section 3 presents our approach. Experiments and discussion are covered in Sect. 4. Related work on coalition formation in smart grids is discussed in Sect. 5. Section 6 presents conclusions and future work.

## 2    Problem Modeling

The scenario presented in our work concerns situations where communities having MGs must rely on their production to meet their demand. In cases of their own energy surpluses or deficits, they cannot get energy supplements from or sell excesses back to the grid, which is now cut off from them. When a community encounters an energy deficit, it will suffer "pain". The pain is the level of discomfort that a community experiences because of the power shortage. We know from previous studies [1,2] that people or communities are willing to pay more than 100 % of the original electric tariff if the power outage last for more than 24 hours. So we have assumed that there is a continuous polynomial function that can represent the pain of the community. When pain increases, the pain level increases exponentially. Supposing that $dmd_i$ is the demand of the community at given time i, where i is any hour of the day. $Gen_i$ is the generation of the community at given time i, $d_i$ is the deficit of the community in fraction at time, then we can calculate it as:

$$d_i = \frac{dmd_i - Gen_i}{dmd_i} \tag{1}$$

For simplicity, we normalize the value of $d_i$ between 0 and 10 and represent the normalized value of the deficit by $x_i$, where 0 means no deficit (i.e. generation is more than or equal to the demand) and 10 means extreme deficit (i.e. no generation is produced locally). Normalization of the deficit fraction can be done using Eq. 2.

$$x_i = ((d_i - minRange) * (maxRange - minRange)) \tag{2}$$

where minRange and maxRange represent the minimum and maximum range of normalization(0 and 10 respectively).

The function for calculating the pain level is presented in Eq. 3. The value of pain is assumed to lie between 0 and 10 (where 0 means no pain and 10 means extreme pain). This function takes $x_i$ as an input and gives the pain level for time i. Mathematically this function can be expressed as:

$$f(x_i) = a * x_i + b * (x_i)^2 + c * (x_i)^3 \tag{3}$$

where a = 0.1, b = -0.01 and c = 0.01. A plot of this function is given in Fig. 1. For example, at a particular hour of the day, say at 10 am, a community generates the electric power of 200 kWh and its demand for that hour is 350 kWh. So, by using Eqs. 1 and 2, we calculate the normalized deficit value (x) to be 4.28. By inserting this value into Eq. 3 the value of pain for this hour becomes 1.02. The specific values used in this function are not important and have been chosen for illustration. We do believe, however, that the exponential shape of this function is generally representative of how discomfort is related to power consumption deficits.

Communities are assumed to be dispersed across a varied geography such that some communities may have surplus power generation due to good wind or sun, while at the same time others may face deficits and thereby suffer pain. The idea of coalition formation among the communities is to help communities that suffer from extreme pain by those who have a much smaller level of pain. A community in a coalition that offers assistance at one time would expect to receive reciprocal assistance when it encounters energy deficits at a later point in

**Pain level**

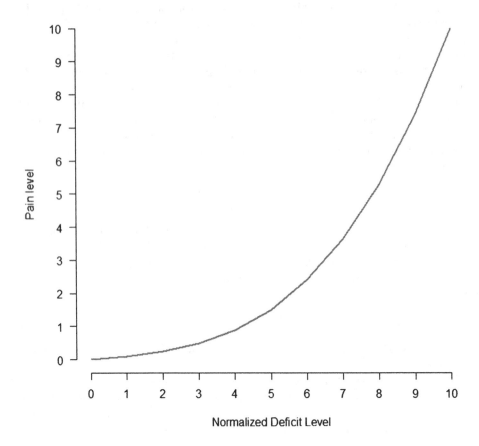

**Fig. 1.** Pain because of deficit

time. To illustrate why this would be beneficial consider a simplified example of just two communities, C1 and C2. Suppose that during a certain 2-hour period of the day C1 has enough energy generation that exactly matches its demand (and hence has a pain level of 0), while C2 has no energy generation at all (and so has a pain level of 10). During a second 2-hour period of the day, both communities C1 and C2 each have a power deficit level of 5 and so have pain levels of 1.5. This means that during the first 2-hour period the aggregate pain of C1 and C2 is 10, and during the second 2-hour period the aggregate pain level of the two is 3. So over the two 2-hour periods this aggregate pain level is 13.0.

If C1 and C2 were to form a coalition for mutual assistance, then during the first 2-hour period C1 might offer 10 % of its power to C2. This would result in a pain level for C1 of 0.1 and a pain level for C2 of 7.48. Then during the second 2-hour period of the day that we mentioned, C2 would reciprocate by giving 10 % of its power back to C1. This means that during this latter period,

C2 will have a power deficit of 6 and C1 will have a power deficit level of 4. Their corresponding pain values for this period would then be 2.4 for C2 and 0.88 for C1. Thus the coalition's aggregate pain level is $7.48 + 0.1 + 2.4 + 0.88 = 10.86$, which is lower than the non-coalition pain level of 13.0. So even though C2 gave up some power when it was in a deficit, it benefited from being in the coalition by obtaining assistance during its most painful period (an overall pain level of 9.88 rather than 11.5). Similarly C1 also benefited from being in the coalition (an overall pain level of 0.98 rather than 1.5).

So operating within a coalition is likely to have beneficial results for all parties. The most effective coalitions will be those for which the excesses and deficits of community members complement each other. The worst periods for some coalition members match up with better periods for others, who may even have energy excesses during those periods.

Of course, energy generation conditions may change over time, and so the most effective coalition combinations over a geographic area may thereby change, too. It would be best of we would allow MG communities to have the autonomy of moving to a new coalition if it so desires. So in the following we present our examination of communities that operate:

- Standalone: there are no coalitions
- Fixed coalitions: there is a single fixed coalition arrangement that does not change.
- Dynamic coalitions: communities have the option of joining a different coalition at the beginning of every month.

In the standalone configuration, no community shares power with others. In the fixed coalition, communities are permanently in a coalition. In this approach, if a community's original pain level is less than the average pain of the coalition, then the community is supposed to give a certain percentage to the coalition. For example if community has some pain but less than average, then 5 % of its power goes to help those members of the coalition whose pain level is greater than the average for the coalition. Similarly, if a community has no pain, then 10 % of its electric power goes to the helping communities. On the other side, a community can receive power from the coalition if its original pain level is greater than the average pain level of the coalition. In this fixed coalition approach, a community cannot leave and join another coalition. In contrast to the fixed coalition, a dynamic coalition allows communities to change coalitions in order to reduce their overall pain level. The working mechanism of the dynamic coalition is described in the next section.

## 3   System Model

In this section, we present the dynamic coalition formation mechanism. As with any coalition formation, the goal is to reduce the overall pain level of communities present in the coalition. The value of a coalition ($v(c_j)$) is represented by:

$$v(c_j) = min_{S \in T}\left(\sum pain\_of\_community\_in\_coalition\right) \qquad (4)$$

---

**Algorithm 1.** Distribution of Electric Power within Coalition

---

```
1  foreach hour of the day do
2  │   Calculate average-pain-level of coalition
3  │   if Community_{i∈M} − pain − level < average − pain − level of coalition then
   │   │   // where M is the total no of communities in coalition;
4  │   │   if Community_i − pain − level = 0 then
5  │   │   │   share electric power to other communities until
   │   │   │   community_i-pain-level increased by σ ;
   │   │   │   // where σ is the certain percentage
6  │   │   else
7  │   │   │   share electric power to other communities until
   │   │   │   community_i-pain-level increased by φ ;
   │   │   │   // where φ is the certain percentage, φ < σ
```

---

where j is the coalition number, S is the number of communities present in the coalition j and T is the total number of the communities present in the system.

At the start of every month, a coalition is selected to be the coordinator agent for the coalition. In this work, the community with lowest average pain level of the previous month is selected to become the coordinator agent. The responsibility of the coordinator agent is to broadcast an invitation message to other communities outside its coalition, identify the potential members of the coalition for joining the coalition, and managing the power-sharing distribution within coalition. There are two main phases of our coalition mechanism. The operational phase, deals with the power distribution power within coalition, and the recruitment phase deals with recruiting other communities to join the coalition.

Algorithm 1 gives the pseudo-code of the distribution mechanism in a coalition. At the beginning of each hour, the coordinator agent calculates the average pain level of coalition by collecting the pain levels of all communities in the coalition (we assume that all communities reveal true information about their pain levels). Now communities whose pain level are below the average pain level are expected to help communities whose pain levels are above than the average pain level. Communities who are below the average pain level and have 0 pain level (line 4 of Algorithm 1) are ready to certain percent ($\sigma$) more pain by sharing their power with other communities (whose average pain is above the average coalition pain). However, those communities who are below the average pain level, but do not have 0 pain level (line 7 of Algorithm 1) must also bear some additional pain of some percentage ($\phi$) by sharing their power. In this way the overall pain level of every community goes down.

From a recruitment perspective, we assume that the coalition is always looking for new communities to join the coalition in order to reduce the coalition pain level. The coordinator agent divides the hours of the day into 12 slots, where each slot consists of two hours. Algorithm 2 shows the pseudo-code of

---

**Algorithm 2.** Main Algorithm for community recruitment

---

1   Calculate & declare Best and worst hours slots;
2   Broadcast-invitation with best & worst hours information;
3   Community analysis of invitation (Algorithm 3);
4   **while** *queue of offer recieved from communities not empty* **do**
5       Calculate-impact-on-pain (offered-amount);
6       Rank community in the list ;

7   **while** *Community from the rank list not joined the coalition* **do**
8       Pick the top community from the list and ask to join the coalition;
9       Community makes decision (Algorithm 4);
10      **if** *Community joined the coalition* **then**
11          send refusal message to other communities from rank list;
12      **else**
13          Go to line 8;

---

recruitment process. At the end of every month, the coordinator agent of each coalition calculates the average pain of each slot during the last month. The six slots with the lowest pain are ranked as the "best hours", while the remaining six slots are marked as the "worst hours" (line 1 of Algorithm 2). The "best hours" mean hours of the day during which the coalition can commit to sharing some of its power with newcomer communities. The "worst hours" signify hours when the coalition seeks to gain power assistance from a potential newcomer community. At the end of month, the coordinator agent broadcasts the invitation message to join its coalition along with the information of its average pain for the worst and best hours slots (line 2 of Algorithm 2). A new community must remain with the coalition it joins for at least one month. In addition to what each coalition coordinator agent does, all communities also calculate their own pain level at the end of each month (see Algorithm 3). If the existing pain level of the community is less than its last three months average pain level, then the community is not interested in leaving its present coalition and will reject all invitation messages (line 9 of Algorithm 3). Otherwise, the community analyzes which received coalition invitation suits it the best. If the invitation-receiving community's best and worst hour slots match the inviting coalition's worst and best hours slots.(line 3 of Algorithm 3), then the community sends an offer to the inviting coalition. The offer mentions how much electric power it can expect from coalition during the community's worst hours slots and how much power community can give to the coalition during the coalition's worst hour. The offer is always a certain percentage (say $\alpha$) of its average power generation during its best and worst hours slots. Once a coalition receives an offer from a community, it calculates how much the average coalition pain level would be decreased by inducting this community(line 5 of Algorithm 2). This calculation is done by adding and subtracting the power (the amount offered from the prospective newcomer community) from the last month's data of the coalition and recalculating what the pain level would be. As part of this calculation, the coalition also takes

---
**Algorithm 3.** Community analysis of invitation

---
1 **if** *current's month pain value* ≥ *last three month's average pain plus β value*
  **then**
   // where $\beta$ is the threshold value;
2  Calculate community's best and worst hours slots;
3  **if** *community's best hours = colaition's worst hour & Vice versa* **then**
4   Make-offer;
5   Send offer to coalition;
6  **else**
7   Reject Coalition's invitation
8 **else**
9  Reject Coalition's invitation

---

into consideration the location of the prospective new member by calculating the expected transmission losses associated with this community during power trading. These losses result in deficits that affect the coalition pain level. The coalition then ranks the offers in descending order in terms of how much they would reduce its pain level (line 6 of Algorithm 2), and then it selects the top community from the list and sends willingness to recruit the community (line 8 of Algorithm 2). After receiving the willingness signal from the coalition, the prospective community also perform the same calculations done by the coalition (Algorithm 4) and selects the best coalition that helps in reducing its own pain level. The community then sends joining message to that coalition, while sending a refusal message to any other coalition. Once the community joins the coalition, the community and coalition must fulfill their commitments. We assume that there is no cheating in fulfilling these commitments. However, sometimes the community or the coalition is unable to comply with their commitments because they were not able to generate the required power. At the end of the month, each community assesses its pain level. If the community's pain level is less than its last three month's average plus a certain tolerance value ($\beta$), then the community stays with the same coalition. Otherwise, it will start looking for another coalition to join. If the newly joined community stays in the same coalition for some time (i.e. $\gamma$), then the community considered to be a regular member of the coalition and all commitments between the community and the coalition are dissolved.

---
**Algorithm 4.** Community makes decision

---
1 **while** *queue of joining inviatation from coalitions not empty* **do**
2  calculate-impact-on-pain;
3  Rank the coalition's in the list ;
4  Pick the best coalition from the rank and join the coalition;
5  Send refusal message to other coalitions;

---

# 4    Simulation Result

## 4.1    Experimental Setup

Our experiment involved forty communities (C1 to C40). The communities each have an average hourly consumption of 1150 kWh and a wind turbine of 2000 kW generation capacity. However, the power generation values for an individual community will vary, due to the dispersed geography involving, and different wind speeds. Thus the power produced by each community is also different. The power generated by a wind turbine is calculated by using the formula [8]:

$$P = 1/2 \; \rho \; A \; V^3 \; C_p$$

where

  P is power in watts (W),
  $\rho$ is the air density in kilograms per cubic meter ($kg/m^3$),
  A is the swept rotor area in square meters ($m^2$),
  V is the wind speed in meters per second (m/s), and
  $C_p$ is the power co-efficient.

  We obtained the wind speed (V) data of forty different New Zealand areas from the National Institute of Water and Atmospheric (NIWA) database [16]. We also obtained hourly power consumption data of forty different places from the Property Services office of the University of Otago [11]. The assumptions made while running our experiments are as follows. All communities are situated at sea level. So the air density value of is $1.23 \, kg/m^3$. The blade length of the wind turbines is 45 meter (m). The cut-in and cut-out wind speeds of the turbines is 3 and 25 meters per second (m/s), respectively. Theoretically the maximum value of Cp is 59 %, which is known as the Betz limit [8]. However, in practice the value of Cp is in between 25 %–45 % [8] depending upon the height and size of the turbine. The value of the power co-efficient (Cp) is 0.4 (i.e. 40 %).The values of $\beta, \alpha, \phi, and \sigma$ are 2, 10 %, 10 % and 5 % respectively. The values of minRange and maxRange are 0 and 10 respectively.

  The simulation runs for 4 years (i.e. 48 months). At the start of the simulation, there are eight coalitions present in the environment and each coalition has 5 communities. Communities are initially assigned to each coalition on a random basis of proximity. Transmission losses, which are calculated when power is transfered from one community to another within a coalition, are determined by the following formula:

$$P_i^{Loss} = (Q_i^2 * R/U^2) + \theta * Q_i \tag{5}$$

where

  $P_i^{Loss}$ is the transmission power loss during one hour ii in watts (W) from one community to another,
  $Q_i$ is the total amount of power transmitted during hour i in kWh,
  R is the resistance of the distribution line between two MGs,
  U is the voltage difference between two ends of the line, and

$\theta$ is the fraction of power lost in the transformer during step up and step down process.

The initial value of R in our experimental setup is 0.2 ohms per km. The value of $\theta$ is 0.02. The value of U is 28 kV. We setup the distribution network within a square region of 500 Km x 500 km. The power lost during transmission is converted into the pain and taken into the account of the receiving MG.

## 4.2   Results

All communities in the environment used our dynamic coalition formation mechanism. In order to measure the effects of our dynamic coalition mechanism, we conducted comparative experiments by using two other approaches: standalone and fixed coalition (discussed in Sect. 2). We show the effectiveness of our coalition mechanism at two levels: at the individual community level and at the system level (the aggreagte result of all communities). Due to space constraints, we are not able to show the results of all the communities present in the environment. So at the community level, we have chosen two representative communities (C1 and C2). The total power generation for C1 during the simulated four years period was more than its demand, while the overall generation of C2 was less than its demand during that period. Figure 2 shows the pain level of community C1 over the simulated time period of four years. The results show that the community employing the standalone (no coalition) approach suffers much more pain as no other community is able to help the stand-alone community. The community staying in fixed coalition does better compared to the community in stand alone mode, because, it gets help from other members of the coalition when it has severe pain levels. However, when the community employs our dynamic coalition approach, it experiences lower pain levels compared to using the alternative approaches. During the first three months of the simulation, community behaves like the fixed coalition (i.e. the second approach), but after three months it jumps to the another coalition that it has found. During first year of the simulation (the first 12 months), this community changes to different coalitions and gets settled down once it finds the right coalition. This result also depicts that community using dynamic coalition formation mechanism has reduced by 38 % of its overall average pain level as compared with the community employing fixed coalition by 79 % in the reduction of average pain as compared to the community in the stand-alone mode. Figure 3 illustrates the pain level of community C2 for the simulated time period of four years. Again the community employing dynamic coalition formation suffers less pain compared to the community configuration using the fixed coalition and the stand alone approach. The results here show that community configuration employing dynamic coalition has an overall 68 % reduction in average pain as compared the community employing fixed coalition approach and 84 % reduction in pain as compared to the community in the standalone mode.

At the system level, it was also evident that the aggregate results for the collection of 40 communities was when dynamic coalitions were employed. Figure 4 depicts the initial coalition setup of the system before employing the dynamic

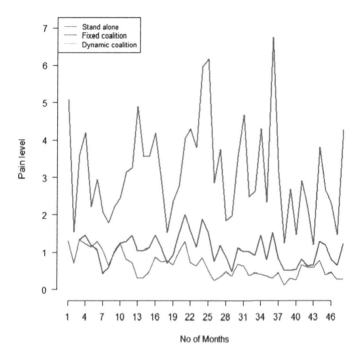

**Fig. 2.** Community (C1) pain level

coalition-forming mechanism. In this figure, house symbols represent a community. Every community is the part of the one of the coalitions, which are initially organized based on proximity. The arrow points to the centroid of the coalition. The communities within a coalition can transfer power among each other by using nearest transmission line point. The transmission lines are the black horizontal and vertical lines intersecting at the center of the figure. Figure 5 shows the final state of the system employing dynamic coalition mechanism after four simulated years. In this figure, communities are no longer part of a coalition on the basis of their proximity to others. They have joined different coalitions to reduce their overall pain level. Communities situated nearby often have similar wind patterns, so they cannot complement each other during their worst and best hour slots. So communities have decided to leave their original coalition (created on the basis of proximity)and joined the coalition that has a contrasting wind pattern. Some coalitions vanished because no community was interested in staying with it or joining it. Similarly, there is a community in the figure that was not able to find any coalition and stand alone, because its wind pattern does not contrast with the any of the existing coalitions. Figure 6 shows the aggregate pain-level results. They reveal that the system employing dynamic coalition formation averaged 33 % less pain than the system using the fixed coalition mechanism. Similarly, on average 65 % of pain is reduced in the system employing dynamic coalition formation as compared to the system where

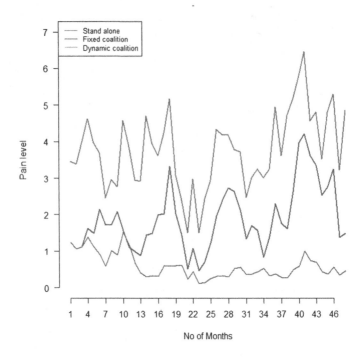

**Fig. 3.** Community (C2) pain level

all communities are on their own (i.e. stand alone mode). We also conducted the t test on the these approaches (i.e. dynamic coalition, fixed coalition, stand alone) and found that two tailed P values between dynamic coalition and fixed coalition and dynamic coalition and stand alone approaches are less than 0.0001, showing very high significance.

# 5  Related Work

Coalition formation in smart grids has been widely used in the multi-agent system community (see for example [5,7,12,14]). In [13] the authors presented an algorithm for coalition formation among micro-grids. By using this algorithm the authors demonstrated the the reduction of power losses over the distribution line is possible by forming the coalition among micro-grids. By forming coalitions among micro-grids, not only are the distribution losses reduced, but so is the load on the transmission lines (transfer of power between micro-grid and sub-station). In [9], the authors demonstrated the idea of dynamic coalition formation for effective utilization of the power. In their work, the coalition is always formed between one micro-grid and the customers. Power is only transferred within the coalition and one coalition cannot sell power to the another coalition. The goal of the coalition formation is to distribute the power optimally i.e. with less energy loss. In their simulation environment, a sub-station

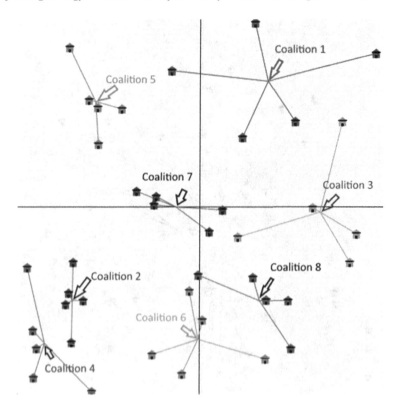

**Fig. 4.** System's initial configuration

is connected to the many micro-grids. Each micro-grid is allowed to provide power to the local customers, which reduces the power load from the sub-station. A micro-grid inside the coalition tries to earn revenue by selling the maximum amount of generated power, whereas the customers present in the coalition want to get the required amount of power at a low price. In [3], the authors presented an algorithm for the dynamic constrained coalition formation (DCCF), which uses heuristic-based method for constrained coalition structure generation in a dynamic environment. The coalition is formed among electric vehicles to sell the power from their batteries to the nearby grid. The goal of the coalition formation is to increase the monetary value given by the grid, which is directly proportional to the amount of power supplied (up to certain limits). In [4], the authors demonstrated the coalition formation among the electric vehicles. The goal of coalition formation was to aggregate the electric power stored in the electric vehicle and participate in the Vehicle to Grid (V2G) market. The coalition is not only used for selling power from the batteries but also is used to buy power for charging the batteries of the vehicles. In [17] the authors, considered a coalition of consumers to buy power from the electricity market. The goal of their algorithm is to improve the grid efficiency through demand-side

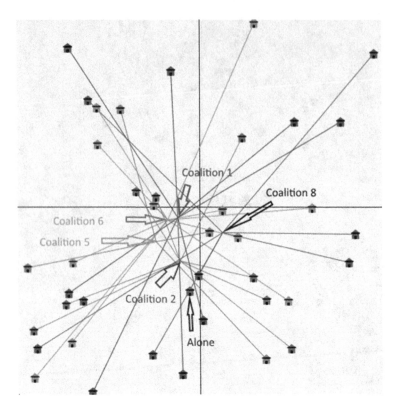

**Fig. 5.** System's final configuration

management and reduce the joint payments (made in the electric market)of consumers present in the coalition.

For the aforementioned systems, the goal of coalition formation is to improve the monetary value. In two of the models [9,13] discussed above, the goal of coalition formation is to reduce the transmission and distribution losses among communities. However, there is no notion discussed in these models of decision making present concerning joining or leaving the coalition. The purpose of coalition formation in [3] is to increase monetary returns for the grid by supplying power. In this model, all electric vehicles share the same amount of power in the coalition, which aids in simplifying the system. As discussed, due to same amount of power shared by electric vehicles, there is no mechanism of distribution of payoff within coalition as discussed. In [4], the goal of the coalition formation is to form virtual power plant for selling and buying power for electric vehicles in the V2G market. In their approach, the coalition aggregator runs the algorithm and makes the feasible coalition of electric vehicles. In that approach, electric vehicles do not have local autonomy to make decisions about staying or leaving the existing coalition.

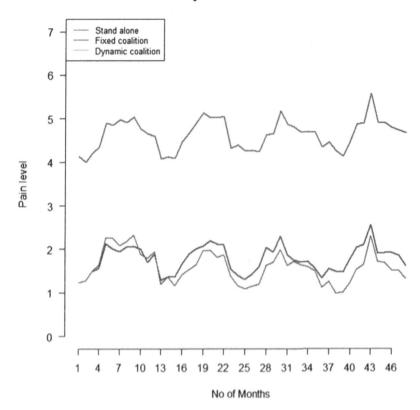

**Fig. 6.** System's pain level

In contrast, the goal of our coalition formation mechanism is to reduce the discomfort (pain level) of a community operating without access to a power grid. And in our model, each community has the autonomy to join or leave the coalition by considering demands, generation and pain.

## 6   Conclusion and Future Work

In this paper we have presented the our dynamic coalition-formation mechanism for micro-grids when they operate in a situation where there is no available support from a main power grid. The goal of the coalition formation is to reduce the discomfort of communities cause because of deficit power generation.

Our experiments show that our mechanism of dynamic coalition formation is effective in reducing pain level (i.e. discomfort) of a communities. We have shown that, compared to the stand-alone and fixed coalition approaches, our approach outperforms and reduced the pain level at community level by considerable amounts (in our examples up to 84 % and 68 % respectively). Similarly, at the system we observed a 33 % reduction in pain compared to the fixed coalition and a 65 % reduction in pain compared to the stand alone approach.

For future work, we intend to introduce the split and merge algorithm for the coalition, so that coalitions have a mechanism to merge into one coalition in order to reduce transmission losses. Also, we intend to develop strategies whereby communities can make more complex and dynamic offers for attracting a coalition. Currently, all communities make fixed offers of a certain percentage of their generation.

# References

1. Carlsson, F., Martinsson, P.: Does it matter when a power outage occurs? A choice experiment study on the willingness to pay to avoid power outages. Energy Econ. **30**(3), 1232–1245 (2008)
2. Carlsson, F., Martinsson, P., Akay, A.: The effect of power outages and cheap talk on willingness to pay to reduce outages. Energy Econ. **33**(5), 790–798 (2011)
3. de O Ramos, G., Burguillo, J.C., Bazzan, A.L.: Dynamic constrained coalition formation among electric vehicles. J. Braz. Comput. Soc. **20**(1), 8 (2014)
4. Decker, K.S., Kamboj, S., Kempton, W.: Deploying power grid-integrated electric vehicles as a multi-agent system. In: 10th International Conference on Autonomous Agents and Multi-agent Systems, Number Aamas, Taipei, pp. 13–20 (2011)
5. Fadlullah, Z.M., Nozaki, Y., Takeuch, A., Kato, N.: A survey of game theoretic approaches in smart grid. In: International Conference on Wireless Communications and Signal Processing, Number WCSP, Nanjing (2011)
6. Jacobson, M.Z., Delucchi, M.A.: Providing all global energy with wind, water, and solar power, part i: technologies, energy resources, quantities and areas of infrastructure, and materials. Energy Policy **39**(3), 1154–1169 (2011)
7. McArthur, S., Davidson, E., Catterson, V., Dimeas, A.: Multi-agent systems for power engineering applicationspart i: concepts, approaches, and technical challenges. Power Syst. **22**(4), 1743–1752 (2007)
8. Miller, A., Muljadi, E., Zinger, D.S.: A variable speed wind turbine power control. Energy Convers. **12**(2), 181–186 (1997)
9. Mondal, A., Misra, S.: Dynamic coalition formation in a smart grid: a game theoretic approach. In: 2013 IEEE International Conference on Communications Workshops (ICC), pp. 1067–1071. IEEE, Budapest (2013)
10. Oliveira, P., Pinto, T., Morais, H., Vale, Z.A., Praça, I.: MASCEM an electricity market simulator providing coalition support for virtual power players. In: 15th International Conference on Intelligent System Applications to Power Systems, 2009. ISAP 2009, pp. 1–6. IEEE, Curitiba (2009)
11. Pietsch, H.: Property service division, http://www.propserv.otago.ac.nz/. Accessed 25 Sept 2014
12. Ramchurn, S.D., Vytelingum, P., Rogers, A., Jennings, N.R.: Putting the 'Smarts' into the smart grid: a grand challenge for artificial intelligence. Commun. ACM **55**(4), 86–97 (2012)
13. Saad, W., Han, Z., Poor, H.: Coalitional game theory for cooperative micro-grid distribution networks. In: 2011 IEEE International Conference on Communications Workshops (ICC), pp. 1–5. IEEE, Kyoto (2011)
14. Saad, W., Han, Z., Poor, H.V., Bas, T.: Game theoretic methods for the smart grid. IEEE Sig. Process. Mag. **29**(5), 86–105 (2012)

15. Sandholm, T., Larson, K., Andersson, M., Shehory, O., Tohmé, F.: Coalition structure generation with worst case. Artif. Intell. **111**(1–2), 209–238 (1999)
16. The National Climate Database. NIWA, The National Institute of Water and Atmospheric Research. http://www.niwa.co.nz/. Accessed Sept 25 2014
17. Vinyals, M., Bistaffa, F., Rogers, A.: Stable coalition formation among energy consumers in the smart grid. In: 3rd International Workshop on Agent Technologies for Energy Systems (ATES 2012), Number i (2012)
18. Yasir, M., Purvis, M.K., Purvis, M., Savarimuthu, B.T.R.: Agent-based community coordination of local energy distribution. Ai & Society, December 2013

# Author Index

Printed in the United States
By Bookmasters